THE WESTERN THEORY OF TRADITION

The Western Theory of Tradition

Terms and Paradigms of the Cultural Sublime

SANFORD BUDICK

Yale University Press   New Haven and London

Designed by James J. Johnson and set in Baskerville Roman type
by The Composing Room of Michigan, Inc., Grand Rapids
Michigan. Printed in the United States of America by Sheridan
Books, Chelsea, Michigan.

Library of Congress Cataloging-in-Publication Data

Budick, Sanford, 1942–
      The western theory of tradition : terms and paradigms
      of the cultural sublime / Sanford Budick.
          p.   cm.
      Includes bibliographical references (p.   ) and index.
      ISBN 0-300-08151-0 (alk. paper)
      1. Sublime, The—History.   2. Tradition (Philosophy)—
      History.   3. Civilization, Western—History.   I. Title.

BH301.S7 B83   2000
111'.85—dc21   99-086678

A catalogue record for this book is available from the
British Library.

The paper in this book meets the guidelines for perma-
nence and durability of the Committee on Production
Guidelines for Book Longevity of the Council on Library
Resources.

10   9   8   7   6   5   4   3   2   1

For Rachel and Ayelet

and

In Memory of Yochanan

Contents

Figures

Preface

This book proposes a quiet revolution in our understanding of the Western theory of tradition. Yet the qualifier *Western* underlines the fact that the theory presented here does not pretend to be a description of a universal condition. Nor, as used here, does the word *theory* imply predictive value.[1] I describe only how Western cultures have implicitly theorized the making of tradition on occasions when they have actually engaged in such making. The deep-seated pervasiveness of this theory in the West, however, sometimes gives it the appearance of being both universal and predictive.

Principally, I have tried to bring to daylight a half-open secret of Western cultures: namely, that in the undercurrent lines of thought of these cultures the act of achieving freedom in sublime representation and the act of making cultural tradition are one and the same phenomenon. Viewed in this double, linked manifestation—which I have called the cultural sublime—the constituent terms of making tradition become available for formal analysis. I will try to show how, for any given Western culture, the effect of losing the capacity for the cultural sublime is that tradition becomes pure coercion while the sublime degenerates into a pseudosublime that is itself an instrument of enforcement. In fact, we will see that in Western cultures the act of making traditions is in resistance to the representations of a pseudosublime. In this resistance, cultural traditions—in their workings *as* cultural traditions—both derive and generate anew structures of representation which momentarily enable the freedom of sublime experience.

These structures and this freedom have nothing whatever to do with whether or not a given cultural tradition—"high" or "popular"—professes (or pretends to) freedom or, indeed, any other value. I would emphasize, accordingly, that the following chapters about how cultural tradition is made are not concerned with "substantive traditionality." Here I draw on the distinction between "tradition" and "substantive traditionality" proposed by the sociologist Edward Shils. Substantive traditionality, he explains, is "the appreciation of the accomplishments and wisdom of the past and of the institutions especially impregnated with tradition, as well as the desirability of regarding patterns inherited from the past as valid guides." "The decisive criterion" of a tradition, on the other hand, is only that, "having been created through human actions, through thought and imagination, it is handed down from one generation to the next." Shils emphasizes that this criterion, definitive of tradition, equally obtains in the so-called "'antitraditions' of originality, scientism, and progressivism" which are closely identified with modernity and which are "addressed to the task of dismantling substantive traditions."

Strangely enough, Shils notes, the "mechanism of recurrent self-reproduction" or repetition that creates tradition has not been described by the social sciences. Shils's identification of a primary reason for this "oversight" also locates what especially eludes description in the mechanism itself: "The 'here and now' postulate of much of modern science, and not least, of the more systematic and theoretical social sciences, has led to an oversight. The temporal dimension is obscured by the concept of equilibrium, stressing as it does the immediately present function of each of the variables in the system. Whatever history each of these variables possesses has been deposited in its present state."[2]

This insight is indispensable for moving toward an understanding of the experience of cultural tradition. The temporal dimension that Shils specifies is totally different from the mere effects, in the present (grasped as equilibrium), of the past. It should not be confused with that which history has deposited in the present state of each of the variables in the system. In other words, in order to describe tradition in these terms an account of something is required which may, in itself, seem an inconceivable leap into temporal disequilibrium: an experience of the time of the past within the time of the present.[3] Shils too, in fact, has not described this temporal dimension of tradition or the conditions of subjectivity in which it is experienced. Nor has he described either the overall mechanism of making tradition or its specific tools and media.

A description of these things is possible, I believe, but it needs to be derived from experiences of works which themselves produce the temporal dimension of cultural tradition. With regard to the question of what makes cultural tradition, the first task of scholarship is to reproduce and to identify the experience of this temporal dimension. I believe that, although Kant avoids acknowledg-

ing it, this is what he is doing in the "Analytic of the Sublime." We will hear
Kant say explicitly that the experience of sublime freedom is the keystone of
his entire philosophy. What he does not say is that the experience of deriving
sublime freedom is the keystone of the Western cultural tradition from which
he has derived his experience. In other words, already in Kant the experience
of the sublime is identical with the acculturated Western experience of this
temporal dimension. Kant's representation of the sublime, including that
which he represses (yet which remains traceable) within that representation, is
itself a representation of both the history of sublime experience and (though he
does not acknowledge it) the experience of cultural tradition in the West. What
Kant specifically represses, in my view, is that the repetitions within sublime experience are always of specifically cultural representations; and that these are
representations which (to use Kant's formulation) show us their inadequacy as
representations. Kant's repressions have a good deal to do with the "oversight"
that modern thought has experienced vis-à-vis the temporal dimension of tradition.

When I put together what Kant says and what he represses about the cultural dimensions of sublime experience, the working description of the sublime
that emerges, in Kantian shorthand, is this: the experience of the sublime is the
effect of encountering an effectively endless repetition of cultural representations each of which is partially withdrawn from representation. Kant was himself experiencing the continuous representation of a Western sublime when he
observed that the effects of this encounter are the experiences of a partial loss
of consciousness, an instant of mental freedom from all coercion, and thereby
the possibility of undetermined moral feeling and moral choice. In fact, I believe that the ground assumption in the West has most often been that the
unique work of cultural tradition is to provide at least intermittent access to experience of freedom and moral feeling. In the West, from antiquity to modernity, it has been acknowledged that an individual can be forced to do or say
something, but that that something will not become his or her act or word except as free choice. At the earliest opportunity he or she, or their descendants,
will escape enforcement. This is not to claim that a condition of freedom at
a given moment of tradition is obvious from outside, or even from inside.
Hypocrisy, deception, and self-deception have long been understood to be as
common in tradition as in any other sphere of human activity. For these reasons, we may not detect a moment of coercion in the mind, just as we may not
detect exactly when a given tradition goes dead. Nevertheless, over a period of
time the demise of freedom in a given tradition as well as the death of the tradition itself is not hard to make out.

In the West, those traditions which have had significant durations have rep-

resented the demise of freedom as scenes of coercion. These scenes are themselves one of the main preoccupations of tradition and of sublime experience.
Yet, again, the importance of this preoccupation for the making of tradition
qua tradition is not a matter of substantive traditionality. We will see that for
any given tradition the recurring representation of a scene of coercion and of
resistance to coercion is a crucial part of Shils's sought-after "mechanism of recurrent self-reproduction." The experience of these particular kinds of representation, in repetition, creates the sublime freedom and moral feeling required
for cultural transmission. This is the freedom with which one may freely inherit
one's past and the moral feeling with which one may uncoercively—and even
in what Goethe terms self-endangerment—reach from one's present toward
the next moment and another human being. Understood in this way, the making and experience of tradition, and, identically, the cultural experience of the
sublime, are never a safe haven.

It may seem surprising, or raise doubts, that an equivalence of cultural tradition and of sublime experience such as I am claiming, which is said to apply
to vast areas of human experience, has not been recognized and become commonplace long before now. I believe it has been so recognized and even become
commonplace; but not, as we say, on a conscious level. The reasons for the hidden status of this commonplaceness are also intrinsic to the experience of tradition. As I have noted, the experience of the sublime, at least as it has been experienced in the West, entails the mind's partial loss of consciousness upon
encountering an endless progression of representations; and it entails resistance to repetition of those representations. Representations which have been,
in effect, endlessly repeated are precisely what we call commonplaces. I will try
to show that our virtually unnoticed and deeply transformative experience of
commonplaces is central to sublime experience in cultural tradition.[4]

If we are now more capable of acknowledging the experience of living with
partial consciousness it may well be because of having been accustomed to the
modern analysis of the psyche into parts, especially parts of consciousness that
we call *un*conscious or even beyond consciousness. Yet by and large we have
been slow to come to grips with the implications of this acknowledgment, especially of the temporal experience of fragmentary consciousness. Kant, however, was only employing our Western language for sublime experience with extraordinary precision when he observed that in the sublime ecstasy the mind
experiences a momentary deprivation of its life force, in effect, an experience of
temporary death.[5] Even at our contemporary, hypermodern moment, many of
us, I think, continue to associate the deepest human capacities with sublime experience, even if, seen in Kant's terms, this kind of experience is certainly not
what we usually think of as normal.[6] I will try to show that in the West

what we call the experience of the continuity of cultural tradition is only the instantaneous experience of a continuum of such special or "abnormal" experiences.

At this moment of beginning to represent a series of experiences of tradition and of the sublime, I would emphasize that this book proposes no extenuations of the crimes of coercion which have been perpetrated in the name of any given tradition of belief or thought—especially of pseudosublimes—whether of ancient religions or modern progressivisms. These are the slow-accruing, partly invisible, often deadly crimes produced by what Milton called "the sour leaven of human Traditions mixed in one putrefied Mass with the poisonous dregs of hypocrisy." As I have already suggested, traditions that have ceased to function as traditions typically employ a pseudosublime, which Milton terms a "spiritual Babel."[7] Yet it would be as simpleminded to wish away all making of tradition or the sublime as of any other pervasive activities and their institutionalizations, such as sex or marriage, imaginative representation and the arts, or investigation of nature and what we call science. At various distant and recent times proposals have been advanced, wholesale, against each of these activities and/or their institutionalizations.

In fact, it may well be that the sustaining of Western traditions is always in resistance to the petrifications and coercions of substantive traditionalities. Walter Benjamin is especially enlightening here, though not in the way he is usually cited. In our time one of the most frequently quoted apparent dismissals of tradition, or the heritage of works of culture, is Benjamin's statement, "There is no document of civilization which is not at the same time a document of barbarism." Yet Benjamin's very next words are these: "And just as such a document is not free of barbarism, barbarism taints also the manner in which it was transmitted from one owner to another." Even if we knew nothing of Benjamin's cherishing of a variety of cultural traditions, this second sentence would compel us to consider the possibility that for Benjamin the historian's task is not to jettison cultural traditions or the documents of civilization on the grounds that none of them is free of barbarism. Rather, his or her task is to transmit the documents of history with the least possible barbarous taint of ownership of his or her own. And, indeed, Benjamin gives us a hint of just what such a transmission or "historiography" might entail when he says, in the same place, "Thinking involves not only the flow of thoughts, but their arrest as well."[8] It has recently been suggested, in fact, that Benjamin conceived of tradition as an "entwinement of elements of continuity and discontinuity," a "figure of an antinomy" that in itself must retrieve and represent what he called "the tradition of the oppressed" within any given tradition.[9] (One figure of antinomy—chiasmus—that is a recurring concern in many of the following chapters has had a good deal to do with representing traditions of the oppressed.)

Within what I am calling the Western idea of tradition per se, we will see that the flow and arrest of thinking do explicitly, repeatedly highlight the scene of barbarism that is potential within the thinking of ownership and its transmission. Reexamined from this point of view, Marx's fillip, in the *The Eighteenth Brumaire of Louis Bonaparte,* that "the tradition of all the dead generations weighs like a nightmare on the brain of the living"[10] should perhaps be seen as an evasion of the need to think out the relations, fateful for freedom in the brain of the living, between cultural tradition (including what Marxists sometimes call "Marxist tradition" or "Marxist cultural tradition") and nightmare scenes of coercion.[11]

The experiences of tradition that I have chosen to recreate are a minuscule selection from the vast range of documents of Western culture. Aside from the constraints of my knowledge, my choices have been determined by a need to identify works that, prima facie, seem to offer a high density of implication for each other. This density of implication is created in these works not so much by similarity of themes but by the shared experience of recurrent commonplaces and techniques. I have reasoned (somewhat circularly, no doubt) that for the study of the theory of tradition in given cultures only a density of experience of this sort could crystalize terms and paradigms in a limited space. In this, I have tried to follow Erwin Panofsky's and Erich Auerbach's suggestion that "an accurate type of spiritual history [*Geistesgeschichte*]" or new scholarly "synthesis" of "*Weltliteratur*" might emerge from tracing, over many centuries, interpretations of "a concrete point of departure" that is "found to coerce the general theme." Thus each such point of departure for the study of Western cultures, they propose, "should not be a generality imposed on a theme from the outside, but ought rather to be an organic inner part of the theme itself." Each should possess both "concreteness" and what Auerbach calls a "potential for centrifugal radiation."[12] Each of the documents studied here, and their ensemble, concretely provides opportunities for study of this kind. I have found, paradoxically, that the grounds of "synthesis" among the documents studied is their blockage of synthesis (especially thematic synthesis) as we usually conceive it. Of late one hears the apothegm that no one can stand outside culture. By this is meant, I assume, that one cannot ever remove oneself from the deepest ideological prejudices of one's given line of culture or language. Yet in the Western tradition at least, the experience of a cultural sublime suggests something very different, namely, that there has been no generating and sustaining of culture without a continual, intermittent suspension of—and momentary standing outside of—culture.

The discussions of ancient paradigms in my opening chapters may seem to attach a special status—or unique power of suspension—to classical cultures. Let me make clear at the outset, therefore, that in the course of writing this book I have not found that, as far as the making of tradition is concerned, works of classicism and neoclassicism (even broadly defined) are characterized by any inherent superiority to those of romanticism and postromanticism. The experience of the sublime which, in my view of Western traditions, is indispensable for achieving cultural transmission as well as sublime freedom and moral feeling is equally in evidence in all the sustained traditions known to me in Western cultures. Thus Goethe, Delacroix, and Baudelaire, who are in so many ways types of romantic culture, are also, as I have tried to show, colossal exemplars of Western cultural transmission. So is Wordsworth. Beyond what I have shown in chapter 6, this could be demonstrated in all of Wordsworth's greatest poetry (though such a demonstration would not, I think, add any term for tradition to those that are better seen in other works that I have described). The economy of my choice of exemplifications has been shaped by the aim of describing significant terms of tradition in a spectrum of diverse Western periods and cultures and of different kinds of cultural documents. I have hoped that by this means my chapters might achieve a certain broad relevance, while not swelling beyond a size that can provide a cogent reading experience.

What may seem to create the impression of a romantic opposition to the earlier articulation of the Western theory of tradition is—besides the internal logic of what I have called counterperiodization—a recurrent romantic desire to appear to be totally new (which some lately call originary), that is, over and above the need, felt in common by all, to sustain freedom within cultural transmission. But this opposition, or self-declared newness, on the part of some romantic writers, by no means defines an essential difference, regarding tradition, between writers of any of these periods. Virgil, after all, was one of the poets who most moved and most significantly formed Wordsworth.

Further to these last two paragraphs, I would like to offer a kind of *profession de foi* of what I have tried to achieve and of what I have avoided in writing this book. In the "Analytic of the Sublime" Kant distinguishes between the "Fanaticism" of "positive representation" and the "Enthusiasm" of sublime experience. Speaking of enthusiasm Kant says, "This pure, elevating, merely negative presentation of morality involves . . . no fear of *fanaticism*, which is a *delusion* that would *will some* VISION *beyond all the bounds of sensibility;* i.e. would dream according to principles. . . . The safeguard is the purely negative character of the presentation. For *the inscrutability of the idea of freedom* precludes all positive presentation."[13] As I have suggested, Kant achieves these perspectives by experiencing them within the tradition in which he found himself. That is, what he describes applies extensively, in my view, to the Western theory of tradition. This is what occurs in sublime experience of a line of negative representations, which are representations of negativity achieved in the withdrawal from positive representation. The astonishing and strange thing that Kant shows us (partly beyond what he thinks he is showing us) is that, for this Western tradition at least, moral empathy with prefigured suffering is achieved only in impersonal participation in the experience of a sublime line of tradition. This initially impersonal activity alone can produce personal freedom and moral feeling, which are not otherwise stored in the mind, waiting to be drawn upon. As part of this moral feeling, we may freely choose to participate, once again, in the line of sublime representations.

In a spirit of passionate dispassion, my aim has been to represent the terms of the Western theory of tradition in the only way that, according to those terms, such a representation can achieve authenticity. A representation of this kind must both emerge from an experience of a line of sublime representations and it must represent a self-skeptical withdrawal within the moment of one's merely personal declaration of principles. This, at least, is the enthusiastic principle that I have tried to follow. Thus I have tried to show that the representation of alternating states of consciousness and unconsciousness (and negativity) is at the heart of the experience of the Western theory and practice of tradition. In order to maintain the status of a fragmented resisting self that is alternative to a Hegelian concept of a reconsolidated self, which is moreover recuperated in a scene of victimization, it has been especially important for me to avoid my own scenario of victimization. To do otherwise would have meant only mirroring Wordsworth punishing Dryden and Pope for their alleged sins; not that there aren't real Shadwells and Cibbers, but the medium for punishing them is always open to the most serious moral questioning. Throughout the writing of this book I have tried to overcome the illusion of having achieved an independently sustained self-consciousness or solitary personal culture. I believe that what I have described emerges from the experience of these traditions. My role on the scene of this book, as I have seen it, has been to try to achieve and to write from a certain calm of mind, all passion spent on tracing the sublime—which is to say, "negative" and repeating—representations of this Western experience of tradition and of freedom and moral feeling. I hope that at least some portion of any freedom and moral feeling that I may have myself derived from tracing these representations has been used to carry me through the writing of this book. But that is for the reader to judge.

One more prefatory note. Although the works discussed in the following chapters are most often presented in roughly chronological order, my discussions of Descartes, Kant, Hegel, and Rembrandt have been placed near the beginning because of the comprehensiveness of the terms for tradition that they develop or provoke. At the same time, a document deriving from late medieval culture has been saved for the last chapter because, for reasons explained there, this document is located at the outer limit of my experience of tradition.

Acknowledgments

For encouragement, good cheer, and intellectual stimulation during the years this book has been in the writing I wish to express my gratitude to family and friends: to my wife, Emily Budick, our daughters, Rachel and Ayelet, our son-in-law, Shaul, and to Moshe Barasch, Lawrence Besserman, Gerald Bruns, Arthur Budick, Harry Budick, Stanley Cavell, Jacques Derrida, Wolfgang Iser, Alfred Ivry, Michael Kaufman, Frank Kermode, and Zephyra Parat. Karlheinz Stierle and Patricia Stierle have been the good angels of this undertaking almost from beginning to end.

The Guggenheim Foundation and the Institute for Advanced Studies of The Hebrew University of Jerusalem provided year-long fellowships that enabled me to embark on this project. In the final stage of my writing Jonathan Brent, Sally Anne Brown, Larisa Heimert, and Lawrence Kenney of Yale University Press greatly facilitated and improved my efforts. So did the press's anonymous reader. Zoe Beenstock prepared the index.

Those of my chapters, or portions of them, which have been previously published have undergone sea changes or have been completely rewritten in becoming parts of this book. Those earlier incarnations appeared as follows: of chapter 1, in *Modern Language Quarterly* 58 (1997), reprinted in *Eighteenth-Century Literary History: An MLQ Reader*, ed. Marshall Brown (Durham: Duke Univ. Press, 1998); of chapter 2, in *Journal of the Warburg and Courtauld Institutes* 51 (1988) and *Social Research* 58 (1991); of chapter 3, in *New Literary History* 25 (1994); of chapter 4, in *New Literary History* 22 (1991); of chapter 5, in *Languages of the Unsayable: The Play of Negativity in Literature and Literary Theory*, ed. Sanford Budick and Wolfgang Iser (New York: Columbia Univ. Press, 1989); of chapter 6, in

ELH 60 (1993), reprinted in *The Challenge of Periodization: Old Paradigms and New Perspectives*, ed. Lawrence Besserman (New York: Garland, 1996); of chapter 8, in *The Translatability of Cultures: Figurations of the Space Between*, ed. Sanford Budick and Wolfgang Iser (Stanford: Stanford Univ. Press, 1996); of chapter 12, in *Common Knowledge* 5 (1996).

THE WESTERN THEORY OF TRADITION

The Cultural Sublime:
Descartes, Kant, and Rembrandt

In this they appear to me similar to a blind man who
wishes to fight on even terms with one who can see,
and so brings him to the back of some very dark cellar. These people, I may say, are interested in my abstaining from the publication of my principles of philosophy; for since these are very simple and evident, I
would be doing much the same to them as though I
opened some windows and let the light of day enter
into that cellar where they had descended to fight.
—Descartes, *Discourse on Method*

There is an *interesting* sadness, such as is inspired by
the sight of some desolate place into which men
might fain withdraw themselves so as to hear no more
of the world without, and be no longer versed in its
affairs, a place, however, which must yet not be so altogether inhospitable as only to afford a most miserable retreat for a human being.—I only make this observation as a reminder that even melancholy, (but
not dispirited sadness,) may take its place among the
vigorous affections, provided it has its root in moral
ideas.
—Kant, "Analytic of the Sublime"

As a way of first entering the world of experience that I call the cultural
sublime, I seek to demonstrate that a hitherto unnoticed intimacy of
consciousness links Descartes, Kant, and Rembrandt. These three figures can be understood as bound together by their connection with a particular
place, namely, Amsterdam. Even work so unworldly as that of the philosophers
may share worldly imagery with certain paintings by Rembrandt.

Descartes's record of the experience of his cogito ("I think, therefore I am")
prompts us to search for a strange intimacy of this kind. Indeed, it provokes in
us the deepest questions about what a shared intimacy of consciousness—perhaps the most powerful and the most difficult of all the implicit claims of cultural tradition—would have to entail. Bernard Williams has made clear that in

Descartes's cogito the move from a consciousness of thinking to the existence of a thinker ("A is thinking") logically requires an impersonal formulation, but Descartes does not and cannot supply it. Achieving the "separateness" of an impersonal formulation, Williams argues, would imply "relativizing the content of the impersonally occurring thoughts."[1] In other words, if a place could be found for the subject to stand outside first-person thoughts (such as the thought of the cogito), the relativized subject could prove that *it* thinks and hence that it exists substantively, beyond consciousness, where others might have access to it. But any such "literal place" or "concrete relativization . . . even if it could fall short of requiring a subject who has the thoughts . . . has to exist in the form of something outside pure thought. . . . The Cartesian reflection merely presents, or rather invites us into, the perspective of consciousness" (pp. 98–100).

Williams repeatedly suggests that "it is not at all clear that we really can grasp . . . in the abstract" the difference between thought in Descartes's first-person form and thought in Williams's impersonal form (p. 96). Thus a concrete relativization might offer some unexpected clarity. In fact, the cue for my line of questioning is Williams's imagining for Descartes—to be sure, as a problem—a possible "relation between the 'I think' in the content of the thought" and "what is objectively involved in the state of affairs which constitutes its being thought" (p. 100). As I interpret this suggestion, Williams wants to reconceive the relation of thought to its contents, such that the state of affairs being thought is not merely assumed but recognized as necessary. Following this interpretation, my informal proposal is that without the existence of Amsterdam and Rembrandt, Descartes's thoughts of himself would not be what they are. The cultural achievements of the Amsterdam of that period and of Rembrandt in his images are the conditions needed for Descartes's supposing of presence. These achievements liberate his thought from an illusory and perhaps fetishized immediacy and dispose it to a subjunctive mood that may well be the hallmark of what we think of as works, or the work, of culture. This disposition of thought amounts to a significant kind of freedom.

Informally, then, I propose that the semantic requirement that Williams sees in Descartes's cogito, but which Descartes does not satisfy, has a cultural realization.[2] At the end of this chapter I will specify as nearly as I can the implications of this proposal for the materials I have presented.

Descartes lays special emphasis on freedom of choice as one kind of thinking. Even in the Second Meditation he includes *affirming* and *denying, willing* and *rejecting*, on his short list of what a thinking being thinks (*PE*, p. 85).[3] In the Fourth Meditation "volition" is said to be "the liberty of the free will"; moreover, it is the highest, the divine, mark of human thinking because it is the freedom to decide between "two contraries" while no "external force" constrains the mind.[4] In the *Discourse on Method*, in Descartes's description of the moment when he came to his cogito, the central term for representing the thinking of freedom is *resolving* or *choosing*. After years of delay Descartes finally set down his system because he was "honest enough not to desire to be esteemed as different from what I am" (*Works* 1:100). In the same paragraph he commences to lay the groundwork of the sameness or repetition of his "I am" and does so by resolving. I refer to Descartes's first resolve ("résoudre" [p. 31]), which is to remove himself from all acquaintances, to Holland. In the following paragraph he again resolves ("résolus" [p. 32]), this time to choose the hyperbolic doubt of "everything that ever entered into my mind." This resolve is what makes possible the experience of the cogito itself.

It is striking that the first resolve sketches many, perhaps all, of the second resolve's principal elements, most especially something very like hyperbolic doubt:

[1] It is just eight years ago that this desire made me resolve to remove myself ["me fit résoudre à m'éloigner"] from all places where any acquaintances were possible, and to retire to a country such as this, where the long-continued war has caused such order to be established that the armies which are maintained seem only to be of use in allowing the inhabitants to enjoy the fruits of peace with so much the more security; and where, in the crowded throng of a great and very active nation, which is more concerned with its own affairs than curious about those of others, without missing any of the conveniences of the most populous towns, I can live as solitary and retired as in deserts the most remote ["j'ai pu vivre aussi solitaire et retiré que dans les déserts les plus écartés"].

(*Works* 1:100)

[2] I resolved ["résolus"] to assume that everything that ever entered into my mind was no more true than the illusions of my dreams. But immediately afterwards I noticed that whilst I thus wished to think all things false, it was absolutely essential that the "I" who thought this should be something. . . . remarking that this truth "*I think, therefore I am*" was so certain and so assured that all the most extravagant suppositions brought forward by the sceptics were incapable of shaking it.

(*Works* 1:101)[5]

How are we to understand the verb to *resolve*, either in the first resolve, which apparently describes no more than Descartes's account of his removal to Amsterdam, a place of estrangement, he says, where no acquaintances were possible; or, in the next paragraph, in his resolve to assume that everything that had ever entered his mind was no more true than the illusions of his dreams?

I propose that in his representation of the origins of his philosophy Descartes's resolve to experience hyperbolic doubt is occasioned by a line of representations—each of which lets us see its inadequacy as a representation—

that together form a particular culture. By *culture* I mean no more or less than the patterns of cultural transmission specified by the works of given cultures. Focusing the term *culture* in the subterm *cultural transmission* is, I believe, commensurate with widely accepted usage. Clifford Geertz, for example, writes, "The culture concept to which I adhere has neither multiple referents nor, so far as I can see, any unusual ambiguity: it denotes an historically transmitted pattern of meanings embodied in symbols, a system of inherited conceptions expressed in symbolic forms by means of which men communicate, perpetuate, and develop their knowledge about and attitudes toward life. Of course, terms such as 'meaning,' 'symbol,' and 'conception' cry out for explication. But that is precisely where the widening, the broadening, and the expanding come in."[6]

Among other things, the present chapter explores the possibility that in a given history of culture the means of cultural transmission (or communication, perpetuation, bequeathing / inheriting, or development from one generation to another) already determine the meanings, symbols, and conceptions of that culture. If so, then the means of cultural transmission are central to what culture is.

I am therefore particularly concerned with the fact that Descartes resolves to remove himself not just to anywhere but to a culture transmitted by partially dispossessed representations. Already in his opening words he shows (although he camouflages it) that the line of transmission that he experiences in, or *as*, this culture holds open the opportunity of hyperbolic doubt, which enables his freedom of choice.

I wish to note certain symmetries among the representations that make up Descartes's first resolve. Each representation is dual. Each is constituted by delineating first a totality suggestive of great activity or even material turbulence and then a withdrawal from part of the totality, leaving a place of emptiness within the maelstrom. In ways that are not immediately clear, Descartes locates his "I am" in a line of points within vortices.

Descartes's first representation is of the peculiar activity of the Dutch: "a great and very active nation . . . more concerned with its own affairs than curious about those of others." The great, divided activity of Dutch life—that is, its active concern with worldly affairs side by side with its indifference to neighbors or acquaintances—is conserved by an equally paradoxical representation of armies that "seem only to be of use in allowing the inhabitants to enjoy the fruits of peace with so much the more security." Thus Descartes's resolve "to remove myself from all places where any acquaintances were possible, and to retire to a country such as this"—which is to say, to remove or withdraw or retire to "peace"—is formally symmetrical with the prior representations constituted by the paradox of self-immersion in the activity of the world and then, somehow as a result, withdrawal from it to the place where the condition of "I can live" is attained: "In the crowded throng of a great and very active nation . . . I can live as solitary and retired as in deserts the most remote."

The continuing line of representations of subtraction in Descartes's first resolve already heralds his cogito with a veiled announcement from the depths of his withdrawal into a condition highly congenial and perhaps indispensable to his hyperbolic doubt. Into "les déserts les plus écartés," that is, Descartes withdraws from everything but the pronouncement, by way of an anagram, of his own name: here "I . . . live," or, here I am, in *les déserts écartés*.[7]

From this serially emptied place Descartes immediately sets out to represent his resolve to hyperbolic doubt. When in the first sentence of part 4 he speaks of "the first meditations there [y (p. 31)] made by me," he means the meditations experienced in *les déserts écartés*, which is his thinking of freedom and his "I am," in other words, his cogito.

There is thus an indispensable continuity between the first and second resolves. The first is a series of representations of subtraction or removal, each of which reveals its own incompleteness of representation; thus each succeeding representation is chosen from the freedom of a nothingness (a space of withdrawal or occlusion) opened by a previous representation. Continually removed from all external objects or forces that might constrain his freedom of thinking and choosing, Descartes remains solitary, unconstrained, in the remotest desert, "there," and in this void his second, apparently more significant resolve is freely enacted.

Despite the very continuity of the representations that culminate in the freedom prerequisite to his cogito, Descartes will soon claim that an infinite series of representations must be denied or halted. He is well aware, however, of at least his initial experience of that continuity. In the Third Meditation he lays down the propositions "One idea gives birth to another idea" and "Ideas in me are like paintings or pictures" (*PE,* p. 98). But Descartes is silent about the kind of nothingness opened, in the *Discourse* at least, within each chosen representation (or painting or idea). Instead he ascribes the freedom of volition in his "present" moment of being to God's *concursus* (concurrence), which alone allows him to return from nothingness. Moreover, the concursus of God's being and his own nothingness is the very image in which the continuous "regress" of representations comes to a halt: "Step by step we finally arrive at an ultimate cause which will turn out to be God. And it is very obvious that in this case there cannot be an infinite regress, since it is not so much a question of the cause which produced me in the past as of that which conserves me in the present" (*PE,* p. 106). "To be conserved at every moment that it endures," Descartes explains, "a substance . . . needs the same power and the same action which would be necessary to produce it and create it anew if it did not yet exist" (*PE*, p. 105). The scene of the concursus is therefore the most fateful moment imaginable for human being per se. God alone gives Descartes the present experience of both nothingness and being. To be created "at every moment . . . anew" means to be created at every moment ex nihilo; hence at every moment every created thing must have just been nothing.

In the Fourth Meditation Descartes says precisely the same about his own thinking and being in his cogito: "There is present in my thought not only a real and positive idea of God, or rather of a supremely perfect being, but also, so to speak, a certain negative idea of nothingness. . . . I see that I am, as it were, a mean between God and nothingness. . . . Placed between the supreme Being and not-being . . . I consider myself as somehow participating in nothingness or not-being" (*PE*, 110). In Descartes's experience, every created thing not only tends constantly to slip out of existence but in fact has already slipped, at every moment, into the nothingness from which God at every moment newly creates it.[8]

Yet Descartes's claims about his experience of nothingness diverge from his representations of it. No doubt Descartes believed that his slipping into nothingness was a quasi-religious experience. But his representation of his oscillation between being and nothingness, as well as of his freedom to choose from nothingness, is accounted for within the structure of his representations, especially those in which he is engaged in his first and second resolves.[9] I propose that his sketch of the concursus of being and nothingness itself points to the freedom that he encounters in his continuous line of culture.[10] Far from identifying a halt to representation in this image, Descartes advances it as his most powerful symbol of necessitated transmission in his line of representations, each of which lets us see its own inadequacy as representation.

Nicholas Malebranche, Descartes's disciple, intended to reveal God's direct action in Descartes's picture of the concursus of being and nothingness. Instead he demonstrated how Descartes's picture of the concursus is spectacularly occasioned by the continuity of cultural transmission. Malebranche observed that Descartes's conception of God in the concursus drew on a formulation commonplace in the New Testament, especially in the Pauline epistles. Malebranche, who styled it "that we see all things in God," meant that we see only in the light provided by God; for example, "Not that we are sufficient of ourselves to think any thing as of ourselves; but our sufficiency is of God" (2 Cor. 3:5); or "That which may be known of God is manifest in them [the Gentiles]; for God hath shewed it unto them" (Rom. 1:19).[11]

The provenience that Malebranche gives for the concursus shows that for Descartes the concursus of being and nothingness must be, among other things, the representation of a line of representations of Paul's representation of it. Because of the nothingness described by each representation within the series, each prior representation (whether we can specifically identify it or not) functions as the enabling ground of freedom for thinking and choosing. Descartes's regress of "ideas" or "paintings" is a spiraling line—more precisely, a vortex—of representations of being and nothingness, each of which is a concursus. Part of what is encountered in the concursus—as in all derivations and transmissions of culture in the mode of partial withdrawal of representation—is its endless, unrepresentable repetition from the past. Descartes traces his line of cultural transmission forward in his own representations of his first and second resolves. His experience entails his free choosing from the contraries of being and nothingness endlessly encountered in representations of the concursus.

The Pauline provenience of Descartes's concursus also helps us, I believe, locate the "great and very active" achievements of Dutch culture that so deeply impressed Descartes, even though he declined to specify them. To begin with, I offer a very brief exemplification of the part of the vast map of contemporary Dutch culture that most directly concerns us.

Among such achievements in the culture of partially withdrawn representations, Rembrandt's *Saint Paul in Prison,* painted in 1627, two years before Descartes reached Holland, is virtually a schematic representation of Paul's meditation on the concursus (fig. 1). The light entering the window of the otherwise dark cell is mediated for Paul by the crucifix handle of his "sword of the Spirit" (Eph. 6:17), supported on both sides by such texts as a saint keeps by him, reminding him that he can think nothing by himself. Rather, his sufficiency to think is of God. The pen in his hand indicates that he is writing the very texts that inscribe this scene.[12] Rembrandt strongly suggests that the texts are themselves reworkings, or representations, of sacred commonplaces of the concursus in the piles of scriptures that Paul keeps at his side and on his lap. (Who would not, under the same circumstances, think back, for example, to Psalms 36:9: "With thee is the fountain of life: in thy light shall we see light"?) Within the Rembrandtian iconographic economy it may even be plausible that Paul opens his eyes wide and brings his hand to his mouth because he suddenly realizes that he has just been created anew, from nothing, by the text that he is meditating on or is about to write down. At the very least, the scene is a stark representation of the Pauline concursus of being and nothingness that Malebranche paraphrases.

Aside: If such a philosophical reception of Rembrandt's painting seems

FIGURE I. Rembrandt, *Saint Paul in Prison* (Bredius 601).
Courtesy Staatsgalerie Stuttgart.

unimaginable for 1627–29, I may instance here the intellectual range of Constantijn Huygens, patron to Descartes and Rembrandt and one of the "great and very active" Dutch whom Descartes came to know best after his arrival in Amsterdam in 1629/30. In 1629 Huygens wrote in his diary that Rembrandt, then only twenty-three years old, was already the equal of the most famous painters of Europe and predicted that he would soon surpass them. In 1632 Huygens began the relationship with Descartes that lasted until the end of Descartes's life. Descartes indicates that he composed the first draft of the *Med-*

itations about this time.[13] Rembrandt moved from Leiden to Amsterdam permanently in 1631/32. It seems clear that Rembrandt knew Descartes directly; apparently, he even painted Descartes in a place of honor in *The Hundred Guilder Print*.[14]

To resume: The art historian Jakob Rosenberg observes that the motif of the meditating philosopher "seems particularly close to Rembrandt and can be called one of his most personal choices." Whereas in other, contemporary Dutch painters "the outward attributes" of the philosopher's inquiry are most prominent, in Rembrandt the emphasis is on "the old philosopher enjoying the privilege of meditating in complete seclusion in his search for truth. Light and shade, a penumbral atmosphere, . . . gain a particular importance in connexion with this subject."[15] By the end of the eighteenth century, at the latest, Rembrandt's work was associated in the public mind with a single representation of the philosopher thinking, *Old Man in an Interior with a Winding Staircase* (1633). I believe that this painting already held a special meaning for Descartes when he composed the *Discourse*. In France the painting had come by the following century to be called *Le Philosophe en contemplation* (fig. 2).[16] A recurrent feature in Rem-

FIGURE 2. Rembrandt, *Le Philosophe en contemplation* (Bredius 431).
Courtesy Musée du Louvre, Paris. © Photo RMN.

FIGURE 3. Rembrandt, *A Scholar in a Lofty Room* (*"St. Anastasius"*) (Bredius 430).
Courtesy of the Statens Konstmuseer, Stockholm.

brandt's paintings of the philosopher is that he meditates near a window or windows, usually in a darkened room. From roughly the same period as *Le Philosophe
en contemplation* we have other well-known Rembrandtian paintings of the
scholar or philosopher thinking near a window (cf. figs. 3, 4).[17]

In the late 1620s and early 1630s Rembrandt made his mark spectacularly
as the master of chiaroscuro. Can it be purely by accident that in the *Discourse*
Descartes evokes something very like Rembrandtian technique when setting
down his philosophical ways of representing thought and knowledge of "material things"? "I intended to include . . . all that I thought I knew," he writes,
"concerning the nature of material things. But I found myself in the same state
as painters, who cannot equally well represent in a two-dimensional painting
all the various faces of a solid body, and so choose one to bring to the light, and

FIGURE 4. Rembrandt (or his school), *A Scholar in a Lofty Room* (Bredius 427).
Courtesy of the National Gallery, London.

leave the others in shadow" (*PE*, 31–32). For Descartes one face of every material thing, or of every cogito, in every concursus is turned toward nothingness.
For us the significance of the relation of Descartes's ideas to Rembrandt's
highly contrastive chiaroscuro does not lie merely in the models that may have
influenced Descartes.[18] Rather, the transposition of a painter's language of
chiaroscuro into Descartes's language allows us to glimpse something like the
cultural enabling of Descartes's freedom of choice between light and shadow,
being and nothingness. That Descartes neglects to name specific cultural objects or occasions of this kind creates a false impression of his intellectual independence, which is contradicted by the way in which freedom becomes available or is derived in his own representations and resolves. Specific occasions of
partially withdrawn representations, rendered by a painter like Rembrandt—

or by extraordinarily close equivalents of Rembrandt—are, I suggest, the missing terms (the experienced openings of freedom) in Descartes's account.

Thus it may be especially significant for our understanding of how Descartes's cogito was enabled that one begetting representation of his freedom is eerily reproduced in the *Discourse*. In one of Descartes's most striking images of the courage of his philosophical resolve, opponents to his way of thinking "appear . . . similar to a blind man who wishes to fight on even terms with one who can see, and so brings him to the back of some very dark cellar. These people, I may say, are interested in my abstaining from the publication of my principles of philosophy; for since these are very simple and evident, I would be doing much the same to them as though I opened some windows and let the light of day enter into that cellar where they had descended (descendus [71]) to fight" (*PE*, p. 51).[19]

I turn again to *Le Philosophe en contemplation* (see fig. 2), which by 1738 was also called *Tobias, and a Winding Stair*. The subject is unmistakably identified from its relation to the Book of Tobit (in the Jewish Apocrypha) and to the many representations of it that Rembrandt executed. The episode superimposed on the meditating philosopher here is that of the victory of Tobias, blind Tobit's son, over a demon who has attempted to murder him in a dark room below the stairs. Tobias, pictured at the window, overcomes the demon without striking a blow and also restores his father's sight. The advanced age of the man at the window suggests that, in addition to being an exemplum of Rembrandt's philosopher, he is also a composite of son and father, the dual heroes of the Book of Tobit.[20]

This painting and Descartes's pictured scene share the specific combination of familiar primary theme and exotic secondary theme. The former is that of the philosopher and his windows; the latter, that of the battle fought (without blows) between the hero and the demon (one of whom is blind) in an intensely dark room to which they have descended, as from a staircase. The correspondences, though vivid, possess only archival interest in themselves. What may be decisive for Descartes's "principles of philosophy," however, is the location of the opening to his freedom in the repetitions from this regress (or progression) of partially withdrawn images, in paintings or in texts, each a concursus unto itself. Most important, both painting and text are chiaroscuro arrangements of being and nothingness in which the painter and the philosopher, each a mean between being and nothingness, resolve to participate. Each finds a freedom enabled by his inherited images of concursus. Each chooses between the contraries of being and nothingness within his effectively endless line of culture, and each is created anew in his representation within his line of culture.

Hanging on a wall of Descartes's Dutch world, the painting (or its twin) opens a window for Descartes's windows and for his free, peaceful battle on behalf of philosophy. Something very like this unnamed transmission of a concursus enabled the freedom of Descartes's "principles of philosophy." Specifically, Descartes obtained the freedom of his "déserts écartés" and of his cogito in a concrete *there* of this culture.

I turn now to Kant's sublime. In the "Analytic of the Sublime" and even in the *Critique of Judgment* as a whole, the mind's a priori ground of the sublime is announced as the "point of capital importance."[21] Kant claims that the freedom experienced in it is entirely independent of any object or any definite concept (pp. 90, 104). He attaches central import to the independence of sublime experience because, in his view, it is identified with the freedom of aesthetic judgment and its consequence, "moral feeling" (pp. 116–17).

Yet the immediacy of the provocation required by the sublime casts doubt, from the start, on Kant's claim.[22] Thus I will propose a counterclaim: in the "Analytic of the Sublime" Kant's representation of the mind's "*a priori* . . . transcendental" freedom (pp. 116–17) is indispensably occasioned by a particular cultural transmission, signaled by a specific work of art; that is, in his experience of the sublime Kant resists, in freedom, a particular representation of resistance in freedom.[23] This prior representation enables Kant's freedom; furthermore, it is experienced by him in an infinite progression—or infinite regress—of representations, each of which lets us see its own inadequacy as representation. These representations form the immediate (always culturally transmitted) objects of Kant's experience of the sublime. Kant's own language indicates that he takes in this prior representation, in its line of representations, "at one glance" (in einem Augenblick), but he chooses to "resist" (widerstehen) what he has seen and in effect "no longer sees" (nicht . . . ansieht) what he has seen.[24]

It will help clarify the nature of my counterclaim to note that it corresponds to Kant's way of setting off his representation of sublime experience. Kant's framing predicate, near the beginning of section 28, is the phrase "wenn . . . wir uns bloss . . . denken" (p. 103) (our simply imagining in thought [p. 110]). These words clearly indicate a supposition or subjunctive condition or, as we now say, a counterfactual: the very supposition "wenn . . . wir uns bloss . . . denken" denies that the representation (the pictured case or situation) is the reality that it represents.[25] Without specific reference to Kant, F. H. Bradley long ago supplied the basic logic of a supposition. With regard to its givens, Bradley explained that although a supposition is "known to be ideal . . . it is not the mere *idea* of existence that is used. What we use is the real that is always in immediate contact with our minds." With regard to what a supposition produces, he observed that "the real is not qualified by the attribute we apply to it. But, so soon as we judge, we have truth or falsehood, and the real is at once concerned in the matter." Bradley added that what a supposition affirms "is the mere ground of the connection; not the actual existing behavior of the real, but a latent quality of its disposition, a quality which has appeared in the experiment."[26] These comments bear on the apparently loose relations among the representations that I describe in Kant's supposition. Furthermore, the status of the supposition obtains equally in the relations among the representations that I have proposed for Descartes. For the meaning of literary history there are important lessons to be learned from the ways in which Kant's and Descartes's representations leave virtually no traces of influence, anxious or unanxious, even while they are powerfully implicated in the relations of a highly specific cultural transmission. One might indeed object that such relations as I propose amount to no more than strings of possible associations that might just as well have led the viewer in many other directions. Yet the experience of cultural transmission—that is, of cultural transmission that continues to find recipients—is characteristically of this kind.

Just in this way, I suggest, Kant's invoking of the suppositional frame for his representation of sublime experience captures a feature of representations that may be all too easily lost on art critics and historians. That is, the status of supposition that conditions Kant's representation reproduces the status of supposition that necessarily inheres in the representations that he takes in. In addition, in the specific representations that Descartes and Kant encounter, as in their own representations, the status of supposition is highlighted by a form of representation that lets us see its own inadequacy as representation.

In Kant's supposition of sublime experience and moral feeling, no less than in Descartes's resolve to the hyperbolic doubt from which his cogito issues, the thought recorded (including its subtractive elements) could not have come into existence without the real that was in immediate contact with their minds. My supposition, accordingly, is that a significant part of the real, for both Descartes and Kant, was provided by an existing line of representations. The disposition for connection that Descartes and Kant came to share is a recurring quality of the line of representations that they chose to join or, as Descartes would say, to remove themselves to. It follows that my own supposition regarding these matters must be formulated in a subjunctive mood, however immediately real I believe the force of the supposition to be.

Here I briefly summarize what Kant says about the half-dozen chief elements of his supposition, or picture, of sublime experience, that is, the experience that he claims is of the mind "of itself alone":

1. "As is allowable," says Kant, his presentation of the sublime is drawn exclusively according to experience of the sublime occasioned by "objects of nature," not from experience occasioned by objects of art or culture (p. 91).
Thus, for example, Kant asks us to imagine some vast peak whose top we
cannot see, "shapeless mountain masses towering one above the other in
wild disorder" (p. 104).

2. The experience of the sublime occurs in the mind as the result of a contradiction between two mental capacities. While our imagination attempts to
follow a progression that has no end in sight—for example, "masses towering one above the other"—our reason tries to grasp a whole idea of that
progression. Oddly, the incapacity created by this contradiction sets in operation the innate capacity to feel the presence of something unknown to the
senses, or "supersensible." The supersensible is not necessarily supernatural
or divinely mysterious. For Kant the sublime is the mind's capacity or "faculty" to continue to think about a given representation of an object even
though the mind has exhausted its resources for sensory perception (mea-
surement) of that object: "Because there is a striving in our imagination towards progress *ad infinitum,* while reason demands absolute totality, as a real
idea, that same inability . . . is the awakening of a feeling of a supersensible
faculty within us. . . . Consequently it is the state of mind evoked by a particular representation engaging the attention of the reflective judgment, and
not the object, that is to be called sublime" (pp. 97–98).[27] For the logical unfolding of the experience of the sublime Kant offers a shorthand that renders the instantaneous character of the experience. The mind's experience
of the sublime is "owing to the impossibility of the absolute totality of an
endless progression" (p. 104).[28]

3. The experience of the sublime occurs only when the individual mind initiates it by freely inducing its own incapacity, which is the mind's subjection to
"the impossibility of the absolute totality of an endless progression." Thus
the mind's act of freedom is a willed self-deprivation of freedom, which
paradoxically creates greater freedom: "The sublime . . . is a feeling of
imagination by its own act depriving itself of its freedom. . . . In this way it
gains an extension and a might greater than that which it sacrifices. But the
ground of this is concealed from it, and in its place it *feels* the sacrifice or deprivation . . . a deprivation of something—though in the interests of inner
freedom" (pp. 120–23).

4. Only in "a negative presentation" can the mind present to itself the idea of
freedom because "the inscrutability of the idea of freedom precludes all
positive presentation" (p. 128), that is, all presentation in any bounded or defined body.

5. "Melancholy," one of Kant's principal names for the mind's representation to itself of its sublime thought and emotion, is the effect on the mind of combining its "serenity" with the abrupt "movement" of the mind aroused by the object (p. 121). This movement, an "alternating repulsion and attraction" (p. 107), follows from "resistance" or "opposition" to the sensory object (pp. 91, 110, 118–19), which "the mind [which] is all life (the life-principle itself)" experiences in the sublime as a moment of dying. We are reassured that this "momentary check to the vital forces" (p. 91) (augenblicklichen Hemmung der Lebenskräfte [p. 75]) is "followed at once by a discharge all the more powerful." Yet it is not obvious in Kant's account of the sublime, any more than in Descartes's sudden awareness of his "I am" after hyperbolic doubt—or, incidentally, than it becomes in Hegel's Kant-derived account of the birth of self-consciousness after "dying-away" in "sublimation"—how the "vital forces," which have been checked or radically suspended or have died away, are able to recover.[29]

6. Surprisingly, Kant withholds discussion of the feeling that a viewer may have on seeing the Pyramids of Egypt or Saint Peter's in Rome, that is, the feeling when it "comes home to him of the inadequacy of his imagination for presenting the idea of a whole within which that imagination attains its maximum, and, in its fruitless efforts to extend this limit, recoils upon itself [in sich selbst zurück sinkt (p. 88)], but in so doing succumbs to an emotional delight" (p. 100). Kant's withholding, a key element in his representation of the sublime, expresses itself as a refusal "at present . . . to deal with the ground of this delight, connected, as it is, with a representation in which we would least of all look for it—*a representation, namely, that lets us see its own inadequacy,* and consequently its subjective want of finality for our judgment in the estimation of magnitude" (p. 100; emphasis added). Such a representation—a work of art or a representation of culture, in other words—has been crafted to let the viewer see its (the art object's) own inadequacy to full or complete representation. Kant appears to distinguish this withdrawn representation from "works of art, e.g. buildings, statues and the like, where a human end determines the form as well as the magnitude" and also from "things of nature, that in their very concept import a definite end" (p. 100). Inexplicably, Kant is "disposed" (p. 100) to deal only with objects of nature that occasion the sublime by not "import[ing] a definite end," and not with works of art that might do the same negative thing.

Yet Kant's own representation of sublime experience, considered in the array of visualized predicates that constitute that representation, allows us to suppose that another picture, prior to Kant's picture of his "*a priori* . . . transcendental," may enable the freedom that leads to moral feeling, that is, for Kant himself. For the following list of those predicates I use only the details of Kant's own terms and phrases, most of them from sections 28 and 29 of the "Analytic of the Sublime." Using a typical Kantian formulation, I ask, What must a representation be to include the predicates that Kant supposes?

1. The individual experiencing the sublime simply imagines in thought the experience of the sublime.
2. He views a desolate place, isolated from all society.
3. He is withdrawn from the world and its affairs.
4. The place to which he has withdrawn is not altogether inhospitable.
5. His mood is that of melancholy—or *apatheia* or *phlegma in significatu bono* [phlegmatic in a good sense]—or "an interesting sadness."
6. He is helpless.
7. He sees that he is safe.
8. He experiences deprivation as if by his own will.
9. He resists (or has resisted) God's commandments.
10. He is now resigned to God's will or wrath.
11. He is conscious of his own uprightness before God and man.
12. God's wrath is shown in the violence of nature.
13. Nature's violence is shown to be God's outburst of wrath or the pouring forth of the vials of his wrath.
14. The individual who experiences all of this at this moment no longer sees the violence wrought by nature in fulfillment of God's wrath.

In principle it must be possible to identify the specific representation that Kant chose to resist (i.e., not to acknowledge specifically) even while he supposed all of its predicates. Of course, I do not insist that the work of art that I will propose, and suppose, must be the one that "immediately . . . provokes" Kant's sublime experience (p. 90). But, following Kant's own terms, I do insist that his sublime experience was immediately provoked by some work of art virtually identical with the one that I will propose. (It is my hope that other readers will propose other possibilities that include all of Kant's predicates.) In Kant's own terms for experience of the sublime and of freedom, only one work at a time could occasion "at once" (p. 103), "at one glance" (p. 107), the instant of "a momentary check to the vital forces." This immediately experienced, particular work signaled for Kant the experience of a particular endless transmission of culture. In the "Analytic of the Sublime" Kant resists this derivation of sublime experience yet actively, specifically represents it.

That is, Kant's representation of sublime experience must in itself be an experience (as well as a representation) of an effectively endless line of prior representations of that experience. It must be occasioned by a particular object that "immediately . . . provokes" this sublime experience, which thus expresses a definite concept of the line of culture (the line of withdrawn representations) subjunctively directed, with a certain disposition, toward an end.[30] All elements of Kant's representation of the experience of the sublime are necessarily represented as commonplaces (topoi). In the experience of the sublime Kant experiences the utter (sublime) commonplaceness of his own thinking of the sublime, because commonplaces are figures or representational predicates (always expressed in the subjunctive mood) derived from an endless progression or line of prior representations. In the representation of sublime experience the lineage of commonplaceness is itself part of the representation.

This perspective on the function of the commonplace within sublime representation at least partly meets and embraces in advance the objection that Kant surely recalled numerous other representations (including discursive descriptions) of the sublime that were very similar to the one I will suppose. In addition, this perspective suggests that in Kant's experience of the sublime per se only those elements—including selection and arrangement—that are part of an effectively endless progression of prior representation are admissible to Kant's picture of the sublime. Here *prior* can mean only "identical to" or at least "identified with" the latest representations in the progression. Of course, there will always be the individual's fingerprints on the sublime transmission of culture, and there will always be new contextualizations or historical landscapes in which the call and the silence of a transmission of the sublime are heard. These fingerprints and contextualizations may be of great interest in themselves, but they do not occasion the sublime experience per se as Kant describes it. Thus Kant's selection and arrangement of commonplaces must be experienced by Kant as the recurrence of a prior, particular selection and arrangement of commonplaces. In this way Kant's representation represents the experience of a particular line or effectively endless progression of sublime representations, which is to say, the sublime suppositions of a given line of culture.

Within Kant's line of culture, an endless progression of representations frees him to resist or choose the object of culture. Yet since freedom is to resist or choose *something*, Kant is free to resist or choose that something only if it has been part of his experience; if, in this case, he stands within his line of cultural transmission. Otherwise his resistance or choice is only the effect of prejudice, that is, of someone else's resistance or choice imposed, however subtly, on him. Kant's act of freedom in resisting or choosing this line of cultural transmission can have occurred only in his experience of this line of his culture. His act of freedom in resisting is achieved by "simply imagining in thought" (i.e., by simply supposing, counterfactually) a "righteous man" wishing to "resist God and His commandments" (p. 110). Although Kant denies that experience of the sublime intrinsically depends on an experience of culture, he must both resist and repeat this particular, prior representation within his line of culture.

The particular representation that I have in mind and that Kant may very well have had in mind—a widely circulated etching of a painting by Rembrandt—was known in Germany in Kant's time both as *Le Philosophe dans sa grotte* (The philosopher in his cave) and as *Loth in der Höhle* (Lot in the cave).[31] (At the end of the nineteenth century, a hundred years after Kant wrote the "Analytic of the Sublime," the painting received a new title, *Jeremiah Lamenting the Destruction of Jerusalem* [fig. 5], which made the connection with Kant much more difficult to see.[32] A number of the details of Kant's predicates have no place in Jeremiah's situation but correspond closely to Lot's.)

Already in the eighteenth century Rembrandt's works were very popular in Germany, especially in northern (Protestant) Germany. The etching of Rembrandt's painting to which I draw attention became commonly available in Kant's part of the world precisely when he was writing the "Analytic of the Sublime." The copperplate etching was made in Berlin in 1768 by Georg Friedrich Schmidt, engraver to the king of Prussia and one of the most famous engravers of the day. Schmidt's Rembrandt etchings (eight in all) were widely admired as the pinnacle of engraving in that century, surpassing (it was said) the engravings of Rembrandt himself.[33] In the Keyserling palace, where Kant was a frequent guest beginning in 1772, Königsberg (one of the king's official residences) boasted one of the finest collections of copperplate etchings in Europe. Considering the prominence of etchings in everyday artistic education of the times and Kant's particular opportunities for special attentiveness to Schmidt's rendering of Rembrandt's picture of the philosopher (rendered, in turn, from the Bible), it requires an effort to imagine that Kant never at least glanced at it. How he may have been affected by it is, of course, another matter.

The representations that I have in mind, then, side by side, are Schmidt's etching of Rembrandt's *Philosopher in His Cave / Lot in the Cave* and the collection of visual predicates from Kant's "Analytic of the Sublime."[34] In the predicates Kant simply imagines in thought the individual in the moment of experiencing the freedom of the sublime, necessarily in resistance (fig. 6). If we put together the title *Lot in the Cave* and the story told in Genesis, the buildings burning to Lot's right may be supposed to be those of Sodom and Gomorrah. Here God expresses his wrath through violent nature: earthquakes, brimstone, and fire. Formerly fearful of this violence, Lot has for a time resisted even divine counsel to flee the city (Gen. 19:16, 18, 20), but now he sits alone in a desolate cave, apa-

FIGURE 5. Rembrandt, *Jeremiah Lamenting the Destruction of Jerusalem* (Bredius 604).
Courtesy Rijksmuseum, Amsterdam.

thetic or melancholy. (He reclines in the pose that iconographically stands for
melancholy [see Bruyn et al., 1:281].) Aware that he is safe from the conflagra-
tion, out of sight of God's wrath, Lot might be taken (as his daughters take him)
for the last man alive. He has accepted God's decree, having earlier risked his
life (and that of his daughters) to observe the customs of hospitality and to pro-
tect the stranger.

"We may look upon an object as *fearful,* and yet not be afraid of it," says

FIGURE 6. Georg Friedrich Schmidt's etching of Rembrandt's *Le Philosophe dans sa grotte* / *Loth in der Höhle* (*Jeremiah Lamenting the Destruction of Jerusalem*). Courtesy Staatliche Museen zu Berlin. Photo Jörg P. Anders.

Kant, "if . . . our estimate takes the form of our simply imagining in thought the case of our wishing to offer some resistance to it, and recognizing that all such resistance would be quite futile. So the righteous man fears God without being afraid of Him, because he regards the case of his wishing to resist God and His commandments as one which need cause *him* no anxiety. But in every such case, regarded by him as not intrinsically impossible, he cognizes Him as One to be feared" (p. 110). To take the estimate of Kant's true picture of sublime cultural experience, we need to paraphrase his words in something like the following way, that is, in order to suppose (to imagine in thought) Kant's resistance to the prior representation (especially of the inadequacy of representation) that he fears:[35]

> We may look upon an object of culture—"a representation, namely, that lets us see its own inadequacy, and consequently its subjective want of finality for our judgment in the estimation of magnitude" (p. 100)—as fearful and yet not be afraid of it. . . . Our estimate takes the form of our simply imagining in thought the case of our wishing to offer some resistance to this "it" and recognizing that all such resistance would be quite futile.
>
> So the philosopher, or person who experiences the sublime, fears the endless progression of artistic, or cultural, presentations of sublime experience, which enables or moves him to achieve his own freedom of sublime experience without being afraid of it. Yet in every such case, regarded by him as not intrinsically impossible, his experience of the sublime enables him to recognize his own line of culture, or progression of such presentations, as one to be feared, since it occasions "a momentary check to the vital forces."

As in what is seen to occur in *The Philosopher in His Cave / Lot in the Cave,* Kant pictures the enforcement of God's might through the agency of violent nature. Once this connection among Kant's representations, or suppositions, is made, this and the other visual predicates I have cited from the "Analytic of the Sublime" are seen to form one extended supposition of the sublime experience.

My supposition is that Kant resists (averts his eyes from) Schmidt's etching of Rembrandt's biblical painting (or its double) even as he retraces it (thus fulfilling what Kant himself identifies as the sublime commandment to represent the inadequacy of representation [p. 127]). In this way, the figure in Kant's picture and in Schmidt's etching resists God's commandments yet fulfills them in the representation or experience that is resistance in freedom.[36] The engraver or painter draws each such experience or representation of the sublime with, as it were, one hand tied behind his back. The resulting disposition of mind for each protagonist in this ongoing cultural experiment—"Lot," Rembrandt, Schmidt, Kant—is melancholic or apathetic. There is no full recovery for any individual mind but only what Kant calls the "subjective want of finality" or the "contra-final" mind. Yet we see a symmetry with each representation of the given line of such representations that leads into this picture, threads through it, and points beyond it.

In this momentary check to his vital forces Kant is unable to acknowledge that a historical line of cultural transmission—an endless progression of representations of the inadequacy of representation—has occasioned his freedom of self-deprivation. Yet his own free act of self-deprivation is his casting away of the immediacy, for his own experience, of the immediate representation that provokes his recognition of this line of representations, which he now continues.

Ten thousand other pictures contain some, many, or most of the elements that are objects of sublime experiences like the one Kant represents. But to glimpse the moment of freedom in Kant's representation of sublime experience, we must suppose, plausibly, the specific prior representation—and *its* endless progression of prior representations—that "immediately . . . provokes" his resistance, as well as the check to his vital forces. I propose that the picture of effectively endless cultural transmission at which Kant glanced must have provoked him in something very like the guise of Schmidt's etching of Rembrandt's *Philosopher in His Cave/Lot in the Cave*.[37] Yet whether or not this etching of this painting of this biblical scene (and of this philosopher) is the specific identification that we require, my supposition is that the philosopher Kant—simply imagining in thought, withdrawn and resisting in his study in Königsberg—has himself pictured just how particular the cultural provocation to his mind's sublime experience had to have been.

Descartes's freedom and Kant's freedom are both enabled by their experiences of cultural transmission, specifically of a transmission defined by a line of representations, each of which shows its own inadequacy as representation. With hindsight we may say that there was a certain inevitability to the experiences of Descartes and Kant: two of the greatest European philosophers, while thinking about representation, not least the representation of painters, encountered one of the greatest European painters, representing the philosopher thinking. Yet, however the stage was set for these encounters, the nothingness of Descartes's hyperbolic doubt, from which his cogito issued, and the momentary check to Kant's vital forces, from which his sublime freedom for moral feeling issued, were each enabled by this line of representations. Each representation in this line shows its inadequacy as representation (in addition to its status as supposition), even as each is specifically a representation of the philosopher thinking. For Descartes and Kant, Rembrandt's two paintings—*Le Philosophe en contemplation* and *Le Philosophe dans sa grotte*—are of special consequence.

If we happen to think of ourselves as belonging to Descartes's and Kant's lines of cultural transmission, we too, in glancing at these paintings, may experience anew our own strange condition as free individuals within these transmissions of culture. Whatever other, infinitely varied things we do, each of us may thereby be enabled to think, and to resist freely, the occasion of freedom within cultural transmissions of this sort.

The means of cultural transmission are central to what culture is. In thinking about, and from, a line of cultural transmission—in conceiving the connections among objects in the line of transmission—we divest ourselves of a positivity or a wholly determinate causality. Cultural transmission makes available a field of suppositions, which the individual mind experiences as an infinite potentiality of permutation, as an unlimited unknowability of intended interconnection, and as a certain disposition toward ways of connecting. This disposition emerges from the line of transmission itself, in which the recipient takes part. Lines of cultural transmission do not necessarily become less real because of their counterfactual status. The freedom of association created for the individual mind by this subjunctive cultural transmission in fact renders more urgent the recipient's desire to ground the disposition of connection.

For the literary or art historian describing cultural transmission, the requirement of providing the plausibility of a given supposition is in no way suspended by its being, after all, only a supposition. The plausible force of the supposition is the depth of the historical account itself, and this depth can be achieved only through an awareness of specific objects within the line of transmission.

The Present Experience of Priority: Rembrandt and Jeremiah (and Isaiah and Ezekiel)

CHAPTER

INTERFACE: Even though Schmidt traced the lines of Rembrandt's painting with extraordinary care, he got Rembrandt wrong in one massive detail. Schmidt's error seems harmless enough. It is no more than reversing the painting from right to left, a frequent (though not inevitable) effect of the engraver's art (see figs. 5 and 6).[1] Yet in this particular event, the reversal blocked off an immense part of the continuity of this painting's line of cultural reference, thereby obscuring as well Rembrandt's representation of the individual mind's placement in a line of cultural transmission. This is to say that Schmidt's reversal of the painting made it very difficult to grasp its continuities of figuration—its commonplaces—which, as we shall see, depend on Rembrandt's designations of right and left. These commonplaces turn out to be, in fact, the most significant grounds for identifying the personality and the cultural line of the old man before us. An experience that is indispensable for the vitality of cultural tradition is right before our eyes in this painting.

In *Jeremiah Lamenting the Destruction of Jerusalem* Rembrandt's continuities of figuration represent the identity between the experience of the sublime and the experience of the continuity of culture.[2] This identity forms the basis of what I will try to show is the central feature of this painting. For Rembrandt the urgency of the real is created by representation or experience of the priority—the anteriority or history—of the present.

The relevance to the Kantian sublime of those features of the painting that Kant would have seen clearly in Schmidt's etching is in no way diminished in significance by identifying more accurately the painting's historical referents and a specific series of repetitions within the endlessness of its sublime representation. That is, even when we replace the title, "Lot in the Cave," with "Jeremiah Lamenting the Destruction of Jerusalem," we see that Rembrandt's painting exhibits, at very least, the chief elements of all the sublime predicates that Kant represents in the "Analytic of the Sublime."

Thus in the case of the Jeremiah that we see here:

- He is merely deep in thought, presumably about the scene of destruction at his right.
- This righteous man no longer sees that scene of destruction, fulfilling God's wrath, even though it is just beside him.
- Withdrawn from the world and its business, he sits isolated in a desolate but not inhospitable place (on a rich carpet, in company with costly vessels).
- He is helpless to prevent the calamity that he himself has prophesied, but he sees that he is himself safe.
- For his own reasons, his mood is melancholic, apathetic, phlegmatic. His is an interesting (even a fascinating) sadness.
- His posture and expression show that he is now resigned to God's commandments (which have included the commandment to prophesy the destruction of Jerusalem).
- Yet this righteous man, who is now silent, has uttered and recorded a remarkable intensity of resistance to the Lord. He has resisted God right from the beginning of his way: "Then said I, Ah, Lord God! behold, I cannot speak: for I am a child. But the Lord said unto me, Say not, I am a child: for thou shalt go to all that I shall send thee, and whatsoever I command thee thou shalt speak" (1:6–7). And he has continued resistant even in the moment of resigning himself to the execution of God's commandment to prophesy the destruction of Jerusalem: "Cursed be the day wherein I was born: let not the day wherein my mother bare me be blessed. . . . Wherefore came I forth out of the womb to see labour and sorrow, and that my days should be consumed with shame?" (20:14, 18). In addition, even the naked eye sees that this man has suffered a marked deprivation, though it may require explicit comment to bring it to more explicit (yet still only partial) consciousness, especially to explain how much it is a self-willed deprivation.

Highlighting this man's act of self-willed deprivation—the act which is of central significance in Kant's analysis of the sublime—will be one of my principal aims in the following pages. Yet in order to present this painting's specific features of the sublime and of cultural transmission, I will not proceed by a counter-Kantian polemic. Rather, I will try to present the painting's representational components in what seem to me to be Rembrandt's own terms.

On first view, what can be said with confidence about this painting's central figure hardly seems worth saying. His expression is preoccupied and downcast. He is old and alone. He is leaning on his left arm in a melancholy posture. By contrast with his well-lighted face and figure, virtually everything around him is shadowy. On the thematic level, this lack of clarity also applies to the man's relation to the scene of destruction at his right, to the objects at his left, and even to the place in which he abides. Striking in their specificity among the obscure objects that surround him are the insectlike figure that holds a torch above the burning buildings at his right and, at his left, a tassled cloth garment, an open leather pouch, and a dark bottle of crude manufacture.

We might feel inclined to shrug off, as being merely uninteresting, circumstances and details that seem unspecified or merely offhand. Yet in this painting we are compelled to experience the perplexities about what we are seeing. These perplexities, or even doubts, propel us into the line of this man's past experience. Indeed, in this painting the need to investigate the provenience of these circumstances and details begins to define the cultural function of an activity of scholarship or learning, which the old man himself, leaning on his book, also represents (among other things). Even the small or marginal constituents of this painting demand careful probing and meditation since, uneventful as any one of them may seem to be, they are all framed together with the spectacle of violence at the man's right.

The drama of these unexplained relations is only heightened by the variety of ways Rembrandt has distanced the old man from that scene of destruction. The burning buildings and the city gate penetrated by a crowd bearing spears are drawn in much-reduced scale and in blurred detail. And the visible part of the scene of destruction is enclosed with an arched segment of a circle which is mostly inaccessible to our view, beyond the frame of the painting. Between this scene and the old man a cloudy diagonal space intervenes, emphasizing his borderline positioning. Paradoxically, the banal and incidental facts of this man's creaturely condition have thus been made structurally pivotal to the entire composition. Indeed, given the spectacle of violence at his right, even the barest logic of relation among the elements of the painting generates a perplexing intuition: this man's aging body represents a more than usual fatality for everything that is shown in this painting, which must also mean for *the way* everything is shown in this painting.

To describe Rembrandt's method of representation I will attend to just three aspects of this painting, all of which are in fact focused with rigorous precision at the point where the cloudy diagonal abuts the figure of the old man. These aspects are (1) a divergence of times, marked by the diagonal, between the right- and left-hand scenes; (2) a self-willed deprivation that the old man has suffered, exactly at the point where the diagonal abuts the figure; and (3) the relation of the painting's images to the scriptural verses which underwrite this point of self-deprivation.

Even the difference in kinds of representation at the old man's right and left suggests his borderline position. At his right is a scene of catastrophe, shown with all the blurriness attendant upon the reporting of such a scene. At his left is a collection of lifeless objects that jut into the viewer's world as unexplained signs or symbols. But the fatality suggested by the man's borderline position is underlined by his location at the seam of a temporal contradiction. Try as we may, we cannot bring together the time of the scene of destruction at the left and the time of the objects piled at the right. This divergence of times is certainly a quite ordinary feature of representation of any kind. No doubt the force of this contradiction is even intimately represented here in the very fact of the man's aging body, that is, in the everyday ungraspable fact that an aging body (young or, more painfully, old) is and is not the same existence that it was a moment ago. Yet the experience of a divergence of times in this painting does not remain general. Rembrandt deepens and channels it in conjunction with other patterns that I will soon describe. Rembrandt's handling of this ordinary feature reveals something extraordinary within it.

The divergent times of the painting are indicated, for one thing, by scriptural information that Rembrandt surely regarded as common knowledge. In fact, it is especially necessary to emphasize that we are speaking here of no more than common knowledge, since strangely enough a standard modern comment on this painting has been, "The reference seems to be to Jeremiah during the destruction of Jerusalem, but no satisfactory explanation of the details or the implications of the theme has yet been advanced."[3] I believe that we cannot begin to respond to this painting in the terms that Rembrandt has specified if we do not supply the commonplace references and iconographic meanings of the painting's details from precisely those texts where one would have expected to find them, namely, in the texts of Scripture associated with Jeremiah. As a result of the juxtaposition of divergent times that these familiar scenes and objects signify, a dislocation of time and place is represented. Because of the implications of these texts that already picture his situation, the old man seems to have suffered his own kind of dislocation or numbing. Among other things, his muteness, while he leans on the book (whether or not it is understood as being exclusively the Bible),[4] suggests a revolving in his thought of the very portions of Scripture which have determined his fate of dislocation and which are now, more remarkably, being spun out, written graphically, by his fate. The series of objects laid out at the old man's left, for example, are part of this highly detailed and highly graphic representation of scriptural writing. Together with the scene at his right, these objects represent details from verses of Jeremiah, from the Lamentations of Jeremiah, and from a famous Psalm associated with (even sometimes ascribed to) Jeremiah. And, as I have said, the divergent times of these scenes and objects split the painting into halves.

To be specific, Rembrandt's Jeremiah is surrounded by nothing less than the iconography of his chief prophecies for the destruction and redemption of Jerusalem. This iconography consists of the bottle in Jeremiah's prophecy of how the Lord will shatter Jerusalem like a bottle (chapter 19); the girdle or "zone" of his prophecy of how the Lord will "mar" Jerusalem like a rotted girdle (chapter 13); the pouch containing the seventeen shekels, for purchasing the field in Anatoth, in the prophecy of how the Lord will yet redeem and rebuild Jerusalem (chapter 32); and the book (on which Jeremiah leans), which suggests both "the book of the purchase" of the field in Anatoth and the Bible or Book of the Law, which already contains all these prophecies, including the present scene itself, in which "Jeremiah abode in the court of the prison until the day that Jerusalem was taken: and he was there when Jerusalem was taken" (38:28).[5]

What then is the complexity of this Jeremiah's intimate knowledge of the objects seen in this painting, including those objects which, at this moment, he no longer sees, left and right to his preoccupied expression? Since in the biblical texts the destructions (for example) of the bottle and the girdle are Jeremiah's major prefigurations of the destruction of Jerusalem, the painting might almost have lent itself to a chronological interpretation. Because, that is, the city's inhabitants have failed to heed his prophecies (e.g., of the zone and the bottle), Jerusalem is being laid waste. The historical drama thus unfolding in the painting would be seen to move chronologically from Jeremiah's left to his right. Yet the hard facts of these simultaneous representations, and even the possibility of reversing this left to right movement, necessarily haunt us. In other words, there is a force of anachronism or contradiction within this left to right movement. The Jeremiah who is now lamenting the destruction of Jerusalem—which, as represented in the painting, is now clearly taking place—sits alongside at least two objects, the bottle and the girdle, that obviously belong to a different moment. Not only are these objects not yet destroyed, but they are grouped together with an empty pouch that is suggestive of a future redemption. The very presence of a worn, closed book—a *bound book*—in the world of 586 B.C. underscores the use of anachronism in this painting. No doubt this play of anachronism needs to be understood as part of Rembrandt's confrontation of a problematics that is especially severe in historical painting: the representation of ancient or historical event in modern or this-moment solidity. In a painting about a prophet the same problematics is doubled in the depiction of prophetic consciousness, that is, consciousness that experiences both the present and the future, as well as the fact that these are not the same things. In short, the problematics of anachronism in this historical representation deepens a problematics within all representation: namely, that the very presence of an object in representation signifies the absence of the object that it represents, so that representation inherently communicates its own anachronism or, we should say (since anachronism carries the implication of something unintended or defective), its anachrony—or, better yet, its counterfactual force.

On the diagonal which divides this painting in two, there is a zigzag of light that illuminates only a cloudlike space. This highlighted spatial break further suggests the incommensurability between the scenes at the extreme left and right. Moreover this break is not only registered by the diagonal cloudlike space but is also witnessed by the diagonal border formed by the prophet. Not only because of his apparent indifference to what is going on around him but also because of his placement at this border, therefore, it is impossible to identify him fully with either the scene at his left or the one at his right. He abides at this midpoint.

The painting shows far more about this midpoint. The form of the dark-red velvet carpet or cloth which drapes down from the vessels toward the lower left corner of the painting has a peculiar lifelikeness. This dark-red concave area replicates Jeremiah's left leg so closely that, particularly in its detailed following out of his foot and toes, it seems to be a kind of false foot. What might be the function of this highlighting of the left leg? Whatever the answer to this question may be, it probably has a direct relation to an almost equally strange circumstance just beside the left leg. While the left leg is thus emphasized and even doubled, the right foot and the right arm are not to be seen at all. Even the doubled tassles on the *zone* and vessels seem to obtrude themselves as two-legged, ironic comments on Jeremiah's missing right limbs, as do the double pantaloon-like folds just below the vessels.[6] Yet Jeremiah's fate is actually less cruel than these emphases may at first seem to imply. What we see as *his fate*, in fact, is only in part *his*. This function of the midpoint is, I believe, at the heart of the painting's iconography and its relation to the texts of Jeremiah.

The composition's major diagonal is not so much what the editors of the Rembrandt *Corpus* call "the attitude of the figure" of Jeremiah. Rather, the diagonal is formed from the merging of that diagonal figure into the luminous diagonal space that runs through the points that we would expect to be occupied by right arm and right foot. The red-velvet modeling of the left leg and the lack of visible right arm and right foot constrain our attention, on the deepest levels of empathic perception, to adhere precisely to this line plotted along points of absence. Rembrandt's emphasis on Jeremiah's body is entirely in accord with Jeremiah's own bodily language in the autobiographical passages of his prophecy. As the messenger of the Lord, Jeremiah suffers a fearful fate, one which he is powerless to refuse near the end of his life, just as he was powerless to refuse it right at the beginning of his prophecy, when the Lord told him about his pre-embryonic and prenatal time: "Before I formed thee in the belly I knew thee; and before thou camest forth out of the womb I sanctified thee, and I ordained thee a prophet unto the nations" (1:5). Jeremiah's specific "sanctified" or instrumental status is to serve as the prophet of Jerusalem's present destruction and future redemption. His life, body, and experience become the language of the Lord's personification. Because the Lord's inscrutable will is Jeremiah's fate, the human being Jeremiah is the Lord's present embodiment. Strangely enough this continues to be Jeremiah's role even in his present immobile condition, that is, in his role as bystander to either the effectuation or the foreshadowing of God's will.

Thus since the Lord has chosen to personify his presence through Jeremiah, the Lord speaks through, or with, Jeremiah when he says, "Is there no balm in Gilead; is there no physician there? why then is not the health of the daughter of my people recovered? Oh that my head were waters, and mine eyes a fountain of tears, that I might weep day and night for the slain of the daughter of my people!" (8:22–9:1). The Lord's own condition of not (yet) being able to weep is a recurring topos in the book of Jeremiah (cf. 9:18 and 14:17). The images of a "head that is not waters" and of eyes that are denied tears belong as much to the Lord as to Jeremiah, who speaks the Lord's self-description. So too in Rembrandt's painting, the parched, almost baking head and the tearlessness of eyes that cannot blink (moistening themselves) signify the Lord's presence in another state, though now they apparently belong, in that second state, to the prophet Jeremiah.

Most important, according to the same principle of accommodation established by the biblical texts, the withdrawn right hand and foot in Rembrandt's representation of the prophet Jeremiah belong equally to the Lord and to Jeremiah, each in a state of partial withdrawal or self-deprivation. Two biblical texts in particular, I propose, underwrite the sharing of this specific self-deprivation. The first is a passage in Psalm 137, a psalm frequently assigned to Jeremiah's authorship. It is significant for Rembrandt's purposes that over the past two millennia the passage in question has also been endlessly cited and pronounced by innumerable other speakers. Indeed, perhaps no other text concerning the threat of destruction to Jerusalem is so infinitely commonplace. The Psalmist apostrophizes, "If I forget thee, O Jerusalem, let my right [side, arm (and foot)] forget *its dexterity*. Let my tongue cleave to my palate, if I do not remember thee." In the Psalm, the subject or "I" of the entire figuration may at first seem to be only a human speaker, but on reflection we realize that it may equally be the Lord who speaks here. In the Psalm these two verses are part of what is called "the Lord's song" (137:4), which the Psalmist now repeats. On this reading, the Psalmist (? Jeremiah) is reminding the Lord of his promise not to abandon Jerusalem (Zion), sworn against the self-imposed penalty of giving up his "right," meaning his deific main and might. That is, on this other reading of this outcry, it is the Lord who, in the Lord's song, declares, 'If I forget thee, O Jerusalem, in your time of need, let me forget my own right hand.' (In Isaiah 62:8 the Lord swears to Jerusalem "by his right hand.")

Another biblical text has a less obvious but even more extensive bearing on the missing right limbs of the old man and on the scenes in which Rembrandt has placed him in this condition. In the Lamentations of Jeremiah 2:3–4 the Lord's wrath against Jerusalem is specified as follows: "He hath drawn back his right hand from before the enemy, and he burned against Jacob like a flaming fire, which devoureth round about. He hath bent his bow like an enemy: he stood with his right hand as an adversary, and slew all that were pleasant to the eye in the tabernacle of the daughter of Zion: he poured out his fury like fire." (In the Hebrew original the word rendered here as the Lord's "hand" is simply "yimeeno" [his right], which includes foot and hand, while the word translated here as "bent" is "darach," which signifies the joint work of emplaced foot and drawn-back hand in drawing a bow and arrow.)[7]

The destructive work of the Lord's withdrawn hand is explicitly carried out in this painting. In Rembrandt's language of representation, the Lord's hand is withdrawn upon the city. We strain our eyes, but not our imaginations, to see that withdrawn hand materializing above the burning buildings at the man's further right.[8] In the tiny winged figure, holding a just barely visible torch, hovering over the city, Rembrandt recalls Ezekiel's pictorial elaboration of precisely this instant when the Lord wills the destruction of Jerusalem. The scene (concomitant with Jeremiah's) is part of Ezekiel's famous Chariot of the Lord. The Lord orders the cherubs to set Jerusalem alight with divine fire and with "the form of a man's hand": "And one cherub stretched forth his hand from between the cherubims unto the fire. . . . And there appeared in the cherubims the form of a man's hand under their wings" (10:7–8).[9] In Rembrandt's painting the virtually unseeable hand within the blaze above Jerusalem is the actualization of God's fury and Jeremiah's (and Ezekiel's) words. This almost, but not quite, invisible hand confirms the active presence of the Lord's and Jeremiah's withdrawn right hand—withdrawn upon the city that it destroys, as in the verses of Lamentations.

Rembrandt's representation accords perfectly with these biblical accounts of the sharing, between man and God, in the condition of missing limbs. As a result, the human being and God are shown transparent, or alternative, to each other. The withdrawn right hand (and foot) and the body from which it is withdrawn both belong to man and God, by turns. In this configuration the withdrawn right hand paradoxically signifies the active withdrawal of presence in the being—God or Jeremiah—who is present (except for his missing right hand and foot) in this body at the moment that the being of the other is totally withdrawn from this same body. Each being disappears in the other's appearance. Each being reappears in the other's disappearance.

If it seems difficult to credit that Rembrandt could have employed a technique and a conception of such audacity, we should recall the similar situation that has been discovered by Henri van de Waal in Rembrandt's *The Condemnation of Haman.* There too the Lord is present in the guise of one of the human figures. Van de Waal calls this a divine "personality take-over" in which the "Principal Actor remains hidden" while accomplishing his divine will.[10]

With regard to a sharing of presence and absence between divine and human beings, the similarity between the paintings is remarkable. Yet in the case of the *Jeremiah,* at least, we do not see a divine takeover. Instead, Rembrandt represents both a sharing and an opposition of experience, and even of wills, between the human and the divine. In the *Jeremiah* God and the human being are not only represented one within the other but also each in a state of accommodation and resistance to the other's realm of being: God aiding and opposing Jerusalem (and Jeremiah); Jeremiah obeying and resisting God's will. We do not view just one being or one will in the figure of Jeremiah. Rather, the shared being represented here is a movement among realms of being that are both antithetical and symmetrical: the Lord, aiding and opposing; Jeremiah, obeying and resisting. At very least, this man's resistance to the Lord is immediately represented by his—which is also to say, by the Lord's—preoccupied expression at the very moment that the Lord's will, which Jeremiah has prophesied (speaking for the Lord), is being done. The being of Jeremiah and the being of the Lord are preoccupied with *and by* each other, in resistance to each other.

In this painting, therefore, neither the Lord nor Jeremiah is represented as being either whole or wholly present. At the point of the midpoint, God and man each abides with his withdrawn, missing, or forgotten right. (The idea of representing God as freely willing his own partial withdrawal, or retiring, from a part of being may seem exotic, but it was itself a commonplace in Rembrandt's time.)[11] And each oscillates interminably into and out of representation of his being. Each shares, alternately, the time of the present.

Rembrandt delineates other structures of antithetical alternation at this midpoint. I noted earlier that the verses of Lamentation 2:3−4 are part of the historical referent for the missing right and its relation to the scene of destruction. I observe now that in Rembrandt's distribution of objects, left and right, he mirrors the spatialization which is already set out in these verses (reversed left to right in Hebrew):

3. he hath drawn back his right hand from before the enemy,	and he burned against Jacob like a flaming fire . . .
4. he stood with his right hand as an adversary	and slew all that were pleasant to the eye in the tabernacle of the daughter of Zion[12]

Rembrandt's pictorial redeployment of these right-left/left-right movements includes at least the drawn-back right hand of Jeremiah/Lord (right),[13] the burning like a flaming fire (left), as well as the standing or manifestation of the might of that otherwise withdrawn right hand in the hand of the cherub (left). The man/God thinks (and commands/prophesies) the scene which he cannot bear to view in its actual occurrence and therefore turns away, imagining with his inner eye the slaughter that follows. The space of line breaks that runs down the center between these halves of verses is mirrored by the diagonal within Rembrandt's painting that runs through the missing right.

The same mirroring of structures obtains in the relation of the painting's left-to-right/right-to-left movements to those of verses 5−6 in Psalm 137. In the painting those movements are shown as follows:

Jerusalem forgotten and/or destroyed muteness of the figure	missing right of the figure Jerusalem forgotten.

In verses 5−6 of Psalm 137 the left-to-right / right-to-left movements are these:

5. If I forget thee, O Jerusalem,	let my right [side, arm, foot] forget [its dexterity]
6. Let my tongue cleave to my palate	if I do not remember thee.[14]

Here too the vertical line that I have drawn down the center of these halves of verses also traces the diagonal within Rembrandt's painting that runs through the missing right.

Thus, always focused at this midpoint, the back-and-forth or left-right/ right-left movement recurs in this painting in the following configuration:

Jerusalem-not-yet destroyed   Jerusalem-destroyed
Jerusalem-destroyed   Jerusalem-not-yet destroyed.

It might be said, of course, that a countermovement of left-right and right-left vectors is probably present to some extent in all paintings. (Some psychologists of art have tried to correlate it with the relations of the right and left sides of the brain.)[15] Nor, certainly, is the relation of this movement to an intervening space of emptiness a new concern of painting. Moshe Barasch has recently shown that already in the ninth century Theodore of Studion was theorizing that the painted icon must open a place of emptiness, which is the place for the occurrence of the commonplace (the *topos*), between the painting's left and right.[16] In Rembrandt's paintings and engravings this countermovement occurs with unusual frequency and is often assigned prominent representational significance.[17] Our task with regard to the *Jeremiah* is to describe the specificity of these countermovements and the proliferation of such patterns. The line of proliferation itself creates one kind of temporal significance, which I will try to define in a moment. But here, first, are some further instances of the proliferation at which I am pointing.

The left-to-right diagonal (along Jeremiah's right side) and the right-to-left diagonal (along the cover of the book, the sprig of vegetation, and the center of the blaze) also intersect at the point of Jeremiah's missing arm, which is also the slightly off-center center of space of the entire painting (which is all displaced toward the upper left by the dark corner at the lower left). The same uncertainty of right-hand/left-hand : left-hand/right-hand movements is doubled and pivoted at the point of the missing right hand in the mirror perspectives of Jeremiah and the spectator (e.g., between the viewer's right hand—perhaps working with the viewer's eye in the act of tracing the lines and figures of the painting—and Jeremiah's). Similar uncertainties about dominant directionality are thus suggested in the painting, in miniaturized form, by the closed book, which might be read from left to right, as in the writing of Roman characters— if this is indeed a Dutch "Bibel" as the black lettering announces—or from right to left, as in a Hebrew Bible. This subtle, apparently inconsequential placement of uncertainty only repeats the more obvious question of whether this painting is meant to be experienced from Jerusalem-destroyed toward symbols of Jerusalem-not-yet-destroyed (or Jerusalem-made-whole-again), or vice versa; in other words, whether it is meant to be experienced in "Dutch" toward (as yet) abiding wholeness or in "Hebrew" toward destruction. Inevitably we read both ways, as if in an interlinear Bible. As a result the artist's meaning and the viewer's experience are left in the lurch. This hint of left-right/right-left ambiguity is further multiplied, at a dizzying rate, if we factor in uncertainty about whether Jeremiah leans on the beginning or end of the Bible or whether the beginning or the end of the book faces Jeremiah or the spectator. (Would Rembrandt have canceled these movements of perplexity by himself penning the letters "BiBeL" facing the spectator? The authenticity of the Roman lettering on the side of the book—which has, indeed, long been questioned—seems to me ever more doubtful.)

Proliferated back-and-forth perception of this sort enforces uncertainty not merely about which is the correct or primary direction of the spectator's experience. Far more fundamentally, the split that is so emphatic in this painting and that gives rise to the back-and-forth movements challenges the stability or even the possibility of the spectator's or the painter's so-called self-consciousness. There is no evidence here of a reflexive awareness of self, sewn from being one's self and next to one's self, which might come harmoniously into existence in the doubling of tentative viewpoints of the self on itself, on the one hand and on the other, as we say. (In the next chapter I will have more to say about this doubling within the formations of what Hegel calls self-consciousness.) The concept of experience as we usually think of it is itself put in doubt by this painting.

In fact, the book which looms so large both pictorially and iconographically in this biblical painting (and which even generates, from the book-to-fire diagonal, a curved line intersecting at the point of the missing right arm) raises a central question about what experience means here. What can it mean to experience the historical line, or tradition, of representation of this painting at or through a point of withdrawal or absence? Not only are the representations of this painting, including this book, *from* this book, but the features of this painting direct our attention to a particular kind of oscillating line of derivation or progression of image and text which rolls into itself all of the painting's structures and which seems to defy our attempts to experience it. We locate oscillating points along this line in the constructions of anachrony, in the alternations of present being within the old man's body, in the re-representation of the objects and spatializations already represented in the biblical verses, as well as in the back-and-forth movements. As we have seen, all of these features center on the midpoint of the absent right arm, which is to say that these features are organized, and we apparently experience them, at this midpoint of absence which is only the withdrawn right arm of this old man's body. The historical line of representation in this painting hurtles toward endlessness of representation of images of withdrawal through this midpoint of withdrawal. Even the scene which represents the destruction of Jerusalem is employed in this painting as a token (or counter) of withdrawal of representation within the endless line of representations of withdrawal. And Jerusalem-being-destroyed too is only an object on the line intersecting with the point of the absent right arm. How can the recurring disappearance of part of an image itself be part of a language of imagery that we actually experience? What kind of experience can an endless flip-flop of representational moments, out of and back into the present, be?

To try to answer this question I will first comment all too briefly on three well-known views—of Martin Heidegger, Jacques Derrida, and Paul de Man—of the kind of experience that is represented in this painting. Profound as these views are, they do not, I believe, provide satisfying descriptions of the extent of the experience specified by Rembrandt.

Heidegger describes the experience of self-presence or Being in terms that seem to be uncannily like the painting before us. To a considerable extent Heidegger, as he well knew, was only recapitulating Hegel's idea that the experience of self-consciousness is effected by the mind's gathering of fragmentary or opposed elements of consciousness into a whole of consciousness. (I will return to Hegel's thinking on this subject in the next chapter.) But passages like the following from "The Origin of the Work of Art" could have been written, one might think, with Rembrandt's *Jeremiah* before Heidegger's eyes. It would seem that Rembrandt gives sensory form to Heidegger's gnomic expressions: "In the midst of beings as a whole an open place occurs. There is a clearing, a lighting . . . like the Nothing which we scarcely know. . . . Only this clearing grants and guarantees to us humans a passage to those beings that we ourselves are not, and access to the being that we ourselves are. . . . Each being we encounter and which encounters us keeps to this curious opposition of presence in that it always withholds itself at the same time in a concealedness."[18]

Alternatively, we might be tempted to think of Rembrandt's representation as closely equivalent to what Derrida calls a writing of difference. Heidegger's claim that access to Being or self-presence is represented in such works of art is fragmented (deconstructed) by Derrida's counterclaim for the effect of interminable difference.[19] In Derrida's conception there can be no passage or access to one's own being or to other beings. Imagining that such things are possible is the effect of what Derrida calls a "*continuist* prejudice."[20] Clearly, there are important resemblances between elements of the experience that Rembrandt represents and these views of either Heidegger or of Derrida.

De Man's view, derived from both Heidegger's and Derrida's, might seem to be the closest to the experience that Rembrandt represents because de Man attends most closely to matters of style or technique. Indeed, in order to understand de Man's view we must have some familiarity with the form of the trope called chiasmus, which is only another name for the back-and-forth countermovement we have been discussing in Rembrandt's painting. A chiasmus, often labeled AB : BA, is an arrangement of two sets of two elements, each A and B (or A and not-A), in which the sets are both symmetrical and antithetical to each other. Each set says or represents the same elements, but in reverse. The elements of this arrangement can be thought of as tracing the opposed movements drawn by the lines of an X (Greek *chi*), hence the name chiasmus:

$$
\begin{array}{cc}
A & B \\
& X \\
B & A.
\end{array}
$$

All of the back-and-forth movements in this painting certainly do form varieties of chiasmata, as in the verses of Psalm 137 that Rembrandt mirrors:

5.	
A	*B*
If I forget thee, O Jerusalem,	let my right [side, arm, foot] forget [its dexterity]
6.	
B	*A*
Let my tongue cleave to my palate	if I do not remember thee.

The compositional pattern of Rembrandt's painting is accurately described as

L	*R*
Jerusalem forgotten and / or destroyed	missing right of the figure
R	*L*
muteness of the figure	Jerusalem forgotten.

In this painting it would certainly be appropriate to think of Rembrandt as citing not only the painterly tradition of back-and-forth countermovement, but also the ancient poetic traditions (biblical and classical) for which a chiasmus was a commonplace. Rembrandt no doubt was well aware that chiasmata occur with the frequency of a commonplace in the Bible, especially the Hebrew Bible.[21] Indeed, even the chiasmus beginning "If I forget thee, O Jerusalem" is necessarily derived, even if only in part, from these three successive chiasmata in the Lord's speaking (or song) in Isaiah 49, which I reproduce according to their Hebrew syntax. The Lord imagines Jerusalem as lamenting:

14.		
Abandoned me		has the Lord
	X	
the Lord has		forgotten me.

To which the Lord responds:

15.
Forget can a woman   her sucking child . . . ?
                            X
["Thee," actually   I will not forget.
part of the verb "forget"]

16.
On the palms of my hands   I have engraved your image;
                            X
[the image of] your walls   are [is] before me always.

De Man highlights the figure of chiasmus because it shows graphically how language always eliminates its own ground of positive connection with the reality it tries to represent. De Man is surely correct in pointing to the empty X-point, or ungrounded space, within chiasmus. Everything we have seen in Rembrandt's painting confirms this. Also at issue for de Man in the groundlessness that is unmistakable in chiasmus are the possibilities of representation and the experience of history, both of which de Man denies. In fact, closely related to these issues for de Man is the delusion, as he sees it, that we can experience re-presentation or re-presencing in painting. He unmasks this delusion in his critique of Baudelaire's "Le peintre de la vie moderne."[22] (I will return to this claim concerning Baudelaire in chapter 10.)

Yet in his *Jeremiah* Rembrandt represents loss of self-presence within the experience of temporal continuity and priority. Located by the act or point of withdrawal, the focal consciousness of this painting (Jeremiah) is represented experiencing the continuity of a line of fragmentary or partially withdrawn representations. The midpoint of his fragmentation is the empty space representing not only the withdrawn right hand of the painting's central figure—man and (alternately) God—but also the midpoint of absence of the endless back-and-forth movements which are the historical line of his chiastic, commonplace language, with which Rembrandt has chosen to generate this representation. Like the Psalmist-Jeremiah with regard to Isaiah, Rembrandt has chosen (in resistance and resignation to the fragmentation of his own mind) to represent this cultural line of partial withdrawal. Rembrandt's representation is, I believe, wholly characteristic of the experience of thinking or writing or representing in this line of tradition. This is the present experience of the priority of the sublime, of tradition.

Thus Rembrandt's representation of the continuity of difference is also his representation of a sublime experience of a line of culture. His painting is a piece of equipment for living in a line of fragmented language and fragmented reality. (One might think of this piece of equipment as a nesting of miter boxes.) The principal figure in this painting represents neither a whole being nor a whole consciousness, just as no wholly present objects are represented in its world. He is partially withdrawn and so are they. Everything represented here is accompanied by the denial that it sustains its wholeness in either time or space.

The banal facts of this old man's body do indeed represent a more than usual fatality for everything that is shown in this painting, which also means for *the way* everything is shown in this painting. This painting represents a choosing of a particular dying-away within a line of language. (Not that any of us has a choice of whether or not to die away, one way or another, in our use of language. We will see that Hegel leaves no room for ambiguity on this point.) It shows that our language or instrument of representation is always vertiginous and self-emptying. We are fragments representing (thinking, writing) ourselves with only representations of fragmentation of one kind or another. By learning to think in freedom with the commonplaces of our culture, we may gain the possibility of inheriting the depth of a line of language that has been made of free choices of dying away within that line.

This will not be everyone's affirmative choice, though it is not obvious that any of the available alternatives is more cheering. In one sense Rembrandt represents the scene called out in Marx's indictment: "The tradition of all the dead generations weighs like a nightmare on the brain of the living."[23] But Rembrandt also represents the realities and the potentialities of this scene. Rembrandt represents human experience as being that of a brain that can accommodate the weight of the continuum because of that brain's capacity for freely choosing a particular kind of partial withdrawal from its hold on (or ownership of) consciousness. More than that, in the representation of the free choice of this continuum of representations (of withdrawal) Rembrandt represents the experience of ungraspable endlessness, that which Kant in his mathematical "formula" for sublime experience calls "a striving in our imagination towards progress *ad infinitum*."[24] Rembrandt's representation of sublime experience in his endless nesting of chiasmata is no less mathematical or geometrical than Kant's "mathematical sublime." In Rembrandt's representation of a chosen geometry of experience the point of withdrawal falls away infinitely in an endless line of representations of withdrawal. This kind of free choice of partial withdrawal from self-representation, all along the line, corresponds closely to the willed "deprivation" that Kant experiences in the sublime. But Kant's discontinuist prejudice (like Derrida's, though for different reasons) disables him from acknowledging the priority and the continuity of his line of the sublime. The continuous line of culture that Rembrandt investigates extends to him the possibility of a free choice, including the possibility of a free reaffirmation of this line of priority. Whether or not he consciously wills it, the by-product of his chosen representation of this line is a similar space of free choice that becomes available to unknown others.

The Second-State Self in the Scene of Victimization and Resistance: Hegel and Virgil

The phrases *historical experience* and *historical consciousness,* or their equivalents, are in frequent use in modern Western cultures, yet one might easily decide that each is a contradiction in terms. Contradictions internal to these phrases would seem to be inevitable because of two assumptions that appear to be inscribed as absolutes in the modern history of Western philosophy:

1. Experience is of the present.
2. Self-consciousness is identical with experience and consciousness.

Indeed, what seems to make these assumptions modern is that they deny the significance, and even the possibility, of the experience of tradition. Yet when viewed from within the Western circle of language and experience—including modern philosophy—that we know as tradition, the claim that these are indeed the assumptions of modernity may appear doubtful.

I have so far proposed that the first assumption is left open to question by a present experience of priority, as in a painting of sublime experience by Rembrandt or in a representation of the sublime by Kant. My concern now is with the second of these assumptions, which has been reissued in our time by Heidegger, who in *Hegel's Concept of Experience* cites Hegel's monumental statement, "We in fact arrive at the philosophy of the modern world . . . with Descartes. With him, we in fact enter into an independent philosophy which knows that it is the independent product of reason, and that the consciousness of self, self-consciousness, is an essential moment of truth."[1] I believe that this assumption too is belied by the experience of cultural tradition in the West, including that experience within modern philosophy—at least in Hegel.

My aim in this chapter is to recover, in Hegel's own account of the sublime moment in which, he claims, self-consciousness is constituted, an experience of the cultural sublime or of cultural tradition. Though unremarked by Hegel's commentators, Hegel in that moment reenacts an astonishing earlier moment of literary history. By a moment of literary history I mean no more than a rehearsal—whether in a literary work or in a work about literary works—of a moment in an earlier text. I will try to show in some detail that, as a result of this rehearsal, an experience which is unrecuperable by self-consciousness intervenes in Hegel's sublime moment of allegedly constituting self-consciousness. This intervention has dramatic consequences. Hegel's concept of self-consciousness is defined by a sublime encounter of the self and the double of itself (which Hegel sometimes calls *the other*). In this encounter, Hegel affirms, nothing is finally lost to self-consciousness. I will propose that, because of the intervention of the unrecuperable, the larger experience in each such moment is only the experience of a sublime fragmentariness and of a potentiality of encounter that does not become actual or final or closed. Yet I would emphasize even at this point that this experience is far from being of merely hypothetical interest. It counts as an immense part of our experience of culture, of language, and of the everyday imaging of life. Precisely how conscious Hegel was of the complexity of his own placement, in the way I am claiming, within the cultural sublime, is something that I will not try to gauge. I cannot believe, however, that it is accidental that the specific moment of literary history and historical consciousness that Hegel rehearses is itself the quintessential case, for all of European writing, of the effort to escape self-consciousness—and its inherent forces of coercion and domination.

It is central to what I want to highlight in Hegel's view of the historian's mind in history, as well as what I want to recover about the view that he avoids, that Hegel conceives of this sublime derivation of self-consciousness, and indeed of thinking itself, as "Force." In the *Phenomenology of Spirit* Hegel explains that "what is called Force" is the movement in which matters "posited as independent directly pass over into their unity, and their unity directly unfolds its diversity, and this once again reduces itself to unity." "Force *proper*," he adds, is that in which the independent matters have "disappeared" (section 136). Hegel's oppositional model is a recapitulation of this absorption into Force, the Force, in other words, which subsumes the other within the self.

Indeed, one of the ways in which Hegel exemplifies the oppositional model, both in the *Phenomenology of Spirit* and the *Philosophy of Right,* is by imagining a scene of "revenge" which he reinterprets as rightful "punishment."[2] Hegel employs the scene of punishment to represent not only the sublime birth of self-consciousness in which self and other disappear, but also the actualization of law in which the activity of the law as punishment and the individuality which is opposed to it also disappear.[3] Hegel expresses this relation in the form of a chiasmus, AB:BA, that is typical of his logic: "[A] *like* becomes [B] *unlike* and [B] *unlike* becomes [A] *like*" (section 156), so that self-consciousness is represented as the product of differences, inversions, and repetitions, all turning and, most important to Hegel, returning into the chiastic pattern. In this way Hegel explains what it means to *think* Force. He displays Force in the activity of its own inherent thought form, namely, that of recurring double antitheses—or chiasmus—which would, if followed indefinitely, be seen to reduplicate itself infinitely. When consciousness encounters this prospect of the infinity of chiasmus, self-consciousness—itself a chiasmus containing the other within the self, the self within the other—is born as "explanation" or as "infinity" made "an object for consciousness."[4] For Hegel this experience of infinity is only "this movement of self-sublimation" (diese Bewegung des Sich-aufhebens) and "the absolute unrest of pure self-movement" (diese absolute Unruhe des reinen Sich-selbst-bewegens) which produce "self-consciousness" (*PS,* 162–63; *PG,* 128–29).[5]

(I note in passing that by following out Hegel's sublime birth of self-consciousness in these ways we return to the oppositional moment which, quite likely, is the basis of the influence or, properly, the continuing *Force* of Hegel's historicism in the so-called "oppositional criticism" of our own time.)[6]

Here is the scene of punishment in the *Philosophy of Right,* where, in the context of a discussion of higher right, certain disturbing features of Force (that are also present in the earlier occurrence of the scene in the *Phenomenology*) come into focus:

> Instead of the injured party, the injured *universal* now comes on the scene. . . . It takes over the pursuit and the avenging of crime, and this pursuit consequently ceases to be the subjective and contingent retribution of revenge and is transformed into the genuine reconciliation of right with itself, i.e. into punishment. Objectively, this is the reconciliation of the law with itself; by the annulment of the crime, the law is restored and its authority is thereby actualized. Subjectively, it is the reconciliation of the criminal with himself, i.e. with the law known by him as his own and as valid for him and his protection; when this law is executed upon him, he himself finds in this process the satisfaction of justice and nothing save his own act.[7]

In this scene from the *Philosophy of Right,* no less than in the parallel scene in the *Phenomenology,* we are mesmerized by the transformative, sublime operations of Hegel's concept of a reflexive "negativity" or double negation. Indeed, early in the *Philosophy of Right* Hegel reestablishes the centrality of his concern with the "innermost secret of speculation," namely, "infinity as negativity relating itself [i.e., negativity][8] to itself, this ultimate spring of all activity, life, and consciousness. . . . The will is not a will until it is this self-mediating activity, this return to itself" (section 7). In the scene of revenge we broach this secret of a negativity which is double (which therefore tallies up as a positivity) and is somehow self-relating, mysteriously returning to life and self-consciousness.[9]

Yet Hegel's scene of thought as punishment needs to be opened to direct moral questioning.[10] For questioning of this kind we can turn to Stanley Cavell. Although Cavell does not reproduce a Hegelian contextualization of Hegel's scene of punishment, he responds provocatively to the language of that scene, in the version of the *Philosophy of Right.* Here is Cavell:

> How shall we characterize this as a mode of thought? In its personifications (e.g., "the injured universal now comes on the scene") it sounds like allegory and mythology, hence like some depassé literary mode. It also sounds like history, sort of; anyway, as if opening itself to historical evidence. It would sound more like history if history were regarded as the anthropology of our pasts, of the presents of the distant tribes whose present we are. It sounds like psychology, sort of; anyway, as if opening itself to psychological evidence. But if one applied what *we* are likely to consider psychology to this passage, especially to its concluding sentence (". . . it is the reconciliation of the criminal with himself . . . "), we are more than likely to understand it as a social piety, either perfectly proper (an attempt to elicit soul-saving repentance) or perfectly tyrannical (a soul-destroying attempt to mortify the criminal into bringing peace to those who destroy him).[11]

Especially within the context of my present inquiry it is useful to note Cavell's assertion, soon after this passage, that he finds himself "pushed to pieces of literature to discover the problem of the other" which he finds "largely undiscovered for philosophy." Cavell gives one hope to believe that literary history complements the work of philosophy in some indispensable way. For Cavell literature means "various literary structures" that may help us, in effect, reach beyond the perfectly tyrannical force of Hegel's language in his scene of punishment.[12] In fact, I now want to survey some of the evidence of Hegel's avoidance of a particular literary structure, one which has a special relation to our experience—and Hegel's experience—of literary history.

I believe that the scene of punishment that Hegel uses to stage the emergence of universal self-consciousness already had a specific location in literary history before Hegel used it. Giving the coordinates of this location will, I believe, partly explain the reasons for the language of personification that sounds like allegory or mythology or history, yet is not quite any of these. Hegel's replication of this scene is apparently against all likelihood or plausibility, considering values or preferences or prejudices that he expresses elsewhere. Hegel replicates this scene, I will try to show, because he identifies it, without saying so, as the moment of—this will sound grandiose, but the grandiosity is most immediately Hegel's—the emergence of the European mind, virtually the emergence of Europe. Why, with this much at stake, Hegel does not finally unveil the identity of the scene that he replicates is also of great interest to me. I will soon propose some possible reasons. But first I want to identify the scene itself.

This can be done with Hegel's help, since he has not covered all his tracks. The paragraph in the *Philosophy of Right* in which Hegel repeats the scene begins with the following sentence, which I did not quote earlier: "When the right against crime has the form of revenge (see Paragraph 102), it is only right implicit, not right in the form of right, i.e. no *act* of revenge is justified" (the parenthesis is Hegel's). The earlier paragraph to which Hegel refers deals with the concept of "the annulling of crime" (section 102). There Hegel writes, "In cases where crimes are prosecuted and punished not as *crimina publica* but as *crimina privata* . . . punishment is in principle, at least to some extent, revenge. There is a difference between private revenge and the revenge of heroes, knights-errant, &c., which is part of the founding of states" (section 102, addition). There is nothing incidental about Hegel's differentiation of the hero's right of revenge, or rather of inflicting punishment, in founding states. The statements in section 102 closely follow up, for example, Hegel's assertion that "coercion is annulled by coercion" (section 93). For Hegel the right of this higher coercion belongs to the liminal moment when civilization is established, when history changes, that is, from the state of nature to the rational order of the State: against "a state of nature, a state of affairs where mere force prevails . . . the Idea establishes a right of Heroes" (section 93, addition).[13]

It is not difficult to make one's way to the famous scene, or representation, of history that Hegel has in mind. It is also, however, not difficult to see some of the reasons for Hegel's continued veiling of the identity of the scene, since it explicitly exhibits something shameful—the killing of one's enemy (which Hegel quietly but definitely sanctions)—and because Hegel's theory of history cannot easily accommodate early full-blown embodiments of what he supposes are later evolutionary stages. In *The Philosophy of History*, for example, Hegel rejects the "fiction" that there was "a Roman Epos" possessing all "spiritual truth."[14] Especially by contrast with Hegel's utopian dream of Athens, Rome was certainly not Hegel's fantasy of civic perfection.[15] Yet the scene we seek is very much the climactic scene of the Roman epos, in the greatest and best known of its representations: the final moment of the *Aeneid*. For European civilization this is the preeminent scene of the hero's right of inflicting punishment in founding the state, even and especially of his founding the state and actualizing the idea (or law), simultaneously, by the act of inflicting punishment. This is Virgil's ultimate scene, indeed, not merely of the hero who founds the European state, but of the hero who founds the force of the idea of the European state. Because of its extraordinary content and placement, this Roman scene, which I am claiming that Hegel has in mind,[16] may well be the single most formative representation of the link between art and imperialism in the history of European art. With only slight exaggeration one might say that in this scene Virgil discovered empire.[17] This is the case if we mean by empire the ethos of the state which is continually reconstituted by confronting the places where brute force is said to prevail.

We stand at a juncture of slippings and slidings. In the *Phenomenology* Hegel seems to make extraordinary claims for a duel of epic heroes that appears to be out of the *Iliad*, presumably the encounter of Achilleus and Hektor. This would seem to be the only moment that Hegel can imagine in which two self-consciousnesses are created in an encounter of perfect equality and mutuality (sections 187–88). Yet there is at least a notable instability in Hegel's reference to this epic duel, since there is no such equality of heroes in Homer's account of the duel between Achilleus and Hektor. In fact, we observe that in Hegel's account it is exactly the inequality that produces the famous scene which immediately succeeds the duel: the scene of master and slave. There is thus likely an equivocation even in Hegel's representation of the apparently ideal moment of the duel of epic heroes. Even, that is, in his thinking (in the *Phenomenology*) of the one allegedly perfect moment of mutual self-consciousness, Hegel, to borrow one of Judith Shklar's formulations (not specifically applied to this scene), is already "caught, as it were, between two quite incompatible types of classicism," one of which is the imagined utopia of aesthetic Hellenism that nurtures free self-consciousness, while the other is the here and now neo-Roman republican polity that atomizes self-consciousness by the alien imposition of civic law.[18] For Hegel's scene of the heroic punishment that, most especially, founds the state, the Homeric scene cannot provide a reference point in the history of thought. Instead, for the historical placement and setting as well as for the innermost details of his scene of punishment, Hegel has veered sharply toward the scene in the *Aeneid*.

Readers of the scene of punishment and imposed law in the *Aeneid* long experienced it, certainly, as a moment of the creation of a European mission and destiny. In what Hegel no doubt regarded as his inevitable unfolding of the latent meaning, or reason, of this scene, the newly interpreted scene of founding the state expands to vast dimensions. It becomes no less than coextensive with the full evolutionary extent of Hegel's mind in the *Phenomenology of Spirit* and after. (In a moment I will unfold details of this coextensiveness.) Indeed, the fact that for European thought the august precedent of the scene of punishment, in the *Aeneid,* is perfectly obvious is part of what, in Hegel's view, makes his reenactment of the scene a new scene of perfect right which only seems to us perfectly tyrannical, perfectly vengeful, but is now understood through Hegel's recuperating mind, once and for all, as perfectly punishing. To use some of Hegel's own phrases about the activity of heroes we can say that, as Hegel sees it, in Virgil's staging of the scene the perfect emergence of force was only stored in "the womb of time." Now, in Hegel, it is "ripe for development" as "the species next in order."[19] Hegel imagines that he adheres closely to the philosophically significant details of the scene and brings them to timely self-consciousness. Yet Hegel misses or avoids two of the scene's most philosophical, most vital features: its structure of repetition and its experience of a sublime unrecuperability. To show this I will now describe Virgil's contextualization of the scene and then cite Virgil's language in the scene itself.

Hegel and his readers would no doubt find any one contextualization of Virgil's scene very odd, not least because Virgil's story and the run of his language, like so much of classical literature, were inseparable parts of their language and imagination. (Hegel's diary entries, at the age of seventeen, show him copying long extracts of the *Aeneid.*)[20] The *Aeneid* occupied a place in their language in which allegory, mythology, history, and psychology overlap, constituting a continuously living element of European culture. Yet in commandeering Virgil's scene from literary history to philosophy, Hegel obscures those elements of the scene that give it its generic particularity, so that our rehearsing of the placement of the scene is a remedial exercise aimed at Hegel as well as at twentieth-century readers who no longer breathe the language of the classics.

The concluding scene of the *Aeneid* recalls the climactic scene of the *Iliad.* In Homer's scene—which is, like all of Homer's poetry, vastly, intensively formulaic, which is to say, filled with the awe of the commonplace—Achilleus kills Hektor, thus making inevitable the fall of Troy. Virgil's scene describes how Aeneas kills Turnus, thus making inevitable the founding of Rome. Turnus is the chief warrior of the Rutuli, who violently oppose the settlement of the Trojans in Italy. This final act of Aeneas is heavy with responsibilities both for Aeneas and for Virgil. The act is assigned the symbolic task of opening the possibility of the founding, and at the same time the reconceptualization, of Rome by a partnership of victor and vanquished, or their descendants. Many modern readers are understandably troubled by this final act of the *Aeneid.* In this epic enshrining of Roman values, commissioned by Augustus himself, Virgil seems to give official poetic sanction to the violence of imperialism, present and future.

Virgil leaves no doubt about the heaviness of his heart at this moment. Out of thin air, he invents an instant of hesitation for Aeneas. This instant and what

Aeneas says in it apparently change nothing. Yet they take us into the deepest recesses of Virgil's mind. Having vanquished Turnus, Aeneas momentarily holds back his sword, considering whether to spare Turnus's life. Turnus has ended his plea, saying, "ulterius ne tende odiis" (press not thy hatred further) (12.938).[21] But at this instant Aeneas is moved to kill Turnus by noticing that he wears the baldric of dead Pallas. Thereupon Aeneas pronounces the justification for killing Turnus and plunges his sword into Turnus's breast. Here are the verses, concluding the *Aeneid*, that describe the hesitation, the rationale, and the punishment:

>   stetit acer in armis
> Aeneas, volvens oculos, dextramque repressit;
> et iam iamque magis cunctantem flectere sermo
> coeperat, infelix umero cum apparuit alto
> balteus et notis fulserunt cingula bullis
> Pallantis pueri, victum quem volnere Turnus
> straverat atque umeris inimicum insigne gerebat.
> ille, oculis postquam saevi monumenta doloris
> exuviasque hausit, furiis accensus et ira
> terribilis: "tune hinc spoliis indute meorum
> eripiare mihi? Pallas te hoc volnere, Pallas
> immolat et poenam scelerato ex sanguine sumit,"
> hoc dicens ferrum adverso sub pectore condit
> fervidus. ast illi solvuntur frigore membra
> vitaque cum gemitu fugit indignata sub umbras.

[Fierce in his arms, Aeneas stood with rolling eyes, and stayed his hand; and now more and more, as he paused, these words began to sway him, when lo! high on the shoulder was seen the luckless baldric, and there flashed the belt with its well-known studs—belt of young Pallas, whom Turnus had smitten and stretched vanquished on earth, and now wore on his shoulders his foeman's badge. The other, soon as his eyes drank in the trophy, that memorial of cruel grief, fired with fury and terrible in his wrath: "Art thou, thou clad in my loved one's spoils, to be snatched hence from my hands? 'Tis Pallas, Pallas who with this stroke sacrifices thee, and takes atonement ["poenam": punishment] of thy guilty blood!" So saying, full in his breast he buries the sword with fiery zeal. But the other's limbs grew slack and chill, and with a moan life passed indignant to the Shades below.]

                                                 (12.938–52)

Aeneas's rationale for the punishment of Turnus is that a disembodied force (dead Pallas) performs the sacrifice ("immolat") in order to annul Turnus's crime. Turnus's crime is conceived as being at least as much a crime against himself as against Pallas. The injured Universal has indeed arrived on the scene. It takes over the pursuit and the avenging of crime. It walks in the shadow projected by Aeneas acting not only for Pallas but, remarkably enough, for Turnus as well. Aeneas says that Turnus's crime has profaned his own blood by guilt ("scelerato ex sanguine"). We recall that in Hegel's version of the scene

"this pursuit consequently ceases to be the subjective and contingent retribution of revenge and is transformed into the genuine reconciliation of right with
itself, i.e. into punishment." For Hegel, as we saw, there is a sharp "difference
between private revenge and the revenge of heroes, knights-errant, &c., which
is part of the founding of states" (section 102). For Hegel this difference presupposes that "punishment . . . is only crime made manifest, i.e. is the second half
which necessarily presupposes the first. . . . It is not something personal, but the
concept itself [i.e., the injured Universal] which carries out retribution" (paragraph 101, addition). Both in Hegel and, at least in part, in Virgil, the scene of
punishment that founds the state is a scene of force which actualizes universal
reason—or Spirit or Mind—in the ratios of negation and counternegation
that integrate self-consciousness.

   Of course, it may seem to us that, despite the obvious parallelisms between
the two scenes, a reaching for actualized universal reason is beyond Virgil's possible ken. Yet it should be pointed out that in the conclusion of his scene Virgil
is recurring to his own version of the same Idealist or Neoplatonist problematics (of inverted worlds of appearance and reality)[22] that concerns Hegel. In
more ways than one, as I will try to show in a moment, Virgil is at this moment
glancing back to a metaphysics of *spiritus* and *mens* (Mind) that Anchises pictures for Aeneas during his descent to the world of the dead: "A spirit within
sustains [heaven and earth], and mind, pervading its members, sways the
whole mass and mingles with its mighty frame"(spiritus intus alit, totamque in-
fusa per artus / mens agitat molem et magno se corpore miscet) (ll. 726–27).
For dead Anchises this is the central principle in the recirculation of consciousnesses—of the dead and the living—which integrates Rome and its destiny.
The dead and the living are recirculated in the mind of Roman history. It is
only in this light that we can see that the final words of the final scene of the
Aeneid—which say that Turnus's soul "passed indignant to the Shades
below"—represent what Hegel calls the reconciliation (however unwilling) of
the criminal to law or the universal. At least part of what Virgil signifies here is
that Turnus rejoins Mind itself. The significance of Turnus's passing to the
spirit world no doubt grows even deeper after the poem (beyond this closing
verse) passes into silence. Aeneas, who is merely left standing in this silence, will
soon follow suit (Roman readers knew from other texts that Aeneas would soon
be killed), as will all the Romans who make up the Roman mind in history. But
the chiasmus of negation and counternegation has apparently already integrated self-conscious mind in Virgil's scene of punishment in something like
the following Hegelian, chiastic form: Aeneas's coercion annuls Turnus's coercion; Turnus's reconciliation to law (in accepting the second half of his crime,
i.e., his punishment) actualizes the law and brings Aeneas's state, with its right

to punish, into being. With Hegel, Virgil seems to be saying that force, punishment, the otherness of self, self-conscious Mind, the state, empire, and, indeed, thinking itself are immediately constituted, not merely vindicated, by this chiasmus. There would seem to be no way out of this reading, this thinking—Hegel's reading and thinking—of Virgil's scene.

In fact, however, there is an overt difference between Virgil's scene of punishment and Hegel's. This difference might at first appear to concern Virgil's emphasis on Turnus's passing to the realm of death, where his consciousness will ultimately be circulated back into life. This passing into death and returning to life together undoubtedly constitute the central figure of Virgil's epic. Aeneas's own passing to death, while still in life, not only forms the center of the *Aeneid*'s particular twelve-book design, but also is at the heart of the Anchisean recognition which founds Rome. This recognition concerns something more than the awareness of imminent death that renders more vivid the appreciation of each instant of life. As it is set out in the *Aeneid*—and in the scene of the *Odyssey* which it mirrors—this recognition clearly has to do with the ways in which we already experience death, or the ways we are ourselves in effect among the dead, within our own lifetimes. We may have to remind ourselves that this apparently implausible, even repellent, idea informs the central literary structures of many of the works which seem inseparable from the continuity of Western civilization. Thus in the *Commedia* Dante directly identifies Virgil with the plausibility or reasonableness of the passage to death-within-life. Directly and extensively echoing Virgil, Milton (in the first two books of *Paradise Lost*) establishes the descent to death as the initial reference point for the mind's full ascent to reality. These are only two of numerous indications that after Virgil the passage to death-in-life becomes central to the European mind, up to, and including in obvious ways, the minds of Joyce, Kafka, and T. S. Eliot.

Yet as an experience within thought, at least, the passage to death-in-life seems to be assigned fully as much importance by Hegel as it is by Virgil. Hegel, that is, assigns a central role to the experience of death in the formation of self-consciousness. Indeed, the parallel role signified in the final verses of the *Aeneid* may sound uncannily like what Hegel says about these matters. The grandeur of Hegel's meditation on death can even enrich our understanding of the ways of consciousness in the scene assembled at the end of the *Aeneid*, even if (as I believe) the understanding of death in that final scene of Virgil's epic is finally taken a step beyond what Hegel is willing, or able, to acknowledge.

For Hegel, too, death is not merely something that the mind thinks about. Experiencing death, rather, is a formative element in the making of mind and thinking. The experience of death in thought, Hegel says, makes possible Spirit or universal self-consciousness as well as the self-consciousness of the state, both of which are embodied in individual self-consciousness.[23] This experience of death is elaborated upon in sections 507–09 of the *Phenomenology:*

> The true sacrifice of *being-for-self* is solely that in which it surrenders itself as completely as in death, yet in this renunciation no less preserves itself. It thereby becomes in actuality what it is in itself, becomes the identical unity of itself and of its opposed self. The separated inner Spirit, the self as such, having come forward and renounced itself, the state power is at the same time raised to the position of having a self of its own.

According to Hegel, the mind achieves this experience of death within life through a "self-alienation" made possible by the "alienation [that] takes place solely in language":

> The "I" that utters itself is *heard* or *perceived;* it is an infection in which it has immediately passed into unity with those for whom it is a real existence, and is a universal self-consciousness. That it is *perceived* or *heard* means that its *real existence dies away;* this its otherness has been taken back into itself; and its real existence is just this: that as a self-conscious Now, [here we mark the Hegelian chiasmus] as a real existence, it is *not* a real existence, and through this vanishing it *is* a real existence.

Of course, Hegel's interest in the experience of death is not news. Around the middle of the twentieth century a good deal of excitement was created by Alexandre Kojève's rediscovery of the centrality of experiencing death in Hegel's thinking about language.[24] Specifically with regard to Hegel's concept of a death within life, Kojève clarified how much is at stake in Hegel's oppositional model of self-consciousness. That is, if it is true to say that, setting aside Hegel's metaphysical claims, our response to Hegel's dialectic of self-consciousness depends on whether we credit his reintegration of self-consciousness (after all its chiastic movements through negativity), part of what we are probing in Hegel is his claim for the capacity of self-consciousness to survive this experience of death within thinking.

Yet, despite the central significance that an experience of death undoubtedly has for Hegel, it represents an avoidance of another experience of death, even within life. Hegel does not acknowledge that there is any kind of experience of death that lies somewhere between the experience that he recuperates and the complete death that would obliterate the self. This self-alienation is an experience of death-in-life that does not return to self-consciousness. This experience makes impossible any recuperation of what Hegel calls unity. He does not acknowledge, in other words, an experience of death that is unrecuperable by the self yet affects the self, situating it in the endless line of repetition and making it a fragmentary or partially withdrawn self.

It will be helpful at this juncture to consider a point made by Georges Bataille and Jacques Derrida. (I am relating here to the intertwining of Bataille's and

Derrida's views presented in Derrida's commentary on Bataille and Hegel in "From Restricted to General Economy: A Hegelianism without Reserve.")[25] The point I have in mind concerns the relation of Hegel's model of self-consciousness to what Bataille calls "tradition."[26] Partly responding to Kojève's account of the courage Hegel shows in facing death, Bataille emphasizes that Hegel in fact avoids a radical experience of death (much as I have been suggesting) and that even the death which Hegel seems to face is recuperated by a "subterfuge" (one which is writ large, we may add, in Hegel's scene of punishment). The subterfuge Bataille has in mind is an illusion of sympathetic magic: "In sacrifice, the sacrificer identifies with the animal struck by death. Thus he dies while watching himself die, and even, after a fashion, dies of his own volition, as one with the sacrificial arm."[27] This does not seem to me an inevitable interpretation of Hegel's negations, but it captures the fact that in the experience of death Hegel recovers all losses, gives up nothing. For Derrida, Bataille's critique is itself of historical importance because what it exposes helps liberate us from Hegel's scene of self-consciousness in which, as Derrida puts it, "the entire history of meaning" is represented.[28] Because the Hegelian writing or thinking is self-preserving, self-serving, and capitalizes all its losses Bataille calls it "vulgar"; because this thinking and writing is an expression of the slave's knowledge gained (by a series of displacements) in avoiding death, Bataille calls it "servile." Derrida classifies this as one of "The Two Forms of Writing."[29] He commends Bataille's attempt to commit himself to a different form of writing and thinking. This would be a writing in which a more radical self-alienation might actually make possible the experience of death which Hegel says is unthinkable by the self. In writing of this kind the role of chance in "nonmeaning" would finally be faced. Bataille believes that only this kind of writing and thinking would make possible the "communication" in silence that "cannot take place from one full and intact being to another: it requires beings who have put the being within themselves *at stake*, have placed it at the limit of death, of nothingness."[30] Derrida, however, finally expresses the view that even Bataille's writing is not durable communication of this kind, since it becomes "servile in once more having been read."[31]

This is the background—which I am aware I have presented in highly inadequate form—of the point that concerns me. Bataille and Derrida following him represent tradition as if it always takes only one form of writing, a form which corresponds to Hegel's vulgar knowledge achieved in his murderous scene of self-consciousness. Derrida cites Bataille: "Hegel's reaction is the fundamental human behavior . . . it is par excellence the expression that tradition has repeated infinitely. . . . It was essential for Hegel to *become conscious* of Negativity as such, to grasp its horror, in this case the horror of death, while supporting the work of death and looking at it full in the face."[32] It is necessary to ask, however, whether there is another form of tradition—correlative to, even coextensive with, another form of writing—which is not vulgar.[33] For the European tradition and "the entire history of meaning" that Hegel represents in his scene of punishment, Virgil's *Aeneid,* particularly Virgil's climactic scene of sacrificial punishment and founding of European tradition—which I take to be a scene of literary history par excellence—is undoubtedly one of the most fertile fields for pursuing exactly such a question.

For some time now it has been felt by many commentators that Virgil speaks with two voices, one of which (I am paraphrasing in Hegel's terms) is the imperial voice of the force that founds Roman self-consciousness, in other words, the voice of vulgar tradition par excellence. Concurrently Virgil speaks with another, subtler voice, one that engages in a powerful critique precisely of the vulgar model of his own Augustan moment in history. This other voice has been called pessimistic, melancholy, and tragic.[34] It is also, I would add, in practice, philosophically not-vulgar in the way—even exceeding the way—that Bataille and Derrida would like to imagine is theoretically possible. It may also communicate, as Bataille dreams, between beings who are no longer full or intact, who have "put the being within themselves *at stake,* have placed it at the limit of death, of nothingness." For Virgil, however, the possibility of such communication—for which not-vulgar tradition or the cultural sublime may position us—exists only as the experience of a fragmentary or partially withdrawn self and only as a potentiality of communication.

Virgil participates in the creation of a literary structure that represents the experience of the death-in-life that cannot be recuperated by the self. There is, therefore, good reason for Hegel's avoidance of a more direct acknowledgment of the final scene of the *Aeneid.* The experience of the passage to death-in-life which that scene enacts is the deepest reach of the recognition that can be imparted only by Anchises in the realm of the dead. This experience is a far more radical thing than may at first appear.

To try to show this I turn once again to Aeneas's statement, within the final scene:

> tune hinc spoliis indute meorum
> eripiare mihi? Pallas te hoc volnere, Pallas
> immolat et poenam scelerato ex sanguine sumit.
>
> [Art thou, thou clad in my loved one's spoils, to be snatched hence from my hands? 'Tis Pallas, Pallas who with this stroke sacrifices thee, and takes atonement of (inflicts punishment on) thy guilty blood!]

$$(12.947-49)$$

I would like to focus attention on something about this statement that is in a sense perfectly obvious. I mean the fact that it is virtually a quotation—that is, in each and every component of Aeneas's statement—of the following words of Achilleus in the *Iliad,* shortly before he kills Hektor (who is wearing the armor which he "stripped when he cut down the strength of Patroklos" [22.323]):

οὔ τοι ἔτ' ἔσθ' ὑπάλυξις, ἄφαρ δέ σε Παλλὰς Ἀθήνη
ἔγχει ἐμῷ δαμάα·' νῦν δ' ἀθρόα πάντ' ἀποτίσεις
κήδε' ἐμῶν ἑτάρων, οὓς ἔκτανες ἔγχεϊ θύων.

[There shall be no more escape for you, but Pallas Athene
will kill you soon by my spear. You will pay the penalty of all
at once for those
sorrows of my companions you killed in your spear's fury.]
(22.270–72)[35]

The possible significance of this virtual quotation—that is, as a repetition which becomes an element of the meaning of Aeneas's statement—has not, to my knowledge, been brought to bear on the interpretation of Virgil's final scene. To be sure, readers of the *Aeneid* are well aware that Virgil keeps Homer's poems constantly in mind and that he employs thousands of details of plot, characterization, and wording that are openly derived from Homer.[36] This elaborate construction of secondariness, of Virgil's poetry to Homer's, is clearly of great importance to Virgil. In fact, it seems probable that in the final or imperial moment of Virgil's epic, precisely when a problematics of the relation of self to other is thematically most critical, Virgil openly broaches the moment toward which his derivative relation to Homer's verse, in the whole of the *Aeneid,* has been building. In this way, at least, not only is Aeneas saying that it is not I who acts here or requires this act, but Virgil is saying, with Aeneas, that it is not I who claims ownership or identity in speaking these words. As Hegel foresees, this is the experience of the "I" whose *"real existence dies away."* As a result, a movement of self-alienation that is explicitly thematized within Aeneas's statement about his action is also realized formally and structurally. It is a tangent thrown off by his (and on another level, Virgil's) self-alienating language in the exit of the "I" from self-referentiality.

Yet this is far from all that Virgil's citation has to say about citation. Even within the restricted conditions of citation—that is, of being bound to reduplication—Virgil's way of registering the force operative in the act of citing the other is quite astonishing. And now it is Virgil's relation to his language, more than Aeneas's, that comes to the fore. At this moment Virgil gains access to his second voice. This fragmentary voice comes to articulation only within the line of fragments that are its inherited language. It is vital to recognize that within the parallelisms between Virgil's and Homer's scenes (each of which is climactic for an entire epic of an entire civilization) Virgil's naming of Pallas constitutes a self-alienation which self-consciousness has no way to think or recuperate. It even evokes what Bataille and Derrida seem to suggest is impossible for a narrative (not to speak of a narrative of tradition) to create, a negativity without reserve.[37] To locate this effect—it is something approaching the status of an event—we need to recreate the context in which Virgil's naming of Pallas occurs.

To a great extent Virgil's naming of Pallas is a matter of pure chance and is to a large degree even involuntary. Virgil does not invent the circumstances of the name Pallas, except in the ancient sense of *finding* them as they already exist. In fact, Virgil's inventiveness here consists of a certain placement or positioning of his poetic voice with regard to the circumstances that lie in the path of what he has chosen to think about. The reasons for regarding these circumstances as being primarily the effect of chance, rather than of higher design, poetic or supernatural, emerge from Virgil's way of proceeding. Indeed, it may prove to be relevant to that way of proceeding that the name Pallas is etymologically linked to a leaping forth (*pallomai*) and even to a casting or drawing of lots (*pallein, pallesthai*). There is certainly an association of Pallas with an unexpected leaping forth from within thought itself in the famous moment of Hesiod's *Theogony* when the goddess is said to leap forth, armed for battle, from the brain of Zeus.[38] The vicissitudes of the name Pallas were conspicuously contradictory or random in Greek mythology. Cicero, for example, had recently reminded Virgil's audience that Pallas was also the name of Athena's father, whom she killed because he wanted to rape her and whose skin she then put on.[39] No doubt part of what kept interest alive in these chaotic backgrounds of the name Pallas was the desire of Latin mythographers to bring about a cultural transference, or *translatio studii,* of the stolen Palladion (likely a statue of Pallas)—the Athenian holy of holies—from Greek to Roman culture. Yet no obvious logical principle offers itself to account for the permutations in the fates of those bearing the name, so that the kind of recovery of meaning that we expect of allusion seems difficult or even impossible in the intoning of "Pallas."

With regard to Virgil's naming of "Pallas . . . Pallas" in the final scene of the *Aeneid,* these backgrounds of the name Pallas might still have been of no more than footnote interest were it not for the patterns of displaced identity that Virgil explicitly signifies in that name. Aeneas, after all, claims that it is something called Pallas that is doing the punishing (killing) of Turnus, thereby founding Rome. Even if we knew nothing else about the name Pallas many of us would find the identity of this force worrisome, at very least. The additional fact, striking in this context, that Aeneas's transfer of responsibility to Pallas (human ally of the Trojans) is virtually a quotation, from the *Iliad,* of Achilleus's transfer of responsibility to Pallas (divine enemy of the Trojans) could, we might think, be recouped as an ironic reversal (that is, despite the inherent problems in Pallas's present action and its violent symbolism of emergent Roman character and despite our helplessness before the chaotic, or wild, fortunes of the name Pallas). By careful stipulation of the materials of the final scene, however, Virgil has made this recuperative reversal utterly impossible. Within the final scene of revenge, he attaches a murderous weight to the name which insists upon all the nightmares of shifting, meaningless identity that are the history of that name. As a result, "Pallas" itself stands for the meaningless excess, the hyperbole, of repetition,[40] or even a compulsion to repeat murder.

In Virgil's scene, that is, there is another citation (a further repetition), of another scene of punishment, actually a series of forty-nine scenes of punishment. These other scenes deepen the melancholy movement of self-alienation in a way that is quite alarming, as if beyond anyone's control. I refer to the details engraved on the baldric of Pallas which inflames Aeneas and sets him on the course of his final statement and act of punishment. We have seen that in the verses of the final scene Virgil refers to the baldric and to the scene on Pallas's baldric as "notis" (well-known), as "inimicum insigne" (a badge which is both of the foeman and fatal), and as "saevi monumenta doloris" (a monument to true grief). These might seem to be strange choices of details as an accompaniment to the moment of instituting empire. Yet they do not seem strange at all if they are read as signals of repetition, signs of the recurring forces of self-alienation that Virgil is unleashing here. Virgil's internal reference is unmistakably to lines 495–99 of book 10, in which the baldric of Pallas, taken from Pallas's dead body by Turnus, is described in detail.[41] The phrases in the final scene of the *Aeneid* which refer to the baldric—"well-known," "(fatal) badge of the foeman," "monument to cruel grief"—meticulously refer to these scenes on the baldric as much as to the scene of young Pallas's death or the present scene in which that death is being avenged.[42] The crime engraved on the baldric is that of the forty-nine daughters of Danaus murdering (on order from Danaus) the forty-nine sons of his twin brother Aegyptus on the same wedding night. As Aeneas prepares to send Turnus's soul to the shades below, these scenes within the scene may be said to stare at Aeneas and at us like a nightmare fusion of the wedding and killing scenes on the shield of Achilleus; or, indeed, like an ultimate expression of the *menis* or wrath or avenging anger of Achilleus (for Patroklos), which from the beginning of European epic poetry, as now in Virgil's scene, threatens to reconstitute the self-consciousness of the hero. This self-consciousness appears to be Achilleus's murderous gain from his revenge in sending "souls of warriors to Hades" (*Iliad* 1.1–4). The circumstances that Virgil traces as the sources of this revenge impulse are not an explanation or a justification, but a plunge into barbarous contingency.

Operating within a kind of tradition that is infinitely not-vulgar, Virgil cites the gap that his self-consciousness cannot leap, that between the Pallas of this *Aeneid* moment and the Pallas of the inverse moment of the *Iliad*. Thus a decorum of a maddening kind makes the scene of the Danaïdes perfectly suited to the naming of Pallas the punisher, especially with regard to the recurrent fracturing of identity (both male and female) that that naming entails.[43] If we are inclined to wonder why Virgil should bother with this morass of meaninglessness, our wonderment turns somber when we recall that in the *Aeneid* Virgil acknowledges that what is at issue for him—on his path—is, indeed, a *translatio studii* of the Palladion, from Athens to Rome. When, in book 8, father Tiber prophesies Rome's future from the waters' depths he reminds us that Pallas's grandfather was also named Pallas and that from "this race sprung from Pallas" a city called "Pallanteum"—meaning Rome—is destined to prevail by vast force (ll. 52–65). When, therefore, in the epic's final moment, Aeneas, using Achilleus's invocation of Pallas, invokes Pallas, he is announcing nothing less than the recovery of this meaningless repetition, this Palladion of scenes of revenge, in the Pallanteum that is Rome.

Yet Virgil exploits the experience of this meaninglessness in an astoundingly meaningful way. In the moment that seems to claim to be the imperial moment of constituting self-consciousness, Virgil's way of dissolving toward the history of his scene and of his naming, in Homer's scene and naming, alienates the self beyond any possibility of recuperation. He commits himself to what Hegel thinks we must finally avoid at all costs: the "trial by death" that "does away with the truth which was supposed to issue from it, and so, too, with the certainty of self generally" (*Phenomenology*, section 188). Virgil's second voice speaks here in its sublime, second state. By repeating the name Pallas, Virgil has evoked a counterforce of resistance in the mind's scene of punishment. The truth that issues from this trial is certainly not one that Virgil's self-consciousness speaks here. Virgil's second voice communicates from the silence of incompleteness and pure chance. It indicates that the whole affair (Rome, empire, punishment) cannot even be properly vulgar, in other words, that all assured connections of supposed meaning have dissolved. We may yet want to assume that the effect of this dissolution has been left only partially in doubt. Perhaps, we conjecture, it has been left accessible for someone to construe as yet another disappearance into the Force of self-consciousness, that is, into a power of citation to absorb what it cites in the way that Hegel's model of sublime self-consciousness prescribes. Yet Virgil provides no warrant for such assumptions. On the contrary, in Virgil's representation the force of resistance unnerves the Force of identity, thereby opening thought to the experience (not the recuperation) of a death within life. In Virgil's scene what Hegel views as the Force of identity and integration within the constituting of self-consciousness is not merely rendered problematical. It is neutralized by a force that suspends the identity connections of self-conscious life. In other words, this naming of Pallas reveals a dying-away within the mind and within the experience of life. In the experience of the cultural sublime the mind does not recuperate this dying-away. The experience of literary history and of tradition that is not vulgar recurs precisely here.

Even if Hegel avoids or does not consciously mark the radical self-alienation in the citation that rules Virgil's scene, he is bound by its logic. His own scene of punishment is not as perfectly tyrannical as his logic supposes. His scene too is a repetition that is perfectly obvious and perfectly self-alienating. To the extent, that is, that Hegel's scene of integrating self-consciousness and founding of the state, in the scene of punishment, is itself a citation of Virgil's scene of integrating self-consciousness and founding of the state, specifically in the scene of punishment, Hegel's scene performs an equivalent radical self-alienation. At least in this way, counter to Hegel's oppositional model of Force and recuperated loss, even in Hegel's scene the claim of this experience of the cultural sublime must continue to hold.

To sum up: What is perhaps most deeply unforgettable (even if we are not consciously aware of it) in the closing revenge scene of the *Aeneid* is Virgil's way of being in the world—that is, in a second state within the cultural sublime. While Virgil works through the same scene of revenge that Hegel recreates in the *Phenomenology of Spirit* and the *Philosophy of Right,* and to the same end of situating consciousness in history, Virgil submits, as Hegel at least imagines he does not, to an unrecuperable self-alienation within language. Virgil's dramatized terms are close to Hegel's dying-away of the I within the alienation that takes place solely in language, but Virgil's way of invoking "Pallas" blocks the illusion that language returns us to the I. Having gone forth in the self-alienation of language, we cannot go back. Yet Virgil also shows that in the language at our disposal the dying-away of the I can be the experience of a line of repetition of self-alienations. This is a limited claim. In Virgil's representation of this cultural sublime the resultant dying-away only enables a resisting, partially withdrawn, fragmentary self to act from freedom, resistance, and moral feeling.

The Surrealism of "Respect" for Tradition: Virgil, Homer, Kant

> Happy pair! If aught my verse avail, no day shall ever blot you from the memory of time, so long as the house of Aeneas shall dwell by the Capitol's immovable rock, and the Father of Rome hold sovereign sway!
> —*Aeneid* 9.446–49

> He knows not himself as he runs, nor as he moves, as he raises his hands, or throws the mighty stone; his knees totter, his blood is frozen cold. Yea, the hero's stone itself, whirled through the empty void, traversed not all the space.
> —*Aeneid* 12.903–07

The experience of cultural continuity is at the heart of Virgil's poetry. Yet weighed down by the imperialist claims that political institutions have made on the *Aeneid*, we may become forgetful of the way its poetry continually suspends the institutional authority upon which that experience of continuity might seem to depend.[1]

In a variety of ways Virgil has made the representation of his final scene of revenge climactic for the work of his poetry. By delving further into that representation and its place in the *Aeneid*, I want to show now how Virgil represents a continuity of sublime experience in an effectively endless line of self-alienation and defoundation. Between this and the following chapter, I will try to suggest how this is the case in two ways: first, in the continuity of Virgil's defoundation of the founding rock of Rome; second, in Virgil's placement of the *Aeneid* in a line of apostrophe, the figure of *turning-away*, in which the solidity of a Roman present is negated while the continuity of Roman historical experience is established. Virgil's series of representations of ungrounding do not produce a blockage or aporia of the line of tradition. Rather, together they extend an endless line of language—a lineage of what may be called the surreal unground—that is the object of sublime experience. If there is a chance for freedom and moral feeling to come into Virgil's world it is from this experience of his second voice continually immobilizing and ungrounding the authority of his imperial voice.

The counterplay of Virgil's two voices around the disappearing rock of foundation highlights the dimension of cultural continuity that Kant has glimpsed in his concept of sublime "respect" (Achtung [p. 83]). Kant couples "respect" with our saying "of an object, without qualification, that it is great [in] a mere reflective judgment upon its representation" (p. 96).[2] He makes clear that sublime respect for greatness is attained in a process of shifting attention from the apparently great to the truly great, which he defines as "the intellectual and intrinsically final (moral) good, estimated aesthetically" and the "might which it exerts in us over all *antecedent* motives of the mind." Kant specifies that "it is only through sacrifices that this might makes itself known to us aesthetically . . . and this involves a deprivation of something—though in the interests of inner freedom" (p. 123). Virgil's ungrounding of the imperial rock of his representational authority lays out a logic which is potential but obscured in Kant's formulation: namely, that the greatness and might achieved in a given representation is constituted by sacrifices or deprivation of nothing so much as the might and greatness *of* representation. In other words, Virgil's sublime representation represents the partial withdrawal of the monumental wholeness and force upon which the institution and authority of its representation depend and which it reciprocally represents—like the "immobile saxum" of Rome and Augustus Caesar. Virgil's countervoice renews respect for cultural tradition not in the form of respect for an institution or authority or for a substantive traditionality, but in respect for the experience of cultural tradition or the cultural sublime that enables freedom and moral choice. Virgil mobilizes the everyday culture concept, lacking in Kant's sublime, of a line of language that aesthetically, mightily sacrifices a part of representation in an endless progression of self-deprived representations.

My discussion of Virgil's final revenge scene will now therefore take on something of the multifocal quality that Virgil brings to the representation of the scene. This scene, we will see, is presented by Virgil as one point on a line of continuity which moves in a time of priority. It is this experience of priority that an imperialist reading must deny in order to declare the all-consuming urgency and the absolute moral authority of the present moment of a given institution.[3] Virgil tells his tale of the priority of experience in an unassuming second voice. As is perhaps always the case in cultural tradition, in the first instance the effect of this countervoice is very hard to credit because it is ranged exactly against those forces that appear to have won the day (like empire or, on a different though related level, egoism and radical skepticism). The second voice's work of ungrounding and its achievement of the experience of a cultural sublime can be carried out only in underground, undercurrent movements within the sublayers of language. Yet slowly but surely Virgil's representation of the continuity of a line of defoundation and of the continuity of apostrophe revitalizes a sublime respect for the cultural tradition that he experiences.

In book 9 Virgil addresses dead Nisus and Euryalus in these words:

> Fortunati ambo! si quid mea carmina possunt,
> nulla dies umquam memori vos eximet aevo,
> dum domus Aeneae Capitoli immobile saxum
> accolet imperiumque pater Romanus habebit.
>
> [Happy pair! If aught my verse avail, no day shall ever blot you from the memory of time, so long as the house of Aeneas shall dwell by the Capitol's immovable rock, and the Father of Rome hold sovereign sway!]
>
> (9.446–49)[4]

To say the least, it is not clear what the conditions are that make this moment ripe for such praise of Roman power. The context of these verses indicates that all is far from well in the past and present Roman worlds that are both reflected here. These lines come precisely at the conclusion of Nisus's and Euryalus's riot of killing and their own death at the hands of the Rutulians. Even if we say that a dual meaning of *fortuna*—both good and evil chance—is invoked in the word "Fortunati," we are at a loss to see here the achievement of any final good. It is true that the pair's initial aim of reaching Aeneas to inform him of Turnus's attack was apparently conceived according to some idea of heroism. And the friends do remain loyal, a "pair," to the end. But as Walter R. Johnson asks, "What have their deaths, their romance, their mindless, murderous rampage to do with the destiny of Rome?"[5] Inevitably, our responses to this moment and to the revenge scene, the end-moment of the poem—the founding of Rome's *aevum* or perpetuity in Aeneas's killing of the Rutulian Turnus—are mirrors of each other that seem to produce a merely abyssal meaning.

Yet Virgil gives us credit (at least he was inclined to do so before he left orders for the poem to be burned) for being able to read the poem's scenes against each other. I now therefore switch between Virgil's scenes of punishment in search of a component highlighted in one scene that is intimated more darkly in the other. And I turn here too to Johnson's moral commentary on Virgil's scenes of violence. In the final revenge scene Johnson believes that Virgil comes close to something like a revelation of his metaphysics in the nightmare simile, derived from Homer,[6] that he applies to the despair of Turnus:

ac velut in somnis, oculos ubi languida pressit
nocte quies, nequiquam avidos extendere cursus
velle videmur et in mediis conatibus aegri
succidimus; non lingua valet, non corpore notae
sufficiunt vires, nec vox aut verba sequuntur:
sic Turno, quacumque viam virtute petivit,
successum dea dira negat. *tum pectore sensus*
vertuntur varii; Rutulos aspectat et urbem
cunctaturque metu *telumque instare tremescit,*
nec quo se eripiat, nec qua vi tendat in hostem,
nec currus usquam videt aurigamve sororem.

[And as in dreams of night, when languorous sleep has weighed down our eyes, we seem to strive vainly to press on our eager course, and in mid effort sink helpless: our tongue lacks power, our wonted strength fails our limbs, nor voice nor words ensue: so to Turnus, howsoe'er by valour he sought to win his way, the dread goddess denies fulfilment. *Then through his soul shifting fancies whirl;* he gazes on his Rutulians and the town, he falters in fear, and *trembles at the threatening lance;* neither sees he whither he may escape, nor with what force bear against the foe; nor anywhere is his car, nor his sister, the charioteer.]

(12.908–18; emphases added)

Johnson says of this passage that "it is not so much the despair of Turnus that is being imagined here as the indefinable, larger despair that haunts the entire poem and threatens to overwhelm it. . . . The laws of time and space—like the human capacities for motion, action, and speech—themselves have become void."[7] Johnson correctly registers a representation of the voiding of the laws of space and time—an experience of the surreal—in Virgil's scene. But it seems to me that this representation and experience are for Virgil the effect of the self-alienation and the dying-away which are inherent in language. Moreover, Virgil, I believe, experiences and represents this moment of the surreal in language as a point on a continuous line of language. Still another scene-switch is visible within this continuity of scenes. To show this I will attend to a strange concatenation of details which has not, to my knowledge, been noticed by Virgil's commentators, perhaps because in their very nature the materials of this concatenation dissolve under our gaze or with our breath.

In the dream simile the most consequential object of attention is not, I suggest, the hero Turnus, but the daimon-weighted stone which is represented as withdrawing from Turnus's world. It is not easy to notice this stone, for it has the peculiar quality of obliterating its own significance. Against a background of deadly stones hurtling through the air—thrown by both sides—this stone disappears into a void within the void which the simile of the dream renders. It is especially important to see that this strange disappearance is part of a continuous line of disappearances—a continuous experience of nothing or vacuum—which defines the experience of continuity.

The passage in which this stone appears and disappears is prepared by the advent of one of the twin banes named Dirae—"geminae pestes cognomine *Dirae*" (12.845). Sent by Jove, the Fury flits and screams before Turnus's face, beats wildly against his buckler, and, as a result, "a novel torpor" unknits his limbs "with dread" (formidine [12.865–67]). This chthonic Fury, dragging down the stone, causes Turnus's failure. Aeneas, now merely the agent of that Fury, comes at Turnus with an enormous "*tree-like*" spear ("Aeneas instat contra telumque coruscat / ingens arboreum" [12.887–88]). Aeneas threatens and taunts. Turnus responds and then falls silent, already on his way to the void. Here are the verses directly before those quoted earlier, beginning with Turnus's response:

> "non me tua fervida terrent
> dicta, ferox: *di me terrent* et Iuppiter hostis."
> nec plura effatus *saxum* circumspicit *ingens,*
> *saxum antiquum, ingens,* campo quod forte iacebat,
> *limes* agro positus, litem ut discerneret arvis;
> vix illud lecti bis sex cervice subirent,
> qualia nunc hominum producit corpora tellus:
> ille manu raptum trepida torquebat in hostem,
> altior insurgens et cursu concitus heros.
> sed neque currentem se nec cognoscit euntem
> tollentemve manus saxumve immane moventem;
> genua labant, gelidus concrevit frigore sanguis.
> tum *lapis ipse viri, vacuum per inane volutus,*
> *nec spatium evasit totum* neque pertulit ictum.
> ac velut in somnis . . .

["Thy fiery words, proud one, daunt me not; *'tis the gods daunt [frighten] me,* and the enmity of Jove." No more he speaks, then glancing round, espies *a giant stone, a giant stone and ancient,* which haply lay upon the plain, set for a landmark [*boundary line*], to ward dispute from the fields. This scarce twice six chosen men could uplift upon their shoulders, men of such frames as earth now begets: but the hero, with hurried grasp, seized and hurled it at his foe, rising to his height and at swiftest speed. But he knows not himself as he runs, nor as he moves, as he raises his hands, or throws the mighty stone; his knees totter, his blood is frozen cold. Yea, *the hero's stone itself, whirled through the empty void, traversed not all the space,* nor carried home its blow. And as in dreams of night . . .]

(emphases added)

In Virgil's imagination of the negative, the eruption of the other world of "vacuum . . . inane," of empty suffering and impenetrable darkness, is marked not by the despair of Turnus or even by some welling up of the generalized feeling of despair evoked throughout the poem. Rather it is specifically evoked by the disappearance of "a giant stone, a giant stone and ancient . . . set for a boundary line," into the space which it does not traverse.[8] How does Virgil represent this disappearing boundary stone with which Turnus cannot kill? It is of the essence of Virgil's representation of a line of language that the answer to this question is beyond either Turnus's or Aeneas's ken. The answer is represented in the poem as a history of the defounded boundary stone. In Virgil's representation that history exceeds even the boundaries of his poem. First, the internal history.

During Aeneas's visit to Evander, just after they return from an interrupted rite of sacrifice, just before Aeneas makes the commitment to Evander to take responsibility for his son Pallas (the responsibility that Aeneas will discharge in the immolation of Turnus in the revenge scene: "Pallas immolat," Aeneas will say), Virgil interpolates the following scene:[9]

> hinc ad Tarpeiam sedem et Capitolia ducit,
> aurea nunc, olim silvestribus *horrida* dumis.
> *iam tum religio pavidos terrebat agrestis*
> *dira loci, iam tum silvam saxumque tremebant.*
>
> [Hence he leads him to the Tarpeian rock,[10] and the Capitol—golden now, once *bristling* with woodland thickets. *Even then the dread sanctity of the region [the aura of the god of the place] awed the trembling rustics; even then they shuddered at the forest and the rock.*]
>
> (8.347–50; emphases added)

It follows from these verses that the chthonic Fury or dread goddess ("dea dira") who "denies fulfilment" to Turnus at the end of the poem thereby fulfills the destiny of the Capitol place, specifically of the Tarpeian rock (from which criminals would one day be executed by being thrown off the rock). The detailed parallels between this passage and the stone passages at the end of book 12 are unmistakable. Turnus, we are told, "falters in fear, and trembles at the threatening lance" (12.916)—trembles all the more because Aeneas's spear is "*tree-like*" (12.888). He is hurled into nightmare and nonexistence by his failure to direct the "giant stone, a giant stone and ancient . . . set for a boundary line" that then whirls "through the empty void." The lines from book 8 quoted above therefore strongly suggest that Turnus reincarnates the "trembling rustics" who, in a primeval *once* or *then*, were awed by the dread sanctity of the place and shuddered at the "bristling" forest and the Capitol "rock." The concentric circles drawn by these passages imply that when Turnus "gazes on his Rutulians" while "he knows not himself" his actions speak the continuity of a language which is of his people and his place but which he does not comprehend. The dread sanctity of this language of the stone is that it is constituted by representations each of which shows us its inadequacy as representation and which, moreover, together form the endless line of representation that for Virgil and his reader is the object of sublime experience. This is a language, in fact, in which Turnus's death is the sign of the dying-away of each of us within language and within the experience of the sublime. In Turnus's waning—and in

Aeneas's also, I will try to show—is their painful waxing in the place that is newly defounded by the Fury-laden stone.[11] This stone is the boundary or limit which remains perpetually in the place, but which is itself not experienceable as a solid present. The Rutulians'/Romans' collective, perpetuated being—here called their "all"—carries doomed Turnus backward to the primeval past and forward to the endless recirculation of dead and living Romans that Anchises describes to Aeneas during his visit to the underworld (6.679–751). In the following verses Virgil makes visible one segment of this continuous recirculation:

> incidit ictus
> ingens ad terram duplicato poplite Turnus.
> consurgunt gemitu Rutuli totusque remugit
> mons circum.

> [Under the blow, with knee beneath him bent down to earth, huge Turnus sank. Up spring with a groan the Rutulians all; the whole hill reechoes round about.]
>
> (12.926–29)

Place is the condition of language into which humans beings are born. The echoing of the place—the "whole hill reechoes"—is where language echoes beyond the individual speaker. The language which has gone forth dies away from the individual, who at no point fully comprehends what his or her speech says. The Rutulians groan and spring from the earth toward which Turnus, breathing, groaning his last, has sunk.

The rush of Aeneas's spear is described in a negative form that gives voice to the void and to the disappearing stone cutting through the air: "murali concita numquam / tormento sic saxa fremunt" (12.921–22) (Never stone shot from engine of siege roars so loud). Virgil thus gives Aeneas's "tree-like" spear the full force of the "Never stone" of Turnus's nightmare. Here, in a single representation of withdrawal, we have "the forest and the rock" of the Capitol at which the Rutulian rustics, the shades of the future, knew to shudder, though Anchisean foreknowledge of the full Roman recirculation, of the living and dead, was beyond their grasp of time and place. I turn now to the time outside the chronology of the poem's verses.

An important part of the experience of continuity in Virgil's launching of the line of the "immobile saxum" is the sense that all of these events, including the launching, have happened before within Virgil's inherited (and chosen) line of withdrawing language, indeed, are even now happening in earlier moments. Homer's line of withdrawing language is indispensable for Virgil's representation of this experience of priority. Specifically, in Virgil's choice of the language of the immovable rock (which stands for a recurring defoundation of the illusion of a present), Homer's language of the same rock is enrolled as a timeless background, neither earlier nor later than Virgil's language. In fact, because of the continuity of Homer's and Virgil's language of the immovable rock, we must finally say that Aeneas, as much as Turnus, is his own murder victim in the revenge scene. This sounds fantastic but can be shown in concrete detail.

In the *Iliad* Homer uses the unliftable boundary stone to mark "Aineias"[12] as the hero who will exit the poem to enter and to inherit and bequeath an unknowable world. Taking into account what we have so far seen of Virgil's use of the immovable boundary stone, and considering Virgil's habitual reprocessing of Homer's details, there can be little doubt that Virgil noticed that the two principal episodes in which Aineias appears in the *Iliad* both concern huge (boundary) stones. These are stones which cannot be hurled to kill. They are symmetrically placed, as markers of some unspoken thinking, five books from the beginning and five books from the ending of the poem. In the parallelisms and contrasts of these two episodes, Homer also hints, indeed, at a fantastic, riddling tale. And the special use Virgil makes of the immovable stone is evidence that Virgil stared hard at that tale of the stone, even made it a part of his own way of thinking.

Here is part of Homer's account, in *Iliad* book 5, in which a stone thrown by Diomed hits Aineias in the thigh, bringing him to the ground on one knee, almost precisely as does Virgil's Turnus when he is wounded in almost the same spot by Aeneas:

> ὁ δὲ χερμάδιον λάβε χειρὶ
> Τυδεΐδης, μέγα ἔργον, ὅ οὐ δύο γ' ἄνδρε φέροιεν,
> οἷοι νῦν βροτοί εἰσ'· ὁ δέ μιν ῥέα πάλλε καὶ οἶος.
> τῷ βάλεν Αἰνείαο κατ' ἰσχίον, ἔνθα τε μηρὸς
> ἰσχίῳ ἐνστρέφεται, κοτύλην δέ τέ μιν καλέουσι·
> θλάσσε δέ οἱ κοτύλην, πρός δ' ἄμφω ῥῆξε τένοντε·
> ὦσε δ' ἀπὸ ῥινὸν τρηχὺς λίθος. αὐτὰρ ὅ γ' ἥρως
> ἔστη γνὺξ ἐριπὼν καὶ ἐρείσατο χειρὶ παχείῃ
> γαίης· ἀμφὶ δὲ ὄσσε κελαινὴ νὺξ ἐκάλυψε.
> Καί νύ κεν ἔνθ' ἀπόλοιτο ἄναξ ἀνδρῶν Αἰνείας,
> εἰ μὴ ἄρ' ὀξὺ νόησε Διὸς θυγάτηρ Ἀφροδίτη,
> μήτηρ, ἥ μιν ὑπ' Ἀγχίσῃ τέκε βουκολέοντι·
> ἀμφὶ δ' ἑὸν φίλον υἱὸν ἐχεύατο πήχεε λευκώ

> [Tydeus's son in his hand caught
> up a stone, a huge thing which no two men could carry
> such as men are now, but by himself he lightly hefted it.
> He threw, and caught Aineias in the hip, in the place where
> the hip-bone
> turns inside the thigh, . . . so that the fighter
> dropping to one knee stayed leaning on the ground with his
> heavy
> hand, and a covering of black night came over both eyes.
> Now in this place Aineias lord of men might have perished

had not Aphrodite, Zeus's daughter, been quick to perceive him,
his mother, who had borne him to Anchises the ox-herd;
and about her beloved son came streaming her white arms.]

(5.302–14)

I will return to this passage in a moment, but first let us recall the parallel episode in book 20.

There, after an initial encounter between Achilleus and Aineias in which they instill in each other equal "fright" (20.262, 279), Aineias, like Turnus, turns in desperation to a huge stone. Before he does so, however, he is seized, like Turnus, by world-forgetting fear of the "long spear": "around his eyes gathered the enormous emotion" [down over his eyes was poured enormous distress (*or* mist)] (20.281–82). Then Homer interpolates the space of the heroes' standoff, from which Aineias will disappear into another world and another history:

αὐτὰρ Ἀχιλλεὺς
ἐμμεμαὼς ἐπόρουσεν ἐρυσσάμενος ξίφος ὀξύ,
σμερδαλέα ἰάχων· ὁ δὲ χερμάδιον λάβε χειρὶ
Αἰνείας, μέγα ἔργον, ὃ οὐ δύο γ' ἄνδρε φέροιεν,
οἷοι νῦν βροτοί εἰσ'· ὁ δέ μιν ῥέα πάλλε καὶ οἶος.
ἔνθα κεν Αἰνείας μὲν ἐπεσσύμενον βάλε πέτρῳ
ἢ κόρυθ' ἠὲ σάκος, τό οἱ ἤρκεσε λυγρὸν ὄλεθρον,
τὸν δέ κε Πηλεΐδης σχεδὸν ἄορι θυμὸν ἀπηύρα,
εἰ μὴ ἄρ' ὀξὺ νόησε Ποσειδάων ἐνοσίχθων·
αὐτίκα δ' ἀθανάτοισι θεοῖς μετὰ μῦθον ἔειπεν·

[Now Achilleus
drew his tearing sword and swept in fury upon him
crying a terrible cry, but Aineias now in his hand caught
up a stone, a huge thing which no two men could carry
such as men are now, but by himself he lightly hefted it.
And there Aineias would have hit him with the stone as he
swept in,
on helm or shield, which would have fended the bitter death
from him,
and Peleus' son would have closed with the sword and stripped
the life from him,
had not the shaker of the earth Poseidon sharply perceived all
and immediately spoken his word out among the immortals.]

(20.283–92)

Aineias is frozen in the act of throwing the huge stone. The founding of his kingdom issues from and coincides with his being rapt *away*, as in a dream.[13]

The verses in which this later event is related were of particular importance in forming Virgil's relation to Homer, since they explicitly foreshadow Aineias's founding of his kingdom. From the point of view of literary history or of the relations of later and earlier writers, Homer's way of anticipating a related, later history is a remarkable act of imagination. Homer foretells Aineias's prophesied founding as a *refounding* of a kingdom older even than ancient Troy (20.215–16, 302–08). This strange interpolation has the effect of canceling in advance any indebtedness of inheriting or "anxiety of influence" that a later poet might feel (or of what Harold Bloom thinks of as an anxiety of "belatedness" which stands in the shadow of someone else's "priority"). But why should Homer do this? It might be possible to explain this kind of act in terms of the special form of anxiety that Kierkegaard sees in our relation to freedom and the future (rather, that is, than an anxiety concerning the influence of the past). This "anxiety of the future" or "anxiety of the Nothing" may be said to engender a kind of altruism.[14] It seems to me, however, that Kierkegaard's view of this anxiety is to a large extent a version of Kant's analytic of the sublime, which itself offers a more persuasive account of the place of alienation, freedom, and moral feeling in the experience of the sublime. Kant adheres more closely to the way in which our experience of alienation is an experience of representation or language itself. Yet Kant too (as I have tried to suggest) ignores or represses the cultural continuity of language. In Virgil and in Homer we see that the construction of a specifically cultural continuity is a matter of choosing a line of self-alienation, a line of partially withdrawn representations that can culminate in sublime experience and, if anything can, may enable freedom and even moral feeling.

In Homer and Virgil this line is made of dreamlike interruptions, signaled by the dissolution of immovable stones and of impassable boundaries. Most vividly the stones mark and erase an immovable limit ("limes"), which is to say that they simultaneously signify the delimited solidity of place and the nothing which is essential to its liminality.[15] The fact that Diomed, Aineias, or Turnus attempts to wield such a marker and necessarily fails in his designs is no doubt a function of the impossibility of either invading or wielding the boundary dimension itself. This experience is closely related to what Derrida calls the "spacing" or "dead time within the presence of the living present." But here again the evidence of the Western experience of cultural tradition, in this case of Virgil's poetry, suggests that in our experience of a series of such spacings we need not fear that we have succumbed to what Derrida calls a "*continuist* prejudice."[16] In this experience of the cultural sublime the ancient, outsize boundary stone is from the beginning—before the beginning, that is, in priority—experienced as a perpetual moment that continuously abides between events, acts, or wills. Conversely, the relations examined here may suggest that what is called deconstruction—particularly the deeply learned, multitextual hermeneutics practiced by Derrida—is itself a way of representing the cultural sublime. Like Kant's analytic of the sublime, this hermeneutics may be as profoundly informed by its representation of the history of representation as it is by the analysis of the history of philosophy.

One of the effects reenforced by the repetition of the stone episodes that we have been examining—and, indeed, of Virgil's *and Homer's* repetitions of so many events that are endlessly, formulaically the same—is to make it a figure of a history that never had a discrete present and that is as much a continuous past as a continuous present. In Homer's presentation of these stone episodes, which mark Aineias as he-who-will-exit the poem, a correlative feature is the dance of identity which makes Aineias both the target and the aimer of stones. Each of these stones is described by exactly the same formula: "a huge thing which no two men could carry / such as men are now, but by himself he lightly hefted it." The stone thus measures a traversing that is suspended not only in midair but in or as the nothing that is located within the poem's time and space. This nothing—another key element in these passages—leads out of the poem itself. By its placement within the symmetrical tableau, the stone organizes and contains all of the story's suggested permutations of exchangeability—Aineias for Diomed, for example, or Achilles for Diomed, Aineias for Achilles. In this poem of formulae and equations, such permutations are both innumerable and signs of a beyond.

When, in killing Turnus, Virgil's Aeneas cries, "Pallas immolat," he is only responding to the silent accusation that as the murderer of Turnus he is himself on the verge of moral self-annihilation. Virgil's precise replication of Aineias's wounding by Diomed's stone in Turnus's wounding by Aeneas suggests the activity of a second Virgilian voice in Aeneas's final outcry to Turnus.[17] In his very last words, that is, Aeneas is also made to say, in effect, that "Pallas here immolates (and takes atonement of)[18] Aeneas . . . as well as Diomed, Achilles, Hektor. . . ." From the sibyl, Aeneas knows very well that Turnus is "another Achilles" (6.89). That Turnus is also a primeval Rutulian and that both Turnus and Aeneas are virtually, even now, the *shades* of future Romans (to whom Turnus descends in the last line of the *Aeneid*) cannot come as a surprise to Aeneas. This is the knowledge of the Roman line that he gleans in his descent to the underworld. At that virtual dead midpoint of the poem's full communication, Anchises explains in detail the recirculation of the dead and the living (6.679–751). In the *Aeneid* Anchises' explanation is fleshed out in Virgil's recirculation of his chosen line of language, of the dead and the living.

In all this the relationship of Homer to Virgil (and of untold intermediaries, no doubt including the foundation myths and sacred rocks of Aeschylus and Sophocles)[19] is marked as a line of cultural tradition. Virgil relied on having readers for whom the experience of reading Homer was inseparable from life experience. This kind of reading has nothing to do with believing literally in either Homer's or Virgil's fictions. Virgil's exchanges with the materials of Homer's world cause Virgil's way of being with the continuity or no-time of those materials to dispense with the idea of hierarchy that is usually associated with imitation.[20] With regard to this no-time, there can be no question of what seems prior or belated. The *idem* in this stone *alio* is no one's possession. Virgil's repetitions of the stone episode reinstitute just this kind of priority.

The dread sanctity of Virgil's and Homer's rock is that it shows us its inadequacy as representation both of a present of reality and, by itself, of a moral coherence. Virgil's second voice removes the pretension that the killing done by Aeneas or by Nisus and Euryalus can be a symbol of the good. Virgil does not commend or recommend any of these moments. This second voice speaks counter to the voice of mere Western empire. I have earlier alluded to Erwin Panofsky's beautiful remark concerning Virgil's first eclogue: "With only slight exaggeration one might say that he 'discovered' the evening."[21] In the context of our present discussion we may try to extend Panofsky's insight by saying that the evening or westering quality of Virgil's imagination pervades much of his greatest poetry and that what westering specifically means to Virgil is a movement of countervoices. Virgil is not the only model for this kind of movement in the West, yet after Virgil the Western cultural sublime is often identifiably Virgilian in this westering sense.

In the series of passages that I have examined Virgil constructs each representation of an immovable rock as an immobilization or removal of the apparent solidity of reality and its authority. Together these representations trace part of an endless line of language that is the object of sublime experience or the experience of continuity. This is a language that goes forth, dying-away, from its individual human speakers or authors, each of whom only partly comprehends its recirculations and countermovements. In the *Aeneid* Virgil does not rewrite the record of (Roman) history or propose fantasies of made-over worlds. One may indeed suspect that the deep dissatisfaction which caused Virgil to order the burning of his manuscript of the *Aeneid* (if he left it unfinished at his death—as he did) was tied to his fear that the appearance of proposing such a fantasy would be, for many readers, the effect of his poem. What is crucially at stake for Virgil in the *Aeneid* is the possibility of choosing a sublime line of language that continuously withdraws from representation and foundation. If there is a chance for moral feeling to be born into Virgil's world it is from this difficult experience of continuously immobilizing the authority of his imperial voice, that is, within the life of his poetry. This is perhaps what Virgil most significantly means by an *influence* or *availing* of his poetry as enduring as the immovable rock.

In the verses that represent this rock, at least one other dimension of Virgil's continuous line of defoundation needs to be described. This dimension is the continuity of apostrophe.

5

C H A P T E R

Apostrophe in the Westering Sublime: The Matrilineal Muse of Homer, Virgil, Dryden, Pope, and T. S. Eliot

Why, Patroklos, art thou bathed in tears, like a girl, a
mere babe, that runneth by her mother's side and
biddeth her take her up, and clutcheth at her gown,
and hindereth her in her going, and tearfully looketh
up at her, till the mother take her up?
—*Iliad* 16.7–10

The Mother [Thetis] . . .
Heard his [Achilles'] loud Cries, and answer'd Groan
    for Groan
—Pope's *Iliad,* 18.43–44

In every historical experience there is a turning away from the here and now
to an absent or dead person or object. Yet, in the West at least, this turning
is not a sufficient condition for historical experience. In order for the act of
turning away to enable the experience of history, or what I have termed the experience of priority, that act must be experienced in an effectively endless repetition of such acts or, what is the same thing, in a lineage of commonplaceness.
It is not surprising, therefore, that in the Western cultural sublime the preeminent, but also the most commonplace, figure of cultural tradition is the figure of
speech called apostrophe, from the Greek *apostrephein,* "to turn away." This is
the figure of direct address in which the speaker turns away from present time
or place to an absent or dead person or object. (In visual representation we observe a similar repetitive or commonplace turning away as, say, in a painting of
a historical figure who is an evocation of one or more lines of such figures as,
say, of the resisting yet resigned Servant of the Lord or of Melancholia. In addition, as Moshe Barasch has demonstrated, in an extraordinarily large number of works of visual art we encounter a representation of speaking to the
spectator as if by the mute work of art itself.)[1]

By the act of turning away, the speaker or representer partially withdraws from the temporal and spatial contexts in which the apostrophe is spoken or represented. But we must be careful to describe the kind and extent of this withdrawal. It is temptingly neat to speak of the "O" of apostrophe as if the vocative breathing represents, in absolute little, the whole of the apostrophe and as if this "O" creates an experience of pure interruption.[2] Yet apostrophes that can be recognized as belonging to a given line of apostrophes are necessarily far greater in extent than this "O," and each, including the sounding of the "O," does not cease to represent both the continuity and discontinuity of language or representation when it is spoken. In the Western cultural sublime apostrophe entails something like the following experience, for which the stage must be set by prior experiences within a given line of sublime apostrophe:

1. Each sublime apostrophe is already spoken as a commonplace or *n*th repetition of an effectively endless line of apostrophes.
2. By virtue of its form of turning away, each apostrophe in the line is a representation and experience of partial withdrawal or partial deprivation of representation (with its attendant shift in respect from the apparently great to the truly great).
3. The encounter with the line of apostrophes produces a check to the vital forces or dying-away, which is itself represented in the line of apostrophe as partial interruption, spatial or temporal.
4. The experience of dying-away creates a feeling of freedom or disinterestedness.
5. This in turn allows for moral feeling or moral choosing, not least of the possibilities of (a) choosing to repeat the line of being-in-language represented by the line of apostrophes and (b) experiencing the priority of a given line of apostrophes.

One of my principal subjects in this chapter is a further dimension of Western apostrophe created by sublime experience. As I will soon explain in greater detail, I have been made aware of this possibility by Barbara Johnson's essay on the connection between apostrophe and motherhood. Johnson, however, does not seem to be aware of a functional relation between the lineage of apostrophe and sublime experience. As I see it, this further possibility created by sublime experience of apostrophe is (c) listening in freedom or disinterestedly to someone else's apostrophe and freely choosing to speak an apostrophe that is a listening-speech. Such apostrophe is heard and spoken in an infinite matrilineal repetition of the infant's cry, "Mama." This matrilineal activity is both located within and creative of the cultural sublime.[3]

I will further propose that the matrilineal repetition of an apostrophe that is a hearing-speaking takes place between speakers or worlds that are lost to each other. The sublime apostrophe takes the form of (d) endless repetition of counterfalling and counterrising, disappearing and reappearing, absence and presence, in an occidental or westering movement described—implicitly or explicitly—by the sun's journey of departure and return. (In the next chapter I will note, in fact, Dryden's and Wordsworth's uses of the commonplace solar journey in this way.)

Because, in European culture, it is difficult, perhaps impossible, to think of any sublime line of apostrophe that does not include, from near or far, the apostrophes of Virgil and Homer, I have chosen as a paradigm of sublime apostrophe a Homeric-Virgilian lineage of apostrophe that spans two millennia. It is no accident that Virgil's placement in this lineage occurs in the apostrophe in which he addresses dead Nisus and Euryalus. In fact, in this apostrophe we see that in the *Aeneid* the continuous defoundation of institutionalized power and the continuity of apostrophe are aspects of each other. The texts I will discuss are (1) Homer's apostrophes to Patroklos in book 16 of the *Iliad*, (2) Virgil's apostrophe to Nisus and Euryalus in book 9 and some related passages in book 6 of the *Aeneid*, (3) Dryden's elegy to Oldham (1684), and (4) Pope's Epistle to Oxford (1721). (The texts of Dryden's elegy and Pope's epistle are reproduced at the end of the notes to this chapter.)

Certain aspects of the interrelations among the contexts of these apostrophes are more or less well known. Not only, for example, are Virgil's stories of Nisus and Euryalus presented as suggestive parallels to the Patrokleia, which brings about the major shift in the action of the *Iliad* by precipitating Achilleus's return to the fighting and, therefore, the tragic fulfillment of his destiny, and not only does Dryden's elegy to Oldham turn on the simile of the race run by Nisus and Euryalus and their subsequent death, but in the verses of Pope's epistle that first describe Oxford's relation to Parnell, Pope invokes Dryden's elegy by overt allusion. As Geoffrey Tillotson says, "Pope echoed Dryden's poem, both echoing Virgil."[4] Taken together with the memorializing of a friendship interrupted by death, these filiations suggest separate attempts by Virgil, Dryden, and Pope to retrieve a potentiality of literary relationship with at least one earlier poem, including, potentially, the *Iliad*. In addition to these multiple parallelisms of context, these apostrophes each suggests that an experience of continuity among apostrophes, in this sublime lineage of apostrophes, is inherent in each sublime apostrophe. Indeed, this way of experiencing apostrophe is already represented as a continuity of a line of apostrophe in the *Iliad* itself.

Of the fifteen narrative apostrophes addressed to mortals in the *Iliad*, eight are addressed to Patroklos as he moves toward death in the Patrokleia.[5] This uniquely clear calling out of Homeric apostrophe, heard and spoken at a single narrative juncture, is subsequently listened to and tacitly invoked within the entire sublime lineage of European apostrophe. In our texts from Virgil, Dryden, and Pope, we will observe a sustained recognition of the relation between this Homeric call and the meaning of the cultural sublime. Here are Homer's apostrophes to Patroklos:[6]

Τὸν δὲ βαρὺ στενάχων προσέφης, Πατρόκλεες ἱππεῦ·

ὣς ἰθὺς Λυκίων, Πατρόκλεες ἱπποκέλευθε,
ἔσσυο καὶ Τρώων, κεχόλωσο δὲ κῆρ ἑτάροιο.

  Ἔνθα τίνα πρῶτον, τίνα δ᾽ ὕστατον ἐξενάριξας,
Πατρόκλεις, ὅτε δή σε θεοὶ θάνατόνδε κάλεσσαν

τὸν δ᾽ ἐπικερτομέων προσέφης, Πατρόκλεες ἱππεῦ·

ὣς ἐπὶ Κεβριόνῃ, Πατρόκλεες, ἄλσο μεμαώς.

ἔνθ᾽ ἄρα τοι, Πάτροκλε, φάνη βιότοιο τελευτή·
ἤντετο γάρ τοι Φοῖβος ἐνὶ κρατερῇ ὑσμίνῃ
δεινός.

ὅς τοι πρῶτος ἐφῆκε βέλος, Πατρόκλεες ἱππεῦ,
οὐδὲ δάμασσ᾽· ὁ μὲν αὖτις ἀνέδραμε, μίκτο δ᾽ ὁμίλῳ,
ἐκ χροὸς ἁρπάξας δόρυ μείλινον

Τὸν δ᾽ ὀλιγοδρανέων προσέφης, Πατρόκλεες ἱππεῦ·

[Then with a heavy groan, Patroklos the rider, you addressed/
spoke to (προσέφης)
(16.20)

So straight for the Lykians, o lord of horses, Patroklos,
you swept, and for the Trojans, heart angered for your companion.
(584–85)

Then who was it you slaughtered first, who was the last one,
Patroklos, as the gods called you to your death?
(692–93)

Now
you spoke in bitter mockery over him rider Patroklos.
(743–44)

So in your fury you pounced, Patroklos, above Kebriones,
(754)

there, Patroklos, the end of your life was shown forth,
since Phoibos came against you there in the strong encounter dangerously.
(787–89)

He first hit you with a thrown spear, o rider Patroklos,
nor broke you, but ran away again, snatching out the ash spear
from your body, and lost himself in the crowd.
(812–14)

And now, dying, you answered him, o rider Patroklos.
(843)]

The contents of these apostrophes differ substantially, yet a number of things remain constant. Each apostrophe sustains a speaking from a shadow world, whence each is addressed to a shade among the shadows. One of the semantic features that is markedly invariable here is the repetition of the name Patroklos. The placement of that name within the turning away of apostrophe rips Patroklos untimely from the world. (I cite the word "untimely" from Pope's hearing it, in his apostrophe to Oxford, primarily in Homer's apostrophes, secondarily in Shakespeare and others.) But what exactly is the continuity of this turning away from present time?

Part of an answer to this question is provided by the fact that, even as Homer speaks, he too is already listening carefully to Patroklos's way of marking himself as a dead man with his own address or prayer or apostrophe. In the local line of Homer's Patrokleian apostrophe, at least, the speaking of sublime apostrophe is simultaneously an act of listening to what is itself an apostrophe, that is, to an absent or dead addressee. In fact, the lineage of classical and neoclassical—and post-Enlightenment—apostrophe marks one of its earliest moments in this listening to Patroklos's prayer within Homer's opening apostrophe to Patroklos: "Then with a heavy groan, Patroklos the rider, you addressed / spoke to" [προσ-έφης]. The fact that Homer gives no object for the verb προσέφης is not in itself remarkable. In this case most translators accordingly say "answered" or "responded," as if the principal addressee is Achilleus, who has just spoken to Patroklos. Yet Homer goes on to say that the addressee of Patroklos's address is actually absent. He says that the addressee here is the god(s) of death: "So spake he in prayer [λισσόμενος], fool that he was, for in sooth it was to be his own evil death and fate for which he prayed [λιτέσθαι]" (16.46–47). When in Homer's third apostrophe to Patroklos Homer hears that "the gods called you to your death" (16.693) Homer confirms the fact that Patroklos's calling out has been heard and has been answered by their call from the realm of death.

This placement of Homer's listening to Patroklos addressing the realm of the dead, praying for his own death, within the first of Homer's apostrophes and, moreover, at the outset of a continuous line of eight apostrophes, is itself of great importance for the meaning and function of apostrophe in the European tradition. Noting this placement may correct some misimpressions about the history of sublime apostrophe; and it may help us find the everyday experience of continuity that is of primary significance in that history. Paul de Man claims that there is a "latent threat" in apostrophe: "The fiction of address . . . acquires a sinister connotation that is not only the prefiguration of one's own mortality but of our actual entry into the frozen world of the dead."[7] In the Homeric text the entry into the world of the dead is patent and taken for granted. Yet it is far from sinister because it represents the experience of a dying-away that is indispensable for the life of the cultural sublime and for the individual's experience of freedom within tradition. Thus the *Aeneid* terminates with the pure apostrophic expiry of Turnus (12.952), repeating the pure apostrophic expiry of Camilla (11.831), citing, from the *Iliad*, the pure apostrophic expiry of Hektor (22.363), citing the pure apostrophic expiry of Patroklos (16.857)—immediately after Homer's series of eight apostrophes to Patroklos is concluded. In fact, everything that we observe in Homer's, Virgil's, Dryden's, and Pope's language of sublime apostrophe makes clear that they experience this kind of continuity not only as the formal design but also as the historical power of sublime apostrophe. In their speaking of, and listening to, apostrophe in this line, they experience both a momentary, ecstatic dying-away and a continuity or priority of the sublime lineage.

In Homer's language the interruptive effect of apostrophe is heard in a variety of manifestations of withdrawal from representation. Thus, from the opening apostrophe of the *Iliad,* to the Muse, the unrepresentable dividing line of the "division of conflict" (the διαστήτην ἐρίσαντε [1.6]) describes more than the plot of the epic. It also reflects the ungrounded, atemporal place that the poet experiences within language—in the singing of the goddess or Muse—to which he responds. For Homer this place is part of the condition in which he encounters sublime language. From this same place—caught in the division of conflict between Achilleus and Agamemnon—Kalchas is told (by Achilleus) that he must "speak, interpreting whatever he knows, fearing nothing" (1.85). Like Homer's, Kalchas's courage to fear nothing on the knife's edge of deadly conflict leads him to "speak," in Pope's translation, "Truths invidious to the Great" (1.101–02), thus shifting respect from the apparently great to the truly great.[8] This dimensionless midpoint figures a partial withdrawal of figuration that is highly similar to the disappearing boundary stones traced in chapter 4. In the Patrokleia the recurrence of these unrepresentable midpoints at the bewildered center of conflict repeatedly figures an atemporal emptiness which is linked to the work of apostrophe. I have elsewhere given a number of instances of this Homeric phenomenon.[9] Here, from the Patrokleia, in the background of Homer's apostrophes, is the defiguration of dead Sarpedon that was to be particularly important to Virgil, Dryden, and Pope:

οὐδ' ἂν ἔτι φράδμων περ ἀνὴρ Σαρπηδόνα δῖον
ἔγνω, ἐπεὶ βελέεσσι καὶ αἵματι καὶ κονίῃσιν
ἐκ κεφαλῆς εἴλυτο διαμπερὲς ἐς πόδας ἄκρους.
οἱ δ' αἰεὶ περὶ νεκρὸν ὁμίλεον, ὡς ὅτε μυῖαι
σταθμῷ ἔνι βρομέωσι περιγλαγέας κατὰ πέλλας
ὥρῃ ἐν εἰαρινῇ, ὅτε τε γλάγος ἄγγεα δεύει·

[No longer

could a man, even a knowing one, have made out the godlike
Sarpedon, since he was piled from head to ends of feet under
a mass of weapons, the blood and the dust, while
                    others about him
kept forever swarming over his dead body, as flies
through a sheepfold thunder about the pails overspilling
milk, in the season of spring when the milk splashes
                    in the buckets.]
                    (16.637–43)

The power of this figure derives (among other things) from what it shows that it cannot show. In this simile, dead Sarpedon cannot be made out, not even, in principle, by the knowing maker of the simile. The simile tells us that the reality of death in Sarpedon's dead body is not figurable, not only not by the body itself but not by spilled milk or thundering swarms of flies or anything else. The description of the slippery place, of blood, not milk, is an instance of the withdrawal from figuration in the background of figuration in which the Patrokleian apostrophe is uttered. This kind of negation of an apparently epic claim on the solidity of represented place—Troy or Rome or Augustan England—shifts the terms of respect within the lineage of apostrophe for Homer, Virgil, Dryden, and Pope alike. Yet this withdrawal from figuration in the placement of apostrophe is less decisive than the withdrawal from figuration within the structure of apostrophe itself, at least, that is, of apostrophes within a lineage of a cultural sublime.

The nature of the apostrophe that Homer hears and to which he responds in his own apostrophe is indicated in his poetry in yet another way. This way, indeed, strikingly confirms the hypothesis about apostrophe offered by Barbara Johnson. Johnson is especially interested in what is nonfigural in apostrophe. In the wake of various psychoanalytic speculations concerning the origins of language in the infant's experience of the absent mother, Johnson suggests that "lyric poetry itself—summed up in the figure of apostrophe—comes to look like the fantastically intricate history of endless elaborations and displacements of the single cry, 'Mama!'" As a displacement of this calling of the child for the absent mother, Johnson posits for apostrophe a "connection between motherhood and death that refuses to remain comfortably and conventionally figurative" as it usually does, she says, in the language of male poets. Johnson believes that "when a woman speaks about the death of children in any sense other than that of pure loss, a powerful taboo is being violated."[10] Considering the significance of Homer's series of apostrophes to the history of apostrophe it is worth noting, with Johnson's comments in mind, that Patroklos's "groan" is placed by Homer in a highly specific way. This groan is not only, as I noted earlier, the call—not to Achilleus but to death—that Homer listens to when he utters the first in his series of apostrophes to Patroklos. In addition, Homer has found a way to suggest that this same Achilleus to whom Patroklos responds and calls out, and who is actually the god of death, is also a "mother" [μητρὶ] to whom Patroklos calls out "like a girl baby" [ἠΰτε κούρη νηπίη], "till the mother take her up" [ὄφρ' ἀνέληται]. Achilleus asks,

> τίπτε δεδάκρυσαι, Πατρόκλεες, ἠΰτε κούρη
> νηπίη, ἥ θ' ἅμα μητρὶ θέουσ' ἀνελέσθαι ἀνώγει,
> εἱανοῦ ἁπτομένη, καί τ' ἐσσυμένην κατερύκει,
> δακρυόεσσα δέ μιν ποτιδέρκεται, ὄφρ' ἀνέληται·
>
> [Why, Patroklos, art thou bathed in tears, like a girl, a mere babe, that runneth by her mother's side and biddeth her take her up, and clutcheth at her gown, and hindereth her in her going, and tearfully looketh up at her, till the mother take her up?]
>
> (XVI.7–10)[11]

Johnson's hypothesis about the connection between apostrophe and motherhood and the cry of the infant and death could not, I think, find a more significantly placed attestation in the whole European history of apostrophe. And her emphasis on apostrophe's nonfigural expression of loss is also borne out by Homer's repeated delimitations of the nonfigural dimension of representation, specifically in the place where apostrophe is uttered.[12]

Yet I have two reservations about Johnson's formulation of her hypothesis. The first concerns the impression that she seems to create that there are biological grounds for her claim that only a female speaker addressing a dead child refuses "to remain comfortably and conventionally figurative." Johnson's statement that "when a woman speaks about the death of children in any sense other than that of pure loss, a powerful taboo is being violated" suggests, on the contrary, that this taboo (like all taboos) is culturally created. In fact in the West the male poets who have most effectually recorded the lineage of apostrophe have not only represented a mother's capacity to experience something that is beyond the unaided capacity of male speakers, but have also recognized the defigural necessities of this lineage. For these male poets the mother or "Mama" is the recurring addressee in the line of human cryings-out; she is the mother who hears the child's apostrophe within an infinite line of cryings-out; and she responds, from this hearing, in her own apostrophe that resonates with the endlessness of mothers' apostrophes. By these male poets, therefore, the sublime lineage of apostrophe is substantively defined as a matrilineage. Because our culture's concept (including its taboos) of a mother is correlative to our experience of the cultural sublime—not least the experience enabled by the lineage of sublime apostrophe—we need to know concretely what the features are that, in Western culture, identify matrilineal hearing-speech.

My second, related reservation concerns the connection between apostrophe and what Johnson calls its "history" of something "endless." This connection seems to me of great significance for the experience of sublime priority in any encounter with a lineage of apostrophe. Yet Johnson's reduction of apostrophe's "fantastically intricate history of endless elaborations and displacements" to "the single cry" and to "pure loss" in effect represses the experience of that history of apostrophe, for women as well as men. This repression is also reflected in the isolation of lyric poetry from the continuous history of epic and lyric poetry. In Western culture, I believe, we can discover the elements of the matrilineal hearing-speaking (that creates the cultural sublime) only by marking the continuities of classical, neoclassical, romantic, and postromantic lineages of apostrophe.

One of the achievements of European neoclassicism is its clarification of the elements of the hearing-speaking in sublime apostrophe and its specific connection with the matrilineage of Homeric-Virgilian apostrophe. In Dryden's apostrophe to Oldham and Pope's to Oxford we see that the cry of apostrophe is indeed that of pure loss in that it is a cry for the loss of an entire world that is not retrievable. The experience of the neoclassical—or more precisely, Christian-classical—speaker of apostrophe is vividly of counterworlds alternately passing away and reappearing, like Dioscuri twins, one falling or setting while the other rises. I will now try to show that the neoclassical poet repeatedly locates this westering, hearing-speaking function of apostrophe in a matrilineal language. The mother in this lineage is the speaker who is capable of representing a withdrawal from representation that she does not recuperate.

In his "Parallel betwixt Painting and Poetry" (1695) Dryden has left us painterly hints about how to hear his elegy to Oldham within its Homeric-Virgilian line of apostrophe:

> As in a picture, besides the principal figures which compose it, and are placed in the midst of it, there are less[er] groups or knots of figures disposed at proper distances, which are parts of the piece, and seem to carry on the same design in a more inferior manner; so in epic poetry there are episodes . . . which are members of the action, [but] not inserted into it. Such in the ninth book of the *Æneids* is the episode of Nisus and Euryalus. . . . some parts of a poem require to be amply written, and with all the force and elegance of words; others must be cast into shadows, that is, passed over in silence. . . .
>
> We have the proverb *manum de tabula* [tollere] ["(to withdraw) one's hand from the picture"]. . . . Both Homer and Virgil practised this precept wonderfully well, but Virgil the better of the two.[13]

In his apostrophe to dead Oldham, Dryden reproduces a power of hearing, while withholding speech, in matters to which he yet pays the profoundest attention or respect. These unspoken matters are invoked, even in their absence, by the knot of figures made from an "inferior" episode of the *Aeneid*. In fact, the principal statements of Dryden's apostrophe to Oldham are withheld statements which are communicated within the silences of this represented episode. Thus, Dryden's likening of himself to Nisus falling upon the slippery place is an enormous holding of the breath. It is built on a principle of withheld statement within spoken statement, hearings and speakings from the realms of life and death, into which the speaker, Dryden, and his addressee, Oldham, alternately rotate. By the end of the poem we understand that all the language of Dryden's neoclassical, or classical and Christian, counterworlds is subject to the same rotation. We also understand that the poet's power to hold his breath in this way is derived from a matrilineal capacity that is not his own.

The formulaic and apostrophic nature of Dryden's elegy to Oldham makes possible a listing of propositions that are more or less self-evident. We may argue about the weight that should be given to any one proposition but what is crucial for our purposes is the tableaux of interconnections. What this apostrophe hears and expresses but *does not say* is

- that this apostrophe hears and calls upon, specifically, the apostrophes of Virgil to Nisus and Euryalus and of Homer to Patroklos that emerge from their scenes of death in the slippery place;
- that in their pictures of the slippery place and most especially in their use of apostrophe Homer and Virgil practice the precept of *manum de tabula*—of representations that partially withdraw from representation;
- that Dryden's apostrophe calls upon the episode in book 9 of the *Aeneid* which carries on the design—at a proper distance—of Aeneas's race within that epic, thus raising traumatic moral questions about the most august myth of well-founded civilization available in Augustan culture, the epic race toward the founding of a "pax Romana," the eternal peace of state power;
- that ivy and laurel as well as mortality are thus bound on the brows of the dead child by the topos or commonplace of the mother or "pastoral Muse" famously represented in Virgil's eighth Eclogue (8.1, 12–13);
- that Dryden's calling out to "Marcellus," whom he had begun to think and call his "own," is an apostrophe to a dead (adopted) child, just as Virgil calls out, on Augustus's behalf, to his dead (adopted) child, Marcellus;
- that within Dryden's outcry to Oldham we hear that Dryden's fall upon the slippery place signifies Dryden's confession of personal and moral failure (recalling these verses in the Killigrew ode, Dryden will describe his part in Restoration comedy as a "Second Fall" upon the "lubrique" place [63–66]), yet Dryden feels himself absorbed into the sublime experience of a repetition of a matrilineal tongue that endlessly repeats this experience;

• that all of this unstated statement takes place within the interruption constituted by Dryden's moment of turning away from his world and time, in apostrophe, to dead Oldham.

As I have suggested, beyond all this implied statement, Dryden records yet
another, more vast silent statement. This is the hearing-speaking of the disappearance of the classical world. Dryden speaks out, listening, from a totally
transfigured Christian world to the shades of a pagan world that he infinitely
values but that is irrecoverable. The precociousness of Dryden's "historicism"
has sometimes been noted,[14] but what is most distinctive in that historicism remains to be explored. Dryden grasped that every past epoch is not only singular but significantly lost to us (ceased, as in the Greek sense of marking an *epoché*
or cessation). Dryden's "To the Memory of Mr. Oldham" is an apostrophe
transacted between classical and Christian counterworlds, each setting and rising beside the lost other.[15] Without saying so in so many words, the poem's two
voices tell of mirror fallings of the Nisus/Dryden who "fell upon the slippery
place" (Virgil's verb is "concidit," 5.333), that is, in both pagan and Christian
counterworlds. Dryden's Christian-classical Muse (herself a speaker from the
realms of death as well as life) hears and responds to the deathcry and binds the
brows of both her classical and her Christian twins. She answers one, audibly
and visually, from the realm of a dead and bygone world, with the classical
wreath of ivy and laurel. In the world and the pathos experienced by a seven-
teenth-century Christian, she is, at the same time, necessarily binding the brow
of her other twin with a thornier crown. (Dryden says this infinitely better by
leaving it unsaid.)

In his epistle to Oxford (also named Harley and Mortimer), Pope reaches for the
same double note in double worlds. Just as his opening word "Such" simultaneously points to Parnell's poems and pulls away from them to the greater succession of poetry sung by other dead poets, so the soul that can touch immortals is
identified not as Oxford's but as being "*like*" Oxford's. It is Oxford's soul only by
approximation and mortal succession. Indeed, if that soul can be said to have a
primary identity in any one individual, it is that of Christ himself, whose soul,
Pope intimates, became incarnate in a tradition of human being. The phrase "in
each hard Instance *try'd*"—meaning *tempted, proven*—and the allegorical scenes
evoked by describing Oxford as being not only "Above all Pain, all Passion, and
all Pride," but also beyond the reach of "The Rage of Pow'r, the Blast of public
Breath / The Lust of Lucre, and the Dread of Death" (ll. 25–26) lead suggestively to an image of the man of the Gospels and of *Paradise Regained,* the greater
man tempted in the wilderness, whose archetype dwarfs the little events of

Augustan England: "In vain . . . ," says the Muse to Harley, "In vain to Desarts thy Retreat is made." Harley has already been absorbed into this greater Christian destiny. He is represented here as a distant imitator of a "supreme" original. In this way, Christian intimations, imitations, and counterpoint represent a separation not only of Harley's soul from its earthly existence but of the Christian world of spirit from the pagan-classical world of material power. The experience of these counterworlds, each summoned in a line of westering apostrophes, is a species of repetition and resistance that produces yet another experience of sublime *dying-away*, thereby opening up the possibility of another experience of sublime freedom and of priority.

Most immediately perhaps, in uttering his apostrophe to Oxford, Pope hears the unspoken statements itemized above from Dryden's apostrophe to Oldham. In fact, the fatal logic of doubling that Pope read in Dryden and Virgil is extensively carried over from Dryden's elegy into Pope's epistle. Pope's epistle, that is, is an elegy for both still living Harley and dead Parnell. Much more than Pope is willing to say explicitly, his poem's conclusion, addressed to Harley, reenacts the Muse's death ritual—"Ev'n now she shades thy Evening Walk with Bays"—heard in the conclusion of Dryden's address to his deceased friend: "Thy brows with ivy, and with laurels bound; / But fate and gloomy night encompass thee around." Echoing Virgil's outcry "Fortunati" to dead Nisus and Euryalus, the Harley who is seen hazily "through Fortune's cloud" is already merging with the dead, melting into "the silent shade" or other world in which only "the Muse attends."

But, once again, what does the Muse's attendance—or attention or respect—amount to? What does she hear and speak? How does she create a perpetuity of Harley's spirit? Pope's answer to these questions can be found in his way of hearing Homer. There was a special symmetry, after all, even a completing of a circle, in Pope's hearing of Homer because his elegy and Dryden's are themselves very much a pair that is paired with Virgil's *Aeneid* and Homer's *Iliad*. Pope composed his epistle to Harley soon after completing his great translation of the *Iliad*. The heroic pitch of Pope's exertions as translator of Homer contributed an important part of the epic identity he was creating for himself in the shadow of the most acclaimed English translation of Virgil in the previous century, Dryden's *Aeneid*. Dryden-the-translator-of-Virgil composed his elegy to Oldham by listening to Virgil listening to Homer. Pope, listening to Dryden, returns to the locatable beginning of his line of apostrophe to clarify, one more time, the identity of the matrilineal Muse who has made possible the generation of this sublime line of language, which is at every point a two-way traffic of countervoices.

One effect of Pope's evocation of these counterworlds is to reclaim a Homeric countermovement in the following way: If Homer's *Iliad* represents the apostrophe spoken from the pain of the earthly city being destroyed; if Virgil's *Aeneid*, hearing Homer's apostrophe, speaks, contra Homer, the apostrophe from the pain of the earthly city being born; if Dryden's elegy to Oldham, hearing Virgil's apostrophe, is spoken, contra Virgil, from the pain of the Heavenly City of God being born in the eternal sacrifice of Christ's dying, yet, like Virgil's, also from the neo-Augustan hope for a providential Restoration of the earthly city; then Pope's apostrophe hearing Dryden's, contra Dryden, is spoken from disillusionment and despair of any neo-Augustan hope for rebirth of the earthly city, yet also from the pain of the Heavenly City of God being born in the eternal sacrifice of Christ's dying. This aspect of Pope's return to Homer, in Pope's inherited line of hearing-speakings, is central to the effect of Pope's poem, but it too does not sufficiently explain the meaning or force of the Muse's attendance.

Indeed, for all the strength of Tillotson's close reading of Pope's epistle, the question that he leaves untouched—I believe it is the poem's central question—is what, after all, Pope claims for this Muse. Tillotson says that Pope's "Muse" is "an impersonal agent, an agent working from the days of Homer onwards."[16] But in Pope's poem what is the specific "working" of the Muse? The larger cause of Tillotson's vagueness on this point is itself significant for the history of tradition in the West and for modern attempts to theorize it. Tillotson is relying on T. S. Eliot's vastly influential but strangely uninformative essay "Tradition and the Individual Talent" (1919), which is ostensibly about how tradition is constituted. The most conspicuous addressee of Tillotson's essay (1949) on Pope's epistle is, in fact, the Eliot of *Four Quartets* (1943), who, Tillotson is suggesting, might perhaps now be expected to add a historical and biographical dimension to the views he expressed in his then already classic essay.

Eliot's dicta in that essay have hung heavily over the study of poetry in the twentieth century and may, I think, fairly be described as the greatest modern dissuasive from the meaningful study of poetic tradition. Eliot claimed that his purpose was "to define" the "process of depersonalization and its relation to the sense of tradition" (end section I). Yet rather than define that process or experience Eliot only warned off anyone else from attempting to do so. In effect, he placed off limits the analysis of the relation of personality and of emotion to the experience of poetry in general and of tradition in particular. "Poetry," he ruled, "is not a turning loose of emotion, but an escape from emotion; it is not the expression of personality, but an escape from personality. But, of course, only those who have personality and emotions know what it means to want to escape from these things" (end section II). And rather than define the experience and making of tradition he intoned a mystical metaphysics of "an ideal order" of "the mind of Europe," while saying that his "essay proposes to halt at the frontier of metaphysics and mysticism" (opening of section III).[17]

The historical experience represented by Pope's poem is indeed purely impersonal, as Eliot apparently wished, but Pope goes much further in describing the kind of impersonality that is experienced in tradition. The shortcoming of Eliot's concept of tradition is not that it is too conservative but that, almost to the contrary, it misses the central experience of tradition: this is the sublime experience of a repeating series of representations, each of which is a partial withdrawal of representation. Thus, the occasion of Pope's experience in his epistle to Oxford is his encounter with an infinite regress or endless progression of representations of withdrawal—most especially in the line of apostrophe— that finally produces the radical, sublime effect of a check to the vital forces of the poet in his line of tradition. Without the personal experience of a dying-away in the sublime, the depersonalization which is indeed required to create tradition is both inaccessible and incomprehensible. Moreover, in his achievement of depersonalization Pope records his hearing of a female speaking-from-hearing that is for him the principal identity of the "She . . . she . . . she," the Muse of his line of apostrophe.

Pope's experience is signaled by his apostrophe's opening phrase, even its opening word: "Such were the Notes. . . ." "Such" points forward to the immediately following words of Pope's poem as well as to the volume of Parnell's poems to which Pope's poem is prefixed. And "Such" refers backward to the line of language and poetry, the formulaic "Notes" (therefore not necessarily the same words) that inform the images and feelings of Pope's and Parnell's verses. Any utterance of this "Such" is only one point on a line of infinite regress as well as of endless progression. In this way, the experience of this line or tradition of apostrophe may begin to explain, in experiential terms, the legacy of the Homeric oral style that otherwise remains invisible here. Reuben Brower remarks that after the discoveries of Milman Parry we know that "most of the diction of the Homeric poems, if not all, is formulaic" and therefore apparently foreign to what we usually value in aesthetic experience: "The listener will . . . hardly see a precise image, since he has heard the phrase[s] so often." Brower laments that "no critic with an understanding of the traditional oral style has been very successful in describing this extraordinary literary achievement."[18]

The theory of the cultural sublime may suggest a way of describing this achievement. It can propose that the core of that traditional style is the experience of repetition itself. In other words, the commonplaceness of Homer's formulaic style is a paradigmatic instance of the experience, within cultural traditions, of the sublime traced but not acknowledged by Kant (i.e., encountered in an endless progression of representations of self-deprivation). We can then see that the experience of formulaic repetition within Homer's poetry is perpetuated by the ways the Homeric traditional style of repetition recurs, not least in the line of sublime apostrophe, with its recurrent gesture of withdrawal from representation.

Such formulaic notes are struck in Pope's hearing-speaking response to Dryden's hearing-speaking response to Virgil's "From thee is my beginning; in thy honour shall I end. . . . grant that about thy brows [the Muse's] ivy may creep among the victor's laurel" (Eclogue 8). Already in the beginning of this poem sung for Parnell and Harley we learn that Such Notes were sung "'Till Death untimely stop'd his tuneful Tongue." In this poem's ending the pattern of thus stopping is repeated when we hear that the Muse, shading the dying hero "with Bays" (l. 35) "Thro' Fortune's Cloud One truly Great can see, / Nor fears to tell, that MORTIMER is He." There is a perpetuity even in the Muse's naming of MORTIMER. This naming is fearless not only because it is not afraid to praise a man who has fallen from power, but because it stoically acknowledges the imminent death of Harley. At this moment of concluding we hear suggestions of Latin *mors, mortis* and Greek *moros*—death—woven or *bound* by the Muse upon that name: Harley or Oxford is now addressed as MORTimer or MOR/TIMER, the Muse's child, call him Achilleus, in the realm of the dead. (By the choice of his epigraph from Horace, Pope has alerted us to a paradoxical effect of just this kind: "dignum laude virum Musa vetat mori" [To the man worthy of praise the Muse forbids dying].)[19] Mortimer's death and memorialized life, not only Parnell's, become "untimely" because empirically the encounter of the Muse's line of language affords the experience of their Greek, Latin, and vernacular perpetuity. Pope's overlay of the figure of Achilleus, withdrawn from the battle and bereft of Patroklos, on Harley in retreat from the political fray and bereft of Parnell not only traces a common denominator of experience that is inevitable—all human beings die and, if they live long enough, are bereaved and disappointed—but utters the inherited language that made possible the concept, for Harley, of the Harley who was not daunted (at least at moments) by these facts.

In the same vein, Parnell was a vehicle of the Notes or "Lays" sung Patroklos-like, with the Muse's help, for Achilleus / Harley. Now that Parnell is dead his oblivion forgets Oxford but the repetitions of those lays will yet remember. This does not mean, however, that the line is fulfilled by Pope. The same implications of transience and exchangeability all along the line suggest that the poet Pope too is fated to be submerged in the line in which, even now, he experiences the world in a sublime hearing-speaking. Because Pope exercises, in this poem, the strict depersonalizing discipline of his sublime line of language, he is beside himself, dying-away.

I want to emphasize, finally, that Pope's hearing-speaking in this second state is a representation of a matrilineal Muse. In the concluding section of his poem Pope hears and speaks the apostrophe of the Muse from the scene at the end of Homer's Patrokleia. Homer makes the matrilineal apostrophe that is spoken in that scene symmetrical with a simile in an earlier scene. This is the simile with which Achilleus anticipates Patroklos's "groan" of apostrophe (to death). We recall that this simile places the apostrophe of motherhood and death that Homer hears when he initiates his series of apostrophes to doomed Patroklos. Achilleus's simile, we recall, was this: "Why, Patroklos, art thou bathed in tears, like a girl, a mere babe, that runneth by her mother's side and biddeth her take her up, and clutcheth at her gown, and hindereth her in her going, and tearfully looketh up at her, till the mother take her up?" Now, after Achilleus has lost Patroklos, Homer tells of Thetis's coming to her son. Homer presents the meeting as a response of apostrophic cry for apostrophic cry. In Pope's translation of Homer's verses: "The Mother . . . / Heard his loud Cries, and answer'd Groan for Groan" (18.43–44). Pope's experience and representation of the priority of his language are astonishing and strange. In his epistle the extended figure of Harley's departure from the light is cited from the formulaic and commonplace figure that Achilleus is already citing from Thetis in his apostrophe on the death of Patroklos. There Thetis proceeds to echo Achilleus's citation of that figure, this time in her apostrophe on the imminent death of Achilleus. This is her way of responding to Achilleus's apostrophe. Her formula for expressing her fear for him is that he, like Patroklos, is about "to lose the light of the sun" (leípsein pháos helíoio).[20] Achilleus groans,

> Is this the Day, . . .
> (So Thetis warn'd) when . . .
> The bravest of the Myrmidonian Band
> Should lose the Light? Fulfill'd is that Decree;
> Fal'n is the Warrior, *and Patroclus he!*
>   (Pope's *Iliad*, 18.11–16; emphasis added)

This last verse (Thetis's, Homer's, Pope's) rings in Pope's ear and voice when he writes that the Muse, working from Homer onward, "One truly Great can see, / Nor fears to tell, that MORTIMER is He."

The weavings of this Muse, which attends Harley "to the silent Shade," are sublimely ordinary and commonplace. Pope's *Iliad* gives us Thetis's apostrophe when she goes to find her son. "There sate Achilles, shaded" (18.5). In that shade he speaks in apostrophe what "Thetis warn'd." To this groan she answers,

> So short a space the Light of Heav'n to view,
> So short alas! . . .
> Hear how his Sorrows echo thro' the Shore!
> . . . .
> I go at least to bear a tender part,
> And mourn my lov'd one with a Mother's Heart.
> (Pope's *Iliad*, 18.79–84)

In Pope's epistle the identity of the Muse ("She . . . she . . . she") is in one highly specific sense Homer's Thetis answering her dying child's groan with her groan, but more significantly she is the Thetis of an endless matrilineage. Her dying child is a composite of Harley, of Parnell, and of Pope as well. Pope achieves a sublime depersonalization by representing a hearing-speaking of this matrilineal apostrophe to the line of human mortality. The relationship, in the line of language, of the mother to her mortal child—to the child's mortality—burns through all of Pope's inherited language, from Homer onward, indeed, from the identifiable outset of the endless Western line of sublime apostrophe onward. Pope thus repeats the always matrilineal formula—of "the Muse"—for the endless line of apostrophes that Homer hears and that intervenes between Homer and Virgil and Dryden and Pope, answering groan for groan.

In the entire Homeric-Virgilian line of sublime apostrophe that Pope hears and speaks in this way no experience is more immediate and real—we may want to say surreal—than this matrilineal outcry responding to the cry of the mortal child. In Pope's epistle the Muse has most immediately heard it in Parnell's lays, in Pope's verses, and in Harley's silence. This matrilineal, hearing-speaking apostrophe is westering and sublime. It is westering in that it is addressed from counterworlds that are lost to each other. It is sublime in that it is an apostrophe which represents partial self-withdrawal in an effectively endless line of such apostrophes. Working from Homer onward, and traced back to Homer, this matrilineage of apostrophe creates the Western cultural sublime or cultural tradition. By himself Pope does not have access to the matrilineal apostrophe. Neither does any other male or female by himself or herself. Yet like Homer, Virgil, and Dryden, Pope shows himself capable of representing the indispensable centrality of the matrilineal apostrophe in Western culture.

The very possibility of the westering, hearing-speaking apostrophe depends upon a matrilineal experience of apostrophe. This is a mother's experience of an endless, commonplace line of the infant's cry and her answering cry.

Each of these hearing-speakings is a representation that shows its inadequacy as representation. The mother-Muse who speaks apostrophe derives her sublime status as Muse from the sublime experience and/or representation of freedom and moral choosing. The Muse chooses to hear and speak from the groans of innumerable mothers and children in innumerable apostrophic cryings-out and writings. This is what the Muse is.

Echoing the Muse, Pope does not fear to tell that, in our culture, the courage of apostrophic language is that of the mother who does not fear to hear and tell (within her matrilineal language) that the creature who calls to her and to whom she calls is bound to mortality, is Patroklos, is Mortimer, is her child.

Counterperiodization and the Colloquial: Wordsworth and "the Days of Dryden and Pope"

CHAPTER 6

I am sorry that Wordsworth is likely to be displeased at my praise of Dryden, extremely limited as it is. The vigour of Drydens mind, and of his poetry too, is far beyond the vigour of Wordsworths. Nothing was ever written in *rhyme* equal to the beginning of the Religio Laici, the eleven first lines.—Part of a letter from Walter Savage Landor to Henry Crabb Robinson; the words in italics have not been printed before

In this chapter my larger subject is once again sublime experience in a line of culture. But my immediate subject is only one condition of that experience all along any given line of Western culture. This is the way in which, in a given line, the writings of an earlier and a later writer, each exemplary of their period, form configurations which are not only strongly oppositional, but also reciprocal. Elements of such periodic reciprocity manifest themselves within matched oppositions, where such opposition is expressed both temporally backward (i.e., a later writer contra a writer of an earlier period) and temporally forward (i.e., an earlier writer contra an imagined writer of an anticipated later period). What is distinctive about this pattern of periodic opposition, however, is that it occurs within a set of reciprocal relations that oppose opposition as such.

My focus, then, is on the details of a symmetrical correspondence, forward and backward, oppositionally and reciprocally, between writers of two different periods of the same literary tradition. I will be adducing various half-hidden tracings of the oppositional-reciprocal relations which form such correspondence, in this case between the neoclassical and the romantic periods. It is not surprising that tracings of this correspondence constitute the figure of chiasmus, since chiasmus is only a diagram of the simultaneous occurrence of opposition and reciprocity (in the pattern AB : BA). By entering into this countermovement against what was already a countermovement, counterperiodization plays out a chiastic pattern of language. The formal objective of this chapter is to describe the chiasmus of countermovements that occurs both *be-tween* writers of different periods and within the writings of each author in the counterperiodizing relation. The counterperiodizing chiasmus of the individual writer speaks in at least two voices, one of which represents a hearing of a voice that does not belong to the author or ostensible speaker. The condition of this occurrence in the writing of each author is that (contrary to Hegel's imagining) what looks like the return movement of language (or recuperation of self-consciousness) within a chiasmus does not overcome the dying-away and self-alienation within language. The antithetical, commonplace (endlessly repeated) elements of chiasmus, often highlighted by a figure of apostrophe, constitute a map of presence and absence, fullness and lack, speaking voice and mute, heard voice. These elements remain in reciprocal opposition rather than being brought round or returned to a wholeness. As a result, we do not experience a recuperation of self-consciousness (as if B came again to be A) such as Hegel imagined after the "trial by death" (when A dies away, passing into the condition of B). Rather, in the line of culture the chiastic experience of language represents the experience of encountering and recording the counter-voice and countermovement of another being or world, or generation or period, that is lost to the present speaker in an endless line of countermovements.

Here is a chiastic couplet from Pope's epitaph on Elizabeth Corbet:

>   [A]   [B]
> Heav'n as its purest gold by tortures tried;
>   [B']   [A']
> The Saint sustain'd it, but the Woman died.

In Wordsworth's effort to distance himself from Pope, Wordsworth cites the second half of this couplet as an example of what he brands the hateful "antithesis" of neoclassical verse.[1]

To be sure, each of these verses is made up of antithetical elements. The second verse, which is more obviously antithetical, makes explicit and confirms the antithesis between "Heav'n" and "tortures" deployed in the first. Yet as a whole the couplet engenders a figuration of chiasmus which is not primarily an activity of exclusion or appropriation, such as antithesis alone would produce. Wordsworth is wondrously forgetful of a wholly different working of chiasmus—forgetful of it in this couplet of Pope as well as in neoclassical poetry in general. I will indicate, however, that in other ways he is also wondrously mindful of it: namely, when he sets his own chiastic structures into motion. Wordsworth's doubleness on this score, like Pope's, comes about because chiasmus itself entails recreating an emptiness or obliviousness within language. This emptiness can result in the reachings out of language, from its incompleteness or obliviousness, toward symmetry with other language. It will emerge that in Wordsworth's own writing he is partly forgetful, partly mindful, of the way the neoclassical counterparts to his own use of chiasmus half-form his poetic tradition and his own situation in the line of counterworlds that constitutes his cultural sublime.

We have repeatedly seen that the figure of chiasmus creates a species of absences between its binary terms. These absences are not simply the antitheses or negations of the binary terms themselves. Nor can absence of this kind be identified with a particular location within chiasmus. In fact, the elaborate complexity of neoclassical chiasmus highlights the fact that absence on this order cannot be located spatially. Quite often, for example, the neoclassical chiasmus disorders visual symmetries by enjambing beyond the frame of the couplet itself. This sort of despatialization of relation also has the effect of further unseating the apparently settled identities of the binary terms.[2] This in turn facilitates the metamorphosis of A into B, B into A, so that it becomes inevitable in the movements of neoclassical chiasmus that sameness (AB : BA; AA = BB) must interchange with constancy of difference (AB : AB; AB = AB). As a consequence, each binary term is charged with the potential of becoming its opposite [i.e., A(b) or B(a)]. In brief: the experience of Pope's or any other chiasmus with regard to its nonthematic absences and its binary terms is of a movement of counterturning that is very different from the negation or appropriation effected in antithesis.

The effect of these multiple inversions does not necessarily spell subversion of meaning. In the five couplets of Pope's epitaph these inversions are carried out within an interrogative discourse that resists any tendency toward meaninglessness in the poem:

> Here rests a Woman, good without pretence,
> Blest with plain reason and with sober sense;
> No conquest she but o'er herself desir'd;
> No arts essayed, but not to be admir'd.
> Passion and pride were to her soul unknown,
> Convinc'd that virtue only is our own.
> So unaffected, so compos'd a mind,
> So firm, yet soft, so strong, yet so refin'd,
> Heav'n as its purest gold by tortures tried;
> The Saint sustain'd it, but the Woman died.

These couplets balance their own emergent questions, thus strongly suggesting that the balance they engender mirrors other acts of balancing other questions. To voice a few of these emergent, albeit only implicit questions, one for each polarity in the last couplet: Can spiritual "Heaven" value even an image of material "gold"? What kind of deity tests a woman by torture? What must be the moral cost of thinking of the Saint separately from the victim? And just who does this poet think he is, that he can write off the death agony of "the Woman" as if he were permanently seated in another room? Partly as a result of the balancing of such questions, we do not give up the quest for at least that kind of meaning which is directly a function of balance or adequation itself. Thus, while it is true that, having entered this couplet, the reader abandons all hope of happy poetic resolution, the fact is that the couplet's strenuous quest for meaning is itself not abandoned.

This is the case, I would emphasize, even though neoclassical chiasmus is no less fraught with deep disturbances than the chiastic reversals which modernisms and postmodernisms of various kinds now claim (antithetically) as their peculiar armorial bearings.[3] In the present chapter I will confront the exclusivist claim of the moderns as it is offered by de Man. I focus on de Man for three reasons. First, with other contemporary critics, he explicitly claims that chiasmus is a characteristically modern phenomenon.[4] Second, his claim for the modernity of chiasmus is formulated antithetically against his account of "classical" figuration—an account which requires significant amendment. Third, he directly repeats Wordsworth's antineoclassical allegation; this, despite de Man's own trenchant critique of romanticism. My purpose here is not, however, merely to counter aspects of Wordsworth's and de Man's critiques of neoclassicism. My aim, rather, is to extend my description of the neoclassical chiastic structures that these romantic and postromantic writers seem to miss and to describe the historical line of chiastic counterworlds in which their own antithetical claims are situated together with these structures of neoclassicism. That is, I am particularly concerned with the continuity of neoclassical and romantic language that is achieved in the retrospective and prospective affiliations of chiasmus.

To explore these affiliations, I will discuss two mappings of the countermovements of chiasmus, both of which are *half*-visible in Wordsworth's *Essays upon Epitaphs*, a text to which de Man has drawn special attention.[5] Not surprisingly, both mappings are closely related to Wordsworth's phrase "counterspirit" (p. 85), which itself lies at the heart of one of the most famous accusations in the modern history of periodization. Scholars of the romantic period, de Man among them, are prone to forget that Wordsworth's way of placing this damning phrase does not at all warrant us to appropriate it for an ahistorical theory of language. Quite the contrary, Wordsworth directs it, very much from his own period, specifically against the language of another period, which he calls "the days of Dryden and Pope" (p. 84).

In our first case Wordsworth's conceiving of "Dryden and Pope" as "days" turns out to be synchronous with the counterperiodization in which he participates. Wordsworth charges that the language of "the days of Dryden and Pope" could not overcome the "sense of death." The language of Wordsworth's new days, on the other hand, lays claim to what he calls "the sense of Immortality" (pp. 52–53). In order to vindicate this claim, Wordsworth compares the spirit of his own period to a series of fateful journeys along the sun's route. Even a cursory reading of the passage reveals, however, that these journeys encompass the days of death fully as much as the days of immortality:

> As, in sailing upon the orb of this planet, a voyage towards the regions where the sun sets, conducts gradually to the quarter where we have been accustomed to behold it come forth at its rising; and, in like manner, a voyage towards the east, the birth-place in our imagination of the morning, leads finally to the quarter where the sun is last seen when he departs from our eyes; so the contemplative Soul, traveling in the direction of mortality, advances to the country of everlasting life; and, in like manner, may she continue to explore those cheerful tracts, till she is brought back, for her advantage and benefit, to the land of transitory things—of sorrow and of tears.
>
> (p. 53)

In establishing his own opposition to Wordsworth's claim to meaning, de Man alleges that in this sentence Wordsworth attempts to write a "solar language of cognition." "The sun," says de Man, "becomes a figure of knowledge as well as of nature, the emblem of what the third essay refers to as 'the mind with absolute sovereignty upon itself.'"[6] This description of Wordsworth's sentence (as well as of the phrase cited from the third essay) is, I maintain, like Wordsworth's own account of the relation of his days and Dryden's and Pope's, significantly inaccurate. Wordsworth, after all, traces a movement that is not of the sun, but of three bodies moving in various relations—half the time in counterrelations—to each other. These bodies are the traveler on the earth, the earth, and the sun. (A glance at the third essay shows that it is only the encounter with "a lovely quality" outside the mind that "fastens the mind with absolute sovereignty upon itself; permitting or inciting it to pass . . . to some other kindred quality"—external, that is, to the mind itself [p. 81].) In Wordsworth's sentence, the sun's own westerly movement is, to be sure, part of what is described, but it is decisively only one part. De Man especially obscures the explicit features of countermovement of the sentence itself, while claiming that it harbors a repressed countermovement. This repressed countermovement, de Man alleges, is opposite to the "solar" movement that Wordsworth purveys (solely, singly) as the figure for the mind's (sole) knowledge.

De Man claims that, by remaining skeptical of the alleged unidirectional rotation of the sentence, he has uncovered how that sentence, against its own avowed intention or meaning, conforms to a logic of self-"de-facement." For de Man this allegedly hidden movement is identical with the "turning motion of tropes"—the countermovement or counterspirit within all individual speaking—that is merely subjective (if that) and "not primarily a situation or an event that can be located in a history."[7] Yet, as I have said, not only is it clear that Wordsworth hardly requires help in acknowledging the countermovements of his sentence, but that (as neither de Man nor Wordsworth acknowledge) these countermovements are specifically parts of the historical, linear situation of Wordsworth's apparently antithetical—actually chiastic—allegation against neoclassical "antithesis"—actually chiasmus—thus opening the scene of a historical line plotted by the countermovements of chiasmus.

The principle of structure in Wordsworth's sentence—which forms it as a double chiasmus—is throughout multidirectional. This multiple directionality is itself incomprehensible without the multiple temporality (or present experience of priority) of historical consciousness. Half of the sentence's voyages are openly, that is, in a countermode, from west to east: "a voyage toward the east, the birth-place in our imagination of the morning." These countervoyages have a radical consequence for the representation of Wordsworth's mind, since the place of his imagination's forgotten "birth" in this counterphase can be only the sunless hemisphere where he is absent. That hemisphere is the one which the sun is always vacating. In addition, though less noticeable at first, each of these primary countervoyages entails an about-face at its conclusion (B and A′ in the following vertical notation):

$$A \quad B' \qquad A \quad B'$$
$$\quad B \quad A' \quad B \quad A'$$

As, in sailing upon the orb of this planet, [A] a voyage towards the regions where the sun sets, [B] conducts gradually to the quarter where we have been accustomed to behold it come forth at its rising; and, in like manner, [B′] a voyage towards the east, the birth-place in our imagination of the morning, [A′] leads finally to the quarter where the sun is last seen when he departs from our eyes; so the contemplative Soul, [A] traveling in the direction of mortality, [B] advances to the country of everlasting life; and, in like manner, may she [B′] continue to explore those cheerful tracts, till she is [A′] brought back, for her advantage and benefit, to the land of transitory things—of sorrow and of tears.

Thus Wordsworth's self-described life of the self-providing spirit explicitly includes a double countermovement that is itself retraced whole by the self. Yet I will argue that a counterhemisphere or counterworld as well as a countervoyager is actually figured here; and they remain infinitely separated, like death from life, each locked in its hemisphere. Thus, rather than following the sun in order to trace "a figure of [self- or sole-] knowledge," Wordsworth's sentence comprises a figure of dependency and history, that is, of past being continuous with but separated from present being. Indeed, the historical dimension of this figure is even greater than this initial analysis suggests.

First, however, to deepen our sense of how much is at stake here for Wordsworth, it is useful to note that a virtually polemical version of this solar-countersolar movement was chosen by Wordsworth to serve as nothing less than the epigraph to his collected poems and as an epitaph, moreover, to his own life. This apostrophe to himself even names the counterhemisphere as the poet's counterplace. Here is the epigraph, together with a mapping of its chiasmata:

$$A \quad B' \qquad B(a) \quad A'(b)'^8 \qquad A \quad B'$$
$$B \quad A' \qquad A(b) \quad B'(a)' \qquad B \quad A'$$

If [A] thou indeed derive thy light from [B] Heaven,
Then, [B'] to the measure of that heaven-born light,
[A'] Shine, Poet! in thy place, and be content:—
[B(a)] The stars preeminent in magnitude,
And they that from the zenith dart their beams,   5
(Visible though they be to half the earth,
Though half a sphere be conscious of their brightness)
Are yet of [A(b)] no diviner origin,
[A'(b')] No purer essence, than [B'(a)] the one that burns,
Like an untended watch-fire, on the ridge   10
Of some dark mountain; or than those which seem
Humbly to hang, like twinkling winter lamps,
Among the branches of the leafless trees;
[A] All are the undying offspring of [B] one Sire:
Then, [B'] to the measure of the light vouchsafed,   15
[A'] *Shine, Poet! in thy place, and be content.*[9]

We note that the hemisphere vacated by the direct light of heaven is the "place" in which the buried poet must "Shine." The sun itself is gone from this place or moment of epitaph. Indeed, the sun itself is noticed only indirectly in a plural "they, that from the zenith dart their beams"—beams, in other words, that are now elsewhere. The sun's present visibility is bracketed, in lines 6 and 7, within the poet's protest against the injustice of the sun's eternal half-measures. With regard to the solar sentence in the *Essays upon Epitaphs,* de Man believes that Wordsworth is unconsciously responding to the latent threat within his own chiastic figure of prosopopeia: namely, the danger that in the epitaph's mirror structure of prosopopeia the living poet addressing the dead will be himself frozen in death.[10] Yet in this epitaph, at least, it is clear that Wordsworth believes that this speaking poet can "shine" in his "place," apparently empowered by the counter-"measure" itself.

My second remark about Wordsworth's solar-countersolar sentence in the *Essays upon Epitaphs* directly concerns its embeddedness in history, specifically in the counterrelations of periodization. Wordsworth protests that the language of "the days of Dryden and Pope" are a "counter-spirit" which spells only a "sense of death." While thus protesting, however, Wordsworth, in fact—within a historical experience of a line of counterworlds—very much derives the light and the counterlight of his sentence (as also the figure of the hemisphere and the counterhemisphere of his epigraph poem) from a particular Ciceronian period (here consisting of two sentences) which is the locus classicus of Enlightenment periodization. This neoclassical period is itself completely incomprehensible without the reversibility of its binary terms, which are all variations of reason and revelation, mortality and immortality. The verses in question comprise the famous exordium of Dryden's *Religio Laici*. My point in turning up this relation is to claim that, uncanny as this relation may seem, it is only representative of the recurring relations of counterperiodization, which are always, in the first instance, invisible to us. Here is Dryden's exordium, with a map of its emerging chiasmata:

$A(b)$ $A'\,(b')$ $\times\,3$
$B(a)$ $B'\,(a')$

Dim, as [$A(b)$] the borrow'd beams of Moon and Stars
To [$B(a)$] lonely, weary, wandring Travellers,   2
Is [$A'(b')$] Reason to [$B'(a']$ the Soul: And as on
       high,
[$A(b)$] Those rowling Fires [$B(a)$] discover but the Sky   4
Not light us here; so [$A'b')$] Reason's glimmering [i.e.,
       intermittent] Ray
Was lent, not to assure our doubtfull way,   6
But [$B'(a')$] guide us upward to a better Day.
And as [$A(b)$] those nightly Tapers disappear   8
When [$B(a)$] *Day's bright Lord ascends our Hemisphere;*
So [$A'(b')$] pale grows Reason at Religions sight;   10
So [$B'(a')$] dyes, and so dissolves in Supernatural Light.

These eleven verses were more than simply well known in the days of Wordsworth. No other verses had a greater claim to expressing the *religio* or faith of the solar "days of Dryden and Pope."[11] This is the faith of the ordinary human being, the *laicus,* in that earlier period. In Wordsworth's condemnation of the neoclassical poets as being antithetical to his own faith and his own way of being in the world, Wordsworth actively represses the fact of this other expression of the ordinary. We note further that Dryden's layman is the individual without assured knowledge. Throughout the poem Dryden's faith can be only a *religio laici* in this skeptical sense. The movements of chiasmus, I have already noted (following de Man on this point), whether neoclassical, romantic, or postromantic, depend upon an ungroundedness or negativity within language. Dryden's exordium, pivoting and turning on this *ungroundedness,* which is to say on a gap in correspondence between subject and object—the very gap which de Man specifically denies to "classical" figuration—builds a vast chiastic structure.[12] In fact, this structure constitutes a solar-countersolar language of Dryden's day with another, better Day. Dryden's exordium enacts counter-movements which suggest a carbon (or negative) copy of Wordsworth's sentence—or vice versa.

Close examination of *Religio Laici* shows, that is, that through the length of the poem Dryden explores images of a philosophical, Boehmistic *unground* for the skeptical or negative knowledge that the *Ungrund* harbors.[13] Within Dryden's poem this unground is identified with the sunless other hemisphere in which the most ordinary man and woman, the *laicus*, can find a sufficiency of saving, albeit negative, knowledge. As much as anything else, what makes *Religio Laici* the quintessential *religio* of English neoclassicism is just this poetics of making clear, through reversals of chiasmus, that the experience of what is withheld is our most valuable datum. According to this poem's Enlightenment argument the dim light of reason and the direct light of revelation are inversely related variables. Every section of the poem is part of a formula metamorphosing from blocked antithesis to circulating chiasmus, in the form

$$A(b) \qquad A'(b')$$
$$B(a) \qquad B'(a')$$

Even within the five rhymes of the exordium, these variables undergo staggering modulations which sweep across whole ages of reason, whole ages of revelation. In Aristotle's terms, playing out this "movement and life" of "proportional" comparisons is itself the poem's actuality or *energy*.[14] In the English of Dryden or Pope or Wordsworth, this would be called the poem's "vigour" of imagination. Dryden's poetic vigor or energy consists of his series of inversions of the ratio of reason to revelation, revelation to reason, so that ratio, *ratio* (reason), itself is inverted and reinverted in unceasing movement. This coming into being of reason in the form of metamorphic chiasmus expresses Dryden's counterperiodization of recollection and forgetting. His poem's inverse waning and waxing, in other words, is an equation of the reserve that suffices in the line of language. In the adjustable economy of this reserve, his reason provides only a negative knowledge of the noumenon. And even that knowledge is not necessarily available to him individually. In the exordium's final instance of this equation, revelation of immortality fully comes when all individual pretense to knowledge of revelation "*dyes*" and "*dissolves*."[15] It is clear that for Dryden this equation is replete with prospective as well as retrospective potentialities. The prospective cases are not so much anticipations of formed actualities as openings of possibilities: namely, of a future individual's faith in immortality expressed, say, by a Wordsworth, or even by a postromantic ebbing of faith in, say, an Arnold's *Dover Beach*.

What does it mean, then, that in a Wordsworthian composition in which "the days of Dryden and Pope" are throughout identified with the antithetical "counter-spirit," which allegedly excludes any figuration of immortality, Wordsworth forgot

1. precisely those famous lines of chiasmus or (as they were then called) "rhymes" that formulated and addressed *his* problem of the other *hemisphere* (as had no other poet in English),
2. those rhymes, moreover, that offered the counterparts of his solar-counter-solar journeys,
3. those rhymes that were the *religio laici* of the newly enfranchised *laicus*, the "man speaking to men," as Wordsworth wished to conceive him,
4. those rhymes that were based on a paradox of negative knowledge closely parallel to romantic or Wordsworthian intuitions about the negative phases of our knowledge of immortality?

I have recently discovered an unpublished part of a letter from Walter Savage Landor to Henry Crabb Robinson that may shed light on these questions. In the unpublished part of the letter, Landor says that in Wordsworth's antipathy to Dryden, Wordsworth forgets the superiority to Wordsworth's own mind and poetry of precisely these five *rhymes* of *Religio Laici*. The excellence of these rhymes, says Landor, is their "vigour," meaning their *energeia* or actuality of movement. Behind Wordsworth's back, that is, Landor writes of Dryden's vigorous equations, to which he thinks Wordsworth sadly unequal: "I am sorry that Wordsworth is likely to be displeased at my praise of Dryden, extremely limited as it is.[16] The vigour of Drydens mind, and of his poetry too, is far beyond the vigour of Wordsworths. Nothing was ever written in rhyme equal to the beginning of the Religio Laici, the eleven first lines."[17]

I propose that Dryden and Wordsworth each figures the condition of colloquy or of a colloquial hearing-speaking of colloquial language. In Wordsworth's voyagers' sentence, as in his hemisphere epitaph on himself, Wordsworth's words, those of "a man [listening to and] speaking to men," only half-forget those of Dryden, a *laicus* listening and speaking to *laici* of both hemispheres. In Wordsworth's voyagers' sentence or period, his *peri-hodos*, or *full way*, is never closed but continues spiraling and counterspiraling. His elements of chiasmus encounter those of Dryden's period—"the days of Dryden and Pope"—in two obvious ways. Both periods offer solutions to the ethico-theological problem of the other hemisphere, though Dryden's solution is in the dissolution of mortality within immortality, Wordsworth's in a largely unexplained education to immortality. And both structures of chiasmus are constituted as solar and countersolar motions, while they are markedly counterrhythms to each other's goings and comings, forgettings and recollections. Dryden begins his meditation thinking of a single "Soul," only to transpose his sense of human destiny to a plural "us" and "our" in the succession of mortality. The pathos of Dryden's faith in personal salvation is that it is grounded only in the ungroundedness of his classical creed of individual mortality, so that his own everlasting rest finally "rolls" (spirals) only upon God's providence for the "*Common quiet*" of "*Mankind*" as a plurality.[18] Wordsworth begins with "we" and "our" but completes his voyage in a prayer for the immortality of the individual soul. Dryden's period turns easterly at its beginning and end, while Wordsworth's turns westerly at its beginning and end. Yet each of these periods both turns and counterturns (especially in the shared word "so") and reads both easterly and westerly; and in both periods each segment of matched voyages consists of a full chiasmus of recollection and forgetting. Dryden's exordium to his *religio laici* already heads off any positive claim of language, any pretense to a totality of meaning controlled by one mind. Wordsworth's sentence and Dryden's exordium have all this and more in common, even if they are not perfectly symmetrical with each other's asymmetries. What Dryden's and Wordsworth's chiasmata share, most of all, are the framed absences within chiasmus, not least within the redoubled chiasmus that they form continuously, as counterworlds, together, that is, hearing and speaking within their linear history of counterperiodization.

Wordsworth hoped to block out, to do away with, and to do in Dryden's verse and its scenario of the void. But instead he heard it, cited it, translated it, embraced it, and turned with it. Landor was right in sensing (though perhaps not really comprehending) that Dryden's "rhyme" was part of Wordsworth's "beyond." In other words, through Wordsworth's chiastic relation to Dryden's chiasmus in the *Religio Laici,* Wordsworth confronts that which is beyond Wordsworth. In Wordsworth's solar-countersolar sentence, as if in double spirals, Dryden's "rowling [spiraling] Fires" within his mortality period and Wordsworth's immortality period spiral past each other, never touching or merging, only sharing absence, only, in this way, rhyming.

Dryden's exordium is markedly apostrophic, and its highly specified representation of sublime dying-away brings with it an experience of freedom as well as a present experience of the priority of Christian and pagan history. But I pass over these things here to resume the more limited subject of counterperiodization.

Specifically, I turn to my second case of counterperiodization in order to describe how absence is created and sustained within a colloquy of language, that is, by hearing the colloquial language of another speaker.

As I recalled earlier, the occasion and antiobject of Wordsworth's discourse throughout the *Essays* is his experience of what he calls the unremediated "sense of death" in the poetry of Dryden and Pope. In particular, Wordsworth explains, he encounters this sense of death in the perverted offspring of "the nice balance of pure intellect" (p. 57), the "antithetic discriminations" (p. 58), and the "antithesis" that is Dryden's and Pope's deadly "nonsense" (p. 79). The culture of those two poets, Wordsworth insists, is itself the period of language as "counterspirit" (p. 85). Very much like a shadow to Milton's named Satan, Wordsworth's unnamed opponent to the sense of immortality is the bringer of an inescapable sense of death. He is the counterspirit incarnate. One of his two secret names is Alexander Pope.[19] The previous age of poetry, says Wordsworth, was particularly "seduced by the example of Pope, whose sparkling and tuneful manner had bewitched the men of letters his Contemporaries, and corrupted the judgment of the Nation through all ranks of society" (p. 75).

Wordsworth's way of specifying the *corruption* that Pope's poetry works on the nation may similarly seem inexplicably excessive. Yet he uses it to make his considered point that the "counter-spirit" of language spoken by "Pope" is a species of deadly alien growth. I quote Wordsworth's sentence describing that cancer, that noiseless eating away of life, diametrically opposed to nourishment and health: "Language, if it do not uphold, and feed, and leave in quiet, like the power of gravitation or the air we breathe, is a counter-spirit, unremittingly and noiselessly at work to derange, to subvert, to lay waste, to vitiate, and to dissolve" (p. 85). Wordsworth's sentence derives its power from the fact that it is a chiastic turning and counterturning in which the key term, *spirit,* is left unspoken. This silent breathing-in is as "quiet" as its tandem polarity, "the power of gravitation or the air we breathe." In order to see the counterperiodization operative in this figure, one aspect of Wordsworth's horrific metaphor for the wrong kind of poetic language is very important: this metaphor is itself unwittingly breathed into Wordsworth's system of thought and language from a metaphor of Pope's. This metaphor, in addition to being deeply implicit in the very form of the neoclassical couplet, is furthermore staring Wordsworth in the face in Pope's lines in a particularly unavoidable way. This strangest of Wordsworth's emulations, or inhalations, challenges us, once again, to probe the repressed counterperiodizatons of romanticism with regard to neoclassicism.

Wordsworth notes this metaphor when he cites (with one significant omission, as we shall see in a moment) the title of Pope's epitaph on Elizabeth Corbet as "Mrs. Corbet (who died of a Cancer)" (p. 76).[20] Yet Wordsworth in no way acknowledges the relevance of Pope's way of representing a victim, specifically of cancer, to his attack on the cancerous nature of Pope's language in the lines of the poem. And, in eliding Pope's title, Wordsworth precisely occludes the way in which Pope's language, more than his own, determinedly opens toward the agony of spirit experienced by Mrs. Corbet. In Pope's and Wordsworth's texts we witness the noiseless movements of spirit-counterspirit which Wordsworth finds so daunting. The formal name of these movements, I suggest, is not cancer but chiasmus or, better still, specifically the empty spaces transported by repetition of difference in the neoclassical couplet. I propose that Pope too saw a potential aberrancy within language. Pope, however, also intuited and exploited its benign possibility, namely, the possibility of sublime experience in a line of language that is made up of countermovements, of countervoices hearing-speaking from counterworlds. Wordsworth, however, very much fell in with Pope's motions and countermotions. In other words, half-of-Wordsworth contemplated half-of-Pope contemplating this possibility, contemplating it, moreover, in the actual cancer and the enduring *spirit* of a woman named Elizabeth Corbet. Since the subject I am about to broach is the representation of another person's unrepresentable agony, I want to apologize in advance for breaches in decorum—Wordsworth's, Pope's, or my own.

There is white magic in Wordsworth's invocation, whole, of what he considers to be the deadly language of Pope's epitaph on Elizabeth Corbet:

Here rests a Woman, good without pretence,
Blest with plain reason and with sober sense;
No conquest she but o'er herself desir'd;
No arts essayed, but not to be admir'd.
Passion and pride were to her soul unknown,
Convinc'd that virtue only is our own.
So unaffected, so compos'd a mind,
So firm, yet soft, so strong, yet so refin'd,
Heav'n as its purest gold by tortures tried;
The Saint sustain'd it, but the Woman died.

In the whole of the *Essays upon Epitaphs* no other piece of poetry is as aggressively or as extensively attacked as this. Wordsworth offers it as a paradigm of the "radical and deadly" faults (p. 98) with which Pope had infected English poetry. All of Wordsworth's objections to Pope's lines are organized under the heading of what Wordsworth regards as Pope's lethal aggression against poetry from within. For Wordsworth, Pope's poem is an obliterative thinking via "antithesis." This antithesis, he claims, deprives poetry of humanity, vitality, and the sense of immortality. Pope, says Wordsworth, is always the unfeeling anatomist, coldly dissecting: "Now mark the process by which this is performed. Nothing is represented implicitly, that is, with its accompaniment of circumstances, or conveyed by its effects. The author forgets that it is a living creature that must interest us and not an intellectual Existence" (p. 77). Wordsworth con-

tinues in this way (on these ten lines) for upward of two thousand words, at-
tacking Pope's antitheses as evidence that, "in fact, the Author appears to have
had no precise notion of his own meaning" (p. 78). Wordsworth suggests that
Pope's lines are all headed toward the condition of what Wordsworth calls *non-
sense.*

I will indicate in a moment that Wordsworth's perusal of Pope's epitaph
is hugely uncomprehending. In fact, Wordsworth's "minute criticism" (p. 77)
of this poem must surely be one of the largest-scale blind readings, by one
major poet of another, in the English tradition. Yet my point in adducing
Wordsworth's blindness to his own operations is not to expose a banality in
Wordsworth's statements. Neither do I believe that they primarily provide evidence of an *"intra-*psychical" "misreading" of the kind that Harold Bloom outlines in his theory of poetry.[21] Bloom's antithetical theory is fertile in these matters, but he insists on intrapsychical solipsism too exclusively, as if it is worth
paying any price to keep out T. S. Eliot's idea of a European poetic community.[22] Bloom's and Eliot's theories of poetry, in my view, are themselves counterparts of a larger, stronger enterprise than either of theirs separately.
Wordsworth's antithetical statements open and extend not only beyond his self-
understanding, but toward the situating of a line of counterworlds that creates
cultural tradition. The counterworld that Wordsworth sees and hears but denies becomes vital for him, nevertheless, in the moment of counterperiodization in which he participates. For unwittingly but (as I will suggest) of necessity
Wordsworth calls attention to the ways in which neoclassical poetry achieved its
immense vitality specifically through its capacity for giving way to another's
speech. This is a giving way—one kind of negative way—which few poets have
been better equipped to appreciate than Wordsworth.[23] It is with regard to this
giving way, which Wordsworth is here determined to ignore, that I offer an alternative reading, counter to Wordsworth's reading of Pope's epitaph. I believe
it is this counterreading that Wordsworth was actively forgetting. Here we come
face to face, once again, with the way language can generate an absence which
yet remains available in a shared line of language.

I cite as representative of Wordsworth's exposition of Pope's epitaph
Wordsworth's analysis of two lines of Pope's epitaph, 8 and 10, with which
Wordsworth leads into his peroration in *Essay II:*

> *"So firm yet soft, so strong yet so refined"*—these intellectual operations . . . remind me of
> the motions of a Posture-Master, or of a Man balancing a Sword upon his finger,
> which must be kept from falling at all hazards. *"The Saint sustained it but the Woman
> died"*—Let us look steadily at this antithesis—the *Saint,* that is her soul strength-
> ened by Religion supported the anguish of her disease with patience and resigna-
> tion;—but the *Woman,* that is her *body,* (for if anything else be meant by the word,

woman, it contradicts the former part of the proposition and the passage is non-sense) was overcome. Why was not this simply expressed; without playing with the Reader's fancy to the delusion and dishonour of his Understanding, by a trifling epigrammatic point?

(p. 79)

The evidence of this passage suggests, in fact, that Pope's use of chiasmus makes available to Wordsworth a language for describing the cancer of language. In a way that now needs to be specified, Wordsworth encounters Pope's decorum of abandoning a part of his claim to knowledge of Corbet's experience. Pope's chiastic art is an astonished forgetting within recollection. In this instance it is an encounter with a woman of unimaginable intellectual composure: of "so compos'd a mind" even in the experience of terrifying agony. Corbet's composure, even the way she died, is not mere silence. Corbet's agony turns silence into the speech of a subject, not of an object. Put another way: Pope tries to acknowledge Corbet's womanliness in her sustaining of emptiness, especially, in this case, the horrifying emptiness of the death consuming her life. This emptiness is located in a specifically womanly part of her body, a part which in this epitaph signifies the innermost place of Corbet's language. From within his own mortality of language, Pope attempts to say "the word, woman." Yet Pope discovers that he can say that word only by hearing and citing it in Corbet's saying of it. Dr. Johnson (whose high opinion of this epitaph Wordsworth cites only to do battle) had given the full title, which Wordsworth elides: "*On Mrs.* CORBET, *who died of a Cancer in her Breast.*" If we want to locate that to which Wordsworth responds so blindly in what he perceives as the neoclassical period, we cannot turn a deaf ear to Pope's way of echoing "the word, woman"—of this particular woman—in the "Cancer in her Breast."

I am claiming that Pope's way of saying that specific word is characteristic of one aspect of neoclassical periodization. I am also claiming that this is not only what Wordsworth most avoids in Pope's language, but that this avoidance describes half the figure of Wordsworth's mind—as well as of romantic-neoclassical counterperiodization. These are difficult claims primarily because, as I will now indicate, they entail matters which our understanding resists in intimate ways.

Perhaps even in our age, when every medical fact can apparently be voiced without flinching, many of us may continue to blink at the words in Pope's title that Wordsworth omitted: "in her breast." In this sense—of our need to forget, momentarily, horrific pain and lonely death—Wordsworth cannot be greatly blamed for not recollecting them. The fact is, however, that it is Wordsworth, not Pope, who forgets that it is this specific suffering of this specific living person that is this epitaph's concern; and that this woman died of a cancer in her breast. It is part of Pope's deferring to the composure and reserve of this woman that, knowing that we already know that brutal fact from the title, forbears to name it as part of the evocation of her life within the poem itself. Yet everything in this poem is represented implicitly—as a half-forgetting within half-recollection—in relation to this fact. Every couplet has this "accompaniment of circumstances" (as Wordsworth would have it) directly "conveyed by its effects."[24] Wordsworth fails to acknowledge how much is poetically, significantly, heard and forgotten of that living part of this woman, while it is simultaneously recollected and spoken, in the very phrase which Wordsworth calls the intellectual operation of the "Posture-Master": "So firm, yet soft." In fact, it is remarkable how precise Wordsworth's half-knowledge is, precisely as half-knowledge. Wordsworth only half-knows what he himself half-senses when he says that in this phrase Pope balances (counterbalances) "a Sword upon his finger, which must be kept from falling at all hazards." The two edges of language, lifepreserving and life-displacing, are poised surgically, both within Wordsworth's phrase and throughout Pope's poem, between a forgetting unto death (a "nonsense" or "sense of death") and a recollection of life as it once was. The "posture" of which Pope seems to be the "master" is only the sustained composure and "posture," not of master Pope, but of mistress Corbet herself: "So unaffected," when the unnamed part of her has been mortally infected. Far from being himself the master of this act of composure, Pope makes way for her unrepresentable self-control. If we ourselves make the effort of imagining her self-control we picture only a human body fading away, yet returning within its own silence—a fullness and emptiness that pass and turn within this woman.

We cannot encounter this doubleness and the movement which relates its elements without entering into the repetitions of difference of the neoclassical chiasmus. Specifically this work of the neoclassical chiasmus is forgotten (and, though unnoticed, recollected) by Wordsworth, by de Man, by scholars of romanticism in general, and, I want to suggest further, by our romantic (and postromantic) period as a whole. The counterforgetting of our period (including de Man's aporias of modernity), I am proposing, is located within an experience of historical consciousness which is itself shared along the line of counterworlds and counterperiods. In this case, I refer to the experience of the multiple chiastic features which abound in the neoclassical couplet. Throughout the *Essays upon Epitaphs* Wordsworth says that his enemy, producing the unremediated sense of death, is "antithesis." Whistling in the dark, he would persuade us that the engine of Pope's verse is only two antithetical half-lines. Yet even while he forgets, he knows very well that the force field of neoclassical verse depends upon an effectively endless line of couplets turning on indefinable points of absence or non-sense (or partial withdrawal of representation). This dynamic, in other words, is coextensive with the motor figure—chiasmus—that abounds in neoclassical repetition of difference.

De Man's spatialized description of the operation of chiasmus helps make my point about our postneoclassical blindness to neoclassical-romantic counterperiodization. In de Man's mind the exploitation of the "negativity" of chiasmus signals the emergence of a Rilkean modernity: "Chiasmus, the ground-figure of the *New Poems,* can only come into being as the result of a void, of a lack ["a negativity"] that allows for the rotating motion of the polarities."[25] With regard to Wordsworth's attack on Pope, de Man writes, "From a rhetorical point of view, the *Essays upon Epitaphs* are a treatise on the superiority of [the "chiasmic" figure of] prosopopeia (associated with the names of Milton and Shakespeare) over antithesis (associated with the name of Pope)."[26] But both Wordsworth and de Man are forgetful here. Most spectacularly in the final couplet of the Corbet epitaph, which is Wordsworth's major counterexemplum of the "counter-spirit" in the *Essays upon Epitaphs,* Pope's recurrent figure is chiasmus, not antithesis. This is the chiasmus that can come into being only by acknowledging and making use of the emptiness within language. Experienced, repeatedly, within more than one part of each couplet simultaneously, this is an emptiness among the lines and half-lines, even between the dualities of single words, that allows for the rotating countermotions of the polarities. Here, most specifically, is the recurring hollowness in which Wordsworth sensed the sense of death, the chiasmus, not cancer, of language. This chiasmus, I am suggesting, locates our possibility not only of hearing this woman, but also of finding the line of counterworlds and of chiasmata shared by Wordsworth and Pope.

In the decorum of Pope's epitaph this hollowness is continually displaced from the nameless absences in the interstices of its couplets to their thematized elements, and then back to the absences. At the same time, each of Pope's couplets is constituted as a chiasmus of forgetting and recollecting the cancer that consumed Corbet's body, while she sustained her human composure. In the figures, commonplaces, or suppositions of this epitaph this is the real (as F. H. Bradley would say) with which our minds are constantly in immediate contact. In each couplet the element of hollowness and forgetting within the half-lines is inversely coordinated with what may be called this positivity and recollection.

In the nature of this language of the couplet, each element is turning into something else, interchanging with another part, so that to name any one part in isolation, as Wordsworth thinks he can, is to misrepresent significantly. This misrepresentation (which I am suggesting is only a counterspirit or counterworld) may become all but inevitable when the element on which we must fix our gaze is the nonrepresentation of nonbeing—in this case, the space eaten

out not only by the cancer within this woman, but the nonbeing, or lapsing
from life, within language. For Wordsworth this was itself the dreaded element
in Pope's language, epitomized by and experienced in (at this moment) the
Corbet couplets. Wordsworth calls this experience "the sense of death." This is
the principal item to which he refuses his own relation in the specificity of the
neoclassical couplet. Yet in each of Pope's couplets it is impossible for a serious
reader to disregard totally the place of words where language resists and counters its own representational function. In these five couplets those figurations of
the place of negativity are thematized in the most ordinary language which yet
borders on describing the human withdrawal from existence. I am especially
thinking of the following five phrases: "Here rests a woman" (l. 1), "but not to
be admir'd" (l. 4), "to her soul unknown" (l. 5), "so strong yet so refin'd" (l. 8)
(out of existence), "but the Woman died" (l. 10). All of these phrases tend toward the same disappearance. The *resting* of this woman, for example, teases us
out of thought. Does this phrase identifiably name *her* life—the life of this invoked woman? Does *that* woman come to rest *here?* Or is the body interred beneath these words, beneath this stone inscription, only the weighing dead of
what is no longer that woman? When or how can our saying of the "word,
woman," or the word "human," ever belong to the world of life rather than of
death? How, in other words, can words ever pretend to be more than only the
representation of life, which means the absence of life, which may mean only
death? Inspired by Wordsworth's response to Pope, and (likely) levying upon
Hegel, de Man turned the inverse of this problematics into an apothegm:
"Death is a displaced name for a linguistic predicament" (p. 81). Yet this
apothegm is inadequate as a description of either Wordsworth's or Pope's ways
of experiencing another individual's death as a fact of reality and history—or
priority, which is to say, again, as a part of the sublime line of language with
which they experience that fact. This becomes clear only when we immerse
ourselves in the details which represent Pope's and Wordsworth's participation
in the history which is not ours or even theirs.

In Pope's citing of Corbet's composure across the multiple absences of the
couplet, one other element is of special significance. The poem's final couplet
enacts, in a deliberately astonishing and strange way, the reply feature of
prosopopeia. It is our understanding that is turned to tomb-stone at this final
moment. To experience this we need to recall that prosopopeia is, as de Man reminds us, "the fiction of an apostrophe to an absent, deceased, or voiceless entity, which posits the possibility of the latter's reply and confers upon it the
power of speech."[27] I want to show, finally, that in the closing words of the epitaph Corbet's voice speaks to us beyond (or, equally, before) the language we actually hear. If this is ventriloquism, we must say that the dummy speaker in this

case is Pope, not Corbet. Hearing the composure of this woman's unspoken speech is a matter of speaking and recollection and of hearing and forgetting, in something like the following way.

Within the epitaph itself there is no naming of Corbet, as if that disclosure would be a violation of the decorum of *her* reserve and her destitution.[28] Missing Pope's reserve, Dr. Johnson's one bad word about the Corbet epitaph was a criticism on this score: "Who can forbear to lament," asks Johnson, "that this amiable woman has no name in the verses?" Yet Johnson and Wordsworth, together with Pope's modern editors, are in fact oblivious to Pope's way of hearing *Corbet* within the verses describing the disease that hollowed out her being. This is given as her way of saying the word *woman*. Corbet achieves this in the final line, "The Saint sustain'd it, but the Woman died." Wordsworth looked steadily at this line and read only two possibilities: her lifeless "body" or "nonsense."

Johnson and Wordsworth both forgot what Pope recollected: that *corbet* means a hollow or "hole . . . left in the walls of ancient churches . . . for Images [of saints] to stand in" (*OED*, 1703).[29] Pope's recollection or, more accurately, counterciting of this figure within Corbet's name is beyond the endurance of imagination, bound up as it is with the recollection of an unendurable event: the torture of a human being, a woman—in her womanliness—out of her existence. Only a "Corbet," in the word "Corbet" that Pope surrenders, could make room for the image of her torment.[30] This is the empty space opened only by Corbet. We may be further stunned to discover that at another point in his *Essays upon Epitaphs* Wordsworth directly attests his blindness to this spectacular Corbet language. While accusing Pope of unsocial detachment, he nostalgically celebrates, "How fond our Ancestors were of a play upon the Name of the deceased" (p. 67).

Because Corbet's image of human being/nonbeing is *Corbet's* experience alone, sculpted within her body, within her naming, Pope has no claim on it. Yet he can hear her silent articulation of it. This articulation includes the composure of acknowledgment that she is part of an endless "our" of human, perhaps especially female, language and endurance. Her figuration of death and her name, named in this way, are the image-place of the saint (the condensed image of the line of language) that only she opens up. The element of empty space is unmistakable within that image and within the name read out by Corbet. In this final image, therefore, this composed Corbet frames and passes on, to those who read her epitaph, the absences around which her name and the image of her being circulate. This passing on of absence enables the difference which is the rotating force or energy not only within Pope's and Corbet's relation but within Wordsworth's and Pope's as well. Horrifying as the parallelisms are, the absences within these rotations cannot be differentiated from those within the composure of Corbet's mind acknowledging her own decomposition, hence of Pope's mind recording, in effect, its decomposition. Hence, also of Wordsworth's mind, will he nill he. This too is a sublime dying-away within the line of commonplaces, or topoi, for commonplace human suffering. Here too hearing-speaking (Wordsworth's, Pope's, and Corbet's as well) is a sublime capacity earned in an infinitely long line of language.

We can only be struck dumb by the uncompromising "sense of death" that is undoubtedly one component of these shared absences. Yet our experience of the form of this couplet—or "rhyme"—reminds us that this choice of the chiastic form is also part of the sustained encounter in which Corbet participates. In this encounter, death and life, earth and heaven, mortal woman and immortal saint—hemisphere and hemisphere—are not resolved. Rather, they are counterbalanced upon historical points of absence in a line of language that may itself enable association (not communication) in counterspiraling movements. This line is generated by women and men isolated in different moments, yet constituting (at a distance) this fragmented form of cultural tradition. This line is no less visible in the chiasmus shared between Wordsworth's counterspirit sentence and Pope's epitaph for Elizabeth Corbet. This larger chiasmus turns on a word for the human—the word "woman"—which Corbet and Pope and Wordsworth think successively. This is the way in which, together, they breathe—in and out—the shared half-secrets of their humanity.

One more word about Pope's epitaph on Elizabeth Corbet. In accordance with my assumptions about the half-blindnesses of counterperiodization I am compelled to imagine that Wordsworth was half-correct in his criticism of Pope: in other words, that Pope is himself at cross-purposes with Corbet in the lines of this epitaph, even within the couplet in which he gives way to her Corbet language. I consider it inevitable, in fact, that for Pope the "Saint" who sustains the act of decomposition and survives, while the woman dies, is half Pope himself, "by tortures tried." Much that we know about Pope's sense of his own diseased body enforces the suggestion that this couplet contains an unspoken encomium of Pope's own power to endure suffering. Recall, for example, this couplet in the "Epistle to Dr. Arbuthnot," written almost at the same time as the Corbet lines: "The Muse but serv'd to ease some Friend, not Wife, / To help me thro' this long Disease, my Life" (ll. 131–32). If this last countersuggestion has force, then part of what we experience in the final Corbet couplet is the subconscious of the male "Saint," which, counter to his conscious intentions, in some sense would do away with this woman. This part of Pope's couplet is Y-not-X, indeed.

It would follow that what we encounter here is a movement of cross-purposes which, as language, can only remain unresolved. Lines of thought or counterspirals of this kind are possible in the counterturnings of one chiasmus of language with another. Clearly such counterturnings do not represent pure saintliness. Yet, mixed blessings as they are, these historical configurations of fragmented subjectivities may well constitute the strongest writing in any given town or cultural tradition.

We may well feel a need, however—as Milton did (and as Pope likely understood that Milton did)—to confront more openly the phenomenon of the literary man's undercurrent desire (from which no male author can exempt himself) to do away with his female subject.

The Reinvention of Desire:
Milton's (and Ezekiel's)
Sublime Melancholia

CHAPTER

And the mute Silence hist along,
'Less Philomel will deign a song.
—Milton, "Il Penseroso"

Many things are Philosophically delivered
    concerning right
and left, which admit of some suspension.
—Sir Thomas Browne, "Of the right and left Hand"

I now seek to demonstrate that Milton's representation of sublime melancholia functions as an antidote to a pathology of victimization that he views as being inherent in language. This sublime melancholia is the experience of a line of language constituted by representations that are both self-depriving and cross-gendered. The experience in question is different from what is usually understood as either melancholia or mourning.[1] I believe it can be shown that the representation of sublime melancholia has considerable significance for the Western tradition, ancient as well as modern. But I need, first, to clear the ground for my demonstration.

Kant was only taking inventory of the Western theory and practice of the cultural sublime when he observed that the emotion of sublime experience is a certain strenuous melancholy.[2] Melancholy of this sort, Kant said, is continually in evidence in the mind's act of self-deprivation, in the momentary check to its vital forces, as well as in its experience of freedom and moral feeling. In addition, Kant's description of this melancholy includes something that is physically and morally threatening. This observation may appear to be incidental, but in fact it locates an indispensable, even if coded, element of this experience. I refer to the fact that Kant sites the melancholy of the sublime in the scene of a city's destruction.

Hegel, we have seen, argued that a sublime scene of destruction (by God or by the hero who founds the state) is a scene of lawful punishment. Hegel associated this scene and experience of punishing with the mind's achievement of self-consciousness, namely, in the double countermovements of, first, dying-away, and second, returning to the wholeness of the self. Yet, as we have also observed, Hegel's scene of sublimation is not an accurate reflection of the Western sublime. Nor, in fact, does his claim for the achievement of self-consciousness correspond to the experience of sublime melancholy, though it does correlate with a different sort of melancholy.

Western culture has long recognized radically different kinds of melancholic experience. In the West, a sublime variety of melancholy is experienced in a struggle against a self-centered, vulgar kind of melancholy. This vulgar melancholy, I suggest, closely corresponds to Hegel's punishing scene of sublimation. Without doubt, vulgar melancholy is itself of real historical significance. In *The Gendering of Melancholia* Juliana Schiesari has traced the modern manifestations of "a specifically male subjectivity that characterizes itself through the production of loss."[3] Her accounts of various male melancholic scenarios of fundamental narcissism, fears of castration, persecutionary fantasies as well as fantasies of being the chosen one, all centered in victimization of women and mourning of loss, are for the most part horrifically persuasive. Schiesari has identified this male, neurotic melancholy with various skepticist tendencies which cluster, in her view, around the figure of Tasso and his poetry: "In Tasso's own time Montaigne saw him as representing melancholic madness. Tasso embodied the dilemma of the *belle-âme* who, having directed his imaginative energy in accordance with an insuperable desire for an ontological and epistemological certitude that cannot be had, mourns this loss by incorporating the ideal back into himself as a condition for an idealization of the self. His 'suffering' becomes the incremental sign of an unappreciated, or even persecuted, but nonetheless divinely accredited genius."[4] These are perceptive observations, but they relate to just one kind of Tassovian melancholy. It is an error to imagine that only a modern sensibility is capable of discerning the victimizing character of vulgar melancholy. The problems and dangers that Schiesari sees, Milton at least—in fact, many others (Tasso too, to a considerable extent)—already saw and struggled against. Milton identifies these problems and dangers as aspects of a pathology of victimization that is potential in human language.

Milton's "Il Penseroso" is explicitly located along the line or tradition of the *homo melancholicus* or *pensoso* or *pensieroso*. A Tassovian neighborhood of melancholia is evoked (among other places in the poem) by the description of "great bards" who

> In sage and solemn tunes have sung,
> Of tourneys and of trophies hung;

Of forests, and enchantments drear,
Where more is meant than meets the ear.
                    (ll. 116–19)[5]

These "enchantments" in "forests" refer, among other things, to book 13 of Tasso's *Gerusalemme liberata* and to Tancred's experience in the enchanted wood, where he seems to kill Clorinda a second time. (This is the specific repetition that will engross Freud's attention in *Beyond the Pleasure Principle*.)[6] The "trophies hung" refer (among other things) to the fulfillment of that epic's central prophecy, when, in Tasso's very last stanza, Godfrey is described hanging up the arms of victory in the Holy Sepulchre at Jerusalem. Yet it is notable that in "Il Penseroso" (which is not one of Schiesari's texts) Milton elaborates, contra Schiesari's paradigm, a specifically female identity of melancholia. Milton's poem, indeed, elaborates a discourse that is the precise opposite of that which Schiesari ascribes—correctly in my view—to what I am calling vulgar, male melancholy: "a discourse that would exclude alterity" and which therefore is restricted to "a sort of intra-subjective copulation, the only eros available to the subject within such a self-enclosed system."[7]

Straddling Western premodernity and Western modernity, Milton is representative of the way, before and after him, a sublime variety of melancholy counters the vulgar kind. In the modern age of Western tradition this countering of vulgar melancholia assumes even more explicit importance than in antiquity. In modernity the grasp of human experience as a subjective life of emotions tends to make the experience of melancholy virtually identical with sublime experience. In the merely victimizing kind of melancholy (in which the only loss, or vacancy, is that which is produced by the destruction of the female or, as Schiesari says, of the city that stands for the female) we encounter a form of Hegel's scene of victimization and recuperated self-consciousness. But the sublime distance from a representation of victimization—especially the distance achieved by self-deprivation in representations and the contemplation of an endless series of such victimizations—creates a different experience. This is not merely aestheticized experience. A paradox that is inherent in sublime experience answers to a central paradox in moral experience, namely, that to be moral a response to the need of another must come from distancing and freedom. Otherwise, what seems to be moral response is only a reflexive and self-reflexive projection of self onto an other. Such reflexes may produce morally dubious results, as often as not smiting rather than loving one's neighbor. A notion that is deeply inscribed in sublime tradition is that to become part of a moral imperative even the rule "Thou shalt love thy neighbor as thyself" has to be experienced in a scripture of infinite provenience that effects sublime freedom. It does not matter whether that provenience is regarded as being purely divine, divine and human, or purely human, as in a poem of Pope or Wordsworth which both hears and speaks the sublimity of what I have called colloquial language. In "Il Penseroso" we see this same phenomenon inserted at the point where such colloquial, or listening-speaking, language represents sublime melancholia. Here the sublime melancholia produced by representing the encounter of an endless line of scenes of victimization, as well as a withdrawal from representation and a privation of consciousness, are endured (in different ways) by the male as well as the female representer (poet and reader), in fact by a male subjectivity in counter- and interrelation with a female subjectivity.

This interrelation is not pure or simple. No doubt for the male it represents, in part, a defeat of striving for recovery of phallic strength and of patriarchal appropriation of the feminine. This defeat leaves the male poet in a condition, we may say, of phallic lack or quasi-feminization, which does not, however, make him part of a matriarchal line of language. Nevertheless this defeat is the male's opportunity to participate in the strength of a cross-gendering. In addition, I would emphasize, arranging or embracing this defeat can be an effect of choosing from the freedom and moral feeling produced by prior experience of the cultural sublime. For the male poet the privation or discontinuity in consciousness that is entailed in this choice crystallizes a sublime melancholia.

Very much in this way Milton's sublime melancholia represents what Walter Benjamin called the "discontinuum" within representation that is "the history of the oppressed." A "tradition of the oppressed," Benjamin announced —somewhat quixotically—is the "foundation" (we may add, intermittent defoundation) of "genuine tradition."[8] Benjamin had a way of formulating his deepest insights into culture as tantalizing impossibilities. At least in this instance, however, his discouragements can be discounted to the considerable extent that he owes these insights to what some forms of male participation in culture had already achieved, concretely even if always incompletely. Milton's "Il Penseroso," I am suggesting, is in the tradition of the oppressed that informs Benjamin's remarks, specifically, I am proposing, in the tradition of oppressed women.

Most of the verses that I will now use to demonstrate Milton's cross-gendering of sublime melancholia are embedded in the following passages from "L'Allegro" and "Il Penseroso." For reasons that have never been made clear, readers have long sensed—correctly in my view—that each of these passages forms the heart of the twinned poem from which it comes, that the second passage represents a revised form of the first, and that, most especially or (as Milton says) "chiefest," the extended image of Contemplation in the second passage is the climax of the two poems taken together.

From "L'Allegro":
And in thy right hand lead with thee,   35
The mountain nymph, sweet Liberty;
And if I give thee honour due,
Mirth, admit me of thy crew
To live with her, and live with thee,
In unreproved pleasures free;   40
To hear the lark begin his flight,
And singing startle the dull night,
From his watch-tower in the skies,
Till the dappled dawn doth rise;
Then to come in spite of sorrow,   45
And at my window bid good morrow,
Through the sweet-briar, or the vine,
Or the twisted eglantine.
While the cock with lively din,
Scatters the rear of darkness thin,   50
And to the stack, or the barn door,
Stoutly struts his dames before,
Oft list'ning how the hounds and horn
Cheerly rouse the slumb'ring morn,
From the side of some hoar hill,   55
Through the high wood echoing shrill.
Sometime walking not unseen
By hedgerow elms, on hillocks green,
Right against the eastern gate,
Where the great sun begins his state,   60
Robed in flames, and amber light,
The clouds in thousand liveries dight.

From "Il Penseroso":
But first, and chiefest, with thee bring,
Him that yon soars on golden wing,
Guiding the fiery-wheeled throne,
The cherub Contemplation,
And the mute Silence hist along,   55
'Less Philomel will deign a song,
In her sweetest, saddest plight,
Smoothing the rugged brow of night,
While Cynthia checks her dragon yoke,
Gently o'er the accustomed oak;   60
Sweet bird that shunn'st the noise of folly,
Most musical, most melancholy!
Thee chauntress oft the woods among,
I woo to hear thy even-song;
And missing thee, I walk unseen   65
On the dry smooth-shaven green,
To behold the wandering moon,
Riding near her highest noon,

Like one that had been led astray
Through the heaven's wide pathless way;   70
And oft, as if her head she bowed,
Stooping through a fleecy cloud.

My comments revolve around something highly obtrusive in this second passage, which is yet left half-unsaid. This is the terrifying violence that underlies Philomel's "saddest plight." Terrifying violence actually underlies the passage as a whole, in which the nightingale is one of two recurrent figures, the other being the cherub who is drawn from Ezekiel's account of the fiery chariot that destroys Jerusalem. Ovid tells how Tereus raped his sister-in-law Philomel, made her *mute* by cutting out her tongue, then imprisoned her in distant *woods*. Philomel managed to weave or *plight* her "saddest plight" in a tapestry. Upon receiving the tapestry, her sister, Procne, rescued Philomel and joined her in taking revenge on Tereus. Thereupon Philomel metamorphosed into the nightingale, singer of love's *most melancholy* song. Both the telescoped image of tragic Philomel and the equally telescoped image of Ezekiel's fiery chariot (destroying Jerusalem) preoccupied Milton throughout his poetic career.[9] Only in "Il Penseroso," however, did Milton directly juxtapose these two images and probe the violence and the sublime melancholy of each.

Once we have recalled, in "Il Penseroso," the force of male sexuality that destroys Philomel, the strutting of the "lively" cock in "L'Allegro" (accompanied by sounds of the hunt) is no longer cause for mirth. Retrospectively, what may have only given us half a pause in our swinging along with Mirth appears more fully disquieting. We now remember to ask: How can Liberty be *led* by anyone and still retain her identity as Liberty? What order of "honour" can be won by a "crew" of merrymakers who fantasize, it seems, about One-on-Two's ("To live with her, and live with thee")? The "state" progress of the "great sun" only lightly conceals under his robe the "amber," fiery force of the cock. The sun (parading in "state") struts the "thousand liveries" of the unresisting clouds before him, as if they were his dames. No wonder the speaker of "L'Allegro" is so full of what we might call the self-presencing of eros. He and the sun, hand in hand, walk "not unseen," to put it mildly. In at least these ways, expressed by only a half-heard voice, each of these passages warns that the neighborhoods described here are unsafe for women.

"Il Penseroso" does not represent the elegant busywork of a brain spinning from mere vacancy. Rather the poem exposes a threat offered by a particular form of male vacancy. In men, this is the melancholic vacancy created by eliminating a woman or by destroying a city (Jerusalem or Troy) that stands for a woman. As Milton represents it, this danger is potential in the nexus of form and ethics in poetry, as in art and culture more generally, or, in other words, in what is usually regarded as the creativity of human language, usually meaning male creativity of male language. Thus "Il Penseroso" certainly is in part a citation of a typology (well described by Schiesari) of the male sufferer-creator who wreaks his aggression against women. Yet the complex care of Milton's language is evidence that he is the very opposite of a dupe or tool of the aggression which we, living in a post-Lacanian or post-Foucauldian age, can reveal beyond Milton's restricted or distorted ken. Milton's verse directly acknowledges and works to overcome the repression of women by men that is part and parcel of vulgar, male melancholia. Milton confronts this pathology as much for the sake of his own freedom and well-being as for anyone else's.

I focus now, more narrowly, on lines 55–56 of "Il Penseroso":

> And the mute Silence hist along,
> 'Less Philomel will deign a song.

This couplet is the interface not only of two muted stories and two scenes of horrifying destruction, but also of two voices, two genders, and two cultures. A borderline weaves through them. The preceding story that leaves off here is from Ezekiel's narrative of the fiery-wheeled throne and the cherub. The story taken up here is from Ovid's tale of Philomel. The "mute Silence" tells, on the one hand, of the catastrophic "silence" (Ezek. 16:42) of the Lord—after destroying Jerusalem—which "mute" Ezekiel (3:26; 24:27; 33:22) must prophesy; and it tells, on the other hand, of the terrible "mute silence" (itself an Ovidian phrase) of the woman Philomel after Tereus has raped her and cut out her tongue, as well as the tragic song (punctuated by silence recalling that muteness) of the woman metamorphosed into a bird.[10] (If we hesitate to credit that Milton could have had in mind both contexts of the word *silence*, we should recall that he repeated the linkage of "Silence" with both Ezekiel's chariot and the song of the nightingale in *Paradise Lost*.)[11] The warning of a Judaeo-Christian biblical voice is heard in the first line, sounding Ezekiel's sustained preoccupation with sighing or hissing (as in 9:4, 21:11 [A.V. 21:6], 24:17, 26:15—I will later return to this preoccupation). At the same time the lamentation of a classical, mythological voice is anticipated in the second line, especially in the doubleness of "'Less," which hints at Philomel's singing of being kidnapped, raped, and losing her tongue and even her woman's body. The first voice speaks for the cross-gendered force of the God of fiery loins (I will detail this cross-gendering in a moment), and it speaks through the male prophet who is himself (I will illustrate this) a highly feminized, if sometimes misogynist, victim of that force; the song of the feminine, second voice filters through as if from its captive status in "mute Silence," in "'Less," and in the word "deign," which hints at

Philomel's disdain—from *desdeign*—for a world that is dominated by masculine violence. Yet the cross-gendered voices are interwoven, even if separate, just as the two verses together configure the cultural counterpoint or counterperiodization of Christian-classicism.

The couplet, then, does not at all merge the two stories that it partly tells. The destruction of Jerusalem, we know, will be followed by a promise of future renewal. The devastation of Philomel, we know, will be followed by revenge on Tereus and by Philomel's metamorphosis into a bird. Neither of these latterly turns of story, however, brings comfort to the victims of immediate catastrophe, nor is injustice to the innocent (in either scene of destruction) explained away by the placement of Philomel's victimization by a male after the scene of feminine Jerusalem's destruction by a God of fiery loins.

Yet, in the mouth of the prophet and of the nightingale, Silence undergoes a sea change that is the effect of sublime experience. Painfully hard to credit at first, this effect is a melancholy dying-away, a freedom, and a moral feeling within sublime experience. For an indispensable moment we—women as well as men—experience a metamorphosis of our world of moral catastrophe into a realm of experience which is nothing more or less than a cultural sublime. Only this experience enables anyone to achieve moral feeling and moral action. Here, as I have said, we confront the paradox of the moral necessity of sublime derailment. That is, unless ("'Less") we achieve sublime experience of this silence—by representing (again and again) scenes of victimization and resistance to victimization—we inhabit no space (have achieved no con-templation) for freedom and moral feeling. The halves of this couplet do not add up to wholes, recuperations, or explanations.

This is not the usual way with language and thought. The usual way is summed up by Hegel as an inexorability. Indeed, in the present context of discussion it is worth noting the startlingly different claim that Hegel makes for the "self-satisfaction" of "explanation" produced by sublimating countermovements. Here is Hegel: "The Understanding's 'explanation' [das Erklären] is primarily only the description of what self-consciousness is. It supersedes [sublimates; "hebt . . . auf"] differences . . . and posits them in a single unity, in Force. . . . The reason why 'explaining' affords so much self-satisfaction is just because in it consciousness is, so to speak, communing directly with itself, enjoying only itself; although it seems to be busy with something else, it is in fact occupied only with itself."[12] There is indeed "a sort of intra-subjective copulation" in this intellectual "self-satisfaction." As opposed to such explanation, the countermovements of Milton's couplet explain nothing. Rather, they represent the experience of endless representation of self-deprivation and of dying-away in a line of language. The moral continuation of these tales can only be in the melancholy affect of sublime experience, which is to say the moral feeling and moral action made possible by sublime freedom.

The representation of this affect is not—cannot be, if it is to achieve a sublime impact—original with Milton. Milton hears and sees an endless repetition of such representation (of this affect) in the lines of language that provide the words of his couplet. Milton's use of the words at his disposal acknowledges where they come from—namely, in this case, their biblical and classical origins—recognizes that these origins are endlessly repeating, and recalls that this endless repetition already constitutes, and even earlier originated in, a sublime experience of a sublime line of language. Milton's and Ezekiel's sensitivity to the sublime effect of sublime repetition was no less than Kant's, even if their interests in these matters were different from formulating philosophical propositions. (Yet Kant's special affinity for Milton's poetry as well as for the scenographies of destruction of the Hebrew prophets is no doubt related to their shared sensitivity to sublime effects.) In this couplet what Milton experiences and represents in his version of Ezekiel's language is not just a function of what he understands Ezekiel's words to mean, that is, in a dictionary; neither is it even merely a function of allusions that his words and phrases make to contexts in Ezekiel. Rather, what is of uppermost importance for Milton's experience and representation of Ezekiel's language, in this poem about a higher melancholy, is the melancholy experience—Ezekiel's and the victimized woman's as well as Milton's—of a sublime line of language. This sublime line of language is specifically opposed to the pathological coerciveness of language.

In the next two sections, I would like to offer some comments on those features of Ezekiel's sublime line of language that Milton makes part of his own experience and representation of sublime language. Because Ezekiel's visions and "Il Penseroso" are texts in which surface statements declare their dependency on veiled meanings, or in which, as Milton says, "more is meant than meets the ear" (l. 120), my comments on the nexus of these works attempt to tease out elements and patterns which are not easily described.

Milton sees and repeats the way in which Ezekiel's language relates the punishment of a female who personifies Jerusalem. Milton repeats even the metonymic and anticipatory style of Ezekiel's inaugural vision. In that vision, Ezekiel's mere imaging of the chariot makes it possible to leave in awesome silence not only the power of God but its punishing effect as well. Less obvious in Ezekiel's language, though also seen and repeated by Milton, is the congruence of the destruction described by that language with the experience of being punished or coerced by language per se. That is, in addition to what it describes, Ezekiel's language represents the experience of a coerced, even victimized speaking of the language that is given or commanded to him, which is to say (in Ezekiel's language), the experience of a feminized victim who is coerced, penetrated, and deprived of any being besides that which has penetrated him or her. The full extent of Ezekiel's consciousness, in this speaking, is in the language or "sign" that he must speak to others and of which his life and speech are only signs. Speaking God's words, Ezekiel says, "I will speak unto thee . . . And the spirit entered into me . . . eat this roll, and go speak unto the house of Israel" (2:1–2; 3:1). The endlessly recurring "Emor!" or "Say!" that Ezekiel speaks at God's command is the metonym or sign of God's commanded language. This metonymic relation is unmistakable, for example, in the redoubled metonymic construction, "Emor, Ani mofetchem" (Say, I [I = Ezekiel speaking God's words] am your sign) in verse 12:11. In the rest of the same verse no doubt is left that this experience of coerced language and the experience of punishment described by this language are of a piece for Ezekiel: "Say, I am your sign: like as I have done [i.e., done to Ezekiel, forcing him into captivity (upon the destruction of Jerusalem)], so it shall be done unto them: they shall remove and go into captivity" (12:11).

To be sure, this condition of being situated in language that we, as it were, take with exhaustive seriousness—to the point of being exiled from ourselves, made captive by language—is not restricted to prophets. Yet the situation of the prophet who must ingest and speak God's words and even announce his condition in words which are not his is the extreme case. No doubt this is part of what is permanently gripping about prophetic discourse. In this vein, Ezekiel's fainting- or dying-away ("I fell on my face": 1:28) would seem to be the dramatization of the prophet's commonplace fate of being displaced from his own personhood or personal language or consciousness, that is, by coercion into God's language. Ezekiel's incapacity to speak any but God's words is one meaning of his being "mute."[13] But in the case of Ezekiel's language this negative or victimizing or vulgarly male phenomenon is a feature that is part of a symmetry of counterfeatures and countermovements. On the one hand, for Ezekiel the negative phenomenon represents a pervasive enslaving and pathological feature of language; but, on the other hand, his language's claims to ecstatic experience and to moral feeling are made good by an encounter, simultaneously, with a kind of representation that is inherently, structurally sublime.

That which turns Ezekiel's lineage of language into a sublime occasioning of moral feeling, rather than a recurring scene of coercion, are the elements of self-deprivation and of cross-gendering in representation itself. In Kant's descriptive terms for Western experience of the sublime the element of deprivation appears (Kant does not explain by what power of free choice) in the subject's act of self-deprivation or, correlatively, in the making of a kind of representation that shows its inadequacy as representation. It is inevitable for the cultural tradition that Kant describes that, as one of its greatest paradigms, Ezekiel's vision of the chariot culminates in a representation of God's image (1:27) in which direct imaging has been largely withdrawn. This is in marked contrast to the repletion of details of machinery and beasts in the description of the chariot itself. Arguably even Ezekiel's description of the chariot is on the way to image withdrawal, in that many of the details of the description are drawn, within a vision of the punishing of idolatry, from the idol-worshiping culture that surrounds Israelite culture, in other words, from the encounter with a counterculture.[14] But I focus here on the more obvious fact that Ezekiel's vision of the fiery, wheeled chariot is an iconic metonym for the largely de-iconized figure to which it gives way in verse 1:27, God's likeness of loins that are like fire:

> [27] From the appearance of his loins upward I saw the like of *hashmal*[15] having something with the appearance of fire surrounding it; and from the appearance of his loins downward I saw something with the appearance of fire; and he was surrounded by a radiance.
>
> [28] . . . That was the appearance of the figure of the Majesty of YHWH; when I saw it, I fell on my face—"[16]

This representation shows its inadequacy as representation in its counterfactual language of "appearance" or "like"-ness or indefinite "something" as well as in the blinding or occluding effect of "surrounding" "fire" and "radiance" (i.e., we are told that the thing which is described here is not what has been described), not to speak of the estrangement produced by focusing on the exposed body part (male or female) which, in Western culture, initially rivets then averts the (guilty) gaze. In Milton's Ezekiel-Philomel couplet, coming directly after and partly continuing the invocation of the chariot image, we see corresponding effects of image withdrawal. With respectful audacity—feeling himself in harmony with Ezekiel's unspoken meanings—Milton puts victimized Philomel in the equivalent of Ezekiel's crowning placement of the figure with the fiery loins:

> And the mute Silence hist along,
> 'Less Philomel will deign a song.

Thus in Milton's couplet too the representations of the speaker-prophet, of the cherub, and especially of the agent figure who rides the chariot—the God whose likeness of loins are like fire—are blocked off, left largely in a silence that draws attention to itself by remaining silent (mute) in these circumstances.[17] So too in Milton's couplet, the person of the coerced speaker-prophet and the body of the victimized woman—here representing both destroyed Jerusalem and destroyed Philomel—do not materialize. Instead, they are left largely un-verbalized and unimagined.[18] In Milton's and Ezekiel's line of language sub-lime experience is the effect of encountering an effectively endless repetition of representations each of which shows its inadequacy as representation. And in-deed Ezekiel's representation of the God who makes unrepresentability his self-image is itself a locus classicus of the sublime topos that Kant describes. Yet the symmetry of the two matched topoi that actually constitutes this topos highlights aspects of the sublime that Kant has scanted.

That is, in addition to repeating the topos of representation that shows the in-adequacy of representation, Ezekiel's figure is another representation of the husband-wife topos, which is to say, of God-the-husband bringing or pointing to the punishment of the wife-Jerusalem, who has been unfaithful to their covenanted language of nonrepresentation. (The full love story, including God's first lovemaking with his beloved and his beloved's forsaking him for "big-membered neighbors" [verse 26] is told in Ezekiel 16.) Thus the language of withdrawing representation not only is the basis of God's self-image and of the wedded language that binds God and Israel, but also provides the structure of imagination that keeps the human mind from the moral collapse of totaliz-ing, especially phallic and fetishist, imaging.

Already in Ezekiel this moral potentiality of sublime experience is strongly in evidence. Ezekiel conceives of the punishment that follows from the ignoring of image withdrawal as the collapse, most immediately, not of the human rela-tion to God, but of human interrelations or social-moral feeling. This linkage of idolatrous image worship and moral failure may help explain what Moshe Greenberg calls Ezekiel's "unexpected shift to denunciation of social wrong doing" and to "the scene of punishment" in which "God affirms his ruthless verdict upon the people on the ground of their social wrongdoing" at the end of chapter 8 and the beginning of chapter 9.[19] In the logic of Ezekiel's tradition, idolatry and social wrongdoing are a cause and effect which are precisely anti-thetical to sublime experience. And within the same clockwork logic of human experience (virtually independent of divine initiation) the punishment that follows is largely a self-inflicted effect of the causes of idolatry and social wrongdoing. Human beings, this logic shows, foul their own nests. The interde-pendency of these husband-wife and image-withdrawal topoi underlies the obligations not only of the feminine personification of Jerusalem (or Israel), who is self-punished for unfaithfulness to God's commandments, but also of the feminized Ezekiel, who is commanded to faithful repetition of God's lan-guage. In Ezekiel's use of these topoi the sense of an inherent fulfillment of rep-etition is of the utmost importance. Greenberg has noted many prior biblical instances of the husband-wife topos. In addition he has observed that "the fig-ure of Israel as YHWH's wife derives from the cardinal commandment [of the Decalogue] that Israel worship YHWH alone. To that demand of exclusive fi-delity, the obligation of a wife to her husband offered a parallel. . . . By extend-ing the metaphor in time, Ezekiel provided the adulterous wife of Hosea and Jeremiah with a biography."[20] To the considerable extent that Ezekiel must be specifically aware of this lineage of the topos of enforced fidelity to God's lan-guage, his repetition of that topos is also a representation of the extension of this metaphor or topos in time. This is to say, its commonplace status (which most modern-day readers perhaps see only when a biblical scholar lays it out) means that it is a representation of a special kind. In addition to whatever else it may signify, it represents the experience of endless, successive recurrences of this topos at a single instant of time. (Even God's first recorded speaking of his cardinal commandment cannot be conceived as a new thought of the God whose nature never changes. His Instruction, or Torah, is commonplacely said to have existed from eternity.)

As part of God's Instruction, his self-imaging is a form of representation that shows, insists upon, its inadequacy as representation and declares that—in God's language—this divine self-imaging was, is, and will be endlessly in this form. The self-deprived sublimity of God's self-image is inseparable from his commandment to faithfulness to his language of self-imaging. If there is a ne-cessity for a specifically religious experience, or specific acknowledgment of God's existence in the logic that joins these topoi, it is of the being which has propagated this line of language of image self-deprivation in its common-placeness and who chooses any individual or community for access to this lan-guage. (In this way Ezekiel's speaking of God's language is homologous with Descartes's experience and representation of the *concursus* of being and noth-ingness in the Fourth Meditation.)[21]

Lacking this self-deprivation in the self-image that disseminates this line of language, the divine speaker would be merely the morally impoverished cliché—the self-worshiping oriental tyrant and slave driver—which those who ignore this line of language make of him. Without this defounding line of lan-guage in representation of self-deprivation his words could have no sublime force of freedom and moral feeling. Every word that is uttered in Ezekiel's ver-bal universe is an occurrence within the commonplace species of God's self-deprived self-representation in his cardinal commandment.[22]

Both for Ezekiel and for Milton the direct relation between the husband-wife and image-withdrawal topoi continuously defines their sublime language. There are many ways, certainly, of understanding this relation. One way that is represented by both Ezekiel and Milton is this: The condition of faithfulness to each other of male and female is the representation of self in self-deprivation in both the male's (God's) and the female's (Israel's) languages. Self-*in*sufficiency, desire, and the acceptance of self-insufficiency make Ezekiel's and Milton's worlds go round. For God as for every individual, male or female, the sublime experience of a line of language is indispensable to freedom and moral feeling.

This state of affairs may strike us as being peculiar or unorthodox for the God of any conventional Judaism or Christianity, but it is in fact a perfectly orthodox mystery of God's humanlike nature. In Ezekiel's terms (as in the earliest Pentateuchal representations of a "passionate" or "jealous" God, Exodus 20:5, 34:14) one of the reasons that this line of the commonplace is overwhelming is that, in every one of its representations, it suggests a concept of God that is incomprehensible or representationally inadequate to an unbearable degree. Can God need anything? Can God desire something? Can God momentarily consummate his desire, as if with fiery loins? Can God feel the impulses to annihilation that may also be associated with fiery loins? In his turn, Ezekiel accepts and represents this representation of the insufficiency of representation (and this representation *of* insufficiency, or at least of need) as part of the language of self-imaging that God speaks and that he makes the shared ground of faithfulness with Israel.

Thus, while giving form to each other, both topoi express double countermovements:

- God's self-representation is the statement and representation that God cannot be represented.
- When Israel repeats (in the entire fabric of their language and imagination) the representation that God cannot be represented they are faithful to God's self-representation.
- God (the husband) desires but can never finish needing or completely have his needy Israel (the wife).
- Needy Israel (the wife) longs for but can never finish needing or completely have God (the husband).

For both God and Israel an endless line of this language of self-deprivation and desire is or can be faithfully chosen in the freedom and moral feeling of sublime experience. Here, once again, in other words, we are face to face with the centrality of the figure of chiasmus in sublime experience, only now we see that in this tradition of language the figure harbors a cross-gendered relation.

I return now to Ezekiel's description of the fiery loins—that is, the compound of husband-wife and image-withdrawal topoi in 1:27—this time to examine the compound's cross-gendered and chiastic features:

[27] From the appearance of his loins upward I saw the like of *hashmal* [here masculine; *hashmalah*, feminine, in virtually the same chiasmus of verse 8:2][23] having something with the appearance of fire surrounding her;[24] and from the appearance of his loins downward I saw something with the appearance of fire; and he was surrounded by a radiance.

[28] . . . [25] That was the appearance of the figure of the Majesty of YHWH; when I saw it, I fell on my face—

This representation of the husband-wife topos includes both feminine and masculine elements, even though in a figure that is apparently only of the male. It is true that the representation of this husband-wife relation is shown, as if in opposition, to God's (feminized) prophet, representing the wife-Jerusalem. It is also true that looming within the scene is the announcement of the self-punishment of the wife-Jerusalem who has been unfaithful to God's commanded language. Yet the figure which heralds this self-punishment (of men as well as women) is drawn with a cross-gendered complexity that makes this image of God both feminine and masculine. The effect of this cross-gendering is simultaneously to represent withdrawal or absence of visualization as, in itself, a function of cross-gendered relation. That is, what is represented by not-being-represented is that which each condition of desire, each gender or force of re-production/representation lacks but cannot achieve. Or we may equally say that that which is identified as feminine or masculine corresponds to one of two phases of representing the inadequacy of representation: either the phase of the unrepresented in representation (presumptively feminine); or the phase of the representation of the inadequacy of representation (presumptively masculine). The chiasmus of verse 1:27 represents the fire of God's male loins as first feminine, then masculine. With feminine and masculine pronouns (each referring to fire) tagged at the appropriate places, here is Greenberg's mapping of what he terms this verse's "intricate quasi-balance" and "effect of chiasm":

I saw X ["her," *lah*] / from his loins up
From his loins down / I saw Y ["he" or "him," *loh*][26]

I propose that the chiasmus in this verse is itself the intricate effect of the formal features of its elements. Each element, first and chiefest, is inherently a topos, a repetition, that is, both of the husband-wife topos and of the topos of withdrawn representation. The representation of transcendence in the verse's language is a function of this repetition of an effectively infinite line of these topoi. The formal experience of this endless repetition, specifically of a line of representations each of which shows its inadequacy as representation, is a dying-away or momentary obliteration of consciousness in the representing subject—or in the viewer who takes in this representation ("when I saw it, I fell on my face"). Ezekiel's representation of the husband-wife topos as a likeness of the loins of YHWH appearing at the scene of Jerusalem's destruction is thus the formal experience of what Greenberg, referring to the narrative elaboration of the topos, calls "extending the metaphor in time." That is, the story line that Ezekiel uses to represent the topos is also the representation of endless repetition in the extensibility or feature of recurrence of recounted story.

In addition, in this chiasmus the effect of dying-away or loss of consciousness (i.e., the sublime effect produced by encountering the sublime line of language, in this case of these two topoi) is directly represented in image deprivation. This is the image deprivation that is represented by the blindingly bright or burning (up) elements which cover and withdraw the representation. In other words, the sublime trauma or effect of the sublime tremendum—which is after all itself located in, fed back into, an endless line of representations of this tremendum—is already represented in its fiery elements.

The effect of dying-away in withdrawn images is also represented in the countermovements of this chiasmus. Image deprivation (and the loss of consciousness it represents) is only representable as a movement from image to image deprivation or from representation to the represented inadequacy of representation, from radiance to blindingness. Each phase of this movement represents a desire to represent being. Each reaches for representation of being in a representation which is a withdrawal of representation. Therefore each gives way to the symmetrical withdrawal of representation of the other. The naming of this configuration of movements as a matrix of desire—or "loins"—is a logical outcome of this figuration of desire. (In a moment I will turn briefly to Hegel's apparently similar yet very different naming of desire.) The gender crossings within Ezekiel's language are internally necessitated. Whether or not Ezekiel, who, as I have said, shows marked misogynist tendencies, was consciously aware of this necessitated effect, in his verse the specification of these movements of desire or "loins" as alternately feminine and masculine is an instance of the sublime reinvention of gender. This reinvention shows that the husband-wife topos (which we might have thought of as representing unilateral desire or force) is the husband-*and*-wife topos. This topos of counterdesire and countermovement is congruent with the two stages of the topos of representational withdrawal: from representation to representational withdrawal; then from representational withdrawal to representation.

It is no accident that this sublime reinvention of gender is represented by Ezekiel as the culmination of his inaugural (or cardinal) vision of both destruction and redemption. Both the destruction and the redemption that Ezekiel envisions are the willed effects of alternative formalisms of language, the enslaving and the liberating, that God distinguished in his cardinal commandment. ("I am the God . . . who took you out of . . . the house of slaves [bet avadim]. . . . Thou shalt not make unto thee any graven image, or any likeness of any thing that is in heaven or earth, or under the earth . . . Thou shalt not be enslaved to them [lo ta-avdem = thou shalt not worship them].") And they are both effects of the gendering of language or, more precisely, of the language choices that define gender. In Ezekiel's vision of his language world, at every moment of thinking, speaking, representing, or acting, the individual is fatefully choosing between two grids of desire in language. Ezekiel dramatically represents the difference between these grids of desire. I am proposing that this difference closely corresponds to that between what I have called vulgar melancholia and sublime melancholia.

Milton recurs to Ezekiel's inaugural vision not only in the central image of "Il Penseroso," that of the cherub and the chariot, but also, I believe, from the very beginning to the very end of the poem. In fact, Milton's way of reconstituting the primary elements of Ezekiel's sublime image lays out the larger structure of sublime imaging that Milton reproduces within the key sublime figures of his poem, as if of Ezekiel's wheels within wheels (1:16). We are dealing here, indeed, with structures of imitation that pervade the largest contours and the smallest details of Milton's relation to Ezekiel.

In Ezekiel the fire that he cannot bear to behold represents both a withdrawal of representation and a gendered countermovement. Milton's representation of the "goddess . . . divinest Melancholy" whose "visage is too bright / To hit the sense of human sight" (ll. 11–14) is deployed in a similar cross-gendered structure. This is to say that the whole of "Il Penseroso" is transacted between the poles of this cross-gendering that expresses, as he suggests, the "prophetic strain" (l. 174) to which he aspires. This is compassed in the juxtaposition of the figure of the "pensive nun" at the poem's beginning with the intricately, though mutely related figure of the male poet-hermit-prophet at the poem's conclusion. Here are those two figures:

> Come pensive nun, devout and pure,
> Sober, steadfast, and demure,
> All in a robe of darkest grain,
> Flowing with majestic train,
> And sable stole of cypress lawn,
> Over thy decent shoulders drawn.
> Come, but keep thy wonted state,
> With even step, and musing gait,
> And looks commercing with the skies,
> Thy rapt soul sitting in thine eyes:
> There held in holy passion still,

Forget thyself to marble, till
With a sad leaden downward cast,
Thou fix them on the earth as fast.
And join with thee calm Peace, and Quiet,
Spare Fast, that oft with gods doth diet,
And hears the Muses in a ring,
Ay round about Jove's altar sing.
And add to these retired Leisure,
That in trim gardens takes his pleasure.
                    (ll. 31–50)

But let my due feet never fail,
To walk the studious cloister's pale,
And love the high embowed roof,
With antique pillars' massy proof,
And storied windows richly dight,
Casting a dim religious light.
There let the pealing organ blow,
To the full-voiced choir below,
In service high, and anthems clear,
As may with sweetness, through mine ear,
Dissolve me into ecstasies,
And bring all heaven before mine eyes.
And may at last my weary age
Find out the peaceful hermitage,
The hairy gown and mossy cell,
Where I may sit and rightly spell
Of every star that heaven doth shew,
And every herb that sips the dew;
Till old experience do attain
To something like prophetic strain.
These pleasures Melancholy give,
And I with thee will choose to live.
                    (ll. 155–76)

The poet represents these two figures in a movement toward a *hieros gamos*, or holy marriage, that can be a true marriage only if it is consummated by the imaginations and wills—the desires—of both partners. In other words, each partner must experience and represent his or her consciousness as a cross-gendering that reaches out to the cross-gendering of another. In this strain of representation the male poet calls to the female to "Come . . . With even step, and musing gait," while praying for the strength to move toward her with mirror countermovements, "Let my due feet never fail . . . ." The cross-referencing woven between the two figures is the tissue of their cross-gendered relation. She wears "a robe of darkest grain," he "the hairy gown" (itself a sign of disciplined desire); she has "looks commercing with the skies," he hopes to "bring all heaven before mine eyes"; she can know "Spare Fast, that oft with gods doth diet," he longs to "spell / Of . . . every herb that sips the dew" (i.e., the dew of heaven or the gods); she can be one who "hears the Muses in a ring, / Ay round about Jove's altar sing," he entreats, "let the pealing organ blow, / To the full-voiced choir below"; she will find "retired Leisure," he hopes to "Find out the peaceful hermitage"; she will achieve the demeanor of a sybil or prophet: "till / With a sad leaden downward cast, / Thou fix them [her eyes] on the earth as fast," he aspires to the same elevated humbling of the spirit: "Till old experi-ence do attain / To something like prophetic strain."

Decisive for the structure of each figure and for the structure of their rela-tion to each other is their virtually identical center point. At the heart of the poet's address to the female figure of melancholia, he envisions her achievement of the following condition: "Thy rapt soul sitting in thine eyes: / There held in holy passion still, / Forget thyself to marble." In this picture of holy rape ("rapt . . . held in holy passion") the effectuation and the possession remain only hers, which means the very opposite of physical coercion: hers alone are the effectua-tion and the possession, that is, of being beside herself or of being self-with-drawn in freedom to choose the encounter with an other. Symmetrically, the poet prays for the experience that will "Dissolve me into ecstasies," that is, of be-ing in willing ex-stasis, self-withdrawn in readiness for the free encounter with an other. In other words, the melancholia that each figure achieves is a function not only of being self-divided but of achieving this self-division in relation to a self-divided individual of the opposite gender. The consistency of this complex rela-tion is brought to an astonishing climax in the crossing over of the "pleasure" or "pleasures" or jouissances that they achieve. In the conclusion of the represen-tation of female melancholia, that is, as part of the representation of her subjec-tivity, we find a presumptively masculine pleasure: "And add to these retired Leisure, / That in trim gardens takes his pleasure" (ll. 49–50). Symmetrically and in cross-relation, at the conclusion of the representation of male melancho-lia the pleasures that are represented are those which are in the possession of the female and which are hers to give: "These pleasures Melancholy give, / And I with thee will choose to live." Milton's symmetrical figures of melancholia are an experience or event as well as a representation. As in the case of the experience of the line of topoi that produces Ezekiel's sublime dying-away and cross-gen-dering, Milton's experience of this line of topoi produces a dying-away and cross-gendering of desire. As in the case of Ezekiel, the moral significance of this grid of desire in language is that the choice of loving and living—the erotic choice—is imagined by each as a choosing that can be enacted only with the de-sire and choosing of a counter-other.

The same complexity of cross-gendering informs the poem's most local repre-sentations of melancholia, as, for example, in the couplet at lines 63–64:

Thee chauntress oft the woods among,
I woo to hear thy even-song.

In the chiastic distribution of the couplet's elements Milton suspends the possibility of discriminating the subjects or singers. Who, we are left wondering, is located "oft the woods among"? Is it Philomel among the branches of the trees or the poet seeking her in her various haunts? With whose song does his wooing-to-hear now enchaunt us? We may think, at first, that the subsequent verses answer the question:

And missing thee, I walk unseen
On the dry smooth-shaven green,
To behold the wandering moon,
Riding near her highest noon,
Like one that had been led astray
Through the heaven's wide pathless way;
And oft, as if her head she bowed,
Stooping through a fleecy cloud.

—but here too the phrasing, as of musical leitmotifs, equally suggests the poet's feeling bereft because he cannot see or hear the nightingale and, at the same time though on a different plane of story, the fate of the female who has been tragically led astray, made to wander a pathless fate, even made to bow her head, in shame or despair, all strength of resistance gone. (Bowing the head—after being raped—is Philomel's gesture of overwhelming despair in Ovid's telling.) The poet's melancholy evensong repeats the endlessly repeated lamentation for unrecuperable destruction that he hears (as Keats says, not with the sensual ear) in the unheard but strong melody of Philomel's evensong. In the between time of evening she is unseen and, as a result, he is unseen. She enchaunts or woos, speaking the eros of repetition and dying-away, representation and withdrawn representation, tragic desire and endless unattainability, deferred merging and acknowledged distances. Even rape has not destroyed the integrity of desire that defines her as a woman. All this the poet hears and speaks. This hearing-speaking can be said to be his experience and representation only in part. This eros at least attempts to be totally different from or opposed to the rapist's. Both her song and his song represent the scene of victimization and resistance that has already taken place, endlessly, but their songs join to reinvent gender in an evenly shared part-song or madrigal. If she goes missed in this listening-speaking, he goes unseen. If her subjectivity cannot find a lodging, he too will be "like one that had been led astray." As Milton represents these tragically fragmented subjectivities, they sing and experience vacancy together, even if on different planes of story that never fully merge.

But what is the force of desire that they share? Can one say more precisely what desire is in this eros of sublime melancholia?

To attempt to do so I would like to glance at a passage in Hegel that will lead us to Ezekiel and then, via Ezekiel, back to Milton. My aim here is to show a certain decisive difference between Hegel's representation of desire and Milton's almost identical representation.

Hegel cites a scriptural chiasmus as part of his argument for the way self-consciousness is achieved in sublimation. In this instance too, of course, Hegel is only working another variation on his endlessly repeated chiasmus of the birth of "a self-conscious Now" of the self:

[A]	[B]
as a real existence,	it is *not* a real existence, and
[B]	[A]
through this vanishing	it is a real existence.[27]

This is Hegel's vision of recuperated consciousness. It is more than a curiosity that, as warrant for this vision, Hegel invokes the authority of a scriptural chiasmus that expresses revenge. Hegel cites Paul in Romans 12:19, "Vengeance is mine; I will repay, saith the Lord" in the following passage from the *Philosophy of Right*: "It is not something personal, but the concept itself, which carries out retribution. 'Vengeance is mine [; I will repay], saith the Lord', as the Bible says. And if something in the word '*re*pay' calls up the idea of a particular caprice of the subjective will, it must be pointed out that what is meant is only that the form which crime takes is turned round against itself" (paragraph 101, addition).[28] What is indispensable for Hegel in Paul's verse is its citation of the Lord's chiasmus: vengeance / mine : I / repay. This is "the form . . . turned round against itself," specifically in the Lord's realization of the concept of revenge.

Despite Hegel's disclaimer of "a particular caprice of the subjective will" in the countermovements of "retribution," we note that the countermovements which constitute revenge are for him indifferentiable from those which he believes constitute the "desire" of the subjective will. For Hegel only these countermovements represent, which is to say achieve, the erotic ego which he calls the "self-consciousness" of "desire." Hegel is well aware of the dangers implicit in this equation of revenge with desire. To repel or counterbalance these dangers his representation of self-consciousness includes a requirement, for each consciousness, to be "acknowledged" in a symmetrical "duplication" of alienation, desire, and "independence." Hegel's picture of self-consciousness thus specifies in detail not only [*a*] the vulgar effect of victimizing the other in male melancholia that Schiesari announces, but, in addition, something very close to [*b*] the condition of what I have called sublime melancholia. Hegel writes,

[a] Self-consciousness is . . . certain of itself only by superseding this other that presents itself to self-consciousness as an independent life; self-consciousness is Desire. Certain of the nothingness of this other, it explicitly affirms that this nothingness is *for it* the truth of the other; it destroys the independent object and thereby gives itself the certainty of itself as a *true* certainty, a certainty which has become explicit for self-consciousness itself *in an objective manner.*

[b] In this satisfaction, however, experience makes it [self-consciousness] aware that the object has its own independence. Desire and the self-certainty obtained in its gratification, are conditioned by the object, for self-certainty comes from superseding this other: in order that this supersession can take place, there must be this other. Thus self-consciousness, by its negative relation to the object, is unable to supersede it; it is really because of that relation that it produces ["erzeugt," generates, i.e., in thought—acknowledges] the object again, and the desire as well. It is in fact something other than self-consciousness that is the essence of Desire; and through this experience self-consciousness has itself realized this truth.

(PS, sections 174–75)

This dynamic picture of desire is the four-chambered engine of Hegel's phenomenology of the chiastic spirit, the "'I' that is 'We' and 'We' that is 'I.'" Hegel declares, "A self-consciousness exists *for a self-consciousness*," so that Spirit "is the unity of the different independent self-consciousnesses which, in their opposition, enjoy perfect freedom and independence: 'I' that is 'We' and 'We' that is 'I'" (*PS*, 174–78).

Yet part of Hegel's account of "freedom and independence" is cast in doubt, I propose, by the line of citation and of image-withdrawal from which Hegel's own cited commonplace of revenge emerges. And, even more, it is transformed by the experience of the line of citation. In fact, the chiastic form is itself the representation of the withdrawal of representation in language, that is, in the experience of the line of citation of language that represents the withdrawal of representation. We need to be as clear as possible about the force of the line of image withdrawal that the biblical line of language has declared to be identical with God's self-image. This self-image is the guise in which the God of this language makes himself known. This is how he is.

Since Hegel writes, "as the Bible says," we may assume that he has noticed that when Paul says, "saith the Lord" he has a double meaning. Paul is both citing God's words and explicitly indicating that he is citing one of many sayings in the Hebrew Bible, each of which is explicitly a chiastic representation of revenge. Not least, in Ezekiel 25:14 Paul and Hegel had to have read:

I will lay my vengeance		upon Edom . . . ;
	X	
they [Edom] shall know		my vengeance, saith the Lord God.[29]

Even the contexts of the verses in Ezekiel and Paul are closely parallel. In both cases the argument is being made that justifiable revenge can be willed only by the Lord and that such divine revenge is, indeed, the Lord's moral judgment and punishment, as Ezekiel specifies (twice), for pretending to "vengeance avenged." This human "eternal hatred" is a "spiteful," malignant vengefulness that has nothing to do with revenge as moral action (25:12, 15). On this distinction hangs nothing less than the moral fabric of Ezekiel's (and of Paul's) world and language. At stake here is the very possibility of moral being. In Ezekiel's verse, as in the entirety of his realm of discourse, the emphasis on social wrongdoing or moral failure is inseparable from the polemic against idolatrous imaging. In positive terms, the emphasis on moral failure is inseparable from the counterargument for the moral efficacy of image-withdrawal, specifically in the line of God's language of sublime experience. It is therefore a logical necessity that Ezekiel's citation summons a line of citation. Thus, for example, Ezekiel's "saith the Lord God" cites (besides much else) Moses in Deuteronomy 32:43:

The [shedding of the] blood of his servants   he will avenge,

$$X$$

And vengeance he will render   to his adversaries.

God's servants are those who adhere to this sublime line of language, in which revenge and desire are constituted in the moment of moral choosing. This sublime line of language is chiastic and self-deprived representation. Indeed, it is self-deprived representation even in its experienced form precisely because it is chiastic. And, in addition, it is chiastic because it represents the countermovements of cross-gendered desire that generate language. Yet none of this could occur without the freedom and moral feeling that are effects of experiencing the cultural sublime.

To sum up what we have seen of these effects thus far: The form of thismoment repetition within the chiastic form (the countermovements) of Ezekiel's verse represents or is formed by the pressures of,

1. the line of repetition that has delivered the words of the chiasmus to this moment;
2. the dying-away experienced in the encounter with this line of language or representations;
3. the self-deprived form of each of these representations;
4. the representation of a duplication and mutual acknowledgment of self-consciousnesses;
5. the acknowledgment as well of embeddedness in the line of language, therefore of duplication and mutual acknowledgment of consciousnesses along the line;
6. a cross-gendered desire that is reinvented in representation of representational inadequacy and withdrawal.

All the effects of the chiasm of self and other which are noted and represented by Hegel are also represented by Ezekiel. But Ezekiel has already gone beyond Hegel. As a result, Ezekiel's representation of desire finally differs entirely from Hegel's. Hegel cites "Vengeance is mine; I will repay" because, as he makes clear in *The Phenomenology of Spirit*, for him the "scene" of desire in which two independent egos each "seeks the death of the other" (sect. 187) is a universal paradigm that is allegedly as much independent of culture and tradition as is the allegedly autonomous individual mind. For Hegel God's revenge too is an instance of setting oneself at risk and of seeking freedom in countermovements of desire. For Hegel this is the only way to achieve the allegedly impersonal (or at least not capricious) desire that is self-consciousness and the freedom of the autonomous mind, because "it is only through staking one's life that freedom is won" (*PS*, sections 186–88).[30] Yet because Hegel's representation of this scene (from Romans) in *The Philosophy of Right* is a repetition of the commonplace line of this scene it too actually represents something other than that which Hegel tells us he is representing.

This something else, we have seen, is the lineal or commonplace or culturally sublime component of Ezekiel's commonplace representation. In Ezekiel's representation of his line of language he can win freedom only along the sublime line of language that is traced from the cardinal commandment, with its husband-wife and image-withdrawal topoi. To be *of* this line of language and to live a mental life of image withdrawal amount, no doubt, to a way of staking one's life. It must mean to live in the condition of continually dying-away, that is, in sublime experience. But revenge has an entirely different meaning for Ezekiel. This meaning is very close to the picture of revenge that Kant derived from the neighborhood of Ezekiel's sublime. In other words, Ezekiel's derivation of freedom in sublime dying-away closely resembles Kant's sublime, especially the cultural sublime which, I have argued, Kant actually represents (that is, the dying-away and freedom and moral feeling that are the effect not only of encountering endless repetition of the colossal and of self-deprivation, but, as Kant acknowledges but will not discuss, especially of encountering representations of image-withdrawal in an endless or commonplace line of culture). In addition, Ezekiel's line of language identifies and explains that which is left mysterious in Kant. It identifies and explains how, in the first place, we have access to the freedom to choose self-deprivation or image-withdrawal or, indeed, even to choose to encounter the sublime experience. For Ezekiel this freedom is made available by being located (graced or chosen, if you will) in a line of sublime language, in the cultural sublime.

Thus although Hegel acknowledges none of the lineal features of the line of language that he is citing, he too has found himself placed and has represented his placement in a line of citation. His "as the Bible says" cites Paul's chiasmus of revenge and Paul's "saith the Lord," which in their turn cite the Hebrew Bible, as in Ezekiel's chiasmus of revenge (citing Moses' chiasmus of revenge, speaking for the Lord) and Ezekiel's "saith the Lord God." As a result, there is a decisive difference between what "the Bible says" about revenge and what Hegel says about that saying or representation. The difference, most of all, is in the conceiving of desire. In the prophetic or biblical strain of Milton's poetry this reconceiving or reinventing of desire is a central, recurring event.

In the recurrences of the fidelity topos of the Hebrew Bible the moral meaning of God's punishing of idolaters is provided by the sublime logic of the de-iconization topos, which means, at the base of all, God's self-definition in sublime experience and his sustaining in freedom of everything in creation (as in Descartes's *concursus*). More than anything else this is what Milton proposes in *Paradise Lost* as the most explicit and deepest ground for "justifying the ways of God to men." In Milton's innermost representation of these "ways," in book 7, we hear God's self-revealing description of his self-depriving way: "I am who fill / Infinitude, nor vacuous the space. / Though I uncircumscrib'd myself retire, / And put not forth my goodness, which is free / To act or not" (7.169–72). Exemplified in this way even by the divine mind, retiring and freedom occur as what Kant describes as "a deprivation of something—though in the interests of inner freedom."[31] God's own conformity to this language is the instruction to sublime experience of freedom and the possibility of moral feeling (that which Ezekiel calls breaking "the old hatred"). The alternative to this experience follows the logic of language pathology and moral catastrophe.[32] Representing just such image-withdrawal are the cross-gendered countermovements of the ways of God's Spirit, that "from the first [was] present":

> Dove-like satst brooding on the vast Abyss
> And madst it pregnant.
> (1.21–22)

Masculine and feminine elements of this image of the divine spirit metamorphose into each other. Here too Milton has braided feminine and masculine, masculine and feminine. This braiding necessarily unsettles fixed conventions of gendering. That which *sits* dovelike is only presumptively feminine; that which *broods* is only presumptively masculine (melancholic) or only presumptively feminine (nesting); so that even that which *makes* pregnant (by the spirit) is also only presumptively masculine; and even that which is *pregnant* (with the spirit) is only presumptively feminine. The chiastic effect of unsettling binary distinctions is staggeringly purposive here. In this representation, as a result, even for the transcendent other the return from antithesis is the achievement of a self-consciousness that remains a bilateral countermovement. In "Il Pense-roso," similarly, for the human self which emulates freely chosen self-with-drawal the return from the self-deprivation that produces freedom and moral feeling is also a representation of a bilaterality. This bilaterality is itself achieved in sublime experience. To close this chapter I will comment on how, in "Il Penseroso," Milton represents and experiences the reinvention of desire in a countermovement of bilaterality.

The "strain" of the prophetic (l. 174) that is the announced model and goal of "Il Penseroso" has a number of related meanings. It signifies a particular *lineage* of biblical representation and the defining characteristic of the language of that line or lineage, namely, the sublime imagery or *pulling away* of representa-tion from itself. And it signifies as well the resulting sublime intensity or *pitch* of such representation achieved in representation-withdrawal. This representa-tion is a *tension* or *suspension* of countermovements. Intensively and extensively, Milton's meanings of the prophetic strain are achieved in a bilateral represen-tation of a *bilaterality of consciousness*. The ensemble of these meanings is observ-able in his emulation of Ezekiel's language in the chiasmus

[A]	[B]
And the mute Silence	hist along,
[B]	[A]
'Less Philomel	will deign a song.

We can briefly summarize the features of this chiasmus that prima facie suggest a bilaterality of some kind. The chiasmus is split both thematically and formally. Thematically, it sets in counterpoint Ezekiel's and Philomel's stories of destroying passion. The mute Silence, specifically, is both Ezekiel's (forced into dumbness while he carries the knowledge of feminine Jerusalem's destruction) as well as Philomel's (after she has been raped and disfigured by Tereus). So too the song that is proposed here is the characteristic song of both Philomel's and Ezekiel's silences.[33] The verb "hist" intensifies the tongueless sound of Philo-mel's flitting movements and of her utterances that are blocked from speech. Ezekiel's song and story are also withheld in this telling. And they too, as I said earlier, are parts of a story of withheld speech, that is, a story of muteness and of sighs.

This rotation of holding forth and withholding marks the interchange be-tween the couplet's theme and form. As in the case of Ezekiel's image of the God of fiery loins, what is represented by not-being-represented is that which each motion of representation/reproduction, each condition of desire, or each gender lacks but cannot achieve. Or, as I have suggested, we may equally say that that which is identified as feminine or masculine corresponds to one of two phases of representing the inadequacy of representation: either the phase of the unrepresented-in-representation (presumptively feminine); or the phase of the representation of the inadequacy of representation (presumptively masculine).

Yet in this chiasmus there is a deeper reach of bilaterality, both thematic and formal, that changes the nature of presumption or prehension of meaning, that is, transforms the experience of a taking (*praesumere*) or grasping (*prehendere*) that is unilateral. This change is effected in representation of a reinvented dextrality. By dextrality I mean what Milton's contemporary Sir Thomas Browne meant: the experience not of the dexter, or right, hand, as if by itself, but the experience of the alleged superiority of the right hand over the left.

The twentieth century has had something to say about dextrality. In his essay "The Pre-eminence of the Right Hand" Robert Hertz showed the vast extent (in a variety of cultures) of the identification of the right hand with the masculine, the strong, the sacred, the patriarchal, the self, and the "rightful" or auspicious and legitimated; all this determined as a matter of binary contradistinction from the counteridentification of the left hand with the feminine, the weak, the profane, the other, and the "sinister" or inauspicious and illegitimate. Hertz also outlined the pervasive stunting, or what he called the "mutilation," of the left hand that insures the ascendancy of the right and, with it, the self-certainty of masculine identity. Hertz believed that the agenda of modernity must be to "dream of a humanity gifted with two 'right hands.'"[34] Yet there is a regressive and masculinist positivity in Hertz's dream of rectification, since even here the standard for the fully developed and the human remains the right. (The quotation marks around *right hands* only evade and highlight the unresolved problem.) For Hertz there is no possibility of imagining that the left itself might, in any sense, have something meaningful to tell about the human, except as a fact of repression from being the right. Hertz remains fully embedded in the binary of right and left and of other binaries as well, as in his clear-cut assignment of blame to what he calls "ancient religious ideas" of right and left.

Discourses on the social determination of right and left are at least as old as Aristotle. In Milton's time they reached a kind of peak intensity because of the emergence of the new anatomy. In "Of the right and left Hand" (1646) Thomas Browne wrote eloquently of the many "vulgar errors," including the misogynist myths, that underlie the oppositional structure of dextrality. (According to the *OED* Browne seems to have coined the term *dextrality* in its binary sense.) What is noteworthy about Browne's skepticist argument is that it negates any positivity concerning a human standard of right and left. "And therefore," he says, "many things are Philosophically delivered concerning right and left, which admit of some suspension." By "suspension" Browne means a mental action of staying in suspense or abeyance (the *OED* cites Browne as a first for this usage as well) or a condition of being "unsatisfied unto great dubitation."[35] Rather than a dream of rectification, Browne experiences a "suspension" of right and left in "great dubitation" or, we may say, hyperbolic doubt.

Milton's maintenance of right and left in ceaseless chiastic interchange is a condition of "prophetic strain" of this kind. And the line of language that Milton employs shows that he is aware that ancient religious ideas of right and left exceeded, at least at times, the limits of a binary dextrality. Milton heard and spoke from a language that sets in twisting motion the misogynist fixation of right and left that was indeed pervasive in the ancient world, as it is in the modern, and that is, indeed, one of the paradigms of victimizing thought. This body language and body thinking of right versus left, of dexterity versus the sinister, of recto versus verso—contained in the versus itself, the turning (*versum, vertere*) of right against left—is one of the most deeply founded catastrophes of a humanity turned against itself. Speaking from the limiting condition of this humanity, Hegel turns a blind eye to the cultural sublime that might work him free of his habituated rectification of chiasmus for self-consciousness and unilateral desire. The centrality of this rectification in *The Philosophy of Right* (the *Philosophie des Rechts* or *Rechtsphilosophie*), like the unilateral recuperations of *The Phenomenology of Spirit*, pervasively suggests the reenactment of this dextral or self-righteous catastrophe.

In Milton's couplet

[A]	[B]
And the mute Silence	hist along,
[B]	[A]
'Less Philomel	will deign a song

it is only because his versifying is a sublime suspension, unto great dubitation, of recto versus verso, verso versus recto, that his representation eludes Hegel's kind of unilateral recuperation and rectification. This is to say that Milton's versifying or countermovement of left and right in this and other couplets is coextensive with endless countermovements of the cultural sublime. As in Ezekiel, the form of this-moment repetition within the couplet represents (is formed by the pressures of)

1. the line of repetition that has delivered each word and phrase in the chiasmus to this moment;

2. the dying-away experienced in the encounter with this line of language or representations;

3. the self-deprived form of each of these representations;

4. the representation of a duplication and mutual acknowledgment of self-consciousnesses;

5. the acknowledgment as well of embeddedness in the line of language, therefore of duplication and mutual acknowledgment of other bilateral consciousnesses along the line;

6. desire reinvented in representation of representational inadequacy and withdrawal.

Remarkably, Milton's repetition of his commonplaces in the couplet also includes, as part of his representation, the commonplace status of a sublime versifying of dextrality. One way and another, that is, Milton repeats Ezekiel's own versifying of dextrality.[36] Ezekiel represents the outcry of a saving remnant at the spectacle of phallic abominations as a "sighing," of which the "mark" is, to the letter, a chiasmus or "X": "Now the Majesty of the God of Israel had moved off the cherub, on which it had been. . . . He called to the man . . . with the scribe's kit at his waist, and YHWH said to him, 'Pass through the city, through Jerusalem, and put a mark on the foreheads of those who moan and groan over all the abominations being committed in it. . . . Slay and destroy . . . , but stay away from those who bear the mark'" (9.1–4).[37] Origen (Milton's favorite among the Church Fathers) and Jerome explain that in Ezekiel's verse the Hebrew word for "mark," *tav*—the graphic "mark" for this saving sighing and moaning—names only the last letter of the Hebrew alphabet, *tav*, written X in ancient Hebrew. (They saw in this X as well a sign of the crucifixion and of the cross later written on the foreheads of Christians.[38] Dante uses a variety of the same topos from Ezekiel in *Purgatorio* 9.112–14.) There can be no doubt that Ezekiel represents not only the mark of the sigh of the redeemed but even the uttering of that sigh in the form of the countermovements of a chiasmus, even as the sigh "from broken loins" that (on some level of consciousness) must recall the countermovements of the cross-gendered or bilateral loins in the climactic moment of Ezekiel's inaugural epiphany in 1:27. In verse 21:11 Ezekiel versifies,

> Sigh from broken loins
> From bitterness you will sigh.

From broken loins, Milton's chiastic couplet

> And the mute Silence hist along,
> 'Less Philomel will deign a song

hears and sighs Ezekiel's and Philomel's sighs, groan for groan.

In fact, "Il Penseroso" expires with a sigh that is suspended in bilaterality.

Symmetrically and in cross-relation, at the conclusion of the representation of male melancholia the pleasures (of eros, of life) that are imagined are those which the female has (possesses) and can give for a sublime melancholia and its choosing in freedom:

> These pleasures Melancholy give,
> And I with thee will choose to live.

Here, one more time, Milton's experience of this line of topoi produces a dying-away and cross-gendering of reinvented desire. As in the case of Ezekiel, the moral significance of this reinvented desire in language is that the choice of loving and living—the erotic choice—is represented and experienced by every individual as a choosing that can be enacted only with the desire and choosing of a counter-other. I propose that, in this culminating moment, the syntactic ambiguity of "with thee" in Milton's final verse "And I with thee will choose to live" must partially (brokenly) contain the meaning *Together with thee I will then be able to make my choice, that is, to constitute my desire with your desire—the desire to love and to live,* meaning as male with female, husband with wife, each of which is part feminine, part masculine. We must be clear about the work that language is doing—and not doing—here. This representation is not a record of convictions, let alone of pieties. Rather, this representation makes available only a sublime experience of an endless line of two topoi (husband and wife; withdrawn image). Only this experience of these commonplaces, triggered by the infinite countermovements that are set in motion within the represented and experienced chiasmata, provides the freedom for the choice of self-deprivation, representational withdrawal, and, therefore, the possibility of reinventing the self. Only this freedom for a sublime versifying suspends or promotes the endless interchange of verso and recto, recto and verso.

In Milton's poem the drive of this ecstatic, endless countermovement momentarily suspends victimization. Momentarily the experience of this cultural sublime reinvents desire in a sigh from loins that are not necessarily broken in the sense of being neutered or castrated. Rather, desire of this kind is represented and experienced in endless, broken bilaterality and in cross-genderedness.

Self-Endangerment and Obliviousness in "Personal Culture": Goethe's "Manifold" *Tasso*

In this danger I no longer know myself.
—Tasso to Antonio in Goethe's *Torquato Tasso*

Here in Germany only the nobleman has the possibility of a certain generalized personal culture. . . .
A bourgeois can achieve great merit; at a pinch he can even cultivate his mind; but his personality will be lost.
—Wilhelm in Goethe's *Wilhelm Meister's Apprenticeship*

That which Goethe calls "personal culture" is equivalent, I believe, to what Harold Bloom has termed "being-with-oneself." Before I turn to Goethe, a word is in order about Bloom's concept, even though, in the historical unfolding of my chapters, I have confronted the elements of this concept mostly in the Hegelian form which I take to be Bloom's model, namely, Hegel's "being-for-self" of a "self-consciousness" that is achieved by "antithesis" (*Phenomenology of Spirit*, section 392 and passim).[1] More than any other contemporary critic Bloom has evoked the intensity of intertextual encounter in European literature of the past three hundred years. In *The Anxiety of Influence* he locates such encounters to support his theory of how "every post-enlightenment master" moves toward this "being-with-oneself." Thus Bloom's poets are said to achieve "antithetical completion" by enacting what is, in effect, a Hegelian sublime annihilation of the antagonist other.[2] Yet, challenging as it is, Bloom's theory recapitulates the lacuna in both Kant's and Hegel's accounts of sublime experience. Bloom, too, fails to place the sublime in relation to the individual's experience of the endlessness of his or her line of representations, each of which shows its inadequacy as representation. This lineal experience of the sublime includes not only repetition and resistance, but also the repetition of resistance. This is the lineal experience that I have called the cultural sublime. Bloom's chief terms—the sublime, the personalized countersublime, priority, completion, antithesis, repetition, discontinuity, emptying-out, solitude, melancholy, the return of the dead—have indeed always been indispensable in the Western cultural tradition. But Bloom skews the meaning of each of these terms by neglecting to configure them in the experience—that is, under the extraordinary, everyday impact—of the specifically cultural sublime, which can only be a lineal sublime.

In a present experience of the priority of the endless line, the individual, in Goethe's terms, endangers his possession of personal culture in order to experience a being-*beside*-oneself (a second state or second self) and a sublime freedom. This present experience of priority (unlike the envy of a precursor's priority, in Bloom's theory) is continually achievable by the individual in tradition, even if only at acute risk. At one moment, at least, Bloom seems to be on the verge of acknowledging that his melancholy myth (like Wordsworth's) of a post-Enlightenment sublime that is discontinuous with the language and the sublime of the preceding age is itself only what I have called a doubleness of counterperiodizations. Bloom asks the following question, which, however, he fails to recognize is only half the question: "What of Blake's Counter-Sublime, and Wordsworth's? Is all the *ekstasis*, the final step beyond, of Romantic vision only an intensity of repression previously unmatched in the history of the imagination? Is Romanticism after all only the waning of the Enlightenment?"[3] Goethe, passing remarkably beyond his personal culture, acknowledges the existence of both halves or both counterperiodizations of a cultural sublime. On one occasion he even seems to picture, explicitly, a kind of counterspiraling of cultural experience: "If we . . . ascribe to mankind a spiral movement, it still turns back to that region through which it has already passed."[4] The present chapter is concerned with the ways in which Goethe chooses to endanger his personal culture—and also remains partially oblivious to his line of culture—within the historical movement of such counterspiraling.

Self-endangerment, like sublime melancholia (to which it is closely related), is another feature of the cultural sublime which comes into special prominence in the modern age. In Kant's account of the sublime we may sense a feature of self-endangerment in the possibility of a link between the subject's "helplessness" and the prerequisite of a "self-deprivation." Similarly, in Hegel's account of sublimation and self-consciousness we hear of the need for the radical self-endangerment called the "trial by death." Yet in Goethe's representation of the sublime in *Torquato Tasso*, the experience of sublime self-endangerment is made payable in a way that even Kant and Hegel do not render. With no hope of controlling the outcome, Goethe throws himself into the countermovements of the language that he inherits. He encounters the line of "Weltliteratur"—what we would call the Western cultural tradition—that is in significant part made up of ghosts whose existence he may partially acknowledge but whose being he can never know. For Goethe the resulting representation of sublime experience is that combination of irresistible intimacy and insuperable distance which we are, I think, accustomed to thinking of as the signature of his self-consciousness. In fact, however, Goethe achieves that signature by continually setting his self-consciousness at risk within his experience of Weltliteratur.

Nietzsche suggestively locates a condition of self-endangerment and partial obliviousness in Goethe's poetry. By enlarging upon a picture put on view by Goethe's Faust, Nietzsche proposes the existence of "manifold" fragments of cultural identity—following Faust, he calls them "souls"—working in what may mistakenly be thought to be the unity of consciousness in the German mind:[5] "The German soul is above all manifold, of diverse origins, put together and superimposed rather than actually constructed: the reason for that is its source. A German who would make bold to say 'two souls, alas, within my bosom dwell' would err very widely from the truth, more correctly he would fall short of the truth by a large number of souls."[6] Nietzsche challenges Faust's formula of only two souls in one by proceeding to "vivisect" the halves alleged for the German soul. He also does something more aggressive, first implicitly, then explicitly. He declares that even in the complex, divided mind of the German who possessed the most comprehensive personal culture—Goethe— obliviousness to the participation of apparently alien elements within the manifold is a notable feature of the way the manifold functions. I will later turn to Nietzsche's specification of this obliviousness. But first I want to linger on the picture of the manifold which Nietzsche scrutinizes in Goethe. Goethe very much provides Nietzsche's model, even if Nietzsche deepens Goethe's model by recovering repressed minds within the manifold.

Nietzsche's reference to Faust's outburst is shorthand for an idea of a manifold of mind that recurs—unconsciously, to some extent, as Nietzsche suggests—throughout Goethe's work and, I would emphasize, which Goethe (like Schiller) regularly expresses in the figure of chiasmus.[7] That is, in Goethe's verse it is usual to find the elements of a manifold of mind as interactive binarisms in a relation of AB : BA. To take one Goethean example, in the case of Faust's declaration partially quoted by Nietzsche it may at first glance seem that Goethe offers the idea of a duplex mind and activates the figure of chiasmus merely to represent Faust in an agitation of cross-purposes which Goethe ultimately will set right. Two souls [A] reside uneasily in Faust's one breast [B]; his sense of a unified or predominant identity [B—"Die eine"] would cut loose from its troubling double [A]:

[A]   [B]
Zwei Seelen wohnen, ach! in meiner Brust,

        [B]   [A]
Die eine will sich von der andern trennen.
                (ll.1112–13)
[Two souls dwell, alas, within my breast,
And each would separate from the other.][8]

Yet there is reason to believe that throughout the play Goethe employs the figure of chiasmus as a tool of open-ended exploration whose object is itself open-
ended. A chiastic exploration of an irretrievable manifold of souls is already
launched, for example, in the final couplet of the "Zueignung" to *Faust*. Those
personally resonant verses are Goethe's way of setting in motion his "längst
entwöhntes Sehnen / Nach jenem stillen, ernsten Geisterreich" (long forgotten yearning, / For the sweet solemn tryst those spirits keep) (ll. 25–26), as if in
an elected affinity of minds of the living and minds of the departed. This couplet superimposes and leaves unconstructed (not deconstructed), that is, a manifold scene of thought which is highly similar to Faust's spectacle of the two-
halved soul, though it is also, in respect to other minds, respectful of the
unattainability of a personal unity of experience:

        [A]   [B]
Was ich besitze, seh' ich wie im Weiten,
        [B]   [A]
Und was verschwand, wird mir zu Wirklichkeiten.
                (ll. 31–32)
[All that I have stands off from me afar,
And all I lost is real, my guiding-star (reality)].[9]

The manifold structure of the chiasmus includes participating fractions which
lie totally beyond the poet's ken, so that one effect of the couplet is to open the
possibility of precisely that affiliation with counterworlds—outside a speaker's
putative self and beyond his voice—which Goethe's protagonist will initially
refuse.

    In probing Goethe's language one is dealing with far more than isolated,
technical, or so-called stylistic phenomena. Goethe's language represents a systematic probing of the language that he most intimately inherits and which
constitutes his self. In delving that language he opens the sense of time and history—the temporal dimension of priority—that he experiences within that
language, including the experience of the inaccessibility or invisibility of parts
of his line of language. At the outermost reaches of his language and representations, I believe, Goethe's experience of the impact of that complex line makes
available to him (and to his reader) a sublime freedom within language and
within the world. Thus in *Torquato Tasso* Goethe's framing acknowledgment is
not only that the condition of his inherited language is significantly determined

by the complexity of Tasso's language and its line, but that his interaction with Tasso's language and its line is part of his own most liberating experience of reality.

I now turn to a distich near the close of *Torquato Tasso* to begin enumerating the elements of the foregoing and other Goethean pictures of chiastic counterworlds. This distich is spoken by Tasso at the moment he imagines he has once again annihilated his world, this time by killing the Princess's love for him. "Ist alles denn verloren?" (Is everything then lost?), he asks, "Bin ich Nichts, / Ganz Nichts geworden?" (And have I become / A nothing, an absolute nothing?) (ll. 3409–16). The distich provides the complex answer:

> Nein, es ist alles da, und ich bin nichts;
> Ich bin mir selbst entwandt, sie ist es mir!
>
> [No—it is all there—and I am *nothing*.
> I am wrenched from myself, and she from me!]
> (ll. 3417–18)[10]

Even the first verse, by itself, is rendered intermittently chiastic by the doubleness of its elements. We can perhaps take conscious note of these chiastic effects only in slow motion. Thus in the first line—

[a]	[b]	[b]	[a]
"Nein,	es ist alles da,	und ich bin	nichts"—

"Nein" momentarily creates a vacuum of absolute negation, even while it affirms (denies the denial of) "es ist alles da" (i.e., alles ist *nicht* verloren). So too the "da" which this speaker from the depths of "nichts" can grasp is as much *fort* (as Freud would say) from his self as it is *da*. Splayed between the progressive conjunction "und" (linking with "es ist alles da") and "nichts," the affirmative "ich bin" is totally split. Similarly, the final "nichts" certainly means "nothing," but it is also the obverse and signal of "alles." Even cursory examination of the second line of the distich shows that it invites very much the same analysis in the reverse order of positive and negative elements (i.e., of being and nonbeing), each compacted of its own doubleness. Thus the full distich constitutes a larger chiasmus of jewel-like intricacy in which the highest level of binarism is a movement between the limits of being and not-being:

	[A]		[B]	
[a]	[b]		[b']	[a']
Nein,	es ist alles da,		und ich bin	nichts
	[B']		[A']	
[b]	[a]		[a']	[b']
Ich bin	mir selbst entwandt,		sie ist	es mir!

Within this larger chiasmus, as within each line, all the binary terms whirl and twist at incalculable speed. Instead of a formula of exclusion, A not B, or even a cross drawn in two indelible lines, we experience a continuous circulation of relations both direct and inverse: namely, AB, BA′, A′B′, B′A, AA′, BB′—in addition to smaller wheels both within and beside the larger wheels (ab, aB, etc.)—each of which may be encountered separately and in combinations, forward and reverse. We can begin to describe the X experienced in this chiasmus only by its illimitable circulation. By virtue of the cross-reading it sets in motion, the chiasmus uncovers endless changes in its component antitheses, invariably to discomposing effect.

For the purposes of this discussion of self-endangerment in the representation of a sublime manifold of cultural tradition, I would like to recall here some points made earlier about the commonplace dynamics of chiasmus, which is to say, in a series of chiasmata. Chiasmus, we have seen, creates a species of absence between its binary terms. Because of this special kind of absence (and other related effects that I have detailed earlier) chiasmus is as distinct from antithesis as negativity is from negation. Chiasmus, in fact, comes into being by framing and implicitly by acknowledging the unformulated element or negativity within language. Experienced within more than one part of the chiasmus simultaneously, this is a negativity among the lines and half-lines, even between the dualities of single words, that allows for the rotating countermotions of the polarities. This negativity is continually displaced from the nameless absences in the interstices of visual or audible matter to thematizations of negativity, and then back to the absences. In a series of chiasmata—in which every literary chiasmus is always commonplacely placed—there is no recuperation of this negativity.

With regard to *Torquato Tasso,* I propose that in describing the relations of the chiasmata (and their framings of negativity) of different individuals one often glimpses a reaching out both to some counterworlds that are named within the text (like the world, for Tasso, of the Princess) and to others that are not named or that remain in oblivion or are even repressed, except intertextually (like the referent, frequently, in the protagonist's ["Tasso"'s] figures of lamented absence). As an example of this phenomenon, I am claiming that the distich quoted above locates our possibility not only of hearing the pain of a man called Tasso, but also of locating the potentiality and the self-endangerment represented by a counterspiraling chiasmus of counterworlds shared by Goethe ("the German")—in halves, mind beside mind—with someone else, in fact, with more than one someone else at a time.

In the case of the relations between Wordsworth and Dryden (or Pope) we have seen, indeed, that in a given literary or artistic tradition, the thinking of individual artists of different times may form configurations which are, in relation to each other, both oppositional and reciprocal. Elements of such reciprocity manifest themselves within matched oppositions in which such opposition is expressed both temporally backward (e.g., a later poet contra a remembered poet) and temporally forward (i.e., an earlier poet contra an anticipated poet). What is distinctive about this pattern of oppositions, however, is that it occurs within a set of recurring reciprocal relations that recurringly oppose opposition as such. Identifying this state of affairs, we have seen, is another way of naming a series of chiasmata, since each chiasmus is a diagram of a simultaneous potentiality of opposition and reciprocity. My focus now is on the individual's choice—in this case, Goethe's choice—of self-endangerment that sets this pattern in motion within a given cultural tradition. Goethe's status as a giant of culture is a function of his awareness—far beyond Hegel's—that he achieves the experience of culture and of freedom only in a kind of self-endangerment. With self-endangerment aforethought, Goethe throws himself into a line of sublime representations of culture and freedom.

I return to the moment of Tasso's experience rendered in Goethe's distich, now to note that Goethe's verses correspond closely to the following chiasmus, describing Tancred's experience, in Tasso's *Gerusalemme liberata:*

> Va fuor di sé; presente aver gli è aviso
> l'offesa donna sua che plori e gema
> [He is beside himself; he thinks he is in the presence
> of his injured lady who is weeping and lamenting.]
> $(13.45, 5-6)^{11}$

For Goethe, in *Torquato Tasso,* the fact of this correspondence to this Tassovian moment is primary in the kind of thinking that engages him. That is, the correspondence results from the manifolds of mind posited in the structures of both Tasso's distich in *Gerusalemme liberata* and its repetition (in resistance, as we shall see) by Goethe in *Torquato Tasso.* What is significant here is not any conscious or even unconscious remembering on Goethe's part. On the contrary the kind of thinking we witness here, in both instances, stipulates a self-endangering obliviousness, a condition, partly chosen, of the self beside itself, that only partially acknowledges minds (in the manifold) which the subject cannot know.

It happens that we know a good deal about Goethe's intense involvement, in 1790, in thinking through the pain of his dependency, or even helplessness, as poet at the court of Weimar via Tasso's at least analogous pain at the court of Ferrara two centuries earlier. Tasso's experience was accessible to Goethe primarily through the *Gerusalemme liberata,* the work that Tasso, on the edge of a kind of madness, was struggling to complete at Ferrara. Yet even without prior knowledge of these connections we could not help being struck by the way

Goethe's drama explicitly highlights Tasso's genius as a sublimely melancholic capacity for assembling (*anziehen*) a manifold of mind, as if in the "Geisterreich" longed for in the "Zueignung" to *Faust*. (There are multiple parallels between that passage and the one I am about to cite.) Speaking in a dense series of chiasmata—for which I offer one possible signposting—Leonora Sanvitale says of Tasso,

[A(b)]   [B(a)]
Oft adelt er,   was uns gemein erschien,
    [B(a)]   [A(b)]
Und das Geschätzte   wird vor ihm zu nichts.
                    [A]
In diesem eignen Zauberkreise wandelt
Der wunderbare Mann   [B]
                und *zieht uns an,*
        [B]   [A]
Mit ihm zu wandeln,   teil an ihm zu nehmen:
        [A]   [B]
Er scheint sich uns zu nahn,   und bleibt uns fern;
        [B]
Er scheint uns anzusehn,   [A]
                und *Geister* mögen
An unsrer Stelle seltsam ihm erscheinen.
            (ll. 165–72; emphases added)

[Whatever seems
Most ordinary to us he can at once
Change into wonders, while what we cherish
Means little to him. He is wonderful—
He walks in his own magic world, and draws
Other people in to share it—yet when
He seems to come close by, he is still far away;
For him we could be disembodied spirits.]

Leonora's first two lines directly represent Tasso's chiastic, melancholy state of mind, especially his courage and power of representing a negativity or "nichts." Tasso does not wander alone in his "Zauberkreise" but draws others in, as if they might occupy or own the vacancy of his "nichts." In this process of *anziehen* they share in making the world's enchantment, which itself remains a function of framing the "nichts." For Leonora this work of drawing other minds into a manifold of mind suggests the similar, if lesser, power of "anziehen" in the Princess and the Duke,[12] who have enabled Tasso and those around him to work this magic of the "Zauberkreise." Considered from the perspective of our discussion of chiasmus and a manifold of mind, we need to inquire into the nature of this shared *anziehen* in the "Zauberkreise" of *Torquato Tasso* and, perhaps by the same token of enchantment, of *hinanziehen* shared by the Chorus Mysticus in the closing chiasmus of *Faust:* "Das Unbeschreibliche, / Hier ist's getan; / Das Ewig-Weibliche / *Zieht uns hinan.*"

One way of approaching an inquiry into this *anziehen* is to ask how we might locate the linkage, through negativity, between Tasso's distich

> Va fuor di sé; presente aver gli è aviso
> l'offesa donna sua che plori e gema

and Goethe's

> Nein, es ist alles da, und ich bin nichts;
> Ich bin mir selbst entwandt, sie ist es mir!
> (ll. 3417–18)

In the relation of these distichs we must take seriously their claims that the subjects or consciousnesses represented here are beside themselves. As I have said, I take such a claim to mean that each consciousness is in part constituted by laying itself open to the experience of the inaccessibility of another consciousness. For each participating consciousness this is already one kind of self-endangerment. In each distich the binary half-lines both thematize and create the structure of a manifold of mind that frames both accessible and inaccessible consciousness. In each distich we see the staging for an affiliation of fractional selves, whether of Tancred and Clorinda or of (Goethe's) Tasso and the Princess, in addition to presences and absences of the author Tasso, in the first distich, and of the author Goethe, in the second. On Goethe's part, the presence of a "Tasso" in both distichs may even partly suggest an attempt to lay the framework for a continuous, or reciprocal, shared thinking-through of a given thought. But how might there be a functional linkage, such as I am claiming, specifically between the chiasmata of these distichs? What kinetic quantity in both chiasmata could create the shared potentiality of experience that remains distinctly beside Goethe's individual mind and Tasso's?

A rough listing of the obvious and more or less static correspondences between these distichs is helpful, as a kind of process of elimination, in pointing toward the strange quantity in question. "Va fuor di sé" is matched by "Ich bin mir selbst entwandt"; "presente aver gli è aviso" by "es ist alles da"; "l'offesa donna sua" ("offesa" [injured], very much in the sense of being severed) in "sie ist es mir" (i.e., she is divided from me). Only Tasso's fourth binary, "che plori e gema," does not find its symmetrical correspondent in Goethe's fourth binary, "und ich bin nichts." This latter is the phrase in which Goethe repeatedly names Tasso's power of negativity. In this element of his chiasmus, I want to suggest, Goethe's mind turns counter to Tasso's even and especially in the act of representing the chiasmus of "Tasso's" mind through which he, Goethe, is also thinking but which is partly inaccessible to him. Something is locatable here between

Tasso's and Goethe's verses, something which neither poet can fully control and which endangers the hold on consciousness, or sanity, of each. This uncontrolled quantity is provisionally located by circumstances of possible interaction between texts. It remains potential in the interstices of cultural fragments that run counter to each other. Experienced in history only within configurations of possible encounters, it may be described, in this particular case, in the following way.

Working from Tasso's chiasmus, Goethe creates a kind of secular paradigm of what Erich Auerbach, characterizing Goethe's genius, has felicitously named "sensory truth."[13] In Goethe's chiasmus it is clear that this power over sensory truth consists in a play of intensely felt sensory presence and its equally felt absence (the "nichts"). In the distich from *Gerusalemme liberata* Tasso's play of absence against presence—indexed in the phrase "plori e gema"—is worlds apart from Goethe's in the sense that Goethe forgoes superhuman mediation in the human experience of negativity. Correlatively, Goethe is oblivious to the interactions of his verses, beyond his meanings, with Tasso's Judaeo-Christian framing of negativity. Yet Goethe's framing of negativity in his distich is as unmistakable as Tasso's.

Tasso's chiasmus depends upon the fact that Tancred's vision of his lady "gema" (lamenting) is not a representation of the affect of erotic passion alone. Rather, via the allusion to Lamentations (repeated in "gemiti" [laments], two lines later) it invokes the typological and antitypological meaning which his "l'offesa donna" carries in the sublime line of Old and New Testament representations. The antitypological other world opened up here is the most weighty burden of Tasso's negativity throughout the *Gerusalemme liberata*. This negativity locates the liberated or opened-up world bestowed on the fallen, earthly world by Christ's dying to that world in fulfillment of the type of Christ's crucifixion in the destruction of Jerusalem. Tasso's very next chiasmus, turning on Tancred's and Clorinda's participation in the liberating (opening) power of Christ's self-endangerment and self-sacrifice, makes this clear. The "langue" (languishing sufferer) of these lines recalls the "infermo" (sick man) sixteen lines earlier—who is there Tancred, not Clorinda—reenforcing the manifold effect (of mutual sharers in Christ's condition) achieved in the chiasmus:

[A] né può soffrir	[B] di rimirar quel sangue,
[B] né quei gemiti	[A] udir d'egro che langue.
[A] and he can no longer bear	[B] to see that blood
[B] or hear those laments[14]	[A] of a languishing sufferer.

The complexity of Tasso's mind, behind Tancred's, is implicated in these lines by the fact that this representation of a Christian negativity is in itself a counterfeit vision of what exists in real form elsewhere. In Tasso's epic of Jerusalem delivered, the false Clorinda offering those laments evokes the Lamentations of Jeremiah for the destruction of Jerusalem. In this speaking of the false Clorinda (which will be a central, if subliminal, preoccupation of Freud as well in *Beyond the Pleasure Principle*), Tasso reminds us of the way Dante's fleshly screen for Beatrice explicitly evokes Lamentations in the *Vita Nuova*.[15] Tasso's *Gerusalemme* other world, where laments ("gemiti") are, among other things, necessarily sighs from the Lamentations of Jeremiah, has something to say, side by side, with Goethe's other world, in a counterspiraling of counterworlds. Here we encounter the Goethe who has willingly (even if he is in part unconscious of the object of his willing) endangered his mere personal culture or self-consciousness in order to compass an entirely different order of experience.

Because each chiasmus in a sublime line of language is a motion of turning with negativity toward the negativity of another chiasmus in that line, we experience here the impact of the unwritable history ("Das Unbeschreibliche") of a shared thinking. Such shared thinking is always only between individuals, between texts, between cultural moments, always, therefore, in the experience of the priority of the sublime line of culture. The time of this priority corresponds closely to what Auerbach called Goethe's "extra-temporal spirit of history." We should recall that for Goethe, at least, the extratemporal was an inevitable feature of an authentic historism. Auerbach, following Friedrich Meinecke, has reminded us of how closely identified the age of Goethe is with the formulation of historism, most especially with the belief in this extratemporal spirit of history. Auerbach, however, sees this aspect of Goethe's mind as a limitation entailed in Goethe's tendency to avoid a fully developed realism and, correlatively, to insulate himself from the social realities of his own time. Auerbach's estimate of Goethe is, to be sure, immensely high, but, looking back on German history in 1946, Auerbach wonders whether the development of modern German culture "might have been" different if Goethe had been able to engage his age more fully "in the realm of realism."[16] Considering both the richness of Auerbach's appreciation of Goethe's genius and the catastrophe that contextualizes this remark, one cannot but pause. Yet I wonder whether, without intending to do so, Auerbach has not made it harder to discern the kind of courageous engagement with history—severely limited as it is—which Goethe, with the special limits and capacities of his historism, actually pursued. Undoubtedly it is an insubstantial comfort to anyone who, like Auerbach, directly experienced the impact of modern German history, but I believe that Goethe's poetry opens the door to just such an extratemporal spirit of history, as if in a *Geisterreich* envisioned by his historism. Auerbach's listing of the limitations in Goethe's capacity for historical engagement can serve, in fact, as a picture of the problematics that Goethe confronts directly in *Torquato Tasso* and that therefore forms the context of the manifold of mind on which we are now focused.

Let me review the main points of Auerbach's analysis of Goethe's avoidances of history. Turning Meinecke's praise of Goethe into a gentle form of blame, Auerbach says that those parts of history that Goethe ignored were ones which he could have "mastered by the cognitional principles which were most peculiarly his own . . . if he had loved those parts of history." But, Auerbach laments, his bourgeois longings for aristocratic culture caused him not to love them. Auerbach reads Goethe's own "confession" in Wilhelm Meister's lament that in Germany only the nobleman may attain "a certain generalized personal culture": "I happen to have," says Wilhelm, "an irresistible propensity for the very kind of harmonious development of my nature which is denied me by my birth."[17] Citing an essay of Goethe's, Auerbach notes his too easy acceptance of the fact that "nowhere in Germany is there a center of social *savoir vivre* where authors might congregate and, in their several domains, develop in one common manner and in one common direction." Auerbach cites Goethe's unwillingness to contemplate the revolutions that would be necessary to change this situation: "We shall not wish for upheavals which might prepare classical works in Germany."[18]

Of course, it would be absurd to argue that Goethe engaged history in the way Auerbach would have hoped. Yet Goethe's limited form of historical engagement is still of very great interest, especially since it risks affiliating itself with something far beyond Goethe and German culture. The decisive difference between Goethe's and Auerbach's perspectives is that Goethe thinks in terms of the cross-cultural and the extratemporal while Auerbach is concerned with the responsibilities of a single national culture to a single moment in history. Auerbach would have wished for Germany that which Goethe is unwilling to hope—for Germany. The manifold of mind that Goethe chooses to encounter in the poetry of Tasso does answer in considerable measure, however, to Auerbach's objections, even if that manifold did not sufficiently change the reality of German culture itself. The "cognitional principles" that peculiarly form that manifold, with its drawing in, or "anziehen," of other minds into the "Zauberkreise" of a *savoir vivre*, are strongly suggestive of what Leonora, we have seen, attributes to Tasso and the d'Este court. At Ferrara, Tasso, painfully the commoner, strives to achieve within the manifold—together with the noblemen whom he draws after him—a "generalized personal culture" and "harmonious development." For us as observers of Goethe's relation (from Weimar) to Tasso's poem (which Tasso struggled to complete and left unfinished at Ferrara) it is further clear that the manifold opened in "classical works" in which he participates cannot be a local German affair. One remembers here Goethe's remark to Eckermann that a "Weltliteratur" could be made only by a kind of ongoing colloquium of artists of different cultures who "correct" each other.[19]

The moment is now ripe to introduce Nietzsche's way of blaming Goethe for his obliviousness to a correction of this sort in the manifold of mind that he represents. I mentioned earlier that while Nietzsche borrows Goethe's picture of the multiplex soul he declares that even in the complex, divided mind of the most self-conscious German—"that German," he calls him—obliviousness to the participation of certain minds within the manifold is both an inevitable feature and potentially a dangerous condition of the way the manifold performs. Nietzsche suggests that one of the components of the German soul repressed by Goethe is that of the Jews. Speaking, we may presume, of the orbit of his intellectual acquaintance and not merely of his contemporaries, Nietzsche will soon say in the same place, "I have never met a German who was favorably inclined towards the Jews."[20]

Nietzsche shows how the Jews alternately form components which are external and internal to what appears to be the unitary soul of the Germans (248). The rules of the game in this manifold are always beyond self-knowledge: "Every people has its own tartuffery and calls it its virtues.—The best that one is one does not know—one cannot know" (249). In other words, the full extent of the transactions among the diverse souls in the manifold, like the diversity of souls itself, is not available for direct knowledge by any of the transactors. This is where Nietzsche's famous tribute to, and censure of, the Jews comes in. That tribute-censure is expressed in Nietzsche's own characteristic chiasmus, giving with one hand what he takes away with the other. His binarisms are Europe and the Jews / the Jews and Europe; repetitions of "the best and the worst" in the worst and the best:

> What Europe owes to the Jews?—Many things, good and bad, and above all one thing that is at once of the best and the worst: the grand style in morality, the dreadfulness and majesty of infinite demands, infinite significances, the whole romanticism and sublimity of moral questionabilities—and consequently precisely the most attractive, insidious and choicest part of those iridescences and seductions to life with whose afterglow the sky of our European culture, its evening sky, is now aflame—and perhaps burning itself up. We artists among the spectators and philosophers are—grateful to the Jews for this.
>
> (250)

In this passage the Jews are not merely woven into the chiasmus of Europe and the Jews. Like Kant's linkage of the Jews with the sublime, but with a more movable expiration date on what Kant calls their "moral period,"[21] Nietzsche sees the Jews as bearing a kind of intrinsic X or chiasmus of "sublimity." This is an equation wrought from "moral questionabilities": "infinite demands" / "infinite significances" = "dreadfulness" / "majesty." In the manifold of the German soul the Jews locate a negativity, a ghostliness consequent upon having been repressed within Western tradition, as well as a sign (as Kant would have it) of the representation which represents its inadequacy as representation. Nietzsche certainly points to the danger here that European culture is burning itself up, as if in a kind of madness of the sublime. Yet Nietzsche embraces this danger in the name of Europe's artist-philosophers. This risk is entirely different from the lethal danger posed to repressed cultures by dominant cultures.

As Nietzsche understands it, German or even European culture becomes dangerously inimical to others when its practitioners operate from the illusion of a sustained self-consciousness or achieved personal culture, such as Hegel, preeminently, claimed. Nietzsche warns against what may be called the Hegelian side of Goethe. Nietzsche's highlighting of hypocrisy (or "tartuffery") in Hegel's famous scene of punishment is seen in Nietzsche's caustic rehearsal of that scene in *Thus Spake Zarathustra*: "You do not want to kill, O judges and sacrificers, until the animal has nodded? Behold, the pale criminal has nodded: out of his eyes speaks the great contempt."[22] Even if Hegel often shows explicit awareness of dangers in the way self-consciousness is earned in the scene of punishment, there are moments when he is inebriate of his own lordliness. This is seen clearly, in fact, in a passage in which Hegel claims a kinship of lordly self-consciousness (in effect, of the bourgeois's achievement of aristocratic personal culture) with Goethe. Hegel writes, "'No man is a hero to his *valet-de-chambre*,' is a well-known proverb; I have added—and Goethe repeated it ten years later—'but not because the former is no hero, but because the latter is a valet.' . . . A World-historical individual . . . must trample down many an innocent flower—crush to pieces many an object in its path. The special interest of passion is thus inseparable from the active development of a general principle."[23] This is Hegelian self-consciousness and Hegelian desire with their allegedly inevitable vengeance. Yet Goethe's representation, at least, of Faustian claims to the world-historical desire that crushes Gretchen ultimately requires the production of very different kinds of consciousness and desire. Nietzsche calls attention to necessitated reconfigurations of this sort in the *shattering* efficacies of *Faust*.[24]

In *Torquato Tasso* Goethe is complexly blind to his repression of the Jews in the German soul. His endangering of his personal culture—meaning his blockage of the recuperation of the chiasmus that represents his self-consciousness—is effected by his turning, in his own sensory "Nichts," toward the Judaeo-Christian negativity of Tasso's "lamentations." Goethe's represented circle of countermovements is therefore not completely in his control. Quite aside from the fact that, as in any such set of countermovements, his subjectivity continuously turns on the representation of a negativity, he further experiences a historically framed negativity that is (also) totally unrecuperable. Without directly recognizing or acknowledging what constitutes the line of Tasso's "lamentations," his historism or historical experience is nevertheless of the "extratemporal" priority—the sublime effect of encountering the endless repetition of self-deprived representations (of negativity)—which in his specific line of Western tradition includes the Hebraic or what Nietzsche calls the Jews. Thus Goethe's condition of complex blindness strongly suggests that even in the case of the most capacious minds and most generous spirits the gains of self-endangered personal culture cannot, in principle, be fully credited to—are not known by—the individual personality. In Nietzsche's formula, "The best that one is one does not know—one cannot know." In the individual personality we may discover even a personal cultural prejudice against the very cultural element that that individual's representation of a sublime self-endangerment is able to embrace. This is an aspect of the experience and making of cultural tradition that especially resists sentimentalization or applause. This is one more reason individual personalities who are even strongly identified with their tradition will always be, as personalities, inadequate representations of their tradition.

I am proposing that in the case of Goethe and Tasso, Nietzsche's remarks may help to locate the experience of priority that Goethe and Tasso encounter in the line of culture that includes the Jews. To close this chapter, I will try to describe concretely how a chiasmus of the Jews forms part of the manifold of tradition in which Goethe and Tasso participate.

I offer one final brief collocation of verses: from the very end of *Torquato Tasso,* from the very end of *Gerusalemme liberata,* and, this time, from Lamentations as well. I earlier discussed verses from the closing moment of *Torquato Tasso.* I now focus on the final instant of that moment. Here Goethe's last resort seems to be only a mutuality of destructive cross-purposes suggestive of Faust's "zwei Seelen" (including even the "klammernden Organen" of one of those souls—*Faust,* l. 1115]). This could indeed be seen as a kind of terminal romantic sublime which is inherently beyond identity, even beyond rational meaning. Tasso's aristocratic nemesis and savior, Antonio, has stepped toward Tasso and taken him by the hand. Tasso declares, "Ich kenne mich in der Gefahr nicht mehr" (In this danger I no longer know myself) and seals the play with these words:

Ich fasse dich mit beiden Armen an!
So klammert sich der Schiffer endlich noch
Am Felsen fest, an dem er scheitern sollte.

(ll. 3451–53)

   [A]   [B]   [B]   [A]
[I reach out   to you   with open arms,
                  [A]
Just as the sailor clings fast to that very
  [B]   [B]   [A]
Rock   on which   his vessel should have foundered.][25]

The complexity of the simile defies paraphrase. The already foundered ship (in the immediately preceding verses: "cracking under my feet . . . deck . . . splitting now, rending apart") is the representational vehicle of that part of Tasso's self that he no longer knows. The other part of his self, beside the foundered part, is his self-beside-himself, which is reaching out to Antonio's arms. Closely mirroring the structure of the manifold of mind in the "Zauberkreise," this "Gefahr" or "danger" is a milling of tentacles within the putative self, which are shown to be a relation of elements inside and outside any mere self. As Antonio is both nemesis and savior—destroying rock and steadfast redeemer—so part of Tasso is wrecked (reverts to "nichts") while part of him is saved. Tasso reaches out with arms of his "zwei Seelen" to the extended arm of Antonio, which is itself doubled in horrifying ambiguity. At the heart of this redoubled doubleness is the desire, on all sides, for something that stands outside the scenography itself. This is a negativity that remains framed in darkness. Yet this interaction within Goethe's verses cannot be their whole story because these final lines spoken by Goethe's Tasso encounter the historical Tasso's final verses in *Gerusalemme liberata*.

Describing Godfrey's final act, Tasso writes,

> e qui l'arme sospende, e qui devoto
> il gran Sepolcro adora, e scioglie il voto.
>
> [and here he hangs up his arms, and here devoutly
> adores the great Sepulcher, and discharges his vow.]

Goethe could not have failed to notice that this image and this moment have special visibility in Tasso's poem because they are a repetition and fulfillment, in that poem's very last moment, of the same image in that poem's very first moment. Tasso has made it further unimaginable that any serious reader could have missed the centrality of the image and its repetition in the design of the poem as a whole. In the remarks which conclude his commentary, "The Allegory of the Poem," he writes,

> Proposing Godfrey and Rinaldo as symbols of the rational and irascible faculties, is
> not contrary to or divergent from what Hugh says in the dream, when he compares

the former to the head and the latter to the arm [14.13]. For the head (if we may believe Plato) is the seat of the reason, and the arm, if not the seat of wrath, is at any
rate its principal instrument. . . . The poem concludes with Godfrey's Adoration in
order to show that the intellect wearied in civil affairs ought finally to rest itself in
prayers and in contemplation of the goods of that other life most blessed and immortal.[26]

The "l'arme sospende"—both armor and arm—which discharges Godfrey's
"vow" is in part Tasso's Christian answer to the blood-feuding of pagan—and
Christian—history. Tasso wants us to take note of the difference between Godfrey's final act and that of Aeneas in the final verses of the *Aeneid*. Having noticed Pallas's battle baldric hanging on Turnus's shoulder, Aeneas thrusts his
sword into Turnus's breast—sending him "to the Shades below"—in this way
discharging and fulfilling his "vow" to Evander to kill the killer of that king's
son, Pallas. Although Godfrey's suspension of his killing arm is ushered in with
streams of blood—the kind of upheaval that Goethe was loath to imagine,
even for the salvation of German culture or for the making of classical works—
Tasso asserts the world-changing power of this Christian suspension, itself an
imitation of the divine forgiveness for the killing (and perhaps the suspension-
crucifixion) of the Son of the King of Kings. The Christian's fulfillment of his
vow is thus in the hanging up of the arms, the suspension of the killing arm. Instead of the shades below, humankind has now been liberated in a Jerusalem
which is centered in the Holy Sepulcher of Christ's dying for the world. We can
paraphrase this matching of worlds in many ways, but it seems clear, at least,
that at the heart of this doubling of Godfrey's act, over and against Aeneas's,
Tasso represents a Christian desire to exit the scenes of history for a negativity
that is framed in distinctively Christian ways. Thus it is already impossible not
to hear a certain extratemporal whispering between this Tassovian framing of
negativity and Goethe's at the end of *Torquato Tasso*.

Yet an extratemporal colloquy of another kind speaks louder from the
crossroads of Tasso's and Goethe's texts because for Tasso the cross-cultural
stakes are far higher than a competition of pagan and Christian. How could
they be otherwise in a Christian epic reenacting the liberation of Jerusalem,
when in the view of Christian typology the Old Testament had prefigured that
liberation of Jerusalem in Jeremiah's Lamentations for the destruction of
Jerusalem? Of necessity, in Tasso's verses he is poised—and self-endangered—
on the boundary lines of Christian typology.

During the past two millennia in the West, perhaps no written evidence of
a manifold of mind has been more extensive than Christian typology, and none
has been more inherently structured on obliviousness to the Jews. In Christian
typology, the thinking of the Jews themselves is frozen and subsumed in a thinking constituted by the types or anticipations of Christ—which occur in the Old

Testament and pre-Christian Jewish history—and the antitypes of the New Testament, which have fulfilled and closed off those types. In one sense, therefore, Nietzsche's explicit criticism of Goethe's merely duplex model of the German soul as well as his reminder concerning the place of the Jews in that soul may represent an indirect response to a Christian typological and bipolar thinking. But Nietzsche's insight goes deeper than the issue of displacements from history. His insight concerns, most of all, exclusive claims to negativity, to the unilateral staging of chiasmus, and to the control of thinking itself. One alternative way, that is, of describing the leverage of a Christian typological imagination is to note that the antitype of Christ is defined by his immense power of negativity, by his liberating the world in his dying to it, so that an infinite other world is opened up within the mortal scene. (Nietzsche's explication of the "sublime" in Raphael's *Transfiguration* is explicitly in this vein.)[27] Nietzsche suggests, as we have seen, that the Jews form their own liberating line of chiasmus, equipped with their own framings of negativity, and that this is what makes it inevitable for them to form part of the German manifold of mind. Just so, in the line of priority that we are considering, various chiasmata of Lamentations become, indeed, no less a powerfully silent partner than Goethe and Tasso. That is, Tasso's phrase "l'arme sospende"—suspended at the exact instant in which Jerusalem is delivered—encounters Lamentations no less than the *Aeneid*. It recalls, reciprocally and oppositionally (that is, in the countermovements of chiasmus), the moment when the hand of the Lord is "withdrawn"—at the exact instant in which Jerusalem was destroyed. Tasso would claim (or imagines he claims) that in *Gerusalemme liberata* the "l'arme sospende" fulfills in deliverance what was before an imperfect type. Among the relevant verses in Lamentations the following (2:3–4), which we have met before, are profoundly of that type:

[3]	
[A] he hath drawn back his right hand [fem.] from before the enemy,	[B] and he burned against Jacob like a flaming fire . . .
[4]	
[B] he stood with his right hand [masc.] as an adversary	[A] and slew all that were pleasant to the eye in the tabernacle of the daughter of Zion

This passage offers stylistic evidence as well as substantiating cultural experience for Nietzsche's argument about "the grand style in morality" of the Jews—that is, the style of the Jews which lies hidden, side by side, within the manifold of diverse minds in the German mind. As noted, Nietzsche sees the "sublimity" of this style in its chiasmus of "moral questionabilities": "infinite demands" / "infinite significances" = "dreadfulness" / "majesty." The moment of Jerusalem's destruction in Lamentations, cited above, represents a sublime of this sort. Triumphalism, nationalistic pride, hiding of national failure, fixing the books of history are excluded at this moment. Another sort of history is at stake here. The "enemy" is a term cast into utter questionability, here implicating the Jews and God as much as the enemies of the Jews. In these verses the scriptures of the Jews show us a God of infinite significances who makes infinite demands upon them (including the demand of the commandment to sublime or withdrawn representation), demands which they do not meet. This God is both *withdrawn* from actuality and *standing* unyieldingly within it. He makes moral demands in the realm of this world, yet at the same time he demands a worship of the infinite itself (in "the tabernacle"), centered only in an earthly framing of negativity. The structure of these verses frames a cultus of negativity that is transacted solely in an extratemporal dimension, across the history of the Jews that is recorded in this scripture. This negativity of the Jews is therefore already explicitly formulated within one kind of typological matrix, although here the antitypological dimension is not closed, but rather reaches out, with both arms of the chiasmus, for fulfillments elsewhere. For the Jews this would presumably take place in the continuing history of the Jews themselves, but clearly this opening for interpretation could also open the door to a Christian typology.[28]

In the God's-eye view of moral questionabilities represented in these verses from Lamentations the dialectic resolves nothing, creates no capital idea. The unresolved oppositions of these verses only keep open the significances of the immediate event in an infinite, extratemporal realm. I will mention here only two of the most obvious of these oppositions. First, there is the hand of God, which is initially said to be withdrawn, while in the following verse that hand is said to be not-withdrawn or active. Second, the withdrawn hand of God is shown in cross-relation to the feminine "tabernacle of the daughter of Zion," while the not-withdrawn, destroying hand of God is shown in cross-relation to masculine Jacob-Israel. (In the Hebrew text these crossings are reenforced by a change in gender of the word *hand*, from feminine to masculine, between the two verses.) Read horizontally, in each verse the violence occasioned in the destruction of Jerusalem is pictured in a gendered opposition and reversed gender opposition of God and the Jews (i.e., feminine to masculine, then masculine to feminine). Thus God's negativity is outside (typographically within) the thematizations of these oppositions. Yet that negativity is rendered suggestively feminine insofar as it represents a withdrawal (like the feminine withdrawn hand in verse 3) from any mere present world or temporality, such as is ideally suggested in the invisible presence within "the tabernacle of the daughter of

Zion." The violence pictured in this masculine-to-feminine relation may of course also figure holy rape as well as a purely brutish force very much within temporality. For the Jews (Jacob-Israel), in any case, only God's negativity can give meaning, beyond the immediate catastrophe, to their existence at any moment in history. This feminine negativity can draw them to a realm beyond the present obliteration of their world.

There may well be overt features of translation between Lamentations—*Klagelieder*—and Goethe's final moment in *Torquato Tasso*. Goethe's Tasso even says here that "Natur," "ein Gott," gave him his poet's power "zu klagen" (ll. 3427–31). In addition, the play of hands that in *Gerusalemme liberata* Tasso pursues with regard to the moment of Jerusalem's destruction in Lamentations may find correlatives in Goethe's language. Tasso, who reaches out to Antonio's hand (of nemesis and salvation) with both his arms, is clearly, perhaps even shockingly for Goethe's contemporary audience, the principle of a feminine negativity and creativity. When Antonio extends his hand to him, Tasso tells him what it means to be the feminine, "breast"-like "wave" breaking on Antonio's masculine "rock":

> Du stehest fest und still,
> Ich scheine nur die sturmbewegte Welle.
> Allein bedenk und überhebe nicht
> Dich deiner Kraft! Die mächtige Natur,
> Die diesen Felsen gründete, hat auch
> Der Welle die Beweglichkeit gegeben.
> Sie sendet ihren Sturm, die Welle flieht
> Und schwankt und schwillt und beugt sich schäumend über.
> In dieser Woge spiegelte so schön
> Die Sonne sich, es ruhten die Gestirne
> An dieser Brust, die zärtlich sich bewegte.
> (ll. 3434–44)
> [You stand there firm and quiet,
> I seem to be only the storm-tossed wave.
> But consider this, and do not presume
> Too much on your great strength: for Nature,
> Who set this rock in place, has also given
> A power of ceaseless movement to the wave.
> She sends her tempest and the wave draws back,
> Rears itself up, and seethes, and overturns
> In bursts of outflung spray. Yet this same wave
> Once held the sun, so calmly; and all the stars
> Once rested on its gently stirring breast.]

Antonio may seem to be an Old Testament masculine God who inscrutably destroys and saves, but he is matched by the power of an Old Testament feminine God who "draws back" and holds the world in her bosom. The final verses of the drama therefore rotate upon a negativity which is framed in the same suggestive feminine way as it is in Lamentations. Only this "Ewig-Weibliche" gives meaning, beyond Tasso's immediate catastrophe, to his existence as a poet working in an extratemporal world between texts and between minds. In effect, he is explaining to Antonio that only this feminine negativity creates, in self-endangerment, a potentiality of relation between them that remains beyond their individual realization or personal culture. In other words, only this feminine negativity *zieht uns hinan*.

These correspondences with Lamentations suggest semantic linkages, as if in some individual's system of signs. Yet, as I have said, my point here is not to describe an intertextuality that is a semantic layering, thin or thick, controlled by a given mind. The relations between the chiasmata of these different texts, especially between the framings of negativity in these chiasmata, are—as, I believe, Goethe and Nietzsche understood—beyond the grasp of any individual subjectivity. Even now, we, as individual readers, do not comprehend the full thought that is being thought in the last lines of *Torquato Tasso*. For Goethe's subjectivity and personal culture this self-endangered representation of the line of culture represents its representational inadequacy (with regard to representing that line, at least). This self-endangerment of individual subjectivity and personal culture sets in countermotion the potentiality of sharing in a cultural manifold. This is the potentiality of sharing in a rotation upon negativity between chiasmata, each of which is an encounter, or countermovement, between at least two subjectivities: in this case (in *Torquato Tasso*) Tasso's "open arms" or "zwei Seelen" with Antonio's, as well as of this quadrature turning in countermovement with (in the *Gerusalemme liberata*) Tasso's typological pairings in the final verses of *Gerusalemme liberata* (especially of the humanly divine God-frey and the divinely human Christ, the liberating, freeing-God), in addition to an endless line of such countermovements, here instanced by the counterpairings, in Lamentations, of God and the Jews and of Jerusalem destroyed by withdrawn hands.

This spiraling, dizzying manifold line is experienced by any one mind only as a sublime present of priority. This experience gives at least one circumstantial meaning to what Auerbach, following Meinecke, calls Goethe's belief in the "extra-temporal spirit of history" or to what Nietzsche, also referring to Goethe, sees as a multilayered consciousness that is not brought together in a unity of individual experience but remains "superimposed rather than actually constructed." In this way, in *Torquato Tasso* Tasso's closing representation of self-endangerment also represents Goethe's chosen experience of the endless line of sublime representations that he encounters in Tasso's language. Like his Tasso—and like the Tasso of the *Gerusalemme liberata*—in the representation of sublime countermovements, Goethe stands self-endangered and partly oblivious, beside himself, both within and beyond his personal culture.

The Modernity of Learning: Baudelaire's and Delacroix's Tasso "roulant un manuscrit"

CHAPTER 9

A long time ago now I heard a man [Delacroix] really learned and profound in his art . . . talking of commonplaces, that is, of the vastest and profoundest things.

Everything that is not sublime is useless and culpable.
—Baudelaire, "The Salon of 1859"

Few writers are more directly associated with the advent of modernity—sometimes even with the emergence of our latest modernity or post-modernity—than Baudelaire. This is one of the reasons that Paul de Man chose Baudelaire, specifically his "Le peintre de la vie moderne," as a test case in his provocative essay "Literary History and Literary Modernity."[1] De Man says that "modernity exists in the form of a desire to wipe out whatever came earlier, in the hope of reaching at last a point that could be called a true present, a point of origin that marks a new departure." The result, he argues, is "a paradox that cannot be resolved, an aporia that comes very close to describing the predicament of our own present modernity."[2] Here is de Man's picture of the paradox which, he claims, "Baudelaire experienced as a curse":

As soon as Baudelaire has to replace the single instant of invention, conceived as an act, by a successive movement that involves at least two distinct moments, he enters into a world that assumes the depths and complications of an articulated time, an interdependence between past and future that prevents any present from ever coming into being. . . .

The distinctive character of literature thus becomes manifest as an inability to escape from a condition that is felt to be unbearable. It seems that there can be no end, no respite in the ceaseless pressure of this contradiction, at least as long as we consider it from the point of view of the writer as subject.[3]

De Man is undoubtedly correct in focusing the struggle of Baudelaire's representations in the present experience of "a successive movement that involves at least two distinct moments." De Man's characterization of this experience, however, as "unbearable" and his failure to distinguish what for Baudelaire constitutes the distinctness of a moment shrink the breadth of possibility that Baudelaire explores in this experience. In the same way, calling Baudelaire's experience of this condition "a curse" only casts an emotional or mystical veil over the causes and elements of the experience. As I will try to show, the evidence suggests that the affliction that Baudelaire experiences in representation is an unrecuperable melancholia. That is, Baudelaire's encounter of "successive movement" is his experience of the present upon encountering a sublime line of representation. Correspondingly, the terms that de Man employs to describe Baudelaire's unbearable condition are only versions of Kant's terminology for the Western sublime, especially the "momentary check to the vital forces" (Hegel's "dying-away") that results from the mind's failure to grasp—in a moment of the present—the totality of an endless progression. Thus what is aesthetically significant about Baudelaire's unbearable moment is that, indeed, momentarily he ceases bearing full consciousness. Within a certain consequent obliviousness, therefore, Baudelaire sees and represents a complication of articulated time which is of a sublime priority. This is Baudelaire's achievement of what he calls a "représentation du présent."[4] In Baudelaire's representation if we wish to speak of "the point of view of the writer as subject" we must acknowledge the manifold or lineal view generated from that point and from such a subjectivity. These occur in the experience of the self-beside-itself which is always indispensable to the Western experience and theory of the sublime.

Baudelaire's term of sublime complication is tradition's own most demanding term for experience of tradition: learning. This appears concretely, even if apparently in an offhand fashion, in Baudelaire's description, for example, of Delacroix's *La Montée au Calvaire* as "une composition compliquée, ardente et savante" (a complex, ardent and learned composition) or in his identification of Delacroix as "un homme vraiment savant et profond dans son art" (a man really learned and profound in his art). Both of these descriptions lead, ultimately, to the pronouncement that "tout ce qui n'est pas sublime est inutile et coupable" (everything that is not sublime is useless and culpable).[5] It is Baudelaire's own artistic representation of learning, however, that I wish to examine. Within his representation of learning we experience in highlighted form a modernity—which means a moment of the present, a new departure, an awakening or renascence after dying-away—that in the West is always a chief element of the cultural sublime. This phenomenon of sublime experience is the same as that named by Kant (though not substantively described by him). It is a "discharge all the more powerful" that somehow follows inevitably after the "check to the vital forces."[6] I now turn to one of Baudelaire's representations of a learning that, for him, qualifies as sublime and of the modernity which that experience of learning produces.

My exemplum is Baudelaire's sonnet of 1844 "Sur *Le Tasse en prison* d'Eugène Delacroix," which is *sur* Delacroix's painting of 1839, *Le Tasse dans la maison des fous,* now in Winterthur (fig. 7):

Le poëte au cachot, débraillé, maladif,
Roulant un manuscrit sous son pied convulsif,
Mesure d'un regard que la terreur enflamme
L'escalier de vertige où s'abîme son âme.

Les rires enivrants dont s'emplit la prison
Vers l'étrange et l'absurde invitent sa raison;
Le Doute l'environne, et la Peur ridicule,
Hideuse et multiforme, autour de lui circule.

Ce génie enfermé dans un taudis malsain,
Ces grimaces, ces cris, ces spectres dont l'essaim
Tourbillonne, ameuté derrière son oreille,

Ce rêveur que l'horreur de son logis réveille,
Voilà bien ton emblème, Âme aux songes obscurs,

Que le Réel étouffe entre ses quatre murs!

[The poet in his cell, unkempt and ailing, rolling a manuscript beneath his convulsive foot, measures with terror-inflamed gaze the stair of vertigo in which his soul is engulfed.

The intoxicating bursts of laughter that fill the prison lure his reason into strangeness and absurdity. Doubt encompasses him, and foolish Fear, hideous and multiform, revolves round him.

That man of genius caged in a noisome hovel, those grimaces, those shrieks, those ghosts that whirl in a swarm behind his ear,

That dreamer awakened from his sleep by his lodging's horror—here it is, your true emblem, Soul, you with your darkling dreams, whom Reality suffocates between its four walls.][7]

The editor of the Clarendon catalogue raisonné of Delacroix's paintings remarks (after quoting the first stanza above) that Baudelaire "allows himself . . . poetic license . . . and exaggerates or invents aspects of convulsion and terror. In so doing, he creates his own work of art but does no service to the subtlety and restraint of Delacroix's."[8] In fact, however, Baudelaire has observed and represented Delacroix's painting with rigorous accuracy. Baudelaire's point of departure is Delacroix's own point of departure for the experience of the sublime that he has represented. This is the rolling of the manuscript by the convulsive foot of the ailing poet (epileptic, according to the legend that is only common knowledge). We may not recognize, at first, how this point of depar-

FIGURE 7. Eugène Delacroix, *Le Tasse dans la maison des fous*.
Courtesy Sammlung Oskar Reinhart "Am Römerholz," Winterthur.

ture functions. Yet we gradually learn to see that the reciprocal relations among
the painting's details specify that function. Baudelaire sees that the extraordinary detail of the poet's foot rolling a manuscript back and forth represents in
concentrated or emblematic form an effect that is achieved throughout the
painting. Once one grasps this detail within the ensemble of the painting's details, one sees that it is the representation, in an achieved present, of the experience of a succession of distinct moments. For Delacroix these distinct moments
are, at very least, his own present moment and the moment of this poet in his
cell working on the manuscript of his poem. For Baudelaire in his poem the

succession of distinct moments is further augmented. I will try to show that for Delacroix and Baudelaire the rolling manuscript represents a ruling principle of representing the present in a succession of distinct moments, each of which is rendered distinct by sublime experience, that is, by the experience of a dying-away (suffocated, "étouffe") and of an awakening to the present ("réveille").

In the painting attention is drawn to the foot rolling a manuscript by the poet's total obliviousness to it, as if that foot is not part of his body. He is oblivious, too, of the arm and forefinger of the inmate which point directly not only at the two sheets of paper discarded on the daybed but at the foot rolling the manuscript. In addition, the poet's obliviousness extends to his other foot, which seems to be climbing an invisible stair. Baudelaire has calibrated the condition of consciousness that Delacroix indexed by the half-closed, half-open right eye with which the poet measures his world. This half-awake, half-dreaming state of consciousness is also registered, in a larger schematic way, by the contrast between the poet's mute, frozen calm and the clamorous disturbance of the figures at the window bars. The expressions and open mouths of these figures indicate just such sounds as Baudelaire names. Baudelaire has duly noted, as well, that Delacroix represents the poet in the commonplace attitude of a melancholia whose commonplace symptom is a muteness of *hysterikè pnix*, meaning hysterical suffocation. Baudelaire's language of "réveille" (awakening) and "songes obscurs" (darkling dreams) reproduces Delacroix's representation of the poet's fitful, waking-dreaming condition, which has been underlined by Delacroix's foregrounding of the mechanism of the convertible daybed. The highly anachronistic presence of this late eighteenth- and early-nineteenth-century device in a scene that is apparently set in the late sixteenth century is itself part of Delacroix's way of rolling together different times.

The wit or paradoxical effect of the painting is focused on the state of double consciousness of the poet. The poet is beside himself, dreaming his awakening and awakening his dreams. Among other things, these are dreams of poetic scenes that he writes down and throws away on the sheets of paper strewn around him. We cannot see what he may hold or wish to hold in his clenched right hand, but that hand is held against the head of the daybed, where we are perhaps compelled to imagine sheets of paper—or an easel—to explain the positioning of the hand. In this state of waking his dreams and dreaming his waking, the poet is both specular and spectral. Delacroix has emphasized his spectral quality in the radiance of the gleamingly white shirt that rings his torso against the dun surroundings.

In addition, the gross imbalance of the poet's feet suggests a chronic falling into a repetition of unstable states. Delacroix treats the poet's body—the body of this Torquato—as an elastic solid on a longitudinal axis, so that the force of the roulant applied at the bottom end of the axis creates a twisting or torque toward the blur of the manuscript. It is by no means immediately clear what is represented by the fact that the painting's representation of awakening and dreaming twists and descends ("s'abîme," as Baudelaire says) toward this whirling blur ("vertige"). Neither is it obvious what resources Delacroix provides for learning more about this endlessly successive movement. In the blur of the *manuscrit roulant* we seem even to reach a dead end. Yet I want to propose that both Delacroix and Baudelaire know what the learning represented by this manuscript requires: namely, that this is a scene of reawakening, rebirth, or modernity in a line of learning. This is to say that the extraordinary impression of awakening which Delacroix achieves in representing the poet's waking-dreaming and which Baudelaire (re-)represents as a "réveille" in "songes obscurs" is already the effect of representing the rolling line of representations of waking-dreaming that they inherit.

"T'éveilles-tu d'un songe . . . ? Oui, tu veilles à la fois et tu rêves." (Have you woken from a dream . . . ? Yes, you are awake and at the same time you are dreaming.) These are Tasso's words, spoken to himself alone, in "prison,"[9] at the climax of the text that was the most immediate cause of intense interest in the figure of Tasso in the artistic world of Delacroix and Baudelaire. This was the French translation of Goethe's *Torquato Tasso* (1790), which appeared in Paris in 1823 and was reprinted in 1827.[10] We will see in a moment that Baudelaire strongly implies that this is a text that Delacroix particularly had in mind. But even if we resist this notion, I believe we come to feel that Delacroix had to have encountered something very like this representation of Tasso's "réveille."

Delacroix has placed Tasso's foot "roulant un manuscrit" ironically as a *note en bas de page,* or footnote, yet this footnote signifies neither secondary knowledge nor an ostentation of learning. Rather it is a representation of the impact of learning which creates the moment of the present. Here learning is worn as lightly as a dream, in what Baudelaire called Delacroix's "langage du rêve" (language of dreams) and its "impression extraordinaire qui accompagnait la conception," where "conception" means not only "the birth of the idea," but, as he says in the same place, "une conception, devenue composition" (a conception, become composition).[11] The dream condition of the fragments of learning in Delacroix's *Le Tasse* composition is already represented as a function of experiencing these fragments by a self-beside-itself in the sublime experience, that is, in an experience of dying-away. This, in turn, is the dying-away which is the effect of encountering a sublime composition or an effectively endless repetition of representations, especially representations of partially withdrawn representation or momentary dying-away. To be sure, particular circumstances, intimate knowledge, and intense contemplation had to set the stage for this extraordinary ordinariness which may seem, at first, merely arcane.

To provide background for the plausibility of what I will now propose, I perhaps need to recall that Delacroix's preoccupations with both Tasso and Goethe are, as far as I know, unmatched by any other major painter of this period. Delacroix painted a number of crucial scenes from the *Gerusalemme* (especially a *Clorinda*) based on the prince Lebrun translation (1782 and numerous reprintings), which Delacroix's friend Jean-Baptiste Pierret was long engaged in revising. Delacroix's close interest in Goethe's poetry was notable throughout his career. He made a striking series of illustrations, for example, for a French edition of *Faust*.

As I have mentioned, there is evidence to suggest that Baudelaire represents his own learning about Delacroix's representation in his way of observing Delacroix's joining—in his learning—the line of learned representations that he encounters in Goethe's representation of Tassovian awakening. Without offering explanations, Baudelaire recovers the passage in Goethe's *Torquato Tasso* that may indeed most immediately provide Delacroix with his figuration of awakening. Drawing upon the conclusion of that passage, Baudelaire reverbalizes, turns back into poetry, the ground of awakening which Delacroix had turned from poetry (from Goethe or some other writing) into painting. Specifically, I suggest, Baudelaire recirculates the following excerpt from Goethe's language for Tasso, *en prison*, speaking (or thinking) to himself, in the French of 1827:

Le cortége *hideux* des oiseaux *équivoques,* lugubres compagnons de la vieille nuit, *crie et voltige bruyamment autour de ma tête.* Où donc, *où diriger mes pas?* où fuir *l'ennui qui me dévore? comment échapper à l'abîme qui est devant moi?*

(emphases added)[12]

[Now they swarm and beat around my head,
The loathsome retinue of ancient night,
The equivocal and hateful fiends. O where
Shall I go to escape this nausea (the ennui that
devours me),
To escape this pit that lies before me?][13]
(ll. 2236–40)

Thus the scene of the imaginary which Baudelaire seems to have imposed on Delacroix's painting is from Goethe, which is to say, from the scene of the imaginary which is the inner experience that accompanies the Goethean formula (or its close equivalent) represented by Delacroix, "tu veilles à la fois et tu rêves." Baudelaire certainly could not have imagined that his heavy levying on Goethe's scenography and language, in this climactic passage of the play, would escape notice by anyone even vaguely interested in the subject, least of all by Delacroix. (Baudelaire has echoed all of Goethe's words and phrases italicized above.)[14] Yet Baudelaire was not plagiarizing, any more than was Delacroix. In turning to Delacroix's painting and in returning to Goethe, Baudelaire was representing learning of a specific kind. Whether in Goethe or elsewhere, Delacroix had turned to the history of the language of Tasso's rolling manuscript to achieve a point of entry—or point of departure—for the representation of an essential Tassovian problematics of representation. Both Delacroix and Baudelaire understood and represented the same Goethean and Tassovian response—within the line of representation—to that problematics. For them, as for Goethe, the immediate object of representation is Tasso's agonized experience of the present in the act of representing. Goethe had defined the problematics of this act of representing as being, most especially, the representation of awakening and the present in a successive movement of representations. Early in the play Léonore and Tasso have the following exchange, which sets out Goethe's preoccupation with what he understands as Tassovian representation:

> *Léonore.* Réveille-toi, réveille-toi. Laisse-nous croire que le présent ne t'est pas tout-à-fait étranger.
> *Le Tasse.* C'est le présent qui me ravit; je ne parais que rêveur, et je suis en extase.[15]
> [*Leonora:* Wake up, wake up. Don't let us feel that you have made yourself a stranger to all that is present.
> *Tasso:* It is the present that ravishes me; I only appear to be dreaming, and I am in ecstasy.]

Even before we encounter Baudelaire's representation, in the present, of the present of Delacroix's (and Goethe's) Tasso, or even Delacroix's representation of Goethe's (and no doubt other artists') Tasso, we see that Goethe's representation of what he understands Tasso-the-representer to represent is what it means to awaken or be reborn into the present. And for Goethe and Delacroix, even before Baudelaire, the answer is in awakened or sublime experience of a present of priority or of presently experienced successive movement.

To anyone familiar with Tasso's *Gerusalemme liberata,* moreover, it was immediately obvious that Goethe accurately represented the central problematics of sublime awakening in Tasso's epic. Tasso is not only already aware of but is inspired by the challenge of what de Man calls modernity's hopeless "hope of reaching at last a point that could be called a true present, a point of origin that marks a new departure." This hope, de Man says, is evidenced in the attempt "to wipe out whatever came earlier." But where Tasso, Goethe, Delacroix, and Baudelaire are concerned, the hope or intention is exactly the opposite. Tasso fixes the turning point of his entire epic in a moment of the highlighted present defined exactly in the terms that de Man believes must undo representation. The "eternal Father" announces the precise moment (echoing Virgil's Messianic Eclogue): "To this point let it be that our beloved host has endured its harsh and perilous adversities. . . . Now let a new order of things begin" (13.73). Tasso assigns specific poetic correlatives or causes to this point of opening up a present or turning toward a new beginning. This point is reached, in fact, between two awakenings from two "songes" (dreams), the first of Clorinda speaking to Tancred, the second of Hugh speaking to Godfrey. After the first dream we hear (in the contemporary Lebrun translation of the *Gerusalemme*), "Tancrède se réveille, la sérénité dans l'âme" (12.94); after the second, "Godefroi se réveille, l'âme remplie d'étonnement et de joie" (14.19).[16] What makes the force of awakening unforgettable in Tasso's poetry is that it is represented by states of extreme melancholy or even melancholic hysteria in which the poet himself seems to be turned out of and then returned to his own writing. In such moments we glimpse the line of representation that Goethe continues to generate from this force of melancholy, the line that reaches to Baudelaire's "pöete . . . maladif."

One of the most gripping of such moments in the *Gerusalemme* is in book 13, stanza 44, where the poet constructs a simile that represents Tancred in the state of believing that he has killed Clorinda for the second time. (In the next chapter I will turn to Freud's representation of this moment.) Here, again in the Lebrun translation, is Tasso's description of this dreamlike waking state:

> Le malade qui voit en songe des dragons ou des chimères que la flamme environne, les craint sans les croire; et quoiqu'à demi convaincu de l'erreur de ses sens, il fait pour les fuir d'inutiles efforts, tant l'aspect de ces monstres imaginaires lui imprime de terreur et d'effroi: ainsi . . .

> [As sometimes the sick man who encounters in a dream dragon[s] or tall chimaera girt with flame, although he suspects or partly knows that the simulacrum is no true shape, yet wants to flee, such terror the horrid and dreadful appearance implants in him; even so . . .][17]

The aesthetic effect of this passage is a revolving of states of consciousness. By comparing and even juxtaposing the nightmare of his romance hero, who moves in a fictional world in which dragons are everyday occurrences, with the dream of a man in a nonfictional world in which dragons are only phantasmagoric occurrences of nightmare, Tasso does more than momentarily exit the fictionality of his poem. Rather, the force of the simile is to destabilize our sense of the framing nonfictional world in which the poet and the reader are located. The structure of the dream simile opens a revolving door between Tancred's and the poet's worlds, creating (in a line of representations that stretches back through the dream similes that Virgil applies to Turnus and Homer to Hektor) a sublime alternation of awakening and dying-away (or suffocation).[18] In their versions of Tasso's simile, Goethe, Delacroix (in his more understated way), and Baudelaire specifically affix this "terror" of the guilt-ridden dreamer to Tasso, while also extending the line of his sublime melancholia.

In his sonnet the accuracy of Baudelaire's representation of Delacroix's representation of an awakened present is carefully sustained in his observation of another, equally significant aspect of the *roulant* of learning. This is its impact on individual awakened consciousness. I will yet turn to and conclude this chapter with an account of Baudelaire's representation of the impact of the *roulant* on Delacroix, but first I will point to earlier, distinct moments of that impact registered in Delacroix's line of inherited language.

In the previous chapter I explored the intertextual countermovements that Goethe enters in the relationship between his own chiastic representations of consciousness and his models of such chiastic consciousness in Tasso, as, say, between Tasso's distich

> Va fuor di sé; presente aver gli è aviso
> l'offesa donna sua che plori e gema
> (13.45,5−6)

and Goethe's

> Nein, es ist alles da, und ich bin nichts;
> Ich bin mir selbst entwandt, sie ist es mir!
> (ll. 3417−18)

I pointed out that the binary halves of the two distichs correspond closely, but that Tasso's fourth binary, "che plori e gema," does not find its symmetrical correspondent in Goethe's fourth binary, "und ich bin nichts." The "Nichts" is the term with which Goethe recurrently designates Tasso's power of negativity. In this element of the above chiasmus Goethe's representation of consciousness turns counter to Tasso's—even and especially in the act of representing the double countermovements of "Tasso's" mind through which he, Goethe, is also thinking but which is partly inaccessible to him. In Goethe's chiasmus the representation of a sensory truth consists, as we have seen, in a play of intensely felt sensory presence and its equally felt absence (the "nichts"). In the distich from *Gerusalemme liberata* Tasso's play of absence against presence—indexed in the phrase "plori e gema"—is the diametrical opposite or counterworld of Goethe's in that Goethe's representation dispenses with superhuman mediation of the human experience of negativity. Yet even within Goethe's experience of negativity his verses are configured with Tasso's Judaeo-Christian framing of negativity and with Tasso's own interactions with framings of negativity earlier along his line of language. Thus Tasso's chiasmus depends upon the fact that Tancred's vision of his lady "gema" (lamenting), echoed in "gemiti" (laments) two lines later, articulates with the Old Testament book of the Lamentations of Jeremiah and invokes the typological and antitypological meaning which his "l'offesa donna" carries in the sublime line of Old and New Testament representations. The antitypological other world opened up here, we noted, is the heaviest burden of Tasso's negativity in the *Gerusalemme liberata*.

Especially in this concentrated form, spatialized description of an intertextuality that is a continuity of countermovements rotating on negativity can seem to be a jargon that has no relevance either to art or to experience. Yet this description is only a tracing of the countermovements within individual representations of sublime experience which are located within a given line of such representations. The point of negativity on which these countermovements turn is experienced by individual consciousness as an inaccessible dying-away within representation. This is also the point or moment at which the individual experiences the joining of his or her unrecuperated consciousness (an unclosed circle) with a line of learning (spiraling, back-and-forth). Granted that there is an element of blur in this complexity of motion. Nevertheless, I believe that we are here very much in the neighborhood of the individual's waking-dreaming experience of a sublime representation of the present. In the sonnet of the individual Baudelaire, I am now proposing, he and we experience a colloquium in which Tasso, Goethe, Delacroix, and Baudelaire participate. This colloquium takes on dimensions of a *Weltliteratur* of Western learning. Baudelaire's representations of a line of learning highlight the way in which, in the West, awakening or modernity is experienced as a counterrepresentation within a given line of the commonplace representation. The ecstatic or doubled simultaneity of awakening and dreaming (which, for example, Goethe's Tasso tells Leonora is definitive of his experience of the present) is always present in the Western sublime of learning and modernity.

In a moment I will turn to a continuation in Baudelaire of the kind of literary countermovements that we find in Goethe vis-à-vis Tasso and his line of language. First, however, I would like to offer a comment, in this vein, directly about Delacroix. The specifically painterly element of Delacroix's *roulant* of learning—that is, in his tradition of painting and its "language of dreams"—is no doubt itself of vast dimensions. To suggest, within very strict limits, just one feature of Delacroix's response to his painterly past in the representation of the foot rolling a manuscript, I adduce one of Delacroix's sketches for the *Le Tasse dans la maison des fous* that survives only in a reproduction of poor quality in the Robaut catalogue, *Eugène Delacroix: Peintures Dessins Gravures Lithographes* (1885). This is sketch "No 185: Le Tasse en Prison" (fig. 8).[19] Fortunately, the aspect of

FIGURE 8. Eugène Delacroix, sketch "No 185: Le Tasse en Prison,"
from *L'Oeuvre Complet de Eugène Delacroix: Peintures Dessins Gravures Lithographes Catalogué
et Reproduit par Alfred Robaut*, commenté par Ernest Chesneau, ouvrage publié avec la collaboration
de Fernand Calmettes (Paris: Charavay, 1885), p. 54.

the sketch to which I want to draw attention is unmistakable even in the form
we have it.

The representation of the melancholic with a missing right foot is extremely rare in European painting. Considering that, in his painting, Delacroix
was to represent Tasso's unseen (strangely draped-over rather than clothed)
right foot doing the unusual work of "roulant un manuscrit," the fact that in the
sketch Tasso's right foot is missing is of particular interest. From the sketch it is

clear that Delacroix was experimenting with the iconography of melancholia. The leaning of the figure to the left and the presence of the urn are explicit signs of this intent.[20] If we take into account that Delacroix was also thinking about Tasso's preoccupation with the writing of the *Gerusalemme* and that (as Delacroix's journals abundantly indicate) his knowledge of Rembrandt's paintings was detailed and extensive, it seems clear that the striking resemblance between his Tasso *en prison* (agonizing over the *Gerusalemme*, which he is even in danger of destroying by wild revisions) and Rembrandt's Jeremiah *en prison* (lamenting the destruction of Jerusalem), each beside a window of violence at the left, is not accidental, least of all in the special attention which Delacroix gives to a missing or unseen right foot (see figs. 7 and 8; cf. fig. 5). In fact, Delacroix's placement of the window, the daybed, the abundance of writings, and the raised foot (as well as the depth of complication of an awakening) may suggest that Delacroix was also aware of Rembrandt's *Saint Paul in Prison* (see fig. 1).

I will not repeat here my comments (in chapter 2) on the way in which in Rembrandt's *Jeremiah* the space of separation that coincides with Jeremiah's missing right foot and arm is a representation of negativity. Neither is there any need to insist here, even in the light of Delacroix's interest in the representation of learning or the enfolding of manuscript within painting, that he was aware of the way, for Rembrandt, this empty space of the missing right is the midpoint of the endless back-and-forth movements which are the scriptural and historical line of his chiastic language of representation. Instead, what I would like to emphasize, concretely, are only the potentialities of a countermovement between Delacroix's composition and Rembrandt's.

Jeremiah's right—hand and foot—like Jerusalem "forgotten," is wholly withdrawn in Rembrandt's painting. Tasso's right foot, albeit covered or veiled, is rolling his *Gerusalemme*, while his right hand, however, is almost, we can say, in evidence. As noted earlier, Tasso's right hand seems to hold or at least to ready itself for holding an instrument of some kind against the head of the daybed, as if against sheets of paper or against an easel. This is apparently the instrument with which Tasso has produced the rejected papers strewn around him. The point at which this perplexed writing takes place coincides exactly with the point at which, in Rembrandt's *Jeremiah*, the Bible is located. Jeremiah's left arm rests on this Bible, while Tasso's left arm, only slightly higher, rests on the head of the daybed or the place of writing. The Bible in Rembrandt's painting and the head of the daybed in Delacroix's are each representations of a myth of empowerment. We can debate exactly what these myths should be called, but what is important here is not only that they are counter to each other, but that each also represents the continuity of a line of representations. In both Rembrandt's and

Delacroix's representations, an element of self-deprivation is crucial. (Strikingly, the bound-book exemplar of the Bible and the mechanism-controlled head of the daybed are sharply anachronistic in their setting.) In the case of Rembrandt's painting we have seen that his confrontation of the problematics of representation is represented in an extensive chiastic structuring of representation. The same could be shown for Delacroix's painting, as, say, in (A) the scene of madness at the top left, (B) the rolling manuscript at the bottom left, the (B) place of writing at the top right, and (A) the raised foot climbing to nowhere or madness at the bottom right. This could suggest the further possibility of cross-chiastic relations such as we have seen between Goethe's distichs and Tasso's. The point of encounter or rotation between these sets of double countermovements is the framed negativity of each, which is only thematized either as the Bible (and its representations of the divine) or the artist's tablet of creation. The potentiality for encounter of this kind is related to the phenomenon of the *roulant* (of the line of representation that represents the problematics of representation), which Delacroix has represented and to which Baudelaire calls attention. As in the case of Goethe's countermovements vis-à-vis Tasso's countermovements, Delacroix's countermovements vis-à-vis Rembrandt's countermovements suggest a counterrelation of romantic and Christian humanisms such as I earlier instanced in the counterperiodizations of the cultural sublime.

A contemporaneous and more directly accessible juxtaposition of countermovements is to be seen between Baudelaire's sonnet and Delacroix's painting. A *roulant* motion, back-and-forth, is unmistakable in this juxtaposition. With or without Baudelaire's title we know that his representation of his experience of his present moment of consciousness is "Sur *Le Tasse en prison* d'Eugène Delacroix." The same holds for Delacroix's representation that is *sur* an evocation of Tasso, whether from Tasso's representations of Tasso-like consciousness in the *Gerusalemme* or from intermediate representations of Tassovian representational consciousness in a representation like Goethe's *Torquato Tasso*. Baudelaire plummets in his sonnet into the vertigo of an experience of the present that constitutes itself from a successive movement that involves not only two but endless distinct moments. All the adjectives and adverbs that Baudelaire applies to "Le pöete" are transferred to this experience of a present, or a modernity of learning, that Baudelaire experiences not only with Delacroix "un homme vraiment savant et profond dans son art" but in the learning that Delacroix represents "dans son art," which is to say, the art and learning of Tasso or Goethe or both, and so forth. All of these terms, in other words, are applied to the contempt and suffering of learning of this all-encompassing kind: imprisonment in a cell, ailing, feverishness, terror, vertigo, drowning, strangeness, absurdity, doubt, fear, ridicule, spectres, horror, and suffocation; in addition, of course, to awakening ("réveille") against which all the other terms, "voilà," are balanced, as if by a trick of magic. This is what the "génie" produces. He is the genius, progenitor, and jinni who is not least the title's "Eugène" upon whose work, *sur* or *roulant*, Baudelaire produces his manuscript.

Baudelaire observes that the one movement that is actually shown in motion in the painting, in a blur, is a successive movement back and forth. The painting's circle of magic is here. In the sonnet the idea of a circle of magic is also made explicit. Baudelaire's four-stanza (or Tassovian) sonnet is organized, back-and-forth (AB : BA), around four words for turning movement: "roulant," "circule," "tourbillonne," and "réveille." These words and their effects are arranged in double countermovements, such as, we have seen, are directly associated with the language of Tasso and Goethe alike. It is worth summoning here the passage from the French translation of Goethe's *Torquato Tasso* which names and enacts this magic circle. In the last chapter I analyzed this passage (in Goethe's German) for the chiastic effect that immediately produces Tasso's "Zauberkreise" (l. 167) or "cercle magique." Here is the German verse, then the French prose of 1827 which faithfully reproduces Goethe's redoubled countermovements:

[A]	[B]
Oft adelt er,	was uns gemein erschien,
[B]	[A]
Und das Geschätzte wird	vor ihm zu nichts.
[A]	
In diesem eignen Zauberkreise wandelt	
Der wunderbare Mann	[B]
	und zieht uns an,
[B]	[A]
Mit ihm zu wandeln,	teil an ihm zu nehmen:
[A]	[B]
Er scheint sich uns zu nahn,	und bleibt uns fern;
[B]	
Er scheint uns anzusehn,	[A]
	und Geister mögen
An unsrer Stelle seltsam ihm erscheinen.	

(ll. 165–72)

[A]	[B]
Souvent il ennoblit	ce qui nous semblait commun,
[B]	[A]
et ce qu'on estime	n'est rien à ses yeux.
[A]	
Cet homme merveilleux marche	
dans son cercle magique	

[B]
et nous force
[A]
à nous identifier à lui:

[B]
à l'y suivre,
[A]
il paraît nous approcher,
[B]
il paraît nous regarder,

[B]
et il demeure loin de nous;

[A]
et peut-être à notre place

lui apparaissent de bizarres esprits.[21]

The intense power of the first chiasmus (which even specifies the role of a negativity or "nichts," "rien") is a schematized demonstration of the magic that is described as typifying the work of Tasso's genius. Yet, as the next two chiasmata make clear, there is a cost to this magic that is not recuperated. In the use of language or representation we experience (as Hegel would say) a dying-away in language. In sublime encounters this experience is powerfully intensified. In the sublime or in sublimation we experience one kind of return from this dying-away. This is a return, or awakening, to the present. Yet (contra Hegel) Tasso, Goethe, Delacroix, and Baudelaire know that these double countermovements do not add up to the experience of a present that is whole.

In this language and experience of dreams, of which our consciousnesses are made, we always remain to some extent bizarre, strange, ghostly to each other and to ourselves as well. As Goethe's Tasso puts it to himself—and as Delacroix paints it—"T'éveilles-tu d'un songe . . . ? Oui, tu veilles à la fois et tu rêves" (Have you woken from a dream . . . ? Yes, you are awake and at the same time you are dreaming). The feeling of the awakened present, awakened from dream, is itself dreamlike, even if it is in a different pitch of dream. The extraordinary impression of an achieved present retains, at least, the wonderment of dream. The poet Baudelaire realizes that the expression or "regard" of "the poet" is itself achieved as a double countermovement in Delacroix's painting. As far as the spectator is concerned, there will inevitably be an element of arbitrariness in supplying names for the binaries that move antithetically in this double countermovement. What is certain, however, is that the spectator traces the countermovement among these binaries first in one direction, then in the other. The spectator sees, for example, an awakening from (or of) dreams; then a dreaming of awakening. Or the spectator sees, first, a present experience of doubt, perhaps a Cartesian cogito affirming the "Réel" of the poet's ego, after radical "Doute"; then a doubting or even loss of any presentness or any "Réel." However we name it, this is a *roulant* motion *sur* the *Réel* which brings about both an awakening—a modernity—and an unrecuperated dying-away within a sublime of learning. This kind of struggle to hold on to the present of representation is different from what is generally meant, at least, by art-for-art's-sake. For Baudelaire and Delacroix, the representation of the present is thrown back upon and produced from past suffering and the pain of experiencing the historical continuum within representation.

To return to Baudelaire's countermovements: In the first stanza of Baudelaire's sonnet Tasso is seen actively *"roulant [A] un manuscrit sous son pied convulsif."* This scene of *sur* is seen by Delacroix *sur,* together with Baudelaire *sur.* But in the second stanza the "roulant" motion is alienated from and antithetical to the Tasso who has set it in motion. Besides the social oppression that Tasso experiences, the victimization of the poet in this scene is a victimization within language, which (given the premises of recognizability that define language) is always inherited language. For the poet this oppressive experience of his language, the language of his own dreams, is "Hideuse et multiforme, autour de lui *circule [B]*." In the third stanza the schematization and spatial representation of the experience of a countermovement are rendered in the recurrence [B] of alienation or antithesis, that is, in the motion of *"tourbillonne"* spectres swarming around Tasso. The fourth stanza represents the term toward which the entire sonnet moves. In the *"réveille" [A],* "le pöete" achieves the reawakening into dream that Baudelaire represents upon encountering it in Delacroix's painting of awakening in dream, in Goethe's soliloquy assigned to Tasso, specifying the awakening in dream, and in Tasso's key realization in the *Gerusalemme,* which is itself a rolling forward and backward, of an effectively endless line of representations of dream-awakening. Thus the "réveille" is an awakening or present experienced in the encounter with a succession of distinct representations, each of which is distinct because of its represented sublime experience of dying-away and awakening.

Whatever these stanzas' themes may suggest separately, it is clear that the double countermovements of the four stanzas, read together, form a circular pattern. Despite their apparently closed, recuperative circularity, Baudelaire experiences here, with or *as* the "génie" and with Eugène, not only an exit from repetition, in a "réveille" or awakening to the present, but also and at the same time a kind of death or dying-away or being "étouffe" (suffocated). Here the final element of Baudelaire's *sur* condition, which is also mentioned in the title, is brought into play: "Delacroix." The subject of this poem of four Tassovian stanzas is represented dying "entre . . . quatre murs." Baudelaire's crosswise, *en croix,* construction of his four stanzas suggests that an important part of the identity of "the poet" is *De la croix* himself.[22] (Baudelaire may have found license for his wordplay on *De la croix* in the torque or twisting noted earlier, that Delacroix applied to his representation of Torquato Tasso.) Delacroix's painting represents only two walls. Baudelaire has supplied the other two walls that complete his representation of what he takes Delacroix's representation to be. To this extent openly resisting the visible (as opposed to the dreamed) language of Delacroix's representation, Baudelaire pictures a scene of victimization and resistance that is counter to as well as in fulfillment of Delacroix's.

Baudelaire's suggestion of a crucifixion (punctuated even by a sort of stigmata of suffering in the four words of turning, "roulant," "circule," "tourbillonne," "réveille") is accompanied by a parallel suggestion of resurrection, rebirth, or awakening. Yet any suggestion of religious transcendence is explicable here purely in terms of sublime experience. Near the end of the "Salon of 1859," after saying that "everything that is not sublime is useless or culpable," Baudelaire remarks, "Nothing is more wearisome than having to explain what everyone ought to know." In his sonnet Baudelaire knows and represents but does not explain only "what everyone ought to know" about Delacroix's sublime representation of Tasso and his rolling manuscript. For Delacroix and Baudelaire the rolling manuscript is no more simply Tasso's *Gerusalemme liberata* than the poet figured in the painting or "Le pöete" in the sonnet is only Torquato Tasso. Each is a topos, which is to say, a representation of an endless line of commonplaces. Baudelaire and Delacroix both know that "commonplaces" are "the vastest and profoundest things" (see the epigraphs to this chapter). Delacroix's and Baudelaire's representations are of the learned experience of these lines of commonplaces, most especially of the *manuscrit roulant* in extension. For painter and poet the goal is the representation, in the present, of the successive movement which is inherent in the experience of commonplaces, rather than the representation—as if there could be such a thing—of a single occurrence of a commonplace. For this successive movement and its temporal complication, as well as for awakening to them, a crucial, freely chosen ingredient is the learning of a sublime line of language. Or, conversely, learning of the present, of modernity—in the moment of dying-away and freedom—is only a sublime representation of a succession of distinct moments.

Baudelaire's artistic sublime of learning therefore illuminates the method not only of Western art but of Western learning as well. It is worth recalling here Erwin Panofsky's and Erich Auerbach's suggestion that "an accurate type of spiritual history [*Geistesgeschichte*]" or new scholarly "synthesis" of *Weltliteratur* might emerge from tracing, over centuries, interpretations of "a concrete point of departure" that is "found to coerce the general theme." In order to achieve this new synthesis the concrete point of departure for the study of Western tradition "should not be a generality imposed on a theme from the outside, but ought rather to be an organic inner part of the theme itself." Each should possess both "concreteness" and what Auerbach calls a "potential for centrifugal radiation."[23] The realization of this kind of scholarly goal in the *roulant* constellation that we have been examining may indicate that Panofsky's and Auerbach's suggestion is already implicit, as an idea of learning, within that *Weltliteratur*. To be sure, the representation of this idea also suggests that when learning comes closest to achieving the concrete representational awakenings of art (and is therefore, hopefully, least wearisome in its explanations) the experience of learning, or scholarship, is charged with both awakening and dying-away of the kind that Baudelaire stipulates.

To return to Delacroix's and Baudelaire's learning, and to conclude: The experience of modernity—or awakening—that concerns Delacroix and Baudelaire is of a given sublime line of learning. In this experience the individual artist or spectator is not only beside himself or herself—painfully so—within the experience of the spiraling and counterspiraling line, but he or she also proceeds to experience free, moral identification with a similar victim in a recurring scene of suffering and resistance. Quite aside from its ramifications for other kinds of victimization and resistance, this is first of all a scene of suffering and resistance within representation itself. Delacroix and Baudelaire show that a sublime amelioration of that scene of representation is possible. And, as we have seen, their term for sublime learning even brings news—always as if for the first time—about the latest stage of sublime experience. For them, even the latest stage of an individual's experience of the sublime takes place within the line of a sublime (or partially withdrawn) language. That which Kant calls the sublime "discharge all the more powerful" only discharges, in freedom, the successive movement, backward and forward, of the endless line of sublime representations.[24] Even moral identification with someone else's suffering is a free choice that, in this view, occurs within the line of sublime language.

Limping: Freud's Experience of Death in His Tassovian Line of Thought

CHAPTER 10

Was man nicht erfliegen kann, muss man erhinken.
. . . .
Die Schrift sagt, es ist keine Sünde zu hinken.
[What we cannot reach flying we must reach limping.
. . . .
The Book tells us it is no sin to limp.]
—Freud quoting from Friedrich Rückert's
version of Al-Hariri

I am aware that the term which may seem least credible in my account of the Western theory of a cultural sublime is a dying-away which is not recuperated—made part of life experience—by individual consciousness. It is therefore of special interest to me that the concept which has caused most incredulity in Freud's lexicon of human experience is that of a "death instinct" which, he insists, is unrecuperable by life instincts. This is a term, furthermore, which in *Beyond the Pleasure Principle* becomes available to Freud in his anciently derived "line of thought" (Gedankengang).[1] In *Beyond the Pleasure Principle,* I will propose, the utterly commonplace term "Gedankengang" is shaped into a meaning of repeatability by the hypotheses which Freud is following out in his line of thought. These are the hypotheses of the compulsion to repeat and the hypothesis on which, he says, the compulsion to repeat has put him on the "track," that of death instinct(s) (*SE* 18:56). I will propose that especially in his hypothesis of a death instinct Freud's line of thought rediscovers the cultural sublime for the modernity which he himself, to a considerable extent, created. Within this rediscovery, he highlights a freedom of hypothesis that is closely associated with the spirit of the modern. Yet Freud's derivation of freedom from the self's experience of death may appear to be the very antithesis of the modern spirit. Thus even one of the greatest of Freud's inheritors, Jean Laplanche, speaks incredulously of the "strange chiasmus" of Freud's unrecuperated death instincts. What Laplanche regards as strange (by which he means unintelligible) is not Freud's account of a chiasmus or countermovement in the self between life instincts and death instincts. Rather, the strangeness comes in, for Laplanche, in Freud's insistence that the chiasmus remains "dualistic" (*SE* 18:53) or made of distinct, unresolved elements, so that the experience of a death instinct is not recuperated by the experience of a life instinct.[2]

I will try to show that Freud's relation to his line of thought of a death instinct, or his experience of a dying-away, is indeed constituted by unrecuperated experience of a chiasmus or, more accurately, of a line of unrecuperated chiasmata. Freud's relation to this line is itself formed into a series of unrecuperated chiasmata. He repeatedly finds [A] freedom for a hypothesis of [B] dying-away by [B] dying-away in [A] an inherited line of free hypothesis (of dying-away). Thus although Freud consciously throws himself, as he puts it, into this line of hypothesis, the consciousness of his experience of dying-away remains beyond or beside Freud, who is—as he insists against all the doubters—dualistically split, beside himself. Freud's "dualistic" picture of a self (his own) that is distinctly alongside the self clarifies the experience of sublimation in the Western experience of tradition. I will describe the principal elements of Freud's dualistic picture of this cultural sublime, saving for last that which makes it possible for Freud to begin to draw his picture in the first place.

I begin where Freud concludes:

Both the fascination and the difficulty of *Beyond the Pleasure Principle* are in what Freud calls, at the very end, its "limping." I believe that what Freud means by limping is closely related, if not identical, to his experience of the death instinct. "Limping" is his experience of his line of thought. This experience and thought are of the line of unrecuperated countermovement of the death-instinct hypothesis. It is worth contemplating, as directly as possible, the heavy hints that Freud gives us about limping. Using the verses of "the poet" that he cites as the conclusion of his book, Freud says that limping characterizes the spirit of his hypothesizing. Yet for reasons that are intrinsic to his hypothesizing, what he does not acknowledge is that limping is also the substance of his hypothesis.

The final paragraph of the book begins, "Here might be the starting-point for fresh investigations." A "striking fact," he says, that these fresh investigations should try to explain is that "the life instincts have so much more contact with our internal perception . . . while the death instincts seem to do their work unobtrusively." "At present," he adds, he does not know how this unobtrusive "work" works. The paragraph ends as follows:

> We must be patient and await fresh methods and occasions of research. We must be ready, too, to abandon a path that we have followed for a time, if it seems to be lead-

ing to no good end. Only believers, who demand that science shall be a substitute for the catechism they have given up, will blame an investigator for developing or even transforming his views. We may take comfort, too, for the slow advances of our scientific knowledge in the words of the poet:

Was man nicht erfliegen kann, muss man erhinken.

· ·

Die Schrift sagt, es ist keine Sünde zu hinken.

[What we cannot reach flying we must reach limping.

· ·

The Book tells us it is no sin to limp.]

Freud's choice of concluding his book with these verses from Rückert's famed version of Al-Hariri's third Makamat (second in Rückert) was certainly not a piece of showing off with esoteric knowledge.[3] In the meaning of these verses Freud found not only a mirror of the whole of his present effort, but also a luminous point along his line of thought. *Beyond the Pleasure Principle* moves forward on a hypothesis of two feet—of two principles or instincts—one of which is lamely about a kind of lameness. In fact, this is a book that limps deliberately in a deliberation on what limping is.

In a secondary or tertiary sense "the poet" mentioned by Freud is Rückert or Al-Hariri. But the limping attempted by Freud is a rigorous analogue or repetition of the limping of Al-Hariri's and Rückert's poet-protagonist, Abu Seid. There is a many-layered and integral aptness in Freud's invocation of the Abu Seid in the Makamat from which Freud quotes. Within this story, which Rückert titles "Die beiden Gulden" (The two gold coins), Abu Seid has feigned limping in order to stage a rhetorical tour de force which is entirely built on a principle of limping. Abu Seid says that his existence is split, double, and alternating. He is "bald frisch, bald lahm" (p. 17) (one moment vigorous, the next moment lame).[4] His symmetrical poems, declaimed within the story, somewhat grotesquely form the two legs of a single persona, limping: the first, or "frisch," poem is an encomium of the life-giving power of a gold coin; the second, or "lahm," poem is a lament on the death-entangling power of a second, identical gold coin. Abu Seid assigns a specific meaning to his "lahm" phase. This meaning is a version of Freud's hypothesis of the death instinct:

—Der Tod bleibt unsere Zuflucht vor Bedrängniss;
—wir klagen an das säumende Verhängniss. (p. 15)

[—Death remains (waits as) our shelter from torment;
—we wail for the undoing that comes too slowly.]

By the time he leaves his auditors, declaiming as he goes the verses which Freud quotes, Abu Seid has waned into a "lahm" or dark phase. That is, when his interlocutor Hareth Ben Hammam says to him,

du solltest dich schämen,—Zuflucht zu einem Gebrechen zu nehmen (p. 17)
[you should be ashamed of yourself for taking shelter in an affliction]

the effect on Abu Seid is this:

Da verfinsterten sich seine Mienen,—und er sprach . . . (p. 17)
[Then his expression darkened over,—and he spoke . . .]

What he speaks in this dark, lame, or sheltered phase are the verses about limping, in other words, his language of finding "shelter" in a speaking which encompasses "death." Abu Seid's artificial taking on of his "Gebrechen" (affliction)—
his limping—has issued in what Freud calls "a piece of real experience"—in
this case of limping. In Freud's citation of "the poet's" *lahm* words and in much
else in *Beyond the Pleasure Principle* his own limping is of this kind.

Freud was greatly interested in what he called the concept of "artificial illness" (artefizielle Krankheit [*GW* 10:135]) as a way of understanding the transference as "a piece of real experience." In "Remembering, Repeating, and
Working-Through" he writes, "The transference . . . creates an intermediate
region between illness and real life through which the transition from the one to
the other is made. The new condition has taken over all the features of the illness; but it represents an artificial illness which is at every point accessible to our
intervention. It is a piece of real experience, but one which has been made possible by especially favorable conditions, and it is of a provisional nature" (*SE*
12:154). I will mention now the principal exemplum of artificial illness to which
I will be turning in this chapter. At an early and pivotal point in *Beyond the Pleasure Principle* Freud relates to a particular artistic representation of an artificial
illness. He invokes it as the chief instance in a series of "observations . . . based
upon behavior in the transference." This is his citing of Tasso's picture of Tancred's neurotic repetition compulsion in (his delusion of) mortally wounding
Clorinda a second time (*SE* 18:22). Freud makes no distinction of status between this artistic observation of an artificial illness and the clinical observations that he cites.

My supposition is that the line of artificial illness and hypothesizing of the
death instinct that guides Freud is the arena of his own "behavior in the transference." Freud's closing identification of *Beyond the Pleasure Principle* with the artificial limping of Abu Seid recollects not only a final piece of real experience in
his line of artificial illness of transference, but the awakening of a memory of a
"fragment" of historical experience. As he will say in "Constructions in Analysis" in 1938, for his culture-oriented "line of thought" (unfolded mainly in his
last two decades) a "fragment of historical truth" can be revived in cultural
memory from the artificial illnesses or "delusions" which are an individual's

"method in madness" (*SE* 23:267). Abu Seid closes the Makamat with a blurring of the distinction between feigned limping and real limping. Freud fully accepts the reality of this artificial illness, so that no trace of a distinction between artificial (or feigned) and real is left in the verses that Freud excerpts. In fact, Freud's way of omitting the intermediate verses between the two that he cites is a further blurring, or limping, of the same kind. As a result, for both Abu Seid and Freud the artificial illness not only has become a piece of real experience but also has revived the same fragment of historical truth and even its effect in creating the individual's fragmentary experience of the transference. In Freud's and Abu Seid's line of thought this fragment of historical truth is the experience of a death instinct, a primordial wailing for the undoing that comes too slowly but comes surely. The effect of this undoing (or momentary check of vital force) in Freud's consciousness is even directly felt in Freud's blurring. Thus, confronted with the question, Why should Freud speak of an actual limping of "the poet" when the point of the story is that it is only a feigned limping? we might think we can reply that this is the effect of mere forgetfulness or sloppiness. Yet some definite thing is signaled by this blurring. We shall see that a highly similar blurring occurs in Freud's presentation of the Tassovian exemplum of the repetition compulsion which, he says, first put him on the track of the death instinct. In an observer of Freud's acuity and care, two such similar occurrences of mere forgetfulness or sloppiness at two climactic moments in the same brief book are difficult to credit.

The particular point that I want to explore in *Beyond the Pleasure Principle* is that at least in Freud's case the experience of limping and the awakening of this fragment of historical truth of the "lahm," as well as its effect, does not depend merely on a single, present moment of transference that Freud seems to represent in isolation. Rather, the transference is a function of the line of thought itself, all of limping, that Freud encounters. The history of Freud's concept of transference has recently been called "the last great mystery" in his oeuvre.[5] In *Beyond the Pleasure Principle* an explanation of the relation of Freud's line of thought to the workings of the transference may shed light on this historical mystery and, more important, may illuminate the temporal, cultural, and sublimatory dimension of Freud's concept of transference.[6]

My procedure will now be, first, to set out briefly Freud's account of his major exemplum of the repetition compulsion, the observation "based upon behavior in the transference" that he repeats from Tasso's picture of Tancred's neurotic repetition compulsion. I will then gather a series of passages from the length of *Beyond the Pleasure Principle* to hear Freud's language of a *lahm* consciousness, or other footfall, before suggesting, finally, where Freud finds his energy for limping and how that limping relates to his error in recording his Tasso exemplum.

Speaking of "a repetition of the same fatality," Freud writes,

> The most moving poetic picture of a fate such as this is given by Tasso in his romantic epic *Gerusalemme Liberata*. Its hero, Tancred, unwittingly kills his beloved Clorinda in a duel while she is disguised in the armour of an enemy knight. After her burial he makes his way into a strange magic forest which strikes the Crusaders' army with terror. He slashes with his sword at a tall tree; but blood streams from the cut and the voice of Clorinda, whose soul is imprisoned in the tree, is heard complaining that he has wounded his beloved once again.
>
> If we take into account observations such as these . . . we shall find courage to assume that there really does exist in the mind a compulsion to repeat which overrides the pleasure principle.
>
> (*SE* 18:22)

The blurring to which I refer is that—contrary to what Freud says or implies—the hero suffers only a delusion of a "repetition of the same fatality." It has somehow slipped Freud's mind that Tancred has certainly not wounded Clorinda once again. Freud at this moment recalls only the false voice of the libidinous sorcerer, Ismen, who is counterfeiting Clorinda's voice. Freud, of all people, makes no mention of the truth-telling dream in which dead Clorinda appears to Tancred. At that juncture Tasso specifies and hysterical Tancred acknowledges Clorinda's dream speech. In the dream Clorinda *liberata* thanks Tancred for having delivered or liberated her: "You removed me, by your mistake, from those who are living in the mortal world; you made me worthy, by your act of mercy, to rise to God's bosom [*womb*] amid the blessed and immortal ones [in grembo (*womb / bosom / middle*) a Dio fra gl'immortali e divi]" (12.92).[7] By Tancred's "mistake," Clorinda has been removed beyond the libidinal, beyond the life instincts, and placed "in grembo" (in the womb of God). This dream immediately precedes Clorinda's burial, which Freud specifically recalls. Again, we might want to say that Freud has merely forgotten the dream and its contents. Yet even if Freud had somehow not noticed or had not recalled the dream, how could he have also forgotten what Tasso says immediately after the false "voice of Clorinda," in Freud's phrases, "is heard complaining"? Tasso writes, "The intimidated lover not wholly believes the false deceits, and yet concedes and fears. . . . He is beside himself; he thinks he is in the presence of his injured lady who is weeping and lamenting; . . . a false shape and insubstantial plaint deluded him" (13.44–46). With so much at stake for Freud's hypothesis of the death instincts, why should he blur, or err, in this way?—and in the one extended literary exemplum that he has singled out from his vast knowledge of Western literature (and beyond)? What he illustrates and repeats is after all only Tancred's delusion and doubt about delusion in doubting that Clorinda is in God's womb, untouchable by human violence or the pleasure principle. The "fatality," if it may be called such, that Freud repeats is something that takes place only in Tancred's mind. Of course, this fatality is itself an artificial illness that is a piece of real experience for Tancred. And it is this piece of real experience that principally interests Freud. But why does Freud compound Tancred's delusion? Why has Freud apparently eliminated the border between feigned and actual, just as he seems to do with the limping of Abu Seid?

I propose that Freud is driven to repeat Tancred's error by an experience that his writing sets in motion and that extends beyond his control. This apparently strange experience requires that Freud's thought go beyond what he himself can think, into a fatality of his own consciousness. Traces of this experience have certainly been glimpsed before by Freud's readers. Laplanche asks, for example, whether an interpretation of *Beyond the Pleasure Principle* should try to take into account the possibility of "Freud's permanent familiarity with his own death."[8] But Laplanche is representative of Freud's interpreters in not taking this route. My hypothesis is that there is a sufficiency of evidence, even within *Beyond the Pleasure Principle* itself, not only to confirm the phenomenon of Freud's "familiarity with his own death," but also to explain how he derives this familiarity as well as how the immediate experience of death informs his representation of the death instincts.

My aim, now, is to locate Freud's concepts on the ancient and continuous line of thought that he evokes. Freud shows that this is no merely archival exercise in the history of ideas. Instead, it is an act of reproducing the experience of the history of ideas that produces a certain fragmentary experience of consciousness. For Freud, I am proposing, this is the experience of the death of individual consciousness within a particular repetition of language.

Especially when we begin to think about what that repeated language might be, Hegel's recapitulations of the historical experience of a dying-away in language may inevitably come to mind. In Hegel's recurring usage, language is observed in the process of alienating consciousness from itself so that consciousness incurs, Hegel says, a kind of "death." Here is a passage from Hegel's *Phenomenology of Spirit* which Freud could have used as the epigraph for *Beyond the Pleasure Principle:*

> Whatever is confined within the limits of a natural life cannot by its own efforts go
> *beyond* its immediate existence; but it is driven *beyond* it by something else, and *this up-*
> *rooting entails its death.* Consciousness, however, is explicitly the *Notion* of itself. Hence
> it is something that goes *beyond* limits, and since these limits are its own, it is some-

thing that goes *beyond* itself. With the positing of a single particular the *beyond* is also established for consciousness, even if it is only *alongside* the limited object as in the case of spatial intuition.

(*PS*, section 80; all emphases except for *Notion* and *alongside* added)[9]

Both Hegel and Freud describe how the consciousness of an individual may go "beyond" itself. Both say that consciousness is driven by a hidden something to experience its own "death." And both use the term "death" to describe the mind's experience of this beyond. In fact, what I am proposing about Freud involves a certain fairly intimate nexus between Freud's concepts and Hegel's, even between Freud's blurring of the encounter of Tancred and Clorinda and Hegel's mistake (which I described in chapter 3) in his account of a different epic duel. One does not have to be cleverer than Hegel or Freud to discover the ways in which they block out certain features of the scenes they recall. Their blockages are made inevitable by their logic of beyond in that the knowledge of both Hegel and Freud suffers the effect of a dying-away or partial blackout. Yet we shall see that Freud comes closer than Hegel to acknowledging the immediate and irreversible effects of this experience. Within *Beyond the Pleasure Principle* Freud will openly say that reproducing the effects of the death instinct, beyond any experience that can be grasped by his own self-reflection, is the trajectory of his book.

In earlier chapters I have remarked some of the ways in which Hegel recuperates his dialectic of alienation, reversing it to form self-consciousness. Thus, to take yet another example, despite Hegel's warning (at the end of the above paragraph) about the trivial "vanity" of a "barren Ego" that "seeks only to be for itself," he soon after ends his introduction to the *Phenomenology of Spirit* by heralding the "*experience*" of a "*dialectical* movement" that is a "*reversal of consciousness itself*" (these are Hegel's emphases). He says that when this "new pattern of consciousness comes on the scene . . . consciousness will arrive at a point at which it gets rid of its semblance of being burdened with something alien, with what is only for it, and some sort of 'other'" (*PS*, sections 86–89). Freud too knows dialectical reversals and double countermovements, but he entertains no such image of reconciliation and wholeness for any consciousness at any time.

In a parallel vein of contrast between Freud and Hegel, Michael S. Roth has recently pointed out that the "aspect of Hegel's conception of freedom that is incompatible with Freud's account . . . is the idea of 'reconciliation' found in *The Phenomenology of Spirit*. . . . In Freud's conception of the mind, the dialectic remains unresolved; knowing is not resolution. . . . The freedom of the analysand at the end of the transference is . . . the opportunity to act self-consciously on the basis of this knowing." This is useful, especially in a discussion that Roth

titles "Sublimation and the Transference."[10] Yet to understand what this freedom is we need to identify the feature of Freud's experience of freedom that determines that the dialectic remains unresolved. I am proposing that for Freud
this feature is itself a freely chosen, active experience which is only enabled by
his given line of such experiences. At least in *Beyond the Pleasure Principle* that
which creates Freud's moment of freedom is the same experience of a line of
culture that Hegel has, but which Hegel denies while Freud faces it more or less
squarely. This is the sublime or sublimatory experience of a repetition of un-
reconciled, partial consciousness in his line of thought. In its turn Freud's
achievement of freedom in the transference creates the possibility of self-transformation and of exploring new hypotheses. Moreover, these possibilities are
inherently linked to the hypothesis and the transformative experience of a dying-away within this given line of thought.

We may enrich our sense of what is at issue in Freud's shaping of modernity
by probing, in a similar way, a point made by Hans Blumenberg. Blumenberg
associates Freud with the marking of the "the beginning of the modern age" as
"a repeatable, or at least imitable, paradigm." In Freud this paradigm emerges,
Blumenberg claims, from the anti-Hegelian influence of Ludwig Feuerbach.
Thus, following Feuerbach, Freud rejects what Blumenberg terms a Hegelian
"consolidation" of consciousness. Blumenberg makes clear that what is "novel
in Freud is the combination of theory and therapy in a simultaneous function-
ing" of what Freud (in *Beyond the Pleasure Principle*) calls engaging in "speculation" or deciding "to throw oneself into a line of thought and to follow it wherever it leads out of simple curiosity." In this way, Blumenberg says, Freud avoids
the repression of libidinal energy "through continuity in the process of sublimation."[11] Yet, once again, we need to locate how the process of sublimation
and the rebirth of simple curiosity are occasioned in Freud's experience. In
Freud's simultaneous therapy (or transference) and theory (or hypothesizing)
the sublime experience and the fresh beginnings of curiosity occur in his encounter of the effectively endless given line of thought of the death-instinct hypothesis. Freud's part in legitimizing the modern age is in this way a reaffirmation of the experience of his "Gedankengang" or line of culture. This line of
culture is defined by double countermovements such as Hegel knows so well, at
least as discrete instances of countermovement. But Freud acknowledges that
because of his experience of his "Gedankengang" the impact of dying-away is
not recuperated for self-consciousness. I will later propose how, in my view,
Freud first experiences this impact in the line of thought of *Beyond the Pleasure
Principle*. No matter how or where, however, Freud initially finds the strength or
energy for first encountering—he speaks of "Mut . . . finden" (finding courage)
(*SE* 18:22; *GW* 13:21)—this line of countermovements, it is this experience

which occasions his freedom and the possibility of his self-transformation. Freud cultivates and extends a large vocabulary of such self-transformation.

To follow Freud's self-transformation, I turn first to his language of "breaking off" (*SE* 18:58; "abzubrechen," *GW* 13:63) in his line of thought. (I point out again that except for the transformative effect of the line of hypotheses which Freud is now describing, this language is not essentially different from that in many other of his writings.)[12] There is more than one such usage—in fact, there is an extended line of them—in *Beyond the Pleasure Principle*. The moment in the text that Freud specifically calls a "breaking off" is clearly a turning point rather than a termination. Yet even so it is not at all evident here what Freud is turning *from* or *to*. Having laid out his hypotheses of the repetition compulsion and the death instinct, Freud announces, "—But here, I think, the moment has come for breaking off" (*SE* 18:58). At this moment he launches his hypothesis concerning the making of hypotheses. This rhetorical errancy would perhaps not be worth a second look were it not for the pressures exerted by the two principal hypotheses that precede it. These are "A compulsion to repeat . . . overrides the pleasure principle" (*SE* 18:22) and "The life process of the individual leads for internal reasons to an abolition of chemical tensions, that is to say, to death" (*SE* 18:55). A glance backward reveals a perplexing situation. After the announcement of the termination of argument, Freud, or rather what Freud calls the train or line of thought that he pursues, makes good on that argument in an entirely new way, explicitly placing the entire argument beyond Freud. This new moment or point on the line further extends, beyond questions of belief (as Freud insists), all the plotted points which project the book's line of thought. Immediately after the words "here, I think, the moment has come for breaking off," a new paragraph begins:

> Not, however, without the addition of a few words of critical reflection. It may be asked whether and how far I am myself convinced of the truth of the hypotheses that have been set out in these pages. My answer would be that I am not convinced myself and that I do not seek to persuade other people to believe in them. Or, more precisely, that I do not know how far I believe in them. There is no reason, as it seems to me, why the emotional factor of conviction should enter into this question at all. It is surely possible to throw oneself into a line of thought and to follow it wherever it leads out of simple scientific curiosity, or, if the reader prefers, as an *advocatus diaboli*, who is not on that account himself sold to the devil. . . . It is impossible to pursue an idea of this kind except by repeatedly combining factual material with what is purely speculative and thus diverging widely from empirical observation. . . . People are seldom impartial where ultimate things, the great problems of science and life, are concerned. Each of us is governed in such cases by deep-rooted internal prejudices, into whose hands our speculation unwittingly plays.
>
> (*SE* 18:59)

Laplanche doubts the sincerity of this "critical reflection." He calls it writing "under cover of an extremely 'liberal' argument: the universal right to pursue a train of thought as far as one wants, the sovereign freedom to philosophize and to dream."[13] Freud's interest here, however, is most of all in the "cover" itself or the operation of "internal prejudices" in his argumentation. He acknowledges that his train of thought is a species of repetition following upon a preprojected line of thought that is not sovereignly driven by his private volition. Laplanche seems to assume that Freud uses the concept of a "train of thought" primarily to convey a personal experience of intellectual spontaneity, inventiveness, or private intuition. Yet Freud emphasizes that the line of thought he pursues does not (at least at first) freely belong to him. In his terms, his speculation is a reflection of prejudgments that have been given to him by others, in internal transactions of unseen "hands" which render his knowledge significantly unwitting. Thus Freud quite openly asserts that his philosophizing or dreaming is not his own. His "breaking off" and his finding a way "to throw oneself into a line of thought" would seem to be pointed toward repetition of a line and its priority.

If the importance I am attaching to Freud's language of breaking off seems far-fetched, we should recall Freud's remark about his own "far-fetched speculation" in following (limpingly) his line of thought: "What follows is speculation, often far-fetched speculation [weitausholende Spekulation (*GW* 13:23)], which the reader will consider or dismiss according to his individual predilection. It is further an attempt to follow out an idea consistently, out of curiosity to see where it will lead" (*SE* 18:24). Of course, this might be taken to support Laplanche's dismissal of Freud's "critical reflection," especially if we do not examine Freud's ambiguously worded claim, right at the beginning of *Beyond the Pleasure Principle,* that no "historically established, philosophical system" has been of use in exploring "the most obscure and inaccessible region of the mind" (*SE* 18:7). Does the above statement mean that Freud's "far-fetched speculation" is a brash assertion of intellectual independence, of sovereign freedom to philosophize? Does Freud's allegation of the uselessness of any "historically established, philosophical system" mean its uselessness with regard to Freud's earlier explorations of the pleasure principle or to his present (not yet named) investigation of the death instinct? Or both? The evidence of Freud's book indicates that the answer should be *neither,* since Freud applies directly to Schopenhauer and to Plato for corroborations of both the pleasure principle and the death instinct. This contradiction, too, between intellectual dependence and independence, itself suggests that there are two distinct minds or voices at work in *Beyond the Pleasure Principle:* one that has no use for the history of philosophy, another that repeatedly acts as the spokesman for that same history; one that strongly asserts its self-presence, another that recedes into the mere echo of other voices, particularly those that voice a dying-away of the self.

This kind of contradiction is at least analogous to the major systemic contradiction which, according to Laplanche, underlies *Beyond the Pleasure Principle.* Freud's "zero principle [the heart of the death-instinct hypothesis] and . . . constancy principle," says Laplanche, "are irreducible to each other. . . . What he needs to affirm, against all biological or psychological plausibility, is the *primacy of zero in relation to constancy.*" In Laplanche's view the question is therefore how to restate the meaning of the zero principle, since (agreeing with Daniel Lagache) he regards the principle itself as "absurd." Laplanche's answer is to change radically the form of Freud's opposition, so that instead of an unbridgeable dualism of death instincts and libidinal instincts we view a "chiasmus" that circulates—and that is resolved, reconciled, recuperated—under the umbrella term "libidinal." Laplanche says, "The death drive is the very soul, the constitutive principle, of libidinal circulation."[14]

Nevertheless, Freud insists that the whole of his effort in *Beyond the Pleasure Principle* is to point to "instincts other than the libidinal ones" (*SE* 18:53) and that the greatest threat to his view is a monism of libido that would blur his absolutely separated dualism of libidinal and death instincts. Two sentences which Freud adds at this juncture (in 1921) are decisive in this regard. They suggest that in Laplanche's effort to save the unity of Freud's views, he has realized Freud's worst fear of what he regarded as the patricidal hostility of "innovators like [Carl] Jung" (*SE* 18:52): "Our views have from the very first been *dualistic,* and to-day they are even more definitely dualistic than before—now that we describe the opposition as being, not between ego-instincts and sexual instincts but between life instincts and death instincts. Jung's libido theory is on the contrary *monistic;* the fact that he has called his one instinctual force 'libido' is bound to cause confusion, but need not affect us otherwise" (*SE* 18:53). Is it possible that one of the effects of *Beyond the Pleasure Principle* is, in Freudian terms, to put Freud's thinking of the beyond (in this book) beyond the reach of Oedipal murder by showing that he has himself already achieved his own death in a thinking that goes on, against all innovators, in the line of thought? If the answer is yes, the book might make all such innovators, whether or not they choose to be such, a species of free inheritors, which is to say, inheritors only of the "prejudice" or "predilection" to keep thought open (along the "Gedankengang") by "the least rigid hypothesis" of the death instinct (*SE* 18:7). Freud would like to breathe a sigh of relief: the monistic innovators, he hopes, "need not affect us otherwise." "Otherwise" would then be his word for the aggression he has worked to escape by showing that a part of him disappears, along the line of thought, into the underground or netherworld. If this is the case, Freud here aims—along the aiming of his line of thought—to undo or pass beyond the Oedipal view of inheritance and tradition that he himself formerly promoted.

In this sense *Beyond the Pleasure Principle* is (to adopt Laplanche's terms) Freud's "counterattack" against "the generalized subversion introduced by sexuality."[15] Yet precisely how does Freud trace the counterattacking line of thought into which he has decided (while in the act of writing this book) "to throw" himself (*SE* 18:59)? We recall that his idea of "curiosity" (*SE* 18:24), "simple scientific curiosity" (*SE* 18:59), turns out to be "governed . . . by deep-rooted internal prejudices, into whose hands our speculation unwittingly plays" (*SE* 18:59). Along this line we must therefore inquire into the hypothesis of *transformation* (*SE* 18:64) that Freud envisions for the formation of his own "prejudices." From what point later or earlier along the line of thought does Freud *fetch* his *speculation?* What meaning does the transformation of the self—in transference—have in such a line of speculation, reflection, repetition? Since my hypothesis is that this line of thought is closely associated with what Freud redefines as the thinking that takes place in the transference, I will glance at some of the other points that plot his line.

In a paragraph that begins, "We may pause for a moment over this pre-eminently dualistic view of instinctual life," Freud lays down the hypothesis of the philosopher Arthur Schopenhauer: "There is something . . . that we cannot remain blind to. We have unwittingly steered our course into the harbour of Schopenhauer's philosophy. For him death is the 'true result and to that extent the purpose of life'" (*SE* 18:49–50). This passage is especially interesting with regard to Freud's relation to Hegel's thought, particularly in view of Freud's assertion, which I quoted in part earlier, that "it is of no concern to us in this connection to enquire how far, with this hypothesis of the pleasure principle [i.e., the present "metapsychological" one of "death instincts"], we have approached or adopted any particular, historically established, philosophical system." Schopenhauer's descriptions of the individual's experience of death, within his or her own life, are concerned with the "turning" of the will through a "free denial of itself" or "resignation," which is the same as a "denial of the will-to-live."[16] Schopenhauer was well known as the open antagonist of Hegel (he had even engaged in a philosophical competition or duel with Hegel at Berlin). In Freud's context it would be natural to think of Schopenhauer's insistence, contra Hegel (the author of the premier "historically established, philosophical system"—a quite precise description, in fact, of the *Phenomenology of Spirit*), on the possibility of a radical, death-dealing abnegation or negation by the self of itself in the "turning" of the self's dialectic. The "something" that Freud realizes he cannot remain blind to, therefore, may turn out to be closely related to Hegel's "something" that, says Hegel, drives the self to its "death." Schopenhauer has insisted on this death-directed something more radically than Hegel—irreconcilably, in fact.

Yet, within the structure of Freud's discourse, what is the significance of these alignments or oppositions for Freud's abandoning himself to a line of thought, that is (in the terms he uses) of overcoming the blindness of one kind of thought while proposing, with open eyes, to close one's eyes fatally, in line with another kind of thought? The hypothesis of the death instinct seems to be formulated in purely biological and chemical terms: "The life process of the individual leads for internal reasons to an abolition of chemical tensions, that is to say, to death" (*SE* 18:55). Yet Freud also uses another kind of language to express his hypothesis. This is the language of language's self-alienations. In this language for his hypothesis Freud says that there is a zero "emotional factor of conviction" which is "governed . . . by deep-rooted internal prejudices, into whose hands our speculation unwittingly plays" (*SE* 18:59). What is the consequence for the conception of the self, along this line of hypothesis, of the word "unwittingly"? What, specifically, is the deathly feature (led by "internal reasons . . . to death") of the "internal prejudices" (or "predilection") which fetches to us from afar our unwitting, perhaps even *unknowing*, speculation? Whose *hands* are these?

The drift of these questions raised by the intersections of Freud's text brings us back to his early term for hysteria, "dual consciousness." Already in 1895 Freud had written, "We think it probable that in every hysteria we are dealing with a rudiment of what is called [in French] 'double conscience', dual consciousness, and that a tendency to such a dissociation and with it the emergence of abnormal states of consciousness, which we propose to call 'hypnoid', is the basic phenomenon of hysteria" (*SE* 3:39). Freud's own experience of hysteria would seem to be an unlikely turn of events in an activity—the writing of *Beyond the Pleasure Principle*—in which the forces operating on Freud are only functions of thinking. These are traumas, at most, of insuperable conceptual contradiction. Yet Freud and Breuer had described just such a form of hysteria which was a "paralysis due to ideas," a "hypnoid state" in which the defenses of the ego are overwhelmed.[17] Laplanche remarks even that *Beyond the Pleasure Principle* was "produced in a kind of second state," but he does not pursue the point.[18] I am suggesting that Freud's voice in *Beyond the Pleasure Principle* is a dual voice speaking from deep agitation. This is the voice in which Freud serves as spokesman for the history of philosophy (which, he has just said, has nothing to say in the present matter), in which he says that he is safely beyond the Oedipal reach of Jung's libido, in which he speaks along the line into which he has thrown himself, and in which his self already exemplifies, I propose, *the zero principle*. On this line of thought Freud sets into limping movement the experience, within his consciousness, of his own death: "bald frisch, bald lahm."

Following out Freud's hypothesis, I am supposing a form of hysteria in the writing of *Beyond the Pleasure Principle*. Freud insists that "our views have from the first been dualistic." I am supposing that this statement entails the dualistic familiarity with death in life. At least in *Beyond the Pleasure Principle* this experience points to something which is beyond all of the self's life, conscious and unconscious. When Freud speaks, in "the moment [which] has now come for breaking off," in a state of zero "emotional factor of conviction," he has thrown himself into the line of thought. This suggests that he sublimely encounters the endless line of thought of his hypothesis of dying-away, thereby producing the sublime effect of dying-away. Within that line he experiences his own hysterical paralysis "due to ideas." He can no longer say what he believes. The ideas in this line of ideas or thought have rendered him unwitting. He is unwitting, moreover, within "the harbour of Schopenhauer's philosophy" of "death," within the turn, in other words, of consciousness's unrecuperable negation— which Hegel, too, experiences but does not acknowledge.

I return to Freud's further plottings of the line of thought, approaching his moment of final breaking off in Abu Seid's limping. Along this line of thought, he says, "an investigator" must not be blamed "for developing or even transforming his views" (*SE* 18:64). "Transforming his views" entails a transference or radical change in the site of his self. Points, egos, along the line drawn out in *Beyond the Pleasure Principle* are by definition in themselves without extension or direction. They participate in extending the line only by being aligned in relations or potentialities of relation with other points along the line. In just this way Freud plots a hypothesis of Plato "the poet-philosopher" (*SE* 18:58) who speaks through Aristophanes. He plots Plato in this way between his plottings of philosopher Schopenhauer and his rehearsal, in a footnote, of Heinrich Gomperz's rehearsal of the poetic mythology of the "*Brihadâranyaka-upanishad* . . . the most ancient of all the Upanishads . . . no competent authority dates it later than about the year 800 B.C." Beyond this the only other (and earlier) point of the line of the death-instinct hypothesis that is explicitly plotted within *Beyond the Pleasure Principle* is the end of this long footnote that in the second edition accompanies the moment of breaking off. I quote from the end of the footnote: "In a paper devoted to a systematic examination of this line of thought before the time of Plato, Ziegler (1913) traces it back to Babylonian origins" (*SE* 18:58n.). Beyond this point, "this line of thought" disappears from view in yet earlier zones, beyond historical records.

In Freud's attempt to think the line of thought, poetry is repeatedly associated with unchartable segments of the line of thought. Freud writes of the hypothesis of the death instinct: "We are strengthened in our thought by the writings of our poets" (*SE* 18:44–45). No doubt it is this identification which prompts Laplanche to ask (I now give the full version of the sentence quoted earlier), "Shall we invoke a romantic or Rilkean theme bearing witness to Freud's permanent familiarity with his own death? Perhaps. But. . . ."[19] Laplanche does not invoke such a "theme" or, what would be more challenging, a structure of poetic language that enacts such a thematics. I suggest that Freud's pluralizations "we" and "our thought" reflect a principle of organization in Freud's thinking of the beyond. They help throw or "abandon" the subject into a line of thought in which "the poets" have also abandoned themselves. It is plausible to assume that the phrase "our poets" has a local German meaning, yet, considering what Freud writes about "the poets" just a few pages later, any effort to restrict them to a "romantic or Rilkean" identity is not only an unnecessary foreshortening of the length of Freud's lineage (making it, incidentally, only an aspect of a Rilkean modernity that may be thought—by de Man, for example—to define itself against the ancients), but an incapacitation of the line's infinite extensibility through and beyond the poetic descents of classical and neoclassical poetry.[20] Very much gesturing toward classical poetry, Freud writes, "The libido of our sexual instincts would coincide with the Eros of the poets and philosophers which holds all living things together" (*SE* 18:50). Freud prompts us to ask: In this particular book what do we encounter of the descents of the poets—ancient and modern—not to Eros but to Thanatos?[21] *Beyond the Pleasure Principle* sets out to isolate the nonlibidinal instincts. Do these other instincts perhaps coincide with the imaginings of Thanatos by ancient and modern poets? Are these imaginings dualistic in Freud's terms?

Freud indicates that *Beyond the Pleasure Principle* is an effort to pass beyond "the inclusive unity of the ego" (*SE* 18:11). In his terms the passing beyond cannot figure a chiasmus of turning and returning, that is, of an ego or self that maintains a constant circulation of ego and death drive. We have seen that Laplanche proposes such a monistic chiasmus by redefining Freud's terms, that is, by discarding Freud's thought in favor (in effect) of Alexandre Kojève's presentation of Hegel's chiasmus of consciousness recuperating death. Yet I believe that for Freud in *Beyond the Pleasure Principle* the more appropriate, though quite hysterical, figure is the chiasmus of distinct halves required by the unrecuperable negation of self in the turning of the self *beyond* itself. This chiasmus must seem "absurd" indeed, from a monistic point of view. I turn now to a proposal concerning how, exemplarily, Freud derives and sustains his dualistic, unrecuperated chiasmus.

I proceed now, in other words, to the question of where, or how, Freud derives the power to throw himself into the line of thought in which he experiences his breaking off. Most especially, I ask how it becomes possible for Freud to launch himself into the chiasmus in which he hypothesizes the death instinct: [*A*] finding freedom for a hypothesis of [B] dying-away by [B] dying-away in [A] an inherited line of free hypothesis (of dying-away). Following the line of Freud's hypothesizing, I am hypothesizing that his power even initially to throw himself into this line is derived from the line itself. I therefore look to Freud's text for the evidence of an encounter with an effectively endless repetition of a characteristic double countermovement. This encounter or piece of real experience of the line of thought must at any given moment be of a given immediate point that enables, in unlimited and unforeseeable extension, the experience of the line. Doubtless Freud had, at various moments, various objects of this kind in mind, but we have seen that in *Beyond the Pleasure Principle* he singles out a particular object, his Tassovian "poetische Darstellung" (poetic picture or representation), as "die ergreifendste," the most moving or gripping.

We need not decide upon a specific level of conscious intention on Freud's part in order to recognize the way he has caught the Tassovian trick of speech, quite possibly from the very verses that render the effect on Tancred's consciousness of the event that Freud is recounting. The Tassovian trick of speech is a repetition (with its own lineal or compulsive force) of double countermovements. Here, first, is Freud's "Wiederholung" (repetition), in this case of [A] the hero's unwitting murder of [B] the beloved, [B] whom he recognizes as his beloved only when [A (b)] he has killed her in combat with him:

> [A]
> Held Tankred hat unwissentlich
> > [B]
> > die von ihm geliebte Clorinda getötet,
> > [B]
> als sie in der Rüstung eines feindlichen Ritters
> > > [A (b)]
> > > mit ihm kämpfte.

> [A]
> [The hero Tancred has unwittingly
> > [B]
> > killed his beloved Clorinda,
> > [B]
> when she, in the disguise of an enemy knight,
> > > [A (b)]
> > > has fought with him.][22]

> [A]
> Dort zerhaut er einen hohen Baum mit seinem Schwerte,
> > [B]
> > aber aus der Wunde des Baumes strömt Blut
> > [B]
> und die Stimme Clorindas, deren Seele in diesen Baum gebannt war, klagt ihn an,
> > > [A (b)]
> > > dass er wiederum die Geliebte geschädigt habe.

[A]
[He slashes with his sword at a tall tree;
[B]
but blood streams from the cut
[B]
and the voice of Clorinda, whose soul is imprisoned in the tree, is heard
complaining
[A (b)]
that he has wounded his beloved once again.][23]

Here now are some of the double countermovements in the line of repetitions
with which Tasso represents the on-again, off-again or limping condition of
Tancred's mind. Each of these double countermovements has its own conceptual grounds of opposition, yet it is clear that each is an agitated movement,
back-and-forth, forth-and-back. And it is noteworthy that Tasso's double countermovements are themselves only about hypothesizing an experience of death
that represents the subject's own dying-away:[24]

[A]	[B]
se ben sospetta,	o in parte anco s'accorge
[B]	[A]
che 'l simulacro	sia non forma vera,
[A]	[B]
[he suspects	or partly knows
[B]	[A]
that the simulacrum	is no true shape]
	(13.44.3–4)
[A]	[B]
tal il timido amante	a pien non crede
[B]	[A]
a i falsi inganni,	e pur ne teme e cede.
[A]	[B]
[even so the intimidated lover	not wholly believes
[B]	[A]
the false deceits,	and yet concedes and fears.]
	(13.44.7–8)

Comparison of these materials from Freud and Tasso prompts a number of
speculations about Freud's designation "ergreifendste." Freud's repetition of
countermovements strongly suggests the impact of Tasso's repetition of countermovements. The picture which so moves him is an artificial illness, a delusion, and a hypothesis. It portrays a mind gripped, split, by hysteria. And it recovers the fragment of historical truth—the primordial existence of death
instincts or the experience of dying-away—in its combination of "sadism" and
"primary masochism" (*SE* 18:54–55). (The fact that the picture is the work of
one of the most famous of modern melancholics is no doubt also relevant, at

some distance, to Freud's interests.) By redrawing Tasso's form of counter-movements, which evidence the death instincts, Freud's larger, strange chiasmus in *Beyond the Pleasure Principle* draws on the power of Tasso's larger, strange chiasmus in the *Gerusalemme liberata*.

I do not insist that Freud was necessarily thinking, at the moment of penning his own countermovements, of precisely these verses of Tasso, but I suggest that he was thinking of representations virtually identical with them. In his line of thought Freud encounters an effectively endless, even commonplace, repetition of countermovements such as these. Here we see, indeed, the necessity of Freud's literary (rather than clinical) proof case. The literariness of the exemplum is its status as that which is endlessly retold as well as its emergence from endless repetition of the topoi of representation. Encounters such as these function for him as a kind of "artificial illness" or "transference" in which the "transformation" of his self is the effect of dying-away and of being beside one's self ("frisch" and "lahm") which is inherent in the cultural sublime. This effect is already repeatedly represented within the line of thought that he encounters. Thus at the moment which Freud records in Tasso's poem the agitated condition of Tancred's mind, as we have seen and remarked in previous chapters, is itself that of being-beside-one's-self:

[A]	[B]
Va fuor di sé;	presente aver gli è aviso
[B]	[A]
l'offesa donna sua	che plori e gema.
[A]	[B]
[He is beside himself;	he thinks he is in the presence
[B]	[A]
of his injured lady	who is weeping and lamenting.]

$$(13.45.5-6)$$

The freedom to be moved (to be transformed in this transference) in this way, to hypothesize this hypothesis of dying-away, and even to empathize morally with this pain is won from the experience of this line of thought. This line of thought, of familiarity with one's own dying-away, is necessarily extended without limit from modernity to antiquity and beyond, so that it is inherently far beyond any romantic or Rilkean thematics.

Thus what is perhaps most remarkable about *Beyond the Pleasure Principle* is Freud's strange success in circumscribing precisely that which he cannot do or reach or know, precisely, in other words, what is beyond his life instincts, though not beyond his death instincts. This beyond may also be closely bound up with his omission of the dream of Clorinda's womb location in his representation of Tasso's representation. In closing I would like to suggest a way in which the womb that Freud remarkably omits in this representation may nevertheless represent for him, in its circumscribed absence, the limit of his ego or life instincts (the *frisch*) as well his experience (which is not the experience of the woman whose womb it is) of dying-away or death instincts (the *lahm*).

In Freud's tracing of his line of thought in *Beyond the Pleasure Principle* we repeatedly encounter figurations that suggest or shadow an inaccessible womb. The area of the unknown figured in this way, Freud says—speaking in each case "about the origin of sexuality"—cannot be "penetrated" by the figurations of the pleasure principle. This womblike area of the unknown exists in a different world from the ego apparatus which penetrates to kinds of knowledge which are assimilable to the self. I quote a series of three passages which at least may be thought to imply a figuration of a womb. The third passage is itself a quotation:

> This is the most obscure and inaccessible region of the mind [Es ist das dunkelste und unzugänglichste Gebiet des Seelenlebens], and, since we cannot avoid contact with it, the least rigid hypothesis [die lockerste Annahme], it seems to me, will be the best.

> science has so little to tell us about the origin of sexuality that we can liken the problem to a darkness into which not so much as a ray of a hypothesis has penetrated [man dies Problem einem Dunkel vergleichen kann, im welches auch nicht der Lichtstrahl einer Hypothese gedrungen ist].

> "He then made his Self to fall in two, and then arose husband and wife. Therefore Yagnavalkya said: 'We two are thus (each of us) like half a shell.' Therefore the void which was there, is filled by the wife."
>
> (*SE* 18:7, 57, 58n.; *GW* 13:4, 62)

These passages may imply a sexual symbolization that denies the predominance of phallic symbols in understanding the origins of sexuality as well as the larger human destiny in which sexuality plays its part. Even by itself this countersymbolization may suggest that Freud's way of entering his line of hypothesis involves a "transforming" (*SE* 18:64) of his previous "figurative language" (of "depth psychology") (*SE* 18:60).

It happens that we have another kind of suggestive evidence that Freud cannot be merely forgetting the dream in which Clorinda informs Tancred of her womb location. In *Beyond the Pleasure Principle,* at the moment he broaches the connection between primary masochism and the death instincts, Freud cites Sabina Spielrein's "gedankenreichen" (instructive) paper on the death drive (*GW* 13:59n.; *SE* 18:55n.). Even if Spielrein's paper has nothing directly to say about death instincts it was clearly for Freud part of the line of thought that led him to the hypothesis of the death instincts. The minutes of the Vienna Psychoanalytic Society show that on 29 November 1911 even the first presentation of the paper focused on the interpretation of fantasies of "being transposed into the mother's womb" and of its "being like death, a shadow existence."[25] Spielrein's published version of the same paper (in the journal that Freud edited with Eugen Bleuler and Jung) addresses Freud directly with his own teaching about the connection between dreams of womb fantasies and the death drive. Spielrein writes, "Jugendliche Individuen und besonders Mädchen haben oft im Traume Phantasien vom Liegen im Sarge. Freud lehrt, das Verweilen im Sarge sei ein Symbol des Verweilens im Mutterleibe (Sarg = Mutterleib)" (Young people, especially girls, often have dream fantasies of lying in a coffin. Freud tells us that the lingering in a coffin is a symbol for lingering in the mother's womb [coffin = womb]).[26] Like Clorinda's speaking to Tancred in a dream about a womb which Freud cannot represent, Sabina Spielrein speaks to Freud about the womb (in a woman's dream) which he himself, in another kind of consciousness, certainly knows about but which in the current phase of his consciousness he does not know about, cannot represent, now.

Yet with his second, *lahm* consciousness Freud's nonfigurative language draws upon and throws him into the Tassovian line of representation which circles or spirals around the truth of Clorinda's and Spielrein's, the woman's, identification of a womb space in his experience of the death instincts.[27] In Freud's chiasmata, as in Tasso's, no figural effect—which is to say, no nonfigural or beyond-figural effect—is more emphatic than the space of the unknown and ungraspable (of a negativity) which is generated by each chiasmus and which, most important, remains unrecuperated in the experience of a line of chiasmata. In the line of thought of the death instinct that Freud hypothesizes in *Beyond the Pleasure Principle* this interruptive space is not a figure of castration or impotent limpness or not merely such, since it is capable of locating, even if only negatively, the experience of the death instincts.

We may want to say that Freud's condition of the least rigid hypothesis, of a limp, or *lahm*, is only a dualistic delusion and artificial illness. Yet in Freud's transference within his line of thought it is a piece of real experience of a fragment of historical truth. For him at least, this is the historical and continuously available, albeit fragmentary, experience of his death instinct. Not least, he is helped to this experience by a woman (for whom the womb signifies her life instinct) who speaks to his innermost limping consciousness.

The Real in the Commonplace: Sarraute's Feminine Sublime of Culture

CHAPTER

> . . . leaning over the tombstones . . . in order to read
> the inscriptions; musing about the possible lives of all
> these people, this link in the infinite chain, this
> flash. . . .
> —Nathalie Sarraute, *Portrait d'un inconnu*

In earlier chapters I have at various points noted that, in the West, sublime experiences of cultural transmission have frequently depended upon a line of representations, each a commonplace scene, of female suffering. In these commonplace scenes the female sufferer remains largely without recourse to means of representing her own scene of pain. This lack of recourse to representation has seemed to mean that for the most part women do not participate either in sublime experience or in cultural transmission. Yet on more than one occasion I have noted recurring signs of a feminine force of representation within this recurrent scene.[1]

I turn now to Nathalie Sarraute's *Portrait d'un inconnu* (1948) for the workings of a feminine sublime of culture that transforms our sense of a male sublime and a male line of culture. The breadth and depth of Sarraute's personal culture (literary, philosophical, and painterly; French, British, German, and Russian) positioned her for a resynthesis of the European representational tradition. Sarraute's enterprise is more radical than that of recent feminist theorists who declare the need to produce "women's culture and literary tradition."[2] Her feminine sublime reclaims for women the entire Western line of culture and literary tradition. In her own transmission of a cultural sublime she recovers, in particular, women's experience of the real in the commonplace.

From its opening to its closing words Sarraute's novel transpires only, ascetically, in repetitions of commonplaces. In the course of these repetitions it performs a comprehensive anatomy of the distinctly feminine commonplace and its relation to the cultural sublime. Jean-Paul Sartre's preface to the first publi-

cation of *Portrait d'un inconnu* immediately drew attention to the centrality of
commonplaces—"the realm of the *commonplace*" (p. ix), "le règne du *lieu com-
mun*" (p. 10)—in this novel. Yet I believe Sartre seriously misunderstands Sarraute's use of commonplaces in *Portrait d'un inconnu*. Sartre's misunderstanding
may well be the result of a certain blindness to the role of commonplaces in his
own work. We will see, in fact, that Sarraute locates a blindness of a Sartrean
variety in her novel. Nevertheless, at the outset it is important to note, with
Sartre, that Sarraute overwhelmingly assigns the endless commonplaces in her
book to women, somewhat as she had done in her earlier collection of sketches,
Tropismes. Sartre, however, makes the equation between these two works too su-
perficially and renders the content of that which is being equated too positive:
"In her first book, *Tropismes*, Nathalie Sarraute showed that women pass their
lives in a sort of communion of the commonplace" (p. x). An ambience of this
communion certainly persists in *Portrait d'un inconnu*. It is even true that the commonplaces that are spoken by men in *Portrait d'un inconnu* have overwhelmingly
to do with the commonplace lives of women. Sartre suggests that the repetitions of the commonplace in the novel amount to what Heidegger calls "babble" or a "realm of inauthenticity" (p. xi). By "tenaciously depicting the reas-
suring, dreary world of the inauthentic," Sartre says, Sarraute allows us "to
sense an intangible authenticity, . . . human reality in its very existence" (p. xiv).
Sartre suggests that this "authenticity" emerges when the "commonplaces
break down" (pp. xiii–xiv). But Sarraute never allows the commonplaces to
break down in this book, not even in the moment, cited by Sartre, when the father and daughter are said to go "down as into the bottom of a well . . . as in an
undersea landscape" (p. xiii; p. 176). Sarraute has preserved the commonplace
status of this moment too, from near the beginning, by having the narrator say,
or cite, "I have the impression of having 'touched bottom'—an expression I often use . . . in the half-light of what is poetically termed 'the inner landscape'"
(p. 27). The "frightful protoplasmic nudity" (p. xiii) that Sartre thinks is revealed
there is itself also only a commonplace of forms floating in "the half-light" of
an alleged "inner landscape" which remains (to use Sartre's term) "inauthentic." In the world of *Portrait d'un inconnu* a phrase such as Sartre's "human reality
in its very existence" immediately sinks into the same pure banality of the commonplace as does the recurring word "reality" (e.g., pp. 74, 107, 123).[3] In *Portrait
d'un inconnu*, I repeat, the commonplaces never break down. On the contrary,
they are endlessly repeated in a sublime procedure that in this novel is carefully
discriminated from other claims to sublime procedures. The goal of these procedures is to recover the real in the mere commonplace, which is to say, in the
apparent "babble" of those who are from beginning to end called "the women"
(pp. 19, 222).

Sartre fails to measure the distance in Sarraute's development between the brush strokes of the commonplace in *Tropismes* (1939) and the full-blown novel of commonplace experience that Sarraute gestated and composed, incognita, during the war years. What Sarraute represents, as she herself termed it, *"in nuce"* in *Tropismes* develops and (to use another of her terms, this one pivotal in the novel) *metamorphoses* into a decisively different writing of the "unknown" in *Portrait d'un inconnu*. This distance is crucial for Sarraute's representation of the failed claims for a culture of "authenticity" (Sartre's word) and of alleged self-"recovery" (Sarraute's word)[4]—not just of German culture (including Heidegger's, Hegel's, and Sartre's Heideggerian and Hegelian culture)—that engulfed her.

We need first to identify something of the provenience of Sarraute's term "the women" in its relation to the commonplace and to tradition. Sarraute offhandedly gives us a yardstick for measuring the different reaches of *Tropismes* and *Portrait d'un inconnu*. In *Tropismes* the heavily English allusiveness (including "Shakespeare. Dickens. . . . Thackeray" [pp. 50–51]) points perhaps most directly to T. S. Eliot's "The Love Song of J. Alfred Prufrock" (1915). Not only does she unmistakably echo Eliot's famous internal echoing of verses (ll. 97–98 and 109–10), "No, that is not it, that's not it at all" (p. 47), but the commonplace notion, commonplace in *Tropismes,* that women pass their lives in a sort of communion of the commonplace, is an echoing of Eliot's description of the commonplace "women"—"the women"—endlessly speaking empty commonplaces. Eliot satirizes "the women" and their commonplaces in his repetition of the recurring, stultifying couplet: "In the room the women come and go / Talking of Michelangelo" (ll. 13–14, 35–36). In *Tropismes* Sarraute tells how "they went out together, led the life that women lead. . . . They, they, they, they . . . And they talked and talked, repeating the same things, going over them, then going over them again" (pp. 38–39), talking, for example, of "Van Gogh, Utrillo" (p. 30). In *Tropismes* there is a virtual helplessness or submission ("Be submissive, be submissive" [p.17]) before Eliot's commonplace, at least in the sense that it is not exceeded by any larger figure.

The entirety of *Portrait d'un inconnu* might also be thought to be "submission to the cliché" (p. 73) of Eliot's couplet. In the novel the women endlessly mouth commonplaces, talking, in particular, about painters, most especially "Rembrandt" (p. 91 and extensively). But the figure achieved by the repetitions of commonplaces in *Portrait d'un inconnu* far exceeds that of Eliot's couplet in "Prufrock." It exceeds even Eliot's then-latest work, his figuration of the sublime at the close of "Little Gidding" in *Four Quartets* (1942). This is the internal echoing of verses that Sarraute echoes—and embeds in the language of pure commonplace—from near the end of "Little Gidding," where Eliot built the sublime conclusion to his wartime poem by echoing the words of Dame Julian of Norwich. For Eliot this amounts to "a symbol" (l. 194):

> A symbol perfected in death.
> And all shall be well and
> All manner of thing shall be well
> By the purification of the motive
> In the ground of our beseeching. (ll. 195–199)
>
> And all shall be well and
> All manner of thing shall be well
> When the tongues of flame are in-folded
> Into the crowned knot of fire
> And the fire and the rose are one.
>   (ll. 255–59)

Sarraute closes her record of "the women" coming and going, talking pure commonplaces about "Rembrandt"—and, indeed, Nathalie Sarraute's own seemingly endless and pointless talk (and title) of a "Portrait"—by making merely commonplace (merely a continuation of the commonplace talk of women) her echo of Eliot's pious language beseeching for a time when "all shall be well" in the achievement of purification and of death:

> Piously, I shall mingle my voice with theirs [those of "the women"]. . . .
> Little by little everything will grow calm. The world will take on a smooth, clean purified aspect. Somewhat akin to the air of serene purity that the faces of people are always said to assume after death.
> After death . . . ? But that, too, that is nothing, either.
> . . . Everything will be all right. . . . It will be nothing.
>
>   (pp. 222–23)

Countering the commonplace placement of Eliot's sublime conclusion is of no small significance in Sarraute's reclamation of her cultural line. Eliot had given the European "Tradition" a particularly individual coloring of his talent. Yet Eliot is for Sarraute only one instance of a pervasive condition, exemplified by even more imposing figures, that is by no means merely negative in its effects. To speak commonplaces with "the women" is for Sarraute the condition of sublime experience, of freedom, of moral feeling, and of cultural transmission. For the method of Sarraute's novel this necessarily implies a significant circularity or countermovement that does not jettison any part of the line of that culture. In this countermovement a certain stance toward the commonplace is earned only by sublime experience, while that very sublime experience is from the first made possible only by adopting that stance toward the commonplace. In this cultural sublime we always speak "Once again . . . " "Une fois de plus," as in the opening phrase of *Portrait d'un inconnu*. For Sarraute this countermovement depends upon the fact that we are always already within the condition of the commonplace within our given culture. I will try to be more specific, already, about this condition of the commonplace, which is for Sarraute both the end-product and the prerequisite of her writing in *Portrait d'un inconnu*.

On the face of it *Portrait d'un inconnu* is primarily a story of a particular man and woman, secondarily of many men and many women, but the only thing we know for certain is that "nothing ever happened between them" (p. 203), any of them. The art of this novel is to "detach, very gently" (p. 29) the assertibility, or adhesion to any sense of an actual event, of all of the male narrator's representations. Here is a string of such totally suppositious nonevents about which the narrator, by his own admission, has no evidence:

> For it to come out, they ["the women"] have to be by themselves . . . two women who meet on the doorstep or in the stairway . . . "He's a selfish old man," they're saying, "I always said so, selfish and close-fisted, people like that shouldn't be allowed to have children. As for her, she's just a crank. . . . "
>
> (p. 19)

> It is more than probable—and for my part I am certain of it—that this is the expression that he must always have worn in her presence. It is surely the expression that he had worn at the moment of their first contact, when she was but a child in her cradle; at the moment, doubtless, when he heard for the first time her stubborn, strident cry . . . pierce through him.
>
> (p. 62)

> It must have started in . . . the sort of commonplace conversation that takes place over a tea table. . . . they had probably said: "These days children are certainly spoiled; if we had asked our parents to travel about like that. . . ."
>
> (pp. 94–95)

> Lonely men, women whom 'life,' as they say, has already treated rather badly, widows, their children dead, one of scarlet fever—"You should have seen what a darling he was . . . Why? he used to ask—he could say extraordinary things, he was so cute—why must we love people since one day we shall have to be separated from them? . . . he had blond curls, if you curled them around a stick in the morning, they stayed curled all day . . . what a waste, I always said, such lovely hair on a boy"—women with faded eyes and worn-out bodies get up at daybreak.
>
> (pp. 152–53)

After a few pages of these commonplaces it does not come as a surprise that the apparently heartrending story of the dead child "who could say extraordinary things" represents—contra the narrator's pretended verisimilitude—only the repeatability, or topos, of an event. This applies as well to the apparently principal tale of this book, the story of the selfish old man and the crank, his daughter. It hardly matters whether we are familiar with the explicitly invoked story "of the hero of [Tolstoy's] *War and Peace* old Prince Bolkonski" (p. 64) and "the case of Princess Marie" (p. 66) or with the never named but omnipresent story of Balzac's *Eugénie Grandet*. The ordinary words that recount all of the above, putative events recur so endlessly and predictably that the claim to experience of any actual event, in any instance of what is repeatedly called "Reality" (cf. pp. 107, 123), is rigorously blocked. In fact, these sayings are as austerely detached from anything living as the commonplace words of an epitaph on a tombstone for an unknown man, or woman, who remains both unseen and totally unknown to us. It is in this sense that this novel well describes itself as " . . . leaning over . . . tombstones . . . in order to read the inscriptions; musing about . . . possible lives" (p. 117).

All the statements in this book, then, are no more or less than commonplaces, which is to say that they are all pure suppositions. Sarraute knows well that the nature of a commonplace or supposition is that it is a counterfactual, a denial that what is represented is the reality or experience that it represents. I recall here F. H. Bradley's saying (Sarraute took her B.A. at Oxford just in the wake of the greatest popularity of *The Principles of Logic*) that what a supposition affirms "is the mere ground of connection; not the actual existing behavior of the real, but a latent quality of its disposition, a quality which has appeared in the experiment." In addition, Bradley emphasizes, the deployment of the supposition depends upon our experience of the "real" that is "always in immediate contact with our minds."[5] The ground of connection in the line of commonplaces or suppositions in Sarraute's novel is unvarying. It is the framing of a scene of victimization. This scene is always the same, although the language of supposition creates the transparent illusion of the verge of an actual event: "She was on the verge of a scene, she had that air of helpless anger of a child . . . the look of a weeping widow. . . . He was looking around him for something to crush her with" (p. 186). We may add that the unflinching purity of supposition in this book reveals that the violence of displacement and effacement is at the heart of supposition itself. This is the substitute-placing (*sub-ponere*) that displaces all the life clamoring for the present moment. This violence of supposition becomes all but unbearable in the commonplace rendering of pain at which no one is looking, which is, strictly speaking, not even occurring:

> He knew, without even having to look at her, that the child's eyes, like those of an insect, had turned toward the toys, only ever so slightly, since she didn't want to let it be seen. . . .
>
> But he would not be taken in. For nothing on earth would he have yielded. And as he dragged her away, pressing her little hand hard in his fingers, he experienced a sort of painful enjoyment, a bitter-tasting slightly cloying satisfaction, tearing from him and crushing the soft, flabby little tentacles that clung timidly to him.
>
> (pp. 166–67)

It is decisive for the book that these commonplaces—all framed scenes of victimization—and their endless repetition never break down. Instead these framed scenes of victimization become the occasion of sublime experience and of moral feeling, even of moral speaking. Sarraute's entire novel is a "spinning" by "the women" (p. 43) of these endless threads of commonplaces. Yet it is the framing of scenes of victimization in this novel that is of decisive importance. It is only this that saves *Portrait d'un inconnu* from, in effect, advertising the victimization that is pictured in its scenes and, indeed, even of compulsively inflicting a repetition of the commonplace upon the reader.

Sarraute recreates a feminine sublime by talking (not taking) over the dominant commonplaces—the worlds of supposition—that "the women" and she herself, with the rest of us in her culture, speak. Although her classifications and enactments of these suppositions are managed in what is called "La Désinvolture" (p. 171), offhandedly, they construct a steeltrap logic. The feminine sublime issues from a detached framing, in "La Désinvolture," of the scene of victimization within the alleged masculine sublime of masculine culture. To achieve this Sarraute avails herself, from the beginning, of the leverage of supposition that her sublime experience provides. She never steps outside this circle. Nor does her experience of "La Désinvolture" ever settle or harden into an ideology with which Sarraute is herself identifiable. Inside the circle of *"La Désinvolture" : the commonplace : sublime experience :"La Désinvolture"* the consciousness that she speaks or represents is that of a dying-away or second state within the line of her language. (Analogies, at least, to this circularity of consciousness are even named in the novel, as in "We kept it up for a long time. Dumontet: The Daughter: The Father: I: Dumontet" [p. 217].) As I began to suggest earlier, the commonplace suggestion of a sublime transcendence with which *Portrait d'un inconnu* closes, "Just one more step to be taken" (Juste encore un pas de plus à franchir), is already fulfilled in the commonplace, "Once again . . . " (Une fois de plus . . .), with which it begins. Not only is the phrase "Once again" totally commonplace in being anterior to any subject or object—as if language itself is supplying the formula for the continuity of language—but the phrase enacts the repetition ("again" or "more") of apparent uniqueness (the "once"), which sends the mind careening into the encounter with the endless progression of the commonplace; thence, into sublime experience. In this extreme case of Sarraute's typical style of commonplace repetition, two countertruths are reconciled in the renovation of both the commonplace and the sublime. While the "Just one more step . . . " suggests that the sublime is no more than a commonplace, the "Once again . . . " (which seems to be only a humdrum commonplace) is already experienced within the endless progression of the sublime. The power of Sarraute's renovation of the sublime is therefore a function of her awareness of the inherited constituents of her own sublime language. Yet in Sarraute's sublime all cultural transmission is experienced as women's culture. All literary tradition belongs to women as much as to men, which is to say, in Sarraute's reformulation, that in the feminine sublime we experience the relation to tradition that makes it living tradition, in "La Désinvolture" or the Offhandedness which finds the real in the commonplace itself.

Sarraute achieves a "Désinvolture" of the sublime and of cultural transmission through commonplace repetitions of the representations of the sublime that she experiences most especially in the representations which she associates with Freud, Baudelaire, Hegel (and Homer), and Rembrandt. These representations are neither more nor less than the language in which she finds herself and in which, she implies, her readers find themselves. Her considered choices of commonplaces are also, that is, the inevitable, automatic choices. They are the commonplaces that she and we speak everyday, all day. This would seem to imply a condition of pure enslavement. But the opposite is the case because Sarraute's placing of this language in a purely suppositious repetition of commonplaces, or mere suppositions, makes possible the emergence of both the ground of connection among the commonplaces and the real which is in immediate contact with the mind. In *Portrait d'un inconnu* the ground of connection is the scene of victimization that the speaker of the sublime speaks even now and has spoken from the opening words of *Portrait d'un inconnu*. In the circular construction of the experience of the sublime Sarraute's speaking appears to be only a promise of a future sublime speech joined to the speakers of the commonplace, "the women." In this speaking, the freedom of detachment or disinterestedness or "La Désinvolture" is the condition for first placing the commonplace and the real in the commonplace in the experience of the sublime. "Piously, I shall mingle my voice with theirs . . . " (p. 222), ["Je mêlerai pieusement ma voix aux leurs . . . " (p. 212)], says this woman among the women. By this time in the novel, this speaking can no longer be taken to be merely that of the putative man unknown / narrator. Just before the last-quoted speaking we hear it said of "the women": "They will know right away . . . that I am one of them" (p. 222). For good reasons that I will yet broach, this metamorphosis from the man unknown to the woman unknown is not unambiguous. But its suggestiveness is unmistakable and, I would emphasize here, it already performs the mingling or merging of the narrator's voice with those of "the women." This promise is already an apostrophe to all the victims—in all the commonplace scenes of victimization of this writing—to whom the woman unknown commits herself. She calls out in an experience of freedom that is born of resisting the sensory object, in this case the commonplace scene of victimization. She calls out, therefore, in the condition of dying-away, of remaining in freedom in the second state. By so doing Sarraute "piously" foregrounds a sublime of the empowered victim that has always been resident within the masculine sublime. Sarraute, or the other narrator, the woman unknown ("Madame X" [pp. 45–46]), calls this letting go or laying off "La Désinvolture."

"Freud": The first of the scenes that Sarraute experiences in the language of the commonplace is unmistakably associated with Freud. Since Sarraute's representation of this scene is only already in the condition of "La Désinvolture" or detachment from any positive or nonsuppositious presentation of Freud's scene I will refer to the author of this scene of Sarraute's commonplace language as "Freud." (For the same reason I will soon refer to "Baudelaire," "Hegel," and "Rembrandt.")

In *Portrait d'un inconnu* this is the primal scene of the repetition compulsion that underlies the commonplace. It is the scene of repetition that repeats the aggression of a man against a woman victim. In "Freud"'s writings it occurs (like a tropism of the sublime) in the work *Beyond the Pleasure Principle*, which ends with this last-resort recommendation of cited, commonplace wisdom: "What we cannot reach flying we must reach limping. / . . . The Book tells us it is no sin to limp." Speaking of a purely suppositious class of "doctors" or psychoanalysts giving their recommendation of "last resort to their 'neuropaths'" (p. 28) the narrator of *Portrait d'un inconnu* says, "I can almost hear them, with that air of mealy-mouthed solidarity of theirs, saying: 'When we are unfortunate enough not to be able to walk straight, it's better, don't you agree, to walk backwards, if by so doing we can reach our goal? . . . '" (p. 28). We have seen in the previous chapter that exactly what is or is not a sin of repetition is the principal subject of *Beyond the Pleasure Principle*. The limping, on-again, off-again, syncopated motions of Freud's walking-thinking, in his "Gedankengang," are the alternations that produce the second state, the other view.

Without understanding how he is almost going about Sarraute's business of rehearsing the commonplace scenes of *Portrait d'un inconnu*, the male narrator will explain in clichéd detail how, he thinks, one can get what he calls "the other view" (p. 29): "There's a trick you can use to get it . . . a sort of sleight-of-hand rather similar to the exercises required for solving certain puzzles, or those pictures composed of black and white diamonds so cleverly combined that they form two superimposed geometrical drawings . . . : you detach, very gently, one of the drawings . . . then you bring the other one forward" (p. 29). In this book the black picture, or set of black diamonds, consists of the repetition of pure commonplaces or commonplaces that draw attention to their purely automatic status. These are endless mere suppositions that make totally impossible any contextualization of an experienced reality.

The clichéd "trick" for getting "the other view" in this way, with strong-handed "déxterité," never leads (as the male narrator thinks it will) to "recovery" or superimposition of the other view on the view at hand. It remains in "La Désinvolture." Reading within the line of Sarraute's repetitions, we see, one page earlier, that this trick for getting the other view is only another form of the trick or formula of "last resort" ("en désespoir de cause" [p. 26]) that the narrator has found in "a psychiatric treatise" ("dans un traité de psychiatrie" [p. 28]). Here is the first (already repeated) trick that I am calling "Freud"'s. This might almost have been a moment of anti-Freudian high parody, but the parody too is part of Sarraute's discipline (beside the narrator's voice) of "patient repetition" of the commonplace:

> So I resorted once more to another of my devices—one I employ in desperate cases, similar to the tricks that doctors discover empirically and sometimes recommend as a last resort to their "neuropaths," such as, to practice smiling every day in front of a mirror so that, with patient repetition, this artificial grin may induce gaiety: I can almost hear them, with that air of mealy-mouthed solidarity of theirs, saying: "When we are unfortunate enough not to be able to walk straight, it's better, don't you agree, to walk backwards, if by so doing we can reach our goal? Whatever people may say, putting the cart before the horse sometimes gives good results. . . . "
>
> (p. 28)

In the analogy between the two tricks, the cart is the picture of black diamonds, the horse is the picture of white diamonds, which is the "other view." The "good results" of which this supposititious psychoanalytic spokesman speaks are spelled out by the narrator's analyst—his "specialist"—as "beginning to be 'in contact with reality' . . . a symptom of recovery" (p. 74), "the road to recovery" (p. 220), but it is not obvious what is supposed to constitute this recovery or contact with reality.

Portrait d'un inconnu could hardly be more explicit about the way in which, because of the commonplaces of our language, we remain in contact with a reality within language itself. The novel repeats, that is, the placement of the scene of the repetition compulsion in our language. In an earlier moment the specialist has this to say about the narrator's account of "the 'scenes' between them [the father and daughter], that moment when they confront each other":

> These people of yours are highly nervous individuals. To be convinced of this fact, one has only to consider the predominant role played, in their case, by 'scenes.' And also by the clichés you describe and which, as you say, they affect in order to confront each other, to legitimize their clashes. This is a frequent feature of the neuropath; his submission to the cliché, which you have identified very accurately, in fact, but which, in my opinion, has nothing disquieting or mysterious about it. Don't take offense . . . don't take it to heart, many a literary character, who has since

become famous, was, from our point of view, a neurotic. . . . the case that seems to be plaguing you . . . is apparently very simple. In this connection, you might read quietly ["reposée" (70)] at home my article treating these types of conformity.

(pp. 73–74)

This identification of a famous moment—the crucial "scene" of "a literary character, who has since become famous" (presumably because of the citation, "since," by the psychoanalytic writing more than, or at least as much as, the growth in reputation of the literary work)—is neither homage nor parody. Having read quietly at home with the rest of us, the narrator is only perpetuating what "Freud" (in *Beyond the Pleasure Principle*) calls "the perpetual recurrence of the same thing," "a repetition of the same fatality," "a compulsion to repeat which overrides the pleasure principle."[6] All this "Freud" famously exemplifies in a particular commonplace scene of a particular literary character. This scene is that of the "duel" which becomes, within the method of "La Désinvolture," the perpetually recurring basic scene of *Portrait d'un inconnu*.[7] Speaking more generally of his technique for getting "the other view," the narrator says that he "must have seen it . . . in a psychiatric treatise" (p. 29).[8] In *Portrait d'un inconnu* the ultimate effect of this offhand repetition of the commonplace of the repeating duel scene—in other words, the scene of victimizing the woman—is not only to reenact the attainment of the goal of the death instinct, the second state (the off-again footfall of limping) in Freud's insistent dualism, but to enable the emergence of the unknown woman narrator in that second state. Here too, to attain and sustain this second state means "to throw oneself into a line of thought" (*SE* 18:59). In *Portrait d'un inconnu* this is to say, "Piously, I shall mingle my voice with theirs. . . ." To join the speaking of the commonplaces of "the women" (not least, the duel scene from "Freud"'s psychiatric treatise) in *Portrait d'un inconnu* or to join "Freud"'s "Gedankengang" guarantees that we never succumb to the illusion of what Sarraute's man unknown calls "recovery" or which Freud's Jung sees as the achievement of a "monistic" recuperation. What Sarraute calls "La Désinvolture" (i.e., in her detached placing of the commonplace of the narrator's account of "Freud"'s adage) is "to walk backwards" in the amble which "La Désinvolture" idiomatically describes. Sarraute thus invokes "Freud"'s closing lines about the requirements of a special kind of walking as a way of marking her own duality of narratorial consciousnesses.

"*Baudelaire*": The second of the narrator's "tricks" for getting "the other view"—which remains beyond him—is to play the *flâneur*:

A stranger walking in a strange city. . . . There is nothing better for bringing the other view back into the foreground. . . . I succeeded rather quickly. . . . The streets began to come to life. More and more they assumed the rather sad, tender charm of Utrillo's little streets. . . . With the liberty and sort of offhanded naïveté of a foreigner [avec cette liberté, cette sorte de naïvete désinvolte des étrangers (pp. 29–30)] I asked a little old woman sitting next to me on the bench if she knew the name of that tree. . . . "I believe it's a whitebeam," she replied. And everything became really very gentle and calm. I felt at ease. I had been entirely successful. . . . Not a trace of the slight disquiet [inquiétude (p. 30)] . . . which I always feel before even noticing them [the father and daughter].

(pp. 30–32)

. . . In such cases as mine, a voyage is always advisable. . . . The specialist, in fact, . . . was very much in favor of this voyage. . . . This city seemed to me . . . to guarantee success. For me it was, and had always been, the city of the *Invitation au Voyage*. Its almost imperceptibly rocking boats (Baudelaire had also considered the word 'waddling' [dandinés (p. 78)], he had hesitated, but in the end had found a way of saying it still better), the masts of vessels lying in the old harbor, the sky, the waters, the canals, were all suffused with a sort of rhapsodical softness. The words of the *Invitation au Voyage* . . . one had only to pronounce the words softly: "*les soleils couchants revêtent les champs, les canaux, la ville entière . . . ,*" and at the words: "*la ville entière,*" it rose up in a single impulse, its main street opened out like an oriflamme, hung with flags and banners, waving in the soft sea breeze, through the golden light.

This was purified . . . matter . . . an exquisite dish, ready to eat. In fact, my condition being so close to recovery helped considerably. . . .

It was in this state of benign ravishment . . . that . . . I made slowly for the museum. . . . I felt . . . a feeling somewhat similar to that of a lover hastening to his first tryst. (pp. 81–83)

The narrator's recipe is for "rhapsodical" experience—getting "the other view"—reduced to its commonplace, readily available ingredients. His recipe is guaranteed to produce "an exquisite dish," "quickly" ready to serve no matter what order of steps we follow.

On the face of it these pages about the condition of the Baudelarian flâneur-narrator, who is even directly inspired by a rhapsodic travel poem of Baudelaire's, would seem to describe the condition of the narrator who speaks in the very last pages of the novel. Here the narrator says, "And everything became really very gentle and calm"; at the end we hear, "Little by little everything will grow calm." Here the narrator says, "This was purified . . . matter"; at the end we hear, "The world will take on a smooth, clean, purified aspect." Yet it is obvious that the narrator speaks at the end only of a devoutly, piously wished-for condition that is in fact impossible to attain; while the context of the flâneur-narrator's repetition of his claims to having "succeeded rather quickly" and to having "been entirely successful" are as dubious as his claim to being "so close to recovery."

In fact in Sarraute's largest aesthetic categories in *Portrait d'un inconnu* the success of the emergent, other narrator in the last pages is precisely measured by that voice's abandonment of any sign of recovery. Some readers have felt that *Portrait d'un inconnu* "suffers from the author's failure fully to dramatize the narrator's relation to his story" and that this "defect is remedied" in Sarraute's later "less strange if also less rich" novels.[9] But Sarraute's aim is to produce the strange, rich truth of "La Désinvolture"—parallel, at least, to the "strange" that Laplanche finds in *Beyond the Pleasure Principle*—by the perpetual detachment of her outermost ring of narration from the story that is being narrated. For Sarraute the flâneur-narrator is only an object lesson in failure. His pretense to "offhanded naïveté" is contradicted by his claim to "rhapsodical" experience of nothing less than "la ville entière." As if "Freud" himself were giving the narrator his cues, the rhapsody fantasized here is that of settings for male penetration / female reception: "Masts" and "canals" or "rocking boats"; "it rose up in a single impulse, its main street opened out like an oriflamme" that is orgiastically blazoned "with flags and banners"! Small wonder that "the specialist, in fact, . . . was very much in favor of this voyage." Yet the flâneur-narrator does not show the smallest inkling of the "Freud" who is looking over his shoulder when, in the next sentence, he pronounces, "This was purified . . . matter."

The space of a different sort of intelligence is hinted at, however, in the parenthesis about "Baudelaire"'s "rocking boats": "(Baudelaire had also considered the word 'waddling' [dandinés], but in the end had found a way of saying it still better)." We must wonder what this "it" must be, according to this other narrator's understanding. The word *dandinés* refers to the swaying or wiggle of a provocative woman. How had "Baudelaire" found a way to say this better? This small suggestion, dropped in a parenthesis, precipitates around itself an entirely different, or other, meaning of "voyage" in "Baudelaire"'s *Invitation au Voyage*. The streets of the city visited by the flâneur are the body of a woman, perhaps even the body of a streetwalker or prostitute. The man's voyage is his dream of easy erotic fulfillment. In this reading of *Invitation au Voyage* proposed by the flâneur-narrator's perspective, "Baudelaire"'s "Invitation" is his propositioning of a woman, mostly (whatever "Baudelaire" may pretend or intend) for his own pleasure. The "voyage" would seem to repeat the cliché of being transported by love while it actually repeats a far more commonplace scene of immobilizing a victim to serve the needs of self. By strong implication the flâneur-narrator's *success* or *recovery*, his sense of "ravishment" and of going to a "tryst," as well of standing over "an exquisite dish, ready to eat," is the effect of the very opposite of an offhand, or hands-off, "Désinvolture." More than anything else, I believe, this exposé means that the rhapsodical or sublime scene (complete with "liberty" or freedom) that the flâneur-narrator claims to repeat at will is only a commonplace scene of erotic victimization, repeated from "Baudelaire"'s veiled scene of erotic victimization. The recovery here is a fantasy of recuperated calm (after a version of the Kantian "discharge all the more powerful") achieved at the expense of the victim.

The method of narrative Désinvolture works to insure that we do not attach any reduced representation of "Freud," "Baudelaire," "Hegel," or "Rembrandt" to Sarraute's own views of Freud, Baudelaire, Hegel, or Rembrandt. It is entirely consonant with Sarraute's "La Désinvolture" for her to represent a commonplace scene of "Baudelaire" which is decisively different from her insight into the sublime experience that Baudelaire might himself have detached from the commonplaces of his scene. To grant him his own Désinvolture is only to allow him the possibility of the experience of the beyond, the "just one more step," that the whole of *Portrait d'un inconnu* retrieves and builds from its line of language. So too, as we have seen, is it with "Freud" from Sarraute's point of view. But we must continue with the tracing of Sarraute's progression of the commonplace to get to her "other view" of that progression. This can only be her sublime experience of her line of commonplaces of sublime experience.

"Hegel": If "Freud"'s duel provides "Baudelaire"'s scene of victimization in one sense—that of erotic victimization—"Hegel"'s duel provides it in another—that of the attempt to recuperate or recover consciousness itself (after self-alienation or dying-away) in a scene of punishment. More than any other repeated scene, "Hegel"'s duel provides the commonplace scene of the entire novel. This is the setting for the only narrative climax that the novel offers.

> They were standing firmly, brow to brow, heavy and awkward, in their rigid carapaces, their heavy armor—two giant insects, two enormous dung beetles. . . . "Ah! indeed. . . . I know, I know all about it. I'm your father. You're my daughter. . . . I'm all you have in the world. . . . You're right." He felt his rage boiling up, a desire to take her and shake her, to tear off her mask too, . . . to crack that carapace . . . behind which she dares to defy him, to drag her out into the open, gasping and naked . . .
>
> The trap door was lifted, they had lifted the trap door, the ground had opened up under their feet, they had swayed on the brink of the abyss, they were about to fall in. . . . They were slipping attached to each other, they were falling . . . their carapaces and armors seemed to be cracking on every side, they were naked, without protection, they were slipping, clasped to each other. . . .
>
> (pp. 174–76)

It is possible to view Sarraute's interest in this scene as a reflection of her reading of Sartre's *Being and Nothingness* (1943).[10] In that work Sartre makes extensive use of Hegel's scene of the duel of consciousnesses in the *Phenomenology of Spirit*.[11] But Sarraute's use of Hegel's scene differs decisively from Sartre's in the way she represents its commonplace status. Sarraute's representation of Hegel's scene reflects on the way it had been highlighted and repeated in French intellectual circles during the 1940s.[12] In other words, what interests Sarraute about Hegel's commonplace scene is its role in the experience, *her* other experience, of the commonplace within a line of commonplaces. Hegel's duel scene is also distinctly literary, commonplace. Hegel, after all, is only reproducing a duel of heroes from the representations of epic, apparently from the *Iliad*, presumably the encounter of Achilleus and Hektor. This would seem to be the only moment that Hegel can imagine in which two self-consciousnesses seem to encounter each other in perfect equality. Here is what Hegel calls the "scene" of the duel—the "trial by death"—in which the independent self-consciousness of the "lord" (or "master") is achieved:

> The 'other' is also a self-consciousness; one individual is confronted by another individual. Appearing thus immediately on the scene . . . each seeks the death of the other. . . . The relation of the two self-conscious individuals is such that they prove themselves and each other through a life-and-death struggle. . . . This trial by death, however, does away with the truth which was supposed to issue from it, and so, too, with the certainty of self generally. . . . The two do not reciprocally give and receive one another back from each other consciously, but leave each other free only indifferently, like things ["in the form of *thinghood*"]. . . . In this experience, self-consciousness learns that life is as essential to it as pure self-consciousness. . . . Since to begin with they are unequal and opposed, and their reflection into a unity has not yet been achieved, they exist as two opposed shapes of consciousness; one is the independent consciousness whose essential nature is to be for itself, the other is the dependent consciousness whose essential nature is simply to live or to be for another. The former is lord [master], the other is bondsman [slave].
> (*PS*, sections 186–89)[13]

I am proposing that Sarraute's duel scene—of heroes in armor who are only things or insects[14]—is a repetition of Hegel's repetitions of his duel scene. Even Hegel's baffling language of inverted worlds closely corresponds to Sarraute's division of the space of her novel into a "dark, entirely closed world" and a world "up there" (pp. 186, 189–90) which is known only by inversive implication and in flashes. (This division into underground and aboveground is no doubt also Dostoevskian, which in Sarraute's language of the commonplace may mean that it is another route to the Hegelian commonplace scene.) It is striking that Sarraute's representation of inverted worlds as well as her metaphor of overlaid, separate "black" and "white" worlds both occur in Hegel's introduction to his account of the recovery of self-consciousness (in victimization) in the duel scene:

> According . . . to the law of this inverted world, what is *like* in the first world is *unlike* to itself, and what is *unlike* in the first world is equally *unlike to itself*, or it becomes *like* itself. Expressed in determinate moments, this means that what in the law of the first world . . . is black is, in the other, white. . . . Revenge on an enemy is, according to the *immediate law*, the supreme satisfaction of the injured individual. This law,

however, which bids me confront him as himself a person who does not treat me as such, and in fact bids me destroy him as an individuality—this law is *turned round* by the principle of the other world into its opposite: the reinstatement of myself as a person through the destruction of the alien individuality is turned into self-destruction. If, now, this inversion, which finds expression in the punishment of crime, is made into *law,* it, too, is again the law of one world which is confronted by an *inverted* supersensible world where what is despised in the former is honoured, and what in the former is honoured, meets with contempt. The punishment which under the law of the *first* world disgraces and destroys a man, is transformed in its *inverted* world into the pardon which preserves his essential being and brings him to honour.

(PS, section 158)

In this recurring scene in the *Phenomenology of Spirit* (and, as we saw in chapter 3, in the corresponding scene in the *Philosophy of Right*) Hegel imagines a scene of revenge which he reinterprets as rightful punishment.[15] Hegel thus employs the scene of punishment to represent not only the birth—the higher, sublime recovery—of self-consciousness in which self and other disappear, but also the actualization of law in which the activity of the law as punishment and the individuality which is opposed to it also disappear. Hegel confirms this sublime recovery by finding in it the form of his beloved chiasmus, AB : BA: "[*A*] *like* becomes [*B*] *unlike* and [*B*] *unlike* becomes [*A*] *like*" (*PS,* section 156).

For Sarraute the scene of Hegelian (chiastic) punishment spells no one's recovery. The scene of countermovement in *Portrait d'un inconnu* is irrecoverable by any self-consciousness. The countermovement is traced between a sublime experience of the infinite priority of the commonplace and an experience of the pure commonplaceness of the commonplace which makes possible the sublime experience. In *Portrait d'un inconnu* the commonplace scene of victimization and of claiming sublime recovery for one's self is of interest for its commonplace status within the "literary" or unrecovered line of this commonplace. In that line it shares the same status and fate as the commonplace scenes of "Freud," "Baudelaire," and (as we shall see in a moment) "Rembrandt." The unflinching purity of supposition in this book reveals that the unremitting violence of displacement and effacement, as if by the engenderer of one's being, is at the heart of supposition itself, that is, in its merciless substitute-placing that displaces all the life clamoring, as I have said, for the present moment. This violence of supposition becomes, indeed, all but unendurable in the commonplace rendering of pain at which no one is looking. Irreducibly, this is the commonplace scene of victimization in which the other is seen as an insect, a "thing" or "form of thinghood" (in Hegel's phrases). Seen in this light, here is a passage that I cited earlier:

> He knew, without even having to look at her, that the child's eyes, like those of an insect, had turned toward the toys, only ever so slightly, since she didn't want to let it be seen. . . .

But he would not be taken in. For nothing on earth would he have yielded. And as he dragged her away, pressing her little hand hard in his fingers, he experienced a sort of painful enjoyment, a bitter-tasting slightly cloying satisfaction, tearing from him and crushing the soft, flabby little tentacles that clung timidly to him.

(pp. 166–67)

This representation of the duel scene is different from both Hegel's and Sartre's. In the *Phenomenology of Spirit* Hegel interprets the duel of consciousnesses as the moment when an individual may recover, in a "Aufhebung" or annulment / preservation / transcending = sublimation, the unity of consciousness. In the third part of *Being and Nothingness* Sartre interprets the same duel as a scene of failure in which the individual may achieve "Being-for-others" by becoming an object for the consciousness of others. Maintaining a strict "literary" discipline, Sarraute represents the duel scene as a repetition of a commonplace in a line of commonplaces. The form of Sarraute's representation is the line of commonplaces, each of which is both a scene of victimization and a false allegation of sublime recovery. Yet Sarraute does not simply give up on the connection between the potentialities of the everyday human and the capacity for sublime experience and its freedom. It is decisive for her book that these commonplaces and their endless repetition never break down. Instead they become the occasion of sublime experience of a "purified" kind, a flash of whiteness. Sarraute's representation of "Rembrandt"—which most immediately defines the painterly, portrait framework of her novel—makes this clear.

"Rembrandt": The commonplace line that the narrator travels is painfully obvious. At the climax of his voyage, à la "Baudelaire"—hastening to his "tryst" (p. 83)—the flâneur-narrator repeats, à la "Freud," his scene of victimization, thereby pretending to recover, à la "Hegel," his sublime self-consciousness. By telegraphing still further Sarraute's telegraphic method I will try to reproduce the story line of the novel's "Rembrandt" dimension, which is indeed focused ever more closely on a particular masterpiece of "Rembrandt." This is the dimension of experience that the narrator associates with the major "crime"—"La Désinvolture" (p. 171), "Offhandedness" (p. 180)—for which the victims in this novel are punished. The father says to the flâneur-narrator, "Still making plans this year? Traveling? . . . Museums? . . . Pictures? . . . Eh?" (p. 38); "Still traveling, eh? Works of art? Museums? The Uffizi? Rembrandt, eh? Or Tiepolo? And what about canals?" (p. 91). Or the flâneur-narrator says of the father, merely supposing the father's supposition, "His daughter and myself . . . were defying him now from afar, strutting about somewhere at his expense, parasitically, going into ecstasies before 'masterpieces'" (p. 97). Here is the flâneur-narrator's voyage to the sublime in his experience of a particular masterpiece:

It was in this state of benign ravishment, and without any ulterior motive, at least, it seemed so to me, that, having wandered for a long time through my favorite streets, those peaceful, intimate, gentle little streets to be found in northern cities, I made slowly for the museum.

. . . when I started towards it, I felt no haste and, it seemed to me, had no motive other than the simple curiosity of the disinterested [desintéressé (p. 79)] picture lover who wants to compare his impression with that carried away from earlier visits. . . . There it was . . . *Portrait of a Man Unknown.* I recalled that the picture was not signed: the painter, too, was unknown.

This time it seemed to me, if anything, even more curious than it had before. . . . It was as though all effort, all doubt, all anxiety had been overtaken by sudden catastrophe, and had remained congealed in action, like corpses that have petrified in the position they were in when death overtook them. The eyes alone seemed to have escaped the catastrophe and achieved fulfillment. . . . Their distressing, insistent entreaty made one strangely aware of his silence and the tragedy of it.

And little by little, I became aware that a timid note, an almost forgotten strain from long ago, had sounded within me. . . . And it seemed to me, as I stood there before him, lost, dissolved in him, that this faltering note, this timid response that he had awakened in me, penetrated him and reverberated inside him, that he seized it and gave it back to me . . . a song filled with hope. . . . I saw white birds rise on joyous wing at my approach.

Suddenly I felt free. Liberated. The Unknown Man . . . "The Man with the Waistcoat," as I called him, had liberated me. . . . I was free. The cables were cut. I was sailing along, headed for the open sea.

(pp. 82–85)

For the flâneur-narrator, who is always desperate to find the one "sign of recovery" (p. 99), this account will soon be exposed as a false experience of the sublime and a false liberation: "All I had done was to change masters. Now it was the Unknown Man, the 'Man with Doublet,' who held the leash at the other end of which I was walking" (p. 99). In *Portrait d'un inconnu* only the novelist-narrator, not the flâneur-narrator, continuously walks backwards the line of commonplace language. In this vein or line, it is indispensable for our experience of the method of "walking backwards," the "Désinvolture" of *Portrait d'un inconnu,* that we recall the earlier moment of which the narrator says, "That's how my moments of triumph and beatitude end: by mistaking long-discarded things for fresh discoveries . . . by forever going over old ground" (p. 46). It is at such moments that Sarraute's own "La Désinvolture" breaks through, when, in other words, we get her "other view" in the detaching of her picture of white diamonds, her flash, from the narrator's picture of black diamonds. A flash of this kind is seen when the narrator's "*alter ego*" gives back to him a picture that is pure supposition not of a Man Unknown but of a Woman Unknown, the neighbor of "Madame X," a "Hypersensitive Girl, Cliché-fed," parroting nothing but commonplaces. The father too can be a victim in such a picture, in close analogy with the Portrait of the Man Unknown who is "overtaken by sud-

den catastrophe, . . . congealed in action": "The picture that he was reproducing just now, that of the 'childlike, naïve philosopher who is defenseless before
life,' had restored his self-assurance" (p. 110). In the method of this novel all the
commonplaces mirror or parrot each other, but the experience of the flash—in
the act of detaching—in the marshaled line of commonplaces belongs to the
novelist herself, who is suggestively identified with the woman unknown or
"Madame X" portrayed here, but only in a flash. Here is the flâneur-narrator's
alter ego serving up a supposition—a "supposing"—of maddening elusive-
ness:

> He smiled: "So it's still there, is it? It still gets you? You remember that time we
> laughed so hard. . . . We had been supposing that one day I should be strolling
> about a museum or at an exhibition, and that suddenly I should see on the wall, be-
> side the *Portrait of Madame X* or the *Girl with Parrot,* something which I could recog-
> nize immediately, ten yards away, as having been done by you, something that un-
> questionably bore your signature, your mark. . . . what was it you called it . . . ?
> *Hypersensitive Girl, Cliché-fed.* . . . It was true. . . . My discoveries are always like
> that. . . . forever going over old ground.
>
> (pp. 45−46)

The closest this novel comes to a categorical statement of "La Désinvolture" is expressed by the flâneur-narrator to the daughter as he delivers his negative verdict on a certain painting. By this point in the flâneur-narrator's commonplace tale we know how to discount his claims to success or recovery, even
and especially when he claims that he is only describing failure, incompleteness, offhandedness. The "Désinvolture" that we pry loose from this passage remains floating in thin air, to be claimed by a different voice, the one that will in-
tone (within a group intoning), at the end, "Piously, I shall mingle my voice with
theirs [the women's]" (p. 222):

> I felt myself blushing. . . . "It lacks disquiet . . . a certain . . . I mean to say . . .
> tremor . . . one feels in it too much assurance . . . too much satisfied certainty . . . or
> . . . perhaps . . . complacency. . . . I believe that rather than the most perfectly fin-
> ished works I prefer those in which complete mastery has not been attained . . . in
> which one still feels, just beneath the surface, a sort of anxious groping . . . a certain
> doubt . . . a mental anguish . . . before the immensity . . . the elusiveness of the ma-
> terial world . . . that escapes us just when we think we have got hold of it . . . the goal
> that's never attained . . . the insufficiency of the means at our disposal. . . . There
> are certain pictures, for instance . . . those by Franz Hals when he was nearly blind
> . . . or the later Rembrandts . . . for instance . . . " I looked away . . . "there is a pic-
> ture . . . you've never seen it, probably, . . . it's not very well known . . . a portrait . . .
> in a Dutch museum . . . it isn't even signed . . . the portrait of an Unknown Man . . .
> Man with a Doublet is my name for it . . . well, there's something in that portrait . . .
> a sort of anguish . . . a sort of appeal . . . I . . . I prefer it to anything else . . . there's
> something uplifting" [exaltant (p. 192)].
>
> (pp. 201−02)

At this moment of pretending to "something uplifting" or sublime, the male narrator supposes for the daughter "a mental picture within herself, the one that I saw inside myself" (202). This is the scene of the duel between the father and the daughter, in which "everything was suddenly going to petrify," though "nothing ever happened" (p. 203). The whole of the narrator's claim to "La Désinvolture" is exploded by the daughter's (the woman's) accusation against his self-aggrandizement, his laying on of hands to promote his recovery: "Condescendingly she smiled: 'Ah! yes, so that's it . . . that's what I thought. . . . The way you judge painting. . . . You are just as you always were . . . that sort of too personal contact . . . the pursuit of emotions of that kind . . . '" (p. 203).

The whole of *Portrait d'un inconnu* shows us, however, that there is another possible way of living within the language of the commonplace and with the suspension of complete mastery. The purity and staying power of Sarraute's commitment to the spinning of her commonplace language means that she herself writes, from beginning to end, in the condition of dying-away in which the experience of the sublime issues. The entirety of *Portrait d'un inconnu* is written in this second state that Sarraute has taken upon herself. It is a handing on of the line of the commonplace in a state of "Désinvolture." This occurs only as the product of an experiment. The experiment is only a line of commonplace supposition in search of a ground of connection and of something real beside the supposition, "the real," as Bradley put it, that in the moment of deploying the merely ideal supposition, "is always in immediate contact with our minds."[16] Sarraute's signature on the novel, "*Paris, 1947*" (p. 223), strongly implies this real that has all along been in contact with the mind deploying the commonplaces or suppositions that constitute *Portrait d'un inconnu*. In reading this novel neither we nor the author can exclude the facts that Sarraute, living under an assumed name, wrote *Portrait d'un inconnu* during the German occupation while passing as a non-Jew and as the governess of her own children, whom she had to forbid to call her "Maman."[17] She wrote in this condition while, in the same few years, millions of children, women, and men were being murdered for the very reason that she was living and writing incognita. This contact with the real in the victimized condition of being unknown and of needing to remain unknown, in this writing of mere suppositions, is as undeniable as it is immeasurable.

In this restricted but powerful sense of a speaking of a second voice—of Sarraute in a second state—Sarraute may finally be said to speak her own voice, as if to her own child who would call her "Maman," through this novel. This occurs when "the women" can recognize that the narrator is now "one of them." The voice that speaks at this moment is from a realm of dying-away, within the line of language, that straddles mere supposition and the real author: "Piously, I shall mingle my voice with theirs. . . ." (p. 222). From this apostrophe there is "Just one more step to be taken"—to "*Paris, 1947*"—to a flash of reality that is experienced only in an endless line of repetition of the commonplace. This flash of the real (from the white world beside the black diamonds of supposition) is mirrored in Sarraute's signing of her own place and time. Because of this signal it has become impossible to evade the real that has all along been in immediate contact with our minds, that is, in this line of pure supposition wending its way to Paris, 1947. In Sarraute's formulation, "La Désinvolture" is a letting go, a suspension of complete mastery, a listening-speech of the mother responding to the child at her breast, though in this book both the child and the encounter with "the soft warmth of the breast" (p. 190) are pure suppositions.

Because for Sarraute, in *Portrait d'un inconnu* at least, language can be only pure supposition, endless repetition of commonplaces, it follows that as a writer she must both overcome and inscribe her resistance to her inherited language of commonplaces, that she must experience its trajectory toward her, find herself within its line of language, and join her voice to the experience of the sublime—specifically a sublime of "the women"—that it creates. Yet it is the line of the sublime which she has followed that has brought Sarraute to the possibility of this aperçu, or "flash."

Sarraute's commonplace book does not merely reproduce the experience of a feminine sublime by repeatedly representing commonplace scenes of victimization, primarily (but not exclusively) of women victims. For Sarraute the necessities of her commonplaces leading to the experience of the sublime are entailed by an archaeology of the commonplaces of sublime language itself. This is the language of the sublime that has come down to her. Yet her foregrounding of the victimization of women, within this language of the sublime, amounts to a reclamation of a large part of the Western tradition, on behalf of "the women." Although *Portrait d'un inconnu* is frequently called the first *nouveau roman* it is difficult to imagine another work that is, in fact, so different from what has been called "the *nouveau roman*'s programme of self-liberation from tradition."[18] Like the principal figures in her line of thought Sarraute shows that achieving freedom and producing a transmissible culture requires entering a second state, an experience of self-deprivation, even of death, within sustained life and the continuous line of a language. In each scene of her language and tradition of "Freud," "Baudelaire," "Hegel," and "Rembrandt" she represents her resistance—and their resistances—to the tendency within each of these languages to falsify a sublime recovery of the self. At the same time Sarraute's "Désinvolture" transforms her line of thought. She achieves this by reclaiming the commonplace, sublime, unrecuperable relation of the women—all along her line—to nothing more or less than the real in the commonplace.

Of the Fragment:
In Memory of Our Son Yochanan

> . . . leaning over the tombstones . . . in order to read
> the inscriptions; musing about the possible lives of all
> these people, this link in the infinite chain, this flash.
> —Nathalie Sarraute

What I have to say about the fragment is impersonal in the extreme, but my broaching of it is in the first instance necessarily personal. This is the way with the experience of the fragment, as I will try to show. Allow me to begin by sharing with you a photograph of our son Yochanan, taken at Prague by my wife in July 1991, and an epitaph, inscribed on his tombstone in July 1992. I reproduce the photograph from our family album, as best I can, in words:

In the photograph Yochanan bends forward, fascinated by the legend of the golem, the artificial man. He bends forward among angles of black stone, his head against sunlight on the tombstone of the Maharal.[1] With his gentle right hand, he traces the inscriptions, phrases of the prophets—his most beloved reading—lavished everywhere. He bends forward in the cemetery at Prague.

. . . A year later: in Jerusalem, in a hallway at school, out of nowhere, blood burst in his brain. He fell forward, helpless.

. . . In the cortege a friend heard the newscast item on the Voice of Israel: "This morning four organs of a fifteen-year-old boy were transplanted into the bodies of two men from Jerusalem and a woman from Ramallah."

Our son's tombstone in Jerusalem is inscribed, in Hebrew, with this text from the Maharal's tombstone in Prague:

And they repaired that which was ruined:
And fragment upon fragment are bound together
        Twins below:
And in peace is his tabernacle above
Under the wings of the spirit.[2]

For reasons that I did not grasp at first (and which, no doubt, I have only grasped in part even now), I have urgently wished to trace the commonplaces, or cited fragments of text, arranged in these lines. From the first, of course, one of the reasons for this sense of urgency was clear. This constellation of frequently cited words and phrases, which had absorbed my son's attention almost by sheer chance, stood waiting at the verge of his existence, like traces of what is gone. I have gradually become aware, however, that the impact of this personal circumstance is intensified by another experience which is both personal and impersonal. The above citation, in fact, itself compels an acknowledgment of this experience, which in these verses races along with every word, every thought, of every one of the commonplaces or fragments. This experience—which is the subject of this chapter—is of the fragment of language *as* fragment, the piece of language, even the fragmentary constellation of fragments, that has been broken off, yet forms a part of a line of fragmentary language. A fragment of this kind comes into being within the experience of the cultural sublime. The condition of the fragment is achieved, sustained, and communicated in the encounter with an effectively endless progression of representations of partial representation. Each of these representations is a commonplace fragment. Here too the experience of a cultural sublime is of a dying-away that is not recuperated by anyone's fragmentary consciousness, yet this experience may continue to generate a sublime line of fragmentary consciousness.

For the workings of this epitaph inscription, it is of the utmost importance that these lines are only an assembly of fragmentary quotations, each broken off from verses that might, in a different moment, spring whole to the mind that recalls them. The topic of fragments is broached directly in the inscription. Each fragment of cited text rumors the possibility of assembling pieces of the destroyed Jerusalem tabernacle. In addition, each fragment hints at a return to life or restoration after death. Yet even in the rehearsal of these rumors, certain facts are pushed to the hard surface. To be sure, once we recall the verses that are cited here (for ease of reference, I will list them in a moment), we know that the epitaph insists upon these facts. Indeed, from the tragic historical context of the very first of these cited fragments—Jeremiah's bitterly ironic "And they repaired," *vayirapooh*—we already know that we must deal here with the *denial* of the claims that "they repaired that which was ruined: and fragment upon fragment are bound together." Even before we spell out this form of the denial, however, the denial itself is palpably before us. In unlettered ways we know the same stark facts announced by the inscription:
Facts:

1. *The tabernacle that was destroyed at Jerusalem is* NOT *miraculously repaired.*
2. *The deceased (in Prague or in Jerusalem) who is the subject of this epitaph is* NOT *miraculously revived from the clay beneath the stone.*

I will soon follow after certain other facts that are signaled by the epitaph.
These other facts, which do not refute those just enumerated, are as follows:

1. *A particular kind of life-transforming power is made available by the fragments of this inscription.*
2. *The fashioning of a tabernacle of a certain kind is indeed reported here.*

There is something like a necessary sequence to a viewer's experience of
this epitaph. Even before reading the inscribed letters, we only stare hard at the
reality on which the tombstone lies. This staring is a work almost without thinking. A kind of thoughtlessness must also characterize, at least to a considerable
extent, the experience of reciting the inscribed declarations—declarations
which, in all likelihood, we had not thought to declare in our own voice before
we faced them on the tombstone. If this mute prelude to speech makes us un-
comfortable, there is another aspect of that prelude that is more discomforting.
This inscription is made of unhesitating statements, yet the fragments which,
side by side, momentarily form these declarations are put in question, even before speech, by shattering kinds of knowledge. All the words of these fragments
once belonged to those who are now dead, but the dead do not speak these
words. And the living who cite the words of the dead have nothing to offer the
dead. The living only erect a stone wall of citation. In this wall there are no
crevices (or secret places) of originality, of self, or of communication. The living cite. Nothing more. Their configurations of fragments proliferate this noth-
ing-more.[3]

This way of hearing the language of an epitaph must be disturbing, but it is
only preliminary to a still more disturbing question for those who try to remember the dead. This question must make us doubt whether even the visit of
the living to the site of the dead can avoid a kind of lie. Do the living even bring
the thought of death to the fact of another's demise? In the line of questions
we have been following we ask, Can the living, within their lives, think a
thought of death? In the language of this inscription this is to ask, Do the living
ever *sustain the thought of a fragment*—a mere fragment, in other words, that has
not already been reimagined, or feigned, as a whole? And if we say that the living can manage to sustain the thought of a fragment—of the dead—then
what kind of meaning, or thought, can the living assemble with an assembly of
fragments? At a moment, for example, when a mother and father recite, on
their son's tombstone, the epitaph from another tombstone—seen in a photograph, where their son traces fading inscriptions—what kind of meaning, if
any, are they making? Is this making a form of superstition—or idolatry—or
necromancy? If one is prepared to say that it is one or more of these blameable
things, then must one assign similar blame (even if only to some considerable

extent) to virtually all human language? After all, to be learnable, to be recognizable, language must have first belonged to someone else. The vast majority of our words and phrases are fragments of the dead.

Once again, then, what would an activity be that puts into orbit a constellation of fragments? As a phenomenon of the psyche, must it be only a pathological lingering on fragments? As a phenomenon of the spirit, how might we, indeed, distinguish such lingering, or fixation, from superstition or idolatry or necromancy—or from desecration, or exploitation, of the memory of the dead? As a phenomenon of social discourse—in which we usually identify given acts or utterances with given minds—*whose mind* do we encounter in the activity of handing on a constellation of fragments? All of these questions have public as well as private dimensions. In fact, one of these dimensions, which is both private and public, raises for me, once more, the question of how a cultural tradition is actively made or brought into being. In the present context I will restate what is at stake for me in this question.

Although we are accustomed to thinking of the phenomenon called tradition as a handing down of an integral whole of meaning, I believe it is far more accurate to say that, on the personal as well as the public levels of our experience, cultural tradition exists only as a participation in a constellation of fragments. Custodians of cultural traditions sometimes claim to have grasped fully formed meanings. At least in the West, however, examinable transmissions and transmitted objects belie those claims. Western cultural traditions do not transmit wholes of meanings; they hand on only constellations of fragments. Yet even the phenomenon of only transmitting fragments certainly forms a vast part of our experience. For each of us, in our particle of human experience, the handing-on, or transplant, of the fragment urgently calls for attention.

Only the context of a given repetition—only the context of a life—determines whether a given repetition of a fragment manifests the repeater's own will to repeat or only his or her submission to someone else's coercion to repeat. But, assuming that the combination of the repetition and its context do evince the will to repeat, the consequence is staggering. The repetition of entering the condition of the fragment affirms one's belonging to the vicissitudes of an effectively endless line of language (including every form of language, including body language). I do not speak of language as if it had a will of its own to call on us. It does seem to me a fact of life, however, one which is felt strongly in our inscription, that in repeating a fragment of the line of language we turn toward the unreachable history of that language. Belonging to this priority of language, in repetition, is our line to this continuity of the human that has produced us, produced us specifically in our condition of the fragment, and which opens (through our repetitions) an unpredictable future of that line of language. In repeating the entry into the condition of the fragment, of fragments made available for transplant somewhere down this line, we almost share in it; we are almost not alone.

I repeat, once again, the fragments of the epitaph:

> And they repaired that which was ruined:
> And fragment upon fragment are bound together
>   Twins below:
> And in peace is his tabernacle above
> Under the wings of the spirit.

With regard to the usages in these lines I understand one of the meanings of the term "fragment" (i.e., the one that refers to the fragments of text that are put together in the inscription) to be identical with that of a commonplace, that is—in this context—a saying or phrase (a "place") to which reference is commonly made.[4] A commonplace in this sense is no more and no less than a datum of common knowledge, a repetition that is recognized as a repetition from innumerable unnamed sources. My focus and, I believe, the focus of the epitaph is on the commonplace as substantive, as a fragment of substance. In the epitaph what is especially on view is the border or edge where the commonplace or fragment has been broken off from something else. The fragments or commonplaces (phrases or even single words) which are arranged here are all, as I have begun to say, citations from specific texts. Some are multiple citations that are clearly designated as multiple citations. In fact, part of what is surprising about the repetitions that comprise these lines is that while one would imagine that each word cited must echo an undifferentiable wilderness of references, in fact the range of possibly appropriate immediate references is limited to only a tiny few, even to references which are virtually unavoidable. (Of course, this is to say nothing about possible echoes of secondary citations. A word about this later.) Since each word cited from the source texts can itself be translated several ways, we cannot say how the maker of the epitaph understood those source texts. For example, the Hebrew word *shever* may mean fragment, hurt, or calamity; *rafeh* may equally mean repaired or healed. Yet we can still proceed to one precise kind of relevant understanding of the epitaph text by translating the source texts according to the collocation of denotative meanings indicated by the epitaph text.

Here is a listing of the fragments of the epitaph (given in italics) cited within the verses from which they are taken:

- Jeremiah 6:14 (repeated, almost word for word, in 8:11): "*And they repaired* [i.e., the false prophets claimed to repair][5] *the fragment* of my people, easily, saying, *Peace, peace,* but there is no *peace*"

- Jeremiah 4:20: "*Fragment upon fragment* is cried out [on Jerusalem]" [The phrase *shever al shever* (fragment upon fragment) occurs only once in the Hebrew Bible, in this verse.]
- Jeremiah 8:21–23:[6] "For the *fragment* of the daughter of my people am I *fragmented;* I am made abject / dejected / melancholy;[7] astonishment has taken hold of me.

   Is there no balm in Gilead? Is there no *repairer* there?

   Why hasn't new flesh covered the wound of the daughter of my people?

   Oh that my head were waters, and my eyes a fountain of tears, that I might weep day and night"
- 1 Kings 18:30: "And he *repaired* God's altar, *that which was ruined*"

   [Elijah repaired God's altar by laying out twelve stones in the name of God. The scene is the competition with the four hundred and fifty false prophets of Baal, whom Elijah challenged, before Ahab and the children of Israel, to produce a miraculous flame upon their altar. After the prophets of Baal failed, Elijah repaired God's altar. God then responded with the flame that fell from heaven upon that altar. The word *heharoos* (that which was ruined), cited in the epitaph, occurs only this once in the Hebrew Bible.]
- Job 38:38: "When the dust grows to hardness and the clods *are bound together*"
- Job 41:8:[8] "[The scales of Leviathan"—by whom "sorrow is turned into joy" (41:14 / AV 41:22)] *are bound together* each to his brother, stuck together, and cannot be separated"

   [These verses spoken by God to Job from the whirlwind instance acts of making wholes that are beyond human capacity, both of execution and understanding. Cited with perfect exactitude in the epitaph, this unusual passive form of the Hebrew word is used here in Job, twice: *yidoobakoo* (are bound together). These are the only occurrences of this form of the word in the Hebrew Bible. Note that the word occurs in Job, as in the inscription, with *bound together* and in a statement concerning the joining of fragments.]
- Exodus 26:24: "And they shall be *twins together and below*"

   [Repeated at Exodus 36:29, with the change of one vowel, the phrase refers to two of the boards that form the tabernacle. In the Hebrew Bible these words occur together nowhere else. The word translated "twins," and so spelled in Hebrew in the epitaph, can be read either "coupled" or "twins" in Ex. 26:24, while it can only be read "coupled" in Ex. 36:29.]
- Psalms 76:3: "*And his tabernacle is in peace* [in Salem]"

   [The letters shin, lamed, mem could be read as *shalom* (peace) or, as in the masoretic or traditional vowelization, *shalem* (Salem, i.e., Jerusalem).][9]
- Babylonian Talmud, Sanhedrin, 96b: "*Under the wings of the spirit*"

   [With the preposition *on*, this phrase became part of the traditional prayer for the dead: "Oh God full of mercy . . . grant proper rest on *the wings of the spirit* . . . and may [he or she] rest in *peace.*"][10]

As I have already suggested, the inscription before us denies, from the beginning and pervasively, the very claim to restoration that it seems to make. This is a claim that any mourner might devoutly wish it to make. The denial is made inescapably clear in the razor-sharp ironic doubleness of the very first cited word, *vayirapooh* (And they repaired). Jeremiah uses this word with bitter irony precisely to denounce the claim of the false prophets that they have "repaired the fragment" of Jerusalem and have wrought *shalom* (peace, wholeness). In fact, if there is any one biblical verse which, more prominently than any other, may be said to shadow our inscription it is the frequently cited "*And they repaired the fragment of the daughter of my people, easily,* saying, *Peace, peace,* but there is no *peace.*"[11] The lines of our inscription consist of three sentences separated by colons. In each sentence the most heavily emphasized word—"And they repaired" (one word in the Hebrew), "fragment," "peace"—is a fragment of this bitter verse in Jeremiah, so that the force of the denial is an undercurrent throughout the inscription.

There are countercurrents here as well, to be sure. Yet the force of the denial, even in citation, is overwhelming, especially since it is not limited to citing the words of Jeremiah in the moment of his affliction. A moment of Job's affliction together with God's direct denial of the human capacity to overcome fragmentation is also cited here. In Job the unique word *yidoobakoo* (are bound) is a citation from the whirlwind, whence God reminds Job that human being (that is, the same human being that God was indeed able to bind together from mere clods of earth) is incapable of binding up fragmentation, either of clods of clay or of the scales of Leviathan. In these ways, at least, the fragments cited from Jeremiah and Job strongly *deny* the human possibility of escaping the condition of the fragment. We mortals are false prophets to our own minds.

Yet, as I have said, there are also countercurrents in these lines. In citing the opening verb, "repaired," in company with the unique word *heharoos* (that which was ruined) the inscription also invokes the scene of Elijah's awesome assembly of fragments: *and he repaired that which was ruined* (vayirafeh et heharoos) (Kings 18:30). There too, however, only God produces the flame that consumes the sacrifice whole, including even "the wood, and the stones, and the dust, and . . . the water" (38). This citation of a fragment thus acknowledges the *possibility,* for another or An Other, of just such an encompassing of the whole (in this case, to blot it out) which is impossible for the reciter or for me. In the inscription, the logic for mentioning this possibility of encompassing the whole—most especially together with an acknowledgment of the impossibility, for some or most humans, of any encompassing of the whole—is already contained in the Job verses and, indeed, in the Jeremiah verse (where the implicit counter-claim is that, unlike man, God could certainly repair the fragmentation of Jerusalem and bring peace—or blot it out whole). Just so, more intricately, the change in the fragment cited from Psalms 76:3, *And his tabernacle is in peace*, "in shalom," rather than "in Shalem/Salem/Jerusalem," not only indicates the importance to the inscription of adhering to the contours of Jeremiah's denial (i.e., the denial that is pronounced by the fragments of the triple citation, "And they repaired," "fragment," "peace"), but represents a removal of the possi-bility of any repair of fragmentation from the human or earthly sphere—Jerusalem—to the peace or wholeness that is marked off only as the possibility of the Other, somewhere above.

Everywhere in the epitaph lines, I am suggesting, the effect of this empha-sis on doubleness is inescapable. It is to open the split between the impossibility, for the self, of repairing fragmentation and the possibility, for the other, of do-ing just that. It is to deepen our experience of the condition of the fragment.[12] We too are fragments. We cannot repair fragmentation any more than we can raise the dead from the clay at our feet, any more than we can repair and re-place the divine tabernacle in earthly Jerusalem. We can acknowledge that an other might have the capacity that our self does not have. But this acknowledg-ment only engraves more deeply the condition of our fragmentation.

A weave of cited fragments such as this must prompt us to ask precisely when, to whom, and in what way this field of reference was accessible. I will skirt these questions by proposing that at least one way of experiencing the density of this epitaph text was immediately available all along the particular line of tradi-tion—this language of Jerusalem and its destroyed tabernacle—in which it was composed and repeated. This experience entails a kind of magic. By magic I mean a power of instantaneously transforming our experience of reality, most especially by making the experience of the boundary of the visible a part of our experience of the visible. I am speaking here of a dimension of human experience that corresponds to what Max Weber attributed to the premodern world in his description of the modern condition as "die Entzauberung der Welt" (the demagicalization of the world.) I take it that Weber was locating something more pervasive than (or at least different from) the decline of belief in divine revelation or in the sacredness of Scripture.

The magic in our lines of epitaph, in any case, does not depend upon any belief in the sacred or sacramental nature of the cited fragments. Neither is the magic a function or reenactment of the Maharal's alleged magical making of a golem—as in the famous legend with which the Maharal's name became powerfully linked at some point.[13] In the epitaph text, effects of magic are achieved, I will try to show, merely by a series of acts of citation. Let me point out already, however, that there is abundant historical evidence of a tradition of golem making in which what is called upon is the capacity of language to disclose the possibility of a realm of nonbeing, beside being. In this tradition the fragment's capacity to disclose the border of nonbeing has, I believe, a pivotal role. Given the historical existence of a tradition of this kind, it seems to me plausible to wonder whether the acts of citation in the epitaph do partly allude to a golem power of the fragment. This possibility will stand in our path more vividly later, but even then only as a distinct possibility.

For the present, my concern is merely with the effect of citing the iterated fragment of language (the commonplace) specifically within an effectively endless line of fragments or commonplaces. I understand the specificity of experiencing one's being within a line of language to denote a quality of devotion to the fragments of one's language, that is, a devotion with all of one's resources of language. This quality of being exhaustively absorbed by a line of language, in the condition of the fragment, seems to me to be unaccounted for in current theories of iterability.[14] Perhaps coming close to such a quality, Derrida has drawn together Heidegger's brief comments on a "Frömmigkeit" (piety) of thought and a "Zusage" (promise, agreement, consent) of language. Derrida understands Heidegger to be pointing to "the memory of a language, of an experience of language 'older' than it, always anterior and presupposed, old enough never to have been present in an 'experience' or a 'speech act'—in the usual sense of these words."[15] This is extremely suggestive for the topics treated in this chapter. Yet considering the brevity of Heidegger's comments on this "Frömmigkeit" and taking into account his life-long exclusions of (what I would call) others' lines of language—exclusions that Derrida, in effect, acknowledges—it is difficult for me to free Heidegger's term from the sense that it is also "a piety," which is to say, a dissembled convention of openness in language. I feel more compelled by the openness of Stanley Cavell's "idea of diurnal devotedness," not least to language: "The world must be regained every day, in repetition, regained as gone."[16] More recently Cavell has written, "It is in recognizing this abandonment to my words, as if to unfeasible epitaphs, presaging the leave-taking of death, that I know my voice, recognize my words (no different from yours) as mine."[17] My difference from Cavell regards the issue of the unfeasibility or feasibility of the epitaphs made by our repetitions of words or fragments (repetitions in what I call the condition of the fragment within the effectively endless line of fragments). At least in the case or kind of case of the epitaph lines presently under consideration, a return of language to the individual speaker—a recognition of identity or even momentary possession—

does not, I believe, occur. The reciter of the fragments of the inscription by-passes the feeling of having his or her own voice or his or her own words, even if he or she stands committed to responsibility for those words. The reciter speaks a feasible epitaph in the words which are gone from him or her in the instant the words are recited or regained.

For the inscribers and early readers of this epitaph the experience of the cited fragment was very likely both the cause and the effect of cultivating their scholarly or learned style of speech, namely, the style of citing endless commonplaces or fragments of text. In the citing of fragments they experienced the edge of the cited fragment, the verge of the commonplace, in their given line of language. The experience of the fragment in this style of speech, we may say, is a piety consequent upon the recognition or skeptical critique of limitations in human consciousness. At the same time, this way of life is unreservedly devoted to a line of language, which is to say, to the sustaining of being (of the fragment) in the line of language. In the lines of our epitaph a parallel observation applies to the content shaped by the reflex of citation. Few metaphors for the death of a loved one (especially an esteemed loved one) are more commonplace in this tradition than that of "the destruction," referring to the particular destruction of the Temple and its Tabernacle at Jerusalem. Knowing these local contingencies is certainly not irrelevant even to our present-day experience of this epitaph.

The reflex of citation is of pervasive significance in Western notions of both consciousness and language, even though it is a function of our experience of the border or margin of consciousness. To focus this significance I want to bring to bear, once more, some remarks of Hegel, the philosopher of all-embracing reflexes of sublime consciousness. Without acknowledging the force of a line of citation, Hegel is nevertheless generalizing this very reflex when he speaks of the "alienation" of the "I" that "takes place solely in *language*." "The 'I'," he says, "that utters itself is *heard* or *perceived*. . . . That it is *perceived* or *heard* means that its *real existence dies away*."[18]

With what kind of language does the self utter itself? It seems clear that utterances in which our self is bereft of itself, in which our identification with our own language dies away or is ruined, are not restricted to statements *about* the self. In the act of marking off the field of our consciousness by the uttering of any fragment of language which (at least to some large extent) is not ours, we are jolted toward the self-alienation which Hegel witnesses. When we cite (when we speak) we turn, as Hegel says, from being "I" toward becoming "not-'I.'" In the everyday act of citation—of merely using language which is never merely ours—something extraordinary happens to us. We are pushed to the boundary of our selves. This turning away from—or emptying out of—the "I" in the act of citation does not fundamentally vary with the degree to which we feel sympathy or antipathy to the language that we utter or cite. Neither does it matter whether the utterances, in which the self posits and then alienates itself, are inherently affirming or denying. Since all the language that we learn to recognize and to use for others' recognition is necessarily repeated language, we continually experience this self-alienation merely as a result of using language, with or without specific attribution to another speaker or another writer.

To put the same point somewhat differently: by virtue of this self-alienation in our use (which is to say, our citing) of language, we experience a split or doubleness of reality. We apprehend the visible world, or the world made by language, alongside the boundary of that world. The consciousness that experiences this self-alienating turn is itself, therefore, in the condition of a fragment, that is, in the divided state of "I" / not-"I" or, we may say, of being / not-being. It may be, in fact, that our capacity to make this particular turn in thinking is precisely what makes it possible to conceive of a fragment, which we would otherwise immediately reconstitute as a whole.

This experience is of the fragment of language as fragment, the piece of language (even the fragmentary constellation of fragments) that has been broken off, which yet forms a part of a line of language. The condition of the fragment is achieved, sustained, and communicated in the encounter with an effectively endless progression of representations, each of which is a commonplace fragment. Here too the experience of a cultural sublime is of a dying-away that is not recuperated by anyone's fragmentary consciousness, yet this experience can continue to generate a sublime line of fragmentary consciousness. In this line, the fragmentary citation is a salutation not only of those who are about to die, but of those who have already died or are now dying-away within the line. Salutations of the fragment achieve more than a momentary injection of life into a life that will also soon end. They enable the free placement of the life to which they turn—which is also a fragment—within a sublime line of language.

I do not mean to suggest that this turn in thinking is without cost or pain. Testimonies of various writers suggest, in fact, that this experience of becoming a fragment may be traumatically felt, to the point of becoming agonizingly undifferentiable from an experience of death, that is, a death within our minds.

Earlier in this book we saw that for Hegel this experience of death is only half the story of the "I." Yet Hegel feels it necessary to terrify us with a moment of such death, implying that it has its own continuous reality or at least significant duration in human experience. We have seen one such moment in section 80 of the *Phenomenology of Spirit*. I want to quote that passage once again not because it records the other-than-ordinary experience of an extraordinary intellect. Rather, its value for me is that it represents with extraordinary penetration and clarity a mind contemplating an experience that is only of the common-places, or the cited fragments, that make up language and that are therefore ac-cessible to everyone, most intensively to those for whom the risks of self-alien-ation in language, in commonplaces, are a way of life. The list of those who live this way of life, every day, certainly includes a great many serious participants in literary, painterly, philosophical, and scriptural traditions. In reciting the fol-lowing passage from Hegel I am suggesting, that is, that for anyone engaged in citing the fragments of a tradition—in which citation is a way of life lived along a line of language—the consequences are no less intensely and radically seri-ous than those described in these words of the *Phenomenology:* "Whatever is con-fined within the limits of a natural life cannot by its own efforts go beyond its immediate existence; but it is driven beyond it by something else, and this up-rooting entails its death. Consciousness, however, is explicitly the *Notion* of itself. Hence it is something that goes beyond limits, and since these limits are its own, it is something that goes beyond itself. With the positing of a single particular the beyond is also established for consciousness, even if it is only *alongside* the limited object."

We have earlier traced Hegel's relation to, and *repression* of, the experience of a line of citation, as for example in his citation of an ancient citation from Virgil of a yet more ancient citation from Homer.[19] This unacknowledged force of the line of citation, we may now say, has particular importance for Hegel's "positing of a single particular," which is at least highly suggestive of citing a fragment of language. Indeed, the passage just quoted has extensive implications for a meditation on the lines of epitaph before us. The "positing of a single particular" and, "*alongside*" that positing, the "beyond . . . established for consciousness" describe the condition of the fragment in our "natural life." Yet Hegel's word "positing" hides the experience of citing, within positing, that drives consciousness beyond itself. The "uprooting" (dies Hinausgerissenwer-den) of which Hegel speaks is not of the effectively endless, buried root of lan-guage, but only of consciousness itself, that is, when consciousness dies away in its encounter with the effectively infinite root of a sublime line of language.[20]

In modern thought the negating turn, or what Hegel calls the "negativ-ity,"[21] that produces the experience of doubleness is well known by the pair of terms "Being" and "Nothingness." In modern philosophy, these terms have ac-quired wide currency in various strands of existentialism. In the above passage from Hegel it is clear that an opposition between being and nothingness is strongly felt from first to last. Yet the narrow association of these terms with particular modern thinkers—as if they were the inventors of them—is cer-tainly a form of provincialism that does violence to the meanings of the terms themselves. The experience of self-alienation (in language), to which these writers have only drawn modern attention, always entails placement in an endless line of self-alienations. This must be the case because the experience of self-alienation in language—which must mean, inherited language—is already a commonplace feature of a variety of ancient cultures, where it appears, indeed, in a vast variety of forms. It cannot surprise us that a writer of the late sixteenth century like the Maharal of Prague, who was conversant not only with biblical and rabbinic culture but also (to the extent imported by medieval philosophy) with Greek philosophy, recurringly employs a conceptual lexicon that includes the fragment, being, nonbeing, nothingness (or cessation), absence, doubling, and doubleness.[22] If one were to bring to bear the relevant texts of the Maharal and the traditions behind them, it would become clear that the affinities of this lexicon with, say, Hegelian concepts of being and nothingness are neither incidental nor superficial.

My claim here, however, is not that the epitaph text from the Maharal's tombstone exemplifies conceptions of being and nothingness which anticipate, as it were, conceptions of modern philosophy. The Maharal's writings offer only an added possible resonance, not a source or explanation, for the constellation of fragments which constitutes these lines. The experience of unrecuperated consciousness which is created by encountering the effectively endless line of commonplaces in our epitaph text is a pervasive phenomenon in the West, compared to which the conceptions of the Maharal, as well as those of Hegel, are only epiphenomena. The acuteness of any one thinker who employs these conceptions is particularly manifest, one might say, at the moments when, in addition to exemplifying the concepts themselves, he or she communicates the immemorial everydayness of what is being exemplified.

If, indeed, all language is charged in this way to lesser or greater extents, it is no wonder that the language framed by an epitaph which is exclusively made of self-consciously cited fragments can raise the experience of self-alienation to an intensity that propels the mind toward helplessness. Our experience of reality is transformed painfully here—merely by experiencing (in citation) the visible world or the world of spoken language or the "I" side-by-side with the verge of these worlds.

The constellation of fragments before us exemplifies, to an unusual degree, the way in which a condition of fragmentation and self-alienation is perceived, in the West, as a historical life-function. To varying degrees, that is, we belong to a line of language (it does not belong to us) in the condition of self-alienation and fragmentation. The line of language is the sustaining of the condition of a fragment within a given history or endless line of language of the fragment. Conversely, this same line of language tends to deny that we may recuperate (from) fragmentation and self-alienation or that we may exit the line of language in which fragmentation repeats. The line of language in which the condition of the fragment is generated and sustained is always our particular line. This is the given line within which the fragment is turned toward other fragments of the line.[23]

In this constellation of fragments we can see, for example, how the condition of a fragment is sustained and turned, when we attend to the chiastic pattern in which the cited fragments are disposed. Here we see again that the rhetorical figure of chiasmus is only, in the first instance, the form of a wish fulfillment, namely, that we might return from (or repair) the condition of the fragment. In other words, within the agitations of thought and language the unit reflex that creates the condition of a fragment consists of the positing of an object and of the alienation which produces the antithesis of that object: A then not-A or B. A full chiasmus would be (wishfully) performed or completed by this reflex and its reverse or return (B then A) or, all together, AB : BA.

In transcendental or religious language the transcending of the condition of the fragment is a projection that acknowledges this possibility of return for the other. Then the other is defined as that which might have this possibility which I do not have. In such cases chiasmus is a double figure that maps both the impossibility of overcoming the condition of the fragment—that is, for the self who speaks (or cites)—together with, at the very same time, the possibility of success for an other. Seen from this point of view, this doubleness is usually a melancholy spectacle for human beings (that is, unless we envision a self with transcendental powers). The first two lines of the epitaph text offer, indeed, a spectacle of this melancholy kind. The fragments set out in these lines—from Jeremiah, Kings, Exodus, and Job—form a cross-structure of antitheses. Thus in the lines,

And they *repaired* that which was *ruined:*
And *fragment upon fragment* are *bound together,*

the would-be chiasmus, which is being denied, could not be clearer:

$$\begin{matrix} \text{repaired [A]} & \text{ruined [B]} \\ & X \\ \text{fragment upon fragment [= ruined, B]} & \text{bound together [= repaired, A]}. \end{matrix}$$

In Scripture (as we saw in chapters 2 and 7) the chiastic form is, indeed, regularly used to express the transcendent mind or divine other. This is the form, for example, of such famous (i.e., endlessly cited) verses as, indeed, Psalms 76:3, part of which is cited in our inscription: "And in Salem is his tabernacle, and his resting place in Zion." Here nearness and farness are expressed simultaneously, so that the limit which defines nearness and farness is transcended:

> And *in* [*earthly*] [*Salem*] *peace*   is *his* [*heavenly*] *tabernacle,*
>   X
> And *his* [*heavenly*] *resting place*   in [*earthly*] *Zion.*[24]

Here the chiastic form is strongly suggestive of the capacity of a divine, Other consciousness to synthesize opposite forces or movements. We have seen how Hegel, in fact, explicitly cites a scriptural chiasmus as part of his demonstration of a realized wish fulfillment of recuperating the condition of the fragment in human consciousness, that is, in the dialectical materialization of self-consciousness. We recall that he cites Paul in Romans 12:19, "Vengeance is mine; I will repay, saith the Lord," in the following passage from the *Philosophy of Right:* "It is not something personal, but the concept itself, which carries out retribution. 'Vengeance is mine [; I will repay], saith the Lord', as the Bible says. And if something in the word '*re*pay' calls up the idea of a particular caprice of the subjective will, it must be pointed out that what is meant is only that the form which crime takes is turned round against itself" (paragraph 101, addition).[25] Without repeating the details of my discussion of these matters in chapter 7, I will recall that Hegel's claim here is cast in doubt even by the direct statements in the line of citation and of image-withdrawal from which his cited commonplace of revenge emerges. More important, it is transformed by the experience of the line of citation. In this line of citation chiastic form is the representation of the withdrawal of representation in language, that is, in the experience of the line of citation of language which represents the withdrawal of representation. Because Hegel's representation of this scene in *The Philosophy of Right* is a repetition of the commonplace line of this scene, it too actually represents something other than that which Hegel tells us he is representing. In this line of citation the derivation of freedom in a sublime dying-away closely resembles Kant's sublime, especially the cultural sublime which, I have argued, Kant actually represents. (This is the dying-away and freedom and moral feeling that are the effect not only of encountering endless repetition of the colossal and of self-deprivation, but, as Kant acknowledges but will not discuss, especially of encountering representations of image-withdrawal in an endless or commonplace line.) In addition, this line of citation identifies and explains that which is left mysterious in Kant. It identifies and explains how, in the first place, we have access to the freedom to choose self-deprivation or image-withdrawal, or, indeed, even to choose to encounter the sublime experience. In this line of citation freedom is made available by being located (graced or chosen, some will say), in a line of sublime language, in the cultural sublime.

Thus although Hegel acknowledges none of the lineal features of the line of language that he is citing, he too has found himself placed and has represented his placement in a line of citation. His "as the Bible says" cites Paul's chiasmus of revenge and Paul's "saith the Lord," which in their turn cite the Hebrew Bible, as in Ezekiel's chiasmus of revenge (citing Moses' chiasmus of revenge, speaking for the Lord) and Ezekiel's "saith the Lord God." As a result, there is a decisive difference between what, on the one hand, "the Bible says" not only about the experience of chiasm and citation but also about revenge and, on the other hand, what Hegel says about that saying or representation. Correlative to the representation of this very different formal experience, this line of citation is making the argument that justifiable revenge can be willed only by the Lord and that such divine revenge is, indeed, the Lord's moral judgment and punishment, rather than a vain human pretense to "vengeance avenged" which, Ezekiel (in this line) twice specifies, is no more than "eternal hatred."

To return to the terms of the present discussion: The biblical commonplace that Hegel cites is already a cited fragment in a particular line of language. In citing (uttering) the commonplace along this effectively endless line of citation Hegel (his "I") too remains irremediably self-alienated. He slips to the verge of the commonplace, the cited fragment. Unlike the divine Other whose chiasmus he cites, Hegel does not haul himself back (*turn round*) to wholeness or conceive the totality of "the concept itself" created by the doubling or reflexiveness of chiasmus. For the transcendent other the return from antithesis can be the achievement of self-consciousness from fragmentation. For the human self the exemplifications of this return from fragmentation can only be the acknowledgment of what is beyond performance and self-fulfillment—except, possibly, by an other. In the case of the mind of a divine Other the basis of the reality expressed by scriptural chiasmus is a matter of belief in possibility. To extend this belief to the mind of Hegel must involve another religious institutionalization.

In our epitaph verses the ironic overtext of the first two lines denies exactly a belief in a human fulfillment of self-consciousness. The same denial is readable in the facts that the fourth line stops short after only the first half of the chiasmus from Psalms 76:3 and that even in this first half we read *heavenly* shalom = peace instead of *earthly* Salem = Jerusalem, thus (among other things) further denying at least the presumption of a chiastic recuperation in the human sphere. Our condition is to remain fragmented, disjoined. Almost like a direct comment on this human disjointure, "the wings of the spirit"—two wings of one spirit—are a figure of what is only a matter of belief in the possibilities of the being "above," only, for me, a possibility of imagining the possibility of the other, only, in other words, what remains impossible for me.

On the reverse side of the Maharal's tombstone in Prague is the following chronicle: "This stone sank into the ground to its base: and was already renewed by members of the family and philanthropists of the community in [1724]: and now that the wall of the cemetery fell on it and broke it into fragment of fragment: and even if fragment upon fragment were joined together: even then "they could not read" it [i.e., 'the unique lettering style of this inscription' could never be reproduced]: as it was engraved on the stone: therefore the inscription was reinscribed . . . in [1815]."[26] These statements witness the prophetic power of the original inscription by pointing out that the inscription strongly hinted at the later fate of the stone, when the wall of the cemetery fell upon it, breaking it into fragment upon fragment. It may not be merely accidental, in addition, that the date of the last Prague reinscription mentioned here is 1815. This date evokes the ghostly possibility of a potential encounter with another fragment of history. That is, it may quietly put into orbit the suggestion that the epitaph text foretold the earthshaking events of that year, when, at Waterloo, the empire of Napoleon (and perhaps also a false messianic hope for the aftermath of the French Revolution, false, not least, for the Jews) was shivered in fragments. The phrase cited from Daniel, "but they could not read [the handwriting on the wall]," certainly can propose a chilling prophecy of empire doomed to fragmentation.

Because of the imposing potentiality of this kind of reference, I need to be especially clear here. Not only do I not say that a prophecy of doomed empire is a meaning that the epitaph states or creates. I say that the epitaph *cannot* state or create such a meaning. Possible references of this or any other kind are only in the category of a possible or potential meaning that the fragments of the epitaph propose *only as a possibility or potentiality*. Each possible reference is only a hint at a would-be synthesis of a would-be experience of a would-be historical moment. It becomes clear here that meaning and the desire for meaning are not the same thing. The epitaph's fragmented constellation of fragments precludes the illusion of a whole of experience or of an actual moment. In this sense these fragments cannot, indeed, be "read." We do not fully encounter history—or bring past and present together—here. We do not fully experience the passing of the deceased here. We do not think our own self-consciousness here. But the fragments which we are continue to turn in a constellation with a vast array of other fragments. Detached from us, our fragments, now no longer ours, may even be passed on, transplanted, along the line of language, even, on occasion, to collateral lines of language. This is the making of tradition in all its magic—and melancholy.

In the epitaph text there are no doubt many diverse references to the locale, or contemporary world, in which the stone was erected. Among such possible references we must also confront, with the utmost care, the possibility, the potentiality, that this epitaph text, inscribed on the tombstone of the Maharal of Prague, includes—*in some sense*—the making of a golem, that is, within the epitaph's activity of citing its cited fragments. There are prima facie reasons for contemplating this possibility. There is the highly specified reference, in the word *heharoos* (*that which was ruined*), to Elijah's prompting of God's miraculous fire by laying down pieces of stone "in God's name." Since the Maharal's legendary tracing of the outline of the golem in wet clay was followed by God's instilling of his divine fire, the word *heharoos* (*that which was ruined*) in the epitaph may suggest the hidden play of God's invisible flame here too, that is, in these lines (inscribed on stone) themselves. There are also the uniquely specified Job references—in the word for joined, *yidoobakoo*—to a divine joining together of clods of clay and of a divine making of a divine servant-creature, Leviathan.

There are large obstacles, however, to interpreting these references as, even in part, allusions to the Prague legend. We know neither the date of first inscription of the epitaph (or this part of the epitaph) nor the date when the Maharal first became associated with the legend of the golem, (i.e., the legend of making a protecting golem, which was an artificial man, from clods of clay, by citing certain sacred words and letters). Yet it seems unwarranted to dismiss totally at least the possibility—*possibility is all-important here*—of a potentiality of reference, hovering in the epitaph text, to a magical creation of a golem through the citation of fragments.

In fact, it may be that the mere, virtually invisible creation of only this potentiality is in this epitaph the magical creation of a golem of language. This may occur, that is, in the citation of the fragments of words and letters—in this encounter with an effectively endless line of language—which are turned toward, transplanted toward, these and other fragments. I cannot help thinking, in these terms, that the inscribers of the epitaph associated the citing of these particular fragments of text with the making of a golem of language, only of language—and of consciousness formed, in the condition of the fragment, along this line of language. This association highlights the magical function of citation and fragmentation in an unforgettable way. That is, I do not suggest that reference is necessarily made here to the golem of the Prague legend. Almost to the contrary, I propose that if reference is made here to the Prague legend, the kind of abstract golem making in which the text engages represents an attempt to elude, or even expurgate, the claim to a materialized golem making that was associated (at some point), will he nill he, with the Maharal.

Historians have documented a long and ancient tradition of golem making.[27] According to this tradition, golem making of a magical but only intellectual kind was exemplified by Bezalel's making of the tabernacle (described in Exodus—without elaboration of the means of making) as a microcosmic representation of the entire cosmos, down to details of human vital organs.[28] To be sure there were other, darker traditions of golem making, which were regarded by many as nothing short of idolatry. Within the lore of golem making itself there are, in fact, well-known stories of opposition to abuse of the power of making a golem.

One of the best known of these stories, for example, regards the ancient tradition that Jeremiah had a son, and that father and son together created a golem in the bodily form of a man. But, having done so, Jeremiah and his son recognized the idolatrous implications of such creation and forthwith reduced the artificial man to dust and ashes.[29] A normative rabbinic attitude toward the dangers of golem making is powerfully reflected in this story. Yet, as Gershom Scholem emphasizes, even within the traditions which warn against material golem making, the idea of an intellectually magical or ecstatic creation of a golem is frequently extolled. One fourteenth-century commentator evokes this white magic of golem making in a particularly beautiful phrase. He calls it "thought creation," (*yetsirah mahshavtith*).[30]

Within our epitaph text it is clear that the leitmotif of all the cited fragments—about a possible construction from fragments (or parts)—is the making or reconstituting of a Jerusalem tabernacle. In the epitaph text this leitmotif may itself suggest that the construction of a tabernacle-like text is inherently miraculous, but perhaps only so, or even distinctly so, in the category of a magical "thought creation," a golem as "*yetsirah mahshavtith.*" Here we remind ourselves that aspects of the term *fragment,* in the sense of imperfect or incomplete material, are contained in the rare biblical word *golem* itself (Ps. 139:16), which only means *imperfect substance.* In the case before us the thought creation is the effect of no more than entering the condition of a fragment and of constellating fragments—fragments which remain fragments—within a given line of language.[31]

Here, one more time, is that constellation:

And they repaired that which was ruined:
And fragment upon fragment are bound together
            Twins below:
And in peace is his tabernacle above
Under the wings of the spirit.

To recapitulate and to conclude:

Only the context of a given repetition—only the context of a life in its given line of language—determines whether a given repetition manifests the repeater's own free will to repeat or only submission to someone else's coercion to repeat. But, assuming that the combination of the repetition and its context do evince a free will to repeat, the consequence may be staggering. The repetition of entering the condition of the fragment may affirm one's belonging to the vicissitudes of a line of language (including every form of language, including body language). Belonging to this line of language, in a freedom of repetition, is our line to this sublime continuity of the human that has produced us, produced us specifically in our condition of the fragment, and which opens (through the edges and transplantings of our fragments) an unpredictable future of that line of language.

A fragment of this kind comes into being within the experience of the cultural sublime. The condition of the fragment is achieved, sustained, and communicated in the encounter with an effectively endless progression of representations, each of which is a commonplace fragment or partial representation. Here too the experience of a cultural sublime is of a dying-away that is not recuperated by anyone's fragmentary consciousness. Yet this experience can continue to generate a sublime line of fragmentary consciousness. We may feel impelled to differentiate sharply between a living individual's sublime experience of the freely chosen condition of the fragment in a line of fragments (say, Freud's continuation of a limping thought of both *frisch* and *lahm*, Pleasure Principle and Beyond, within *Beyond the Pleasure Principle*) and the condition of the dead fragment (say, the constellation of fragments called *Beyond the Pleasure Principle*, that is no longer Freud's life) which no longer has free choice of any kind, even if it yet contributes something to the sustaining of another life within the line. A difference between the effects of these handings on, however, may not exist for the recipient individual and the recipient community. This effect will be especially undifferentiable if the hander on has achieved a residuum of identity, which is to say, a traceable record of sublime disposition of one's life while lived, that continues to remove attached strings of self (and to make way for others' freedom) even after death. Thus, in repeating the entry into the condition of the fragment, along the line of a cultural sublime, we almost share in it, both with the living and with the dead; we are almost not alone.

One more word of conclusion:

For me, necessarily, the magical experience of fragments in a line of language—of a Jerusalem-centered cultural tradition or any other—is most of all revealed in flashes by our son's life and death. I do not take hold of it. I do not grasp it. In our son's life this magic of language occurred not only, but also not least, in his motion of turning toward two gravely ill Jewish men and a Moslem woman. Fragments of his being, of his being as living language—fragments now no longer his—passed to their beings. This was the final, unconscious gesture of a dying boy of Jerusalem, our son Yochanan.[32]

Notes

Preface

1. George Steiner, *Real Presences* (Chicago: University of Chicago Press, 1991), pp. 72–75, has recently cautioned that, unlike the case of scientific theory, which has "predictive force," with regard to the productions of culture "the concept of theory . . . is wholly contained within the life and limits of language."

2. Edward Shils, *Tradition* (Chicago: University of Chicago Press, 1981), pp. 21, 12, 235, 7.

3. Indirectly or unconsciously Shils's insights may well derive, in part, from Martin Heidegger's immensely subtle but esoteric and, in one way, more limiting discussion of "Temporality and Historicality" (2.5) in *Being and Time*, trans. John Macquarrie and Edward Robinson (Oxford: Blackwell, 1985), pp. 424–55. Indeed in *Truth and Method*, 2d ed., trans. Joel Weinsheimer and Donald G. Marshall (New York: Crossroad, 1991), pp. 296–98, Hans-Georg Gadamer's remarks on tradition and "the hermeneutic productivity of temporal distance" heavily invoke Heidegger's interpretation of "Dasein's mode of being in terms of time." Gadamer's pages, however, do not help us get at the mechanisms of cultural transmission, partly no doubt because of Gadamer's Heideggerian aversion to anything that seems to be mechanistic practice (see p. 266). With regard to temporal distance what is most significant for my purposes is that the new "ontological orientation" that Gadamer takes from Heidegger does not help him achieve or describe any experience of tradition or of any work of tradition that is not, finally, limited to experience of the present. The reasons for this limitation, or limiting focus, may be traceable to Heidegger. For example, in "Temporality and Historicality" Heidegger makes this statement (highly qualified, to be sure, and set among many other statements expressing other angles of vision): in a "sequence of Experiences, what is 'really' 'actual' is, in each case, just that Experience which is present-at-hand 'in the current "now"'" (p. 425). Elsewhere, more simply, Heidegger lays down this axiom: "Experience is concerned with what is present, in its presence" (Heidegger, *Hegel's Concept of Experience*, trans. Kenley Royce Dove [New York: Harper & Row, 1970], p. 121; and see the opening of chapter 3 below). In the closing sentences of *Being and Time* Heidegger nevertheless is (still) asking how to interpret "the ecstatical projection of Being" which is "made pos-

sible by some primordial way in which ecstatical temporality temporalizes" (p. 488). In largely non-Heideggerian ways, the present study follows out a series of interpretive experiences (many of them ecstatic or of the interpreter beside herself or himself) that may be thought to address this question while yet suspending belief in Heidegger's axiom that experience is concerned with what is present, in its presence.

4. My interest is in the representation of the repetition of commonplaces or topoi and not in the way topoi are said by Ernst Robert Curtius to constitute a "unity," a "whole," or perhaps even the assembled archetypes of European culture: *European Literature and the Latin Middle Ages,* trans. Willard R. Trask [Princeton: Princeton University Press, 1990), pp. vii, 15, 101. If there is a contiguity between my inquiry and Curtius's it is with his comments (in the very last pages of his book) on the importance of "Longinus." Curtius breaks off those comments, saying, "We shall not trace the subsequent career of 'Longinus' in the eighteenth century" (p. 400). This door to a sublime experience and self-understanding of Western tradition—via the deepening of concepts of the sublime in the eighteenth century—is one that I have especially tried to open. Indeed, since a transformative experience of the commonplace is a central concern of my book, I should perhaps also note at this juncture that my conceptions of such transformation differ from those of Arthur Danto in *The Transfiguration of the Commonplace: A Philosophy of Art* (Cambridge: Harvard University Press, 1981). What interests me about the commonplace is how it is located, and how it occasions sublime experience, within an effectively endless line of cultural representations each of which is a fragmentary commonplace.

5. Kant, "Analytic of the Sublime," in *The Critique of Judgement,* trans. James Creed Meredith (Oxford: Clarendon, 1973), p. 91.

6. For Jean-François Lyotard an experience of the sublime is of central importance in postmodernism, as he argues, for example, in *The Postmodern Condition: A Report on Knowledge,* trans. Geoff Bennington and Brian Massumi (Minneapolis: University of Minnesota Press, 1984). As far as I can tell, however, Lyotard's kind of sublime is not (despite his invocations of Kant) significantly a Kantian encounter with a series of objects, especially of scenes of victimization and resistance of victimization, in which freedom and moral feeling are definitive of the sublime experience. For critiques of Lyotard's sublime on other grounds, see Meaghan Morris, *The Pirate's Fiancée: Feminism, reading, postmodernism* (London: Verso, 1988), pp. 213–39, and Dominick LaCapra, *Representing the Holocaust: History, Theory, Trauma* (Ithaca: Cornell University Press, 1994), pp. 96–100. Like Lyotard, however, Morris and LaCapra do not attend directly either to Kant's sublime or to Kant's tradition of sublime culture.

7. John Milton, *Of Reformation Touching Church-Discipline,* in *Milton's Prose,* ed. Malcolm W. Wallace (London: Oxford University Press, 1959), p. 44.

8. Walter Benjamin, "Theses on the Philosophy of History," in *Illuminations,* trans. Harry Zohn (New York: Schocken, 1969), pp. 256, 262.

9. See John McCole, *Walter Benjamin and the Antinomies of Tradition* (Ithaca: Cornell University Press, 1993), pp. 10, 295.

10. Karl Marx, *The Eighteenth Brumaire of Louis Bonaparte* (New York: International Publishers, 1969), p. 15.

11. I cite these phrases from Raymond Williams, "Base and Superstructure in Marxist Cultural Theory," *Problems in Materialism and Culture* (London: Verso, 1980), pp. 48–49. In fact, we must not forget that Marx's fillip comes just a few sentences after his opening shot at Hegel: "Hegel remarks somewhere that all facts and personages of great importance in world history occur, as it were, twice. He forgot to add: the first time as tragedy, the second as farce." By reading Marx's repetition of, and resistance to, Hegel's remark on repetition together with Marx's condemnation of the repetitions of tradition we are led to suspect that

Marx was not quite sure of the status of his living brain or consciousness in Hegel's tradition. Here and elsewhere "living" Marx was to a significant extent repeating "dead" Hegel's famous dialectic of antinomies. Here at least Marx is unsure (hence perhaps what we may feel is the nervousness of his joke on Hegel) of just who is here being forgetful or oblivious or consigned to oblivion in this process of repetition. The "nightmare" that Marx experiences here, not only with regard to the scene of "tradition," where he says the "dead" coerce the "living," but also with regard to leading concepts of Hegel (who at very least is having his say in one fully known location, namely, in Marx's speaking right now, right here), is that Marx partly feels himself dispatched to the ghostly realm of the "dead." In the same vein, insofar as Marx's condemnation of Hegel and the dead generations is part of his effort to foster his own tradition Marx too is identified with the oppressor dead. What may be particularly interesting, therefore, in these statements against tradition is the way they show us, contra Marx's intentions, the flow and arrest that sustain a line of tradition.

12. Erich Auerbach, "Philology and *Weltliteratur*," trans. Maire and Edward Said, *Centennial Review* 13 (1969): 15–16.

13. Kant, *The Critique of Judgement*, trans. Meredith, p. 128.

CHAPTER 1. The Cultural Sublime: Descartes, Kant, and Rembrandt

1. Bernard Williams, *Descartes: The Project of Pure Enquiry* (Atlantic Highlands, N.J.: Humanities, 1978), p. 98.

2. I stress that this possible picture of Descartes's thought as what is objectively involved in the state of affairs that constitutes its being thought is an informal proposal rather than a formal crossing of a logical demarcation. I do not require prior acceptance of this proposal to get on, now, to the presentation of materials that will unhurriedly lead the reader to his or her own judgments.

3. Descartes, *Philosophical Essays*, trans. Laurence J. Lafleur (New York: Bobbs-Merrill, 1964), p. 85. Citations from Descartes in English are either from this collection (hereafter *PE*) or from *The Philosophical Works of Descartes*, trans. Elizabeth S. Haldane and G. R. T. Ross, 2 vols. (New York: Dover, 1955) (hereafter *Works*). Citations from the *Discourse on Method* in French are from *Discours de la méthode: Texte et commentaire*, ed. Étienne Gilson (Paris: Vrin, 1925).

4. "Our free will consists," says Descartes, in behaving "in such a way that we do not feel that any external force has constrained us in our choice . . . of one or the other of . . . two contraries" (*PE*, p. 113).

5. I amend Haldane and Ross's "'I' who thought this should be somewhat" to "'I' who thought this should be something."

6. Geertz, *The Interpretation of Cultures: Selected Essays* (New York: Basic, 1973), p. 89.

7. *René* can be read here, too, in "*et retiré que dans les*," which is perhaps plausible only immediately before "*les déserts les plus écartés*." (If such an interest in anagrams seems out of character for Descartes, think of the anagrammatic side of Saussure.) Two other points about "*les déserts les plus écartés*" are worth making. First, when two paragraphs later, Descartes says that for the "existence" of his cogito "there is no need of any place, nor does it depend on any material thing," he knows that he has already represented such an immaterial place by expressing his solitary cogito as no more than "I . . . live" in "*les déserts écartés*," amid "the crowded throng," which is to say, amid the whirl of unlimited material things in "the most populous towns." Second, the lineage of Descartes's utterance of his "I . . . live" or "I am" is immeasurably long. Given the isolation in this clause of his "I . . . live" or "I am"

together with his self-naming "*les* déserts *les plus* écartés," Descartes is almost certainly thinking not only of God's most explicit Old Testament naming of himself, "Ego sum qui sum" (I am that I am)—whose connection with Descartes's "I am" has been frequently noted—but also of its placement "ad interiora deserti" (behind / after the desert) (Vulg. Exod. 3:1, 14). In this sense Descartes's double resolve and double pronouncement of his "I am" echo God's doubled naming of himself in the deepest desert.

8. Descartes's "doctrine" that "every created thing tends constantly to slip out of existence, being kept in being only by the continuous activity of God" is, Williams remarks, "one of the most genuinely religious elements in Descartes' outlook" (p. 149). I suggest that Williams's statement can be amended as proposed here.

9. There may be another consequence for Descartes's religious outlook in his comments on nothingness. Descartes names being "God" and not-being "nothingness." Insofar as God has created him as "a mean between God and nothingness . . . placed between the supreme Being and not-being," Descartes's freedom of choice requires the freedom to deny one of the two contraries in the midst of which he is placed, namely, the existence of God, for even an instant; otherwise he could never *affirm* the existence of God. The tacit implication of Descartes's freedom of choice may account for the veiled force of the word *somehow* in Descartes's statement that God has created him with the possibility of "somehow participating in nothingness." In effect, Descartes describes a divinely sanctioned oscillation between nothingness and being and between affirming and denying God that is perhaps as bold as the same element of Nietzsche's "death of God" theology.

10. See also Descartes's *Principles of Philosophy*, part 1, principle 51: "We perceive that all other things [besides God] can exist only by the help of the concourse of God" (*Works* 1:239).

11. Nicholas Malebranche, *Recherche de la vérité*, ed. Geneviève Rodis-Lewis, 3 vols. (Paris: CNRS, 1962–64), 1:439–40.

12. Rembrandt seems to join himself to the effects of God's light (and *fiat lux*) and concurrence by writing in large letters, at the top of Paul's page, "Rembrand [*sic*] fecit" [Rembrandt made this], although J. Bruyn et al. express doubt that Rembrandt himself inscribed these words (*A Corpus of Rembrandt Paintings*, trans. D. Cook-Radmore [The Hague: Martinus Nijhoff, 1982], 1:146).

13. See Elizabeth S. Haldane, *Descartes: His Life and Times* (London: John Murray, 1905), p. 121. Haldane largely relies on Descartes's remarks in what I call his first resolve.

14. Howard White precedes me in noting resemblances between Rembrandt's and Descartes's handling of light ("Rembrandt and the Human Condition," *Interpretation* 4 [1974]: 17–37). White also draws special attention to Rembrandt's picturing of philosophers in cavernous rooms with windows and to the possibility that Huygens provided a link between Descartes and Rembrandt. Yet White's interpretations of Rembrandt and Descartes seem to me almost wholly mistaken. They are given as general impressions rather than derived from the structures of thought and object that Rembrandt and Descartes show. Curiously, White does not note Descartes's philosopher-in-the-cellar-with-windows passage, quoted below.

15. Rosenberg, *Rembrandt: Life and Work*, 2d ed. (London: Phaidon, 1964), pp. 266–67.

16. Ironically, although the painting "helped to determine the image of Rembrandt's work to an unwarranted extent" (Bruyn et al., 642), it is currently ascribed (at least by Bruyn et al.) only to his workshop, not to Rembrandt himself. The distinction would, I suspect, have been lost on Descartes and most of his contemporaries. The same point applies to Bredius 427, mentioned below. (Bredius numbers are given according to A. Bredius, ed., *Rembrandt: The Complete Edition of the Paintings*, rev. H. Gerson, 3d ed. [London: Phaidon, 1969].)

17. From Rembrandt's later years we may instance the famous *Scholar in His Study* (1652),

usually called the *Faust Etching*. The status of this setting for European philosophical culture at the end of the eighteenth and the beginning of the nineteenth centuries can hardly have been attested in a more remarkable way than by its free adaptation to illustrate the first edition of Goethe's *Faust* (1808).

18. Moshe Barasch has pointed out to me that the chiaroscuro of the late sixteenth century, say, that of Caravaggio or even that of Dutch Caravaggesque painters, uses shadow to bring into relief the material reality of the bodies on which shadow and light are seen together. In Caravaggio we see the outlines of the body through the shadow. In Rembrandt, however, the outlines of the body tend to be lost in darkness. Descartes's reference to painters' use of shadow therefore corresponds quite closely, even distinctively, to the chiaroscuro that Rembrandt was innovating at the time of Descartes's arrival in Holland.

19. I amend Lafleur's translation "cave," for the French *cave,* to "cellar."

20. Rembrandt painted blind Tobit many times, and more than once at a window where Tobias restores his sight to him. In *Tobias, and a Winding Stair* the female figure at the lower right burns incense, presumably at Tobias's direction, to drive away the demon, as the Book of Tobit requires. Unaccountably, Bruyn et al. claim that the identification of the painting with the story of Tobias "is certainly incorrect since there are two women in the picture and there is no specific motif from the story of Tobias" (1:642). In fact, even the second woman, about to leave at the head of the stairs, is clearly indicated in this episode: "Then they [Tobias's in-laws] went forth and shut the door of the chamber" (Tob. 8:2; cited from *The Book of Tobit,* ed. Frank Zimmermann [New York: Harper, 1958]). The woman who helps Tobias by taking "the liver of the fish and the heart out of the bag"—perhaps like the bag that Rembrandt places under the stairs—and puts them "on the ashes of the incense" (Tob. 8:2) is identifiable with Tobias's bride, Sarah. The result is that "the smell of the fish repelled the demon, and he fled into the upper parts of Egypt" (Tob. 8:3).

This is the moment to recall that in Descartes's third dream of 10 November 1619, which he regarded as an oracle of his philosophical future and of what must happen to him for the rest of his life ("Ce dernier songe . . . marquoit l'avenir selon lui; & il n'étoit que pour ce qui devoit luy arriver dans le reste de sa vie") he saw copperplate etchings ("les petits Portraits de taille-douce") which were at the time inexplicable to him: *Oeuvres de Descartes,* ed. Charles Adam and Paul Tannery (Vrin: Paris, 1966), 10:185.

21. Kant, "Analytic of the Sublime," in *The Critique of Judgement,* trans. James Creed Meredith (Oxford: Clarendon, 1973), pp. 102, 117. I do not reproduce Meredith's capitalizations of certain nouns (e.g., *Object*). Citations from the "Analytic of the Sublime" in German are from *Kants Werke: Akademie-Textausgabe,* vol. 5 (Berlin: Walter de Gruyter, 1968).

22. Kant's contradictions regarding the occasion of the sublime have been noticed before. See, for example, Paul Crowther, *The Kantian Sublime: From Morality to Art* (Oxford: Clarendon, 1989), pp. 108–35. Although my interpretation of Kant's representation of sublime experience is very different from Crowther's, I take heart from his attempt to find in Kant an "artefactual sublime" (p. 162), that is, "a sense of the scope of human artifice" (p. 153) that has gone into the production of a given work of art and that therefore can give us "species solidarity" (p. 173).

If there are grounds for excusing my temerity in trying to describe and give voice to something in the experience of the sublime that is hidden from Kant or that he hides from himself, they are that Kant incurs—even insists upon—a distinct cultural "Epoche" or "stoppage" in his relation to the sublime. Kant views the historical line of his own cultural inheritance as magically—by divine dispensation—*dis*continued, so that as a result of this cultural discontinuance the individual human mind was all at once empowered to fall back upon its own autonomy and its own law of reason. This is the autonomy that Kant renders in his presentation of the mind's experience of the sublime. Three years after the publication of the "Analytic of the Sublime," in his *Religion within the Limits of Reason Alone,* Kant succinctly affirms this divine, historical break and its attendant creation of the universal autonomy of the mind. He does this by citing Christ's epochal response to the Pharisees (those who insisted on the continued authority of the Law) in Luke 17:21–22: "For, behold, the kingdom of God is within you." (*Religion within the Limits of Reason Alone,* trans. Theodore M. Greene and Hoyt H. Hudson [New York: Harper, 1960], p. 126.) For Kant the moment of becoming independent of the continuity of culture is also the moment of the liberation of the human mind.

It may not be immediately apparent, but in the "Analytic of the Sublime" Kant decisively expresses the same historical and philosophical persuasion in his apparently gratuitous qualifying phrase about "the Jewish people." He praises that people for the "enthusiasm" they once felt for the "sublime" "commandment" (i.e., of "the Jewish Law") against graven images. Yet he stipulates that this held true of the Jewish people only "in their moral period" (p. 127) ["Epoche," "Periode"—p. 124]. Kant's translator, James Creed Meredith, says of this phrase, "This unkind qualification is a regrettable concession to continental prejudice." (In this case I quote from the first volume of the two-volume first edition of Meredith's translation [his notes are not included in the one-volume edition], *Kant's Critique of Aesthetic Judgement* [Oxford: Oxford University Press, 1911], p. 267.) Kant's disposition in this matter is of far greater interest than as a reflection of European—and Enlightenment—anti-Semitism. What is at stake here for Kant is establishing the *dis*continuance of culture in human experience, the absence or cessation of any life-principle other than that of the autonomous individual mind "of itself alone." Within the "Analytic of the Sublime" Kant incorporates this particular epochal break in his representation of sublime experience. He locates it as the "Epoche" (meaning *stoppage, cessation, pause*) or "Periode" (here meaning *limited stage*) of "the Jewish people," that is, in the termination of their "moral" and "sublime" period (p. 127). (Kant used the word "Epoche" in the first and second editions; "Periode" in the third edition.) Kant denies the continuance of cultural experience within the human thinking of "Law." That continuance would seem to preclude, or at least make unnecessary, the claim of Kant's "transcendental philosophy" (p. 117) for the experience of the "law (of reason)" (p. 106), that is, by the transcendental mind of the individual.

23. I do not find that Kant maintains a significant distinction between presentation and representation, *Darstellung* and *Vorstellung,* in the "Analytic of the Sublime."

24. To be viewed within Kant's own picture of the sublime, these terms require an appropriate framing, which I try to give below. The terms occur on pages 107, 110, and 114 of *The Critique of Judgement;* on pages 99, 103, and 108 of *Kritik der Urteilskraft.*

25. I am grateful to Dieter Henrich for pointing out to me the counterfactual form of Kant's phrase and for proposing the translation "our simply imagining in thought" in place of Meredith's "simply picturing to ourselves." Meredith's phrase apparently anticipates the emergence of a picture in Kant's text; Henrich's is more neutral.

26. Bradley, *The Principles of Logic,* 2d ed., 2 vols. (London: Oxford University Press, 1922), 1:85–87.

27. I have given "state of mind" for Kant's *Geistesstimmung* (p. 85), where Meredith has "disposition of soul," although Meredith usually translates Kant's words for the location of the supersensible faculty as "mind." J. H. Bernard's translation of the *Critique of Judgment* (New York: Haffner, 1931) gives "state of mind" for *Geistesstimmung.*

28. To avoid later confusion we should perhaps note already that the experience of succession, numericity, repetition, and innumerableness is applied by Kant (perhaps somewhat confusingly) not only to the mathematical sublime but also to the dynamically sublime, so

that it will not do to restrict this experience to one kind of cultural experience. See, for example, section 28, where, in the context of the dynamically sublime, Kant instances "bold, overhanging, and, as it were, threatening rocks, thunderclouds piled up the vault of heaven . . . the boundless ocean" and then speaks of "the immeasurableness of nature and the incompetence of our faculty for adopting a standard proportionate to the aesthetic estimation of the magnitude of its *realm*." At the end of that section he calls this "the faculty which is planted in us of estimating that might [nature's] without fear." This is not to say that there is no difference for Kant between the two kinds of sublime experience, but the difference has to do with the subject's angle of vision, with his or her relation to fear, and with the prioritizing of reason rather than with numericity or estimating the "might" of "magnitude."

29. I comment on Hegel's account of "dying-away" in chapter 3.

30. Stanley Cavell suggested to me the emphasis, at this juncture of my argument, on the expressibility of the concept and on the directedness (of sublime experience) toward an end.

31. Bruyn et al. point out that the painting was called *Loth in der Höhle* as early as 1767 (1:282). They mistakenly suggest, however, that the title *Le Philosophe dans sa grotte* dates from C. Vosmaer, *Rembrandt Harmens van Rijn: Sa vie et ses oeuvres* (The Hague, 1868), pp. 2–3. Already in A. Crayen's *Catalogue raisonné de l'oeuvre de feu George Frédéric Schmidt, graveur du roi de Prusse*, published in London in 1789 (i.e., a year before the publication of Kant's "Analytic of the Sublime"), Schmidt's etching of Rembrandt's painting is itemized as "No. 166 *Le Philosophe dans sa grotte . . .* le nom qu'on donne ordinairement à cette estampe" (p. 104).

32. I comment on the iconography of this painting in the next chapter and in articles (although without reference to Kant) mentioned there in note 5. Schmidt's etching is extremely faithful to Rembrandt's painting, except for a slight change in the shape of the bag (here a kind of hat) beside the old man, the absence of the inscription "BiBeL" (perhaps a late addition to the painting) on the book, and the omission of a tiny, insectlike figure over the fire. In addition, of course, Schmidt's etching (dedicated, left to right, to his friend Hoffrath Johann George Lesser, physician to the king) reproduces Rembrandt's painting in reverse. If the accepted date of the painting (1630) is correct, then it was painted shortly *before* Rembrandt moved permanently to Amsterdam, although most of his paintings in the philosophical genre were painted in Amsterdam.

33. The contemporary art connoisseur Matthias Oesterreich, for example, explicitly made this claim in *Beschreibung der Königlichen Bildergalerie und des Kabinets in Sans-Souci*, 2d ed. (Potsdam, 1770), p. 29. In a similar vein, and with regard to the failure of Schmidt's black-and-white etching to reproduce the richness of Rembrandt's painting, it is interesting to recall Kant's comment that, in our experience of painting, "the *charm* of colors" may distract the aesthetic judgment from "what is essential," namely, "the *design*" (pp. 67–68).

34. Aside from the passages quoted earlier, the principal passages I have in mind are the following: (1) "The irresistibility of the might of nature forces upon us the recognition of our physical helplessness as beings of nature, but at the same time reveals a faculty of estimating ourselves as independent of nature, and discovers a pre-eminence above nature that is the foundation of a self-preservation of quite another kind from that which may be assailed and brought into danger by external nature. This saves humanity in our own person from humiliation, even though as mortal men we have to submit to external violence. . . . We must see ourselves safe in order to feel this soul-stirring delight" (pp. 111–12). (2) "Only when [a man] becomes conscious of having a disposition that is upright and acceptable to God, do those operations of might serve to stir within him the idea of the sublimity of this Being, so far as he recognizes the existence in himself of a sublimity of disposition consonant with His will, and is thus raised above the dread of such operations of nature [i.e., 'God in the tempest, the

storm, the earthquake, and the like, . . . presenting Himself in His wrath'], in which he no longer sees God pouring forth the vials of his wrath [und dadurch über die Furcht vor solchen Wirkungen der Natur, die er nicht als Ausbrüche seines Zorns ansieht, erhoben wird (p. 108)]" (pp. 113–14). (3) "(As seems strange) even *freedom from affection (apatheia, phlegma in significatu bono)* in a mind that strenuously follows its unswerving principles is sublime. . . . Such a stamp of mind is alone called noble" (pp. 124–25). (4) "*Isolation from all society* is looked upon as something sublime, provided it rests upon ideas which disregard all sensible interest. To be self-sufficing, and so not to stand in need of society, yet without being unsociable, i.e. without shunning it, is something approaching the sublime" (p. 129). (5) "There is an *interesting* sadness [eine interessante Traurigkeit (p. 127)], such as is inspired by the sight of some desolate place into which men might fain withdraw themselves so as to hear no more of the world without, and be no longer versed in its affairs, a place, however, which must yet not be so altogether inhospitable as only to afford a most miserable retreat for a human being.—I only make this observation as a reminder that even melancholy, (but not dispirited sadness,) may take its place among the *vigorous* affections, provided it has its root in moral ideas" (p. 130).

35. Kant further specifies the importance of resistance in his experience of the sublime: "The *sublime* is what pleases immediately by reason of its opposition to the interest of sense . . . in . . . *opposition* to sensibility . . . in opposition to our (sensible) interest" (pp. 118–19); "the object of a pure and unconditioned intellectual delight is the moral law in the might which it exerts in us over all *antecedent* motives of the mind. Now, since it is only through sacrifices that this might makes itself known to us aesthetically, (and this involves a deprivation of something—though in the interests of inner freedom—whilst in turn it reveals in us an unfathomable depth of this supersensible faculty, the consequences of which extend beyond reach of the eye of sense,) it follows that the delight, looked at from the aesthetic side (in reference to sensibility) is negative, i.e. opposed to this interest" (p. 123).

36. In the next chapter I say more about the resistance in freedom pictured by Rembrandt in his central figure.

37. Some third-party suggestion of Kant's special attention to Schmidt's and Rembrandt's picture of the philosopher withdrawn to his cave may be available in the four-volume novel *Lebensläufe nach aufsteigender Linie* (Berlin, 1778–81), by Kant's close friend Theodor Gottfried von Hippel. Prior to the publication of Kant's *Critique of Pure Reason* (1781), the first and second volumes of Hippel's novel employed a variety of unmistakably Kantian or pseudo-Kantian views and terms (entries in a "Lexicon der reinen Vernunft" [2:245]). After Hippel's death Kant noted, not disapprovingly, that Hippel had made use of ideas derived from Kant's lectures. (Kant's published letter on the subject, together with the more extensive manuscript draft of the letter, is reproduced in Arthur Warda, "Kants 'Erklärung' wegen der v. Hippelschen Autorschaft," *Altpreussische Monatsschrift* 41 [1904]: 61–93.) It may therefore be of special interest, for example, that Hippel's Kantian philosopher expresses the wish that one of his students might attain to the philosopher's "glance through the crack or opening" [Blick durchs Ritzchen (2:246 and passim)] by locating himself in an antique "place of withdrawal into solitude, a place of hiding, a retired spot" [ein Secessum, Secretum, Angulum (2:252)].

CHAPTER 2. The Present Experience of Priority

1. Schmidt's dedication, written from left to right, at the bottom of the reversed plate makes clear that he saw no particular problem in the fact of the reversal.

2. We can regard the synchronicity of Schmidt's obliviousness with Kant's either as an uncanny coincidence or as an inevitable effect of the same Zeitgeist that was forming Kant.

3. Gary Schwartz, *Rembrandt: His Life, His Paintings* (London: Penguin Books, 1991), p. 100. Essentially the same views are expressed by J. G. van Gelder, "Jeremia treurende over de verwoesting van Jeruzalem," *Openbaar Kunstbezit* 7 (1963): 15a, B. Haak, *Rembrandt: zijn leven, zijn werk, zijn tijd* (Amsterdam, 1969), p. 60, and by Bruyn, *A Corpus of Rembrandt Paintings*, ed. J. Bruyn et al., trans. D. Cook-Radmore (The Hague: Martinus Nijhoff, 1982), 1:282.

4. Since the inscription "BiBeL" does not appear in Schmidt's etching, doubt has been expressed about whether the letters were printed on the book by Rembrandt. See *A Corpus of Rembrandt Paintings*, ed. Bruyn, 1:280.

5. I have commented on the iconography of the painting in "Rembrandt's *Jeremiah*," *Journal of the Warburg and Courtauld Institutes* 51 (1988): 260–64 and plate 41, and "Rembrandt's and Freud's 'Gerusalemme Liberata'," *Social Research* 58 (1991): 189–207.

6. Is there a kind of visual pun in the astragal or small convex molding at the *foot* of the column behind Jeremiah's head, directly along the line where Jeremiah's right foot and arm are missing? An astragal is equally a molding of this kind on a column and an ankle-bone.

7. The Dutch is *zijne rechterhand* and *gespannen*.

8. In fact, the winged figure with a torch in its hand that is firing the city was first noticed in print only forty years ago, by L. Réau, *Iconographie de l'art chrétien* (Paris, 1956), II, i, 371, but there can be no doubt of its existence. Réau thought that this was a demon destroying Jerusalem, as it were, against God's will. The editors of the Rembrandt *Corpus* think Réau's view "may be correct" but regard "the appearance of this figure in a biblical scene [as] nonetheless surprising" (Bruyn, 1:282). A demonic interpretation of the winged figure is indeed unjustified.

9. In fact, numerous interpreters of Jeremiah's prophecy and its fulfillment insisted that "the destruction of the Temple was never achieved by the hand of man, but that the angels (or the heavenly fire) burned it. . . . Michael and Gabriel are mentioned as the angels who carried out the work of destruction": see Louis Ginzberg, *The Legends of the Jews*, vol. 6, (Philadelphia: Jewish Publication Society, 1946), 6:392. For the traditional connection between the destructive activity of God's withdrawn right hand in Lamentations and the "forgetting" of both Jerusalem and right hand in Ps. 137:5, see *Midrash Echa Rabbati: Sammlung agadischer Auslegungen der Klagelieder*, ed. Salomon Buber (Vilna, 1899), pp. 110–11. For other aspects of Rembrandt's relation to texts of Ezekiel in this painting, see chapter 7, n. 36 below.

10. See "Rembrandt and the Feast of Purim," in Henri van de Waal, *Steps towards Rembrandt: Collected Articles, 1937–1972*, ed. R. H. Fuchs, trans. Patricia Wardle and Alan Griffiths (Amsterdam: North-Holland, 1974), pp. 206, 213.

11. Rembrandt's contemporary John Milton, for example, puts the following words into the mouth of God the Father in *Paradise Lost*: "I, uncircumscrib'd myself, retire, / And put not forth my goodness, which is free / To act or not" (7.170–72). I have discussed the background of these lines and their significance for Milton's poem in *The Dividing Muse: Images of Sacred Disjunction in Milton's Poetry* (New Haven: Yale University Press, 1985), pp. 112–15.

12. The translation is quite literal and follows the syntax of the original.

13. In the case of these verses Rembrandt reproduces even the left and right placement of the objects in the typography of Hebrew writing, the reverse of Roman typographies. This is not the case, however, with the verses of Psalms, which do nonetheless, as I have said, offer the same fourfold countermovement of left and right, right and left.

14. In the Authorized Version the syntax of the second verse is reversed from its order, thus undoing the chiastic arrangement of both the Hebrew Bible and the Vulgate.

15. See Rudolf Arnheim, *Art and Visual Perception: A Psychology of the Creative Eye. The New Version* (Berkeley: University of California Press, 1974), pp. 34–36.

16. Moshe Barasch, *Icon: Studies in the History of an Idea* (New York: New York University Press, 1992), pp. 282–83.

17. On these vectors in painting in general and in Rembrandt's etchings in particular, see Mercedes Gaffron, "Right and Left in Pictures," *Art Quarterly* 13 (1950): 312–13 and *Die Radierung Rembrandts Originale und Drucke: Studien über Inhalt und Komposition* (Mainz: Kupferberg, 1950), mentioned by Arnheim.

18. Martin Heidegger, "The Origin of the Work of Art," in *Poetry, Language, Thought*, trans. Albert Hofstadter (New York: Harper & Row, 1971), p. 53.

19. See Jacques Derrida, *Writing and Difference* (Chicago: University of Chicago Press, 1978).

20. Derrida, *Of Grammatology*, trans. Gayatri Chakravorty Spivak (Baltimore: Johns Hopkins University Press, 1976), p. 69.

21. To my knowledge, there has been little philosophical discussion of the use of chiastic form in biblical literature, in any specific period or more generally, though the commentary on the technique of biblical chiasmus is extensive. For examples of this commentary, see M. O'Connor, *Hebrew Verse Structure* (Winona Lake, Ind.: Eisenbrauns, 1980), pp. 135, 144, 391–95, 538, James L. Kugel, *The Idea of Biblical Poetry: Parallelism and Its History* (New Haven: Yale University Press, 1981), pp. 18–19, and *Chiasmus in Antiquity: Structures, Analyses, Exegesis*, ed. John W. Welch (Hildesheim: Gerstenberg, 1981), esp. the essays by Yehuda T. Radday, "Chiasmus in Hebrew Biblical Narrative," pp. 50–117, Wilfred G. E. Watson, "Chiastic Patterns in Biblical Hebrew Poetry," pp. 118–68, and John W. Welch, "Chiasmus in the New Testament," pp. 211–49.

22. See "Tropes (Rilke)," *Allegories of Reading: Figural Language in Rousseau, Nietzsche, Rilke, and Proust* (New Haven: Yale University Press, 1979), esp. pp. 40–49, and "Literary History and Literary Modernity," *Blindness and Insight: Essays in the Rhetoric of Contemporary Criticism*, 2d ed. (London: Methuen, 1983), pp. 142–65. It should be mentioned that Derrida has also pursued his own interest in the role of chiasmus in painting. See *The Truth in Painting*, trans. Geoff Bennington and Ian McLeod (Chicago: University of Chicago Press, 1987), p. 166, for example, where Derrida brings to bear on painting his earlier discussions of chiasmus, or, indeed, in the painting of Valerio Adami which Derrida discusses extensively and which he chose for the cover of *The Truth in Painting*. This painting inscribes Derrida's own words, beginning with ".*X.chiasme*," at the X-point or intersection of the painting's two diagonals.

23. Karl Marx, *The Eighteenth Brumaire of Louis Bonaparte* (New York: International Publishers, 1963), p. 15.

24. Kant, *The Critique of Judgement*, trans. James Creed Meredith (Oxford: Clarendon, 1973), pp. 97–98.

CHAPTER 3. The Second-State Self in the Scene of Victimization

1. Martin Heidegger, *Hegel's Concept of Experience*, trans. Kenley Royce Dove (New York: Harper & Row, 1970), p. 27. With regard to what I list as the first assumption, Heidegger paraphrases Hegel, saying, "Experience is concerned with what is present, in its presence" (p. 121). Hegel says that "experience" is "attention to the here and now [the immediate present—('das Gegenwärtige')] as such": *The Phenomenology of Spirit*, trans. A. V. Miller (Oxford: Clarendon, 1977), section 8; hereafter cited in text as *PS* and section number; *Phänome-*

nologie des Geistes, ed. Lorenz Bruno Puntel (Stuttgart: Reclam, 1987), p. 14; hereafter cited in text as *PG* and page number.

2. With respect to questions of force and right and law, there are significant differences in outlook between the *Phenomenology* and the *Philosophy of Right* (ed. T. M. Knox [Oxford: Oxford University Press, 1967]); hereafter cited in text as *PR*. The earlier work offers what Judith Shklar calls a utopian "lament for Hellas," that is, for a fully integrated consciousness, "the undivided consciousness of free citizens in a free polity." (See Shklar, *Freedom and Independence: A Study of the Political Ideas of Hegel's Phenomenology of Mind* [Cambridge: Cambridge University Press, 1976], p. 74.) Compared to the unity of self-consciousness experienced by each Athenian citizen separately, and by all together, the Hegel of the *Phenomenology* considers Roman civil law "atomizing," Roman justice "an alien imposition" (*Freedom and Independence*, pp. 149, 86). Thus it is by sharp contrast that the Hegel of the *Philosophy of Right* comes to "a new, positive appreciation of the social function of legality. . . . The law is now seen as an integrative institution" (*Freedom and Independence*, p. 205). Yet, given these larger differences in context, the differences between Hegel's two scenes of punishment turn out to be smaller than one might have expected. In both cases the nature of the scene is that it expresses an essential self-division at all times in the construction of self-consciousness. In addition, in both versions of the scene there may well be an element of deep division that refutes the claim for undisturbed "undivided consciousness," that is, in Athens as well as in Rome. Commenting on the *Phenomenology*, Shklar draws attention to Hegel's "deeply troubling silence" and "equivocation" about "physical and political coercion," particularly about slavery, in his Athenian utopia. "Hegel chose," says Shklar, "to avert his eyes . . . and to dwell upon civic freedom" (*Freedom and Independence*, p. 95). Hegel's two scenes of punishment still cannot be said to be identical, but the correspondences between them may suggest some of the ways in which even in the earlier scene (i.e., in the *Phenomenology*) Hegel cannot really avert his eyes from the problematic Force of self-consciousness.

3. Here is the scene of revenge in the *Phenomenology of Spirit* which Hegel uses to exemplify the chiasmus of Force: "Revenge on an enemy is, according to the *immediate law*, the supreme satisfaction of the injured individuality. This law, however, which bids me confront him as himself a person who does not treat me as such, and in fact bids me destroy him as an individuality—this law is *turned round* by the principle of the other world into its opposite: the reinstatement of myself as a person through the destruction of the alien individuality is turned into self-destruction. If, now, this inversion, which finds expression in the punishment of crime, is made into a *law*, it, too, again is the law of one world which is confronted by an *inverted* supersensible world where what is despised in the former is honoured, and what in the former is honoured, meets with contempt. The punishment which under the law of the *first* world disgraces and destroys a man, is transformed in its *inverted* world into the pardon which preserves his essential being and brings him to honour" (section 158). Hegel's language of inverted worlds in this and neighboring passages is somewhat baffling, but for our purposes its significance is clear enough. The worlds that stand in inverse relation to each other and that separately generate an internal negation or antithesis are effects both of the way change occurs in the world and of the way the understanding grasps that change.

4. For Hegel the chiasmus or antinomy of Force is nothing less than the "self-identical essence" of life: "We have to think pure change, or *think antithesis within the antithesis itself*, or *contradiction*. For in the difference which is an inner difference, the opposite is not merely *one of two*—if it were, it would simply *be*, without being an opposite—but it is the opposite of an opposite, or the other is itself immediately present in it. . . . What was called *simple Force duplicates* itself and through its infinity is law. . . . This simple infinity, or the absolute Notion, may be called the simple essence of life. . . . This self-identical essence is therefore related

only to itself; 'to itself' implies relationship to an 'other', and the *relation-to-self* is rather a *self-sundering*" (sections 160–62).

5. What Hegel may be repressing (particularly with regard to the poets) in this picture of the self-conscious experience of infinity, and how central the repression is for him, is suggested at a glance in his way of forcibly changing verses of Schiller to serve as the conclusion of the entire work that he entitled *Phänomenologie des Geistes*. In his "Die Freundschaft" (Friendship) Schiller pictures the relation of souls ("*Geister*") as being, in the case of human friendship or even in God's capacity for oneness, an infinite striving for communion in which Infinity or Eternity ("die Unendlichkeit") remains the companion of uncompounded or fragmentary aloneness. Our fate is like God's in this sense of not being able to find, much less unite with, a soul that is the same ("gleich"):

> Freundloss war der grosse Weltenmeister,
> Fühlte *Mangel*—darum schuf er Geister,
> Selge Spiegel *seiner* Seligkeit!—
> Fand das höchste Wesen schon kein gleiches,
> Aus dem Kelch des ganzen Seelenreiches
> Schäumt *ihm*—die Unendlichkeit.

(Cited from *Friedrich Schiller: Gedichte 1776–1788* [Munich: Deutscher Taschenbuch Verlag, 1965], p. 79).

> [Friendless ruled God His solitary sky;
> He felt the want, and therefore Souls were made,
> The blesséd mirrors of His bliss!—His Eye
> No equal in His loftiest works surveyed;
> And from the source whence souls are quickened—He
> Called His Companion forth—ETERNITY!]

(The translation is from *Schiller's Poems and Plays*, ed. Edward, Lord Lytton et al. [London: Routledge, 1889], p. 20.)

Hegel concludes the *Phenomenology* by writing only,

> aus dem Kelche dieses Geisterreiches
> schäumt ihm seine Unendlichkeit. (*PG*, p. 567)
>
> [from the chalice of this realm of spirits
> foams forth for Him his own infinitude.] (*PS*, sect. 808)

Hegel thus proposes that the "realm of spirits" (Geisterreich) is internalized and transformed into a self-compounding, self-consciousness, and "its"—that is self-consciousness's—experience of its own "infinity" (seine Unendlichkeit). Hegel is perhaps acknowledging something about this difference between his thinking and that of Schiller when he observes in *The Philosophy of History* (trans. J. Sibree [New York: Dover, 1956], p. 35) that the representations of "poets, as *e.g.* Schiller" suffer from "the deeply melancholy conviction" that "Universal Reason" cannot be achieved. Hegel was undoubtedly aware of Schiller's extensive preoccupation with the figure of chiasmus and with its very different meaning for Schiller. (See Elizabeth M. Wilkinson's and L. A. Willoughby's introduction to their edition and translation of Schiller's *On the Aesthetic Education of Man: In a Series of Letters* [Oxford: Clarendon, 1982], esp. pp. lxviii–lxxii, xci–xcv, cxcv–cxcvi.) Hegel published the *Phenomenology* in 1807. It is of special interest to me that a year later, in the "Zueignung" to the first part of *Faust*, Goethe, lamenting his departed friends, not least Schiller, has much to say about the

Geisterreich, and he says it in the spirit of Schiller rather than of Hegel. I will turn to Goethe's *Geisterreich* in chapter 8.

    6. For the axis between Hegel and contemporary historicisms, I am thinking, in Hegel's writings, of accounts such as the following, in which despite, even precisely because of, differences and negations self-consciousness comes firmly into being: "The *relation-to-self* is . . . a *self-sundering;* or, in other words, that very self-identicalness is an inner difference. These *sundered moments* are thus *in and for themselves* each an opposite—*of an other;* thus in each moment the 'other' is at the same time expressed" (*PS,* section 162; the emphases are Hegel's). Yet the question of what is new or not new in contemporary historicisms is in itself trivial compared to the significance of the buried commitments which these historicisms continue to make to Hegel's notion of the balanced oppositions which constitute self-consciousness. This self-consciousness seems to depend upon a psychic reading of the other's mind and even a vicarious living of the other's experience. In Hegel's use of the oppositional model, the mind—contemplating the infinity of self-contradictions between self and other—leaps to the achievement of self-consciousness. Despite the mysteriousness of this leap, for most literary historians up to the present day the triple event of achieving self-consciousness, detailed in Hegel's account, retains something very like the following triple Hegelian significance: in the moment of achieving self-consciousness, (a) the other is comprehended within self-identity, (b) the back-and-forth movement of reality between unity and diversity is grasped, and (c) law (or submission to a way of understanding) is actualized in the foundation of an all-embracing institution, such as the state. To be sure, Hegel believes that this self-consciousness is more than personal or individual. While it is embodied in the individual, it has a more than physical and more than human reality which he calls "Universal" and "Absolute."

    The relation between self-consciousness and the other is simplified in the *Philosophy of Mind.* There Hegel claims that through the mutual recognition of self-consciousnesses, "as it were, fused with one another" (Zusatz 436), self-consciousness is elevated to the condition of "universal self-consciousness." In Zusatz 437 he adds, "Universal self-consciousness has revealed itself to us as this unity, for we have seen that this, in its absolute difference from its Other, is yet at the same time absolutely identical with it." (I quote from *Philosophy of Mind,* trans. William Wallace, together with the *Zusätze,* trans. A. V. Miller [Oxford: Clarendon, 1971].)

    Derrida, whose commitment is to letting deconstruction or "writing" happen, rather than to either writing histories or denying the possibility of writing history, has no difficulty in acknowledging that Hegel was "the first thinker of writing": *Of Grammatology,* trans. Gayatri Chakravorty Spivak (Baltimore: Johns Hopkins University Press, 1976), p. 26.

    Whether or not they acknowledge it, the historicisms of Harold Bloom, Paul de Man, and Stephen J. Greenblatt are built upon versions of this Hegelian chiasmus. Thus, although he does not seem to be aware of it, Bloom's "revisionary ratios" described in *The Anxiety of Influence: A Theory of Poetry* (New York: Oxford University Press, 1973), pp. 14–16, are a rich and elaborate reissuing of Hegel's chiasmus of self-consciousness in its moment within the historical process. One could make a list of Bloom's terminology—"swerve," "completion and antithesis," "breaking-device," "repetition," "discontinuity," "emptying-out," "ebbing," "Sublime" and "Counter-Sublime," "solitude," "return of the dead"—and then mine Hegel's descriptions in the *Phenomenology* for very close equivalents. Most especially, Bloom's revisionary ratios turn like Hegel's chiamsus by experiencing the dying-away and alienation of negativity and then recuperating all losses within self-consciousness. When Bloom says later that "every post-enlightenment master moves, not towards a sharing-with-others as

Dante does . . . , but towards a being-with-oneself" (p. 123), he is citing the force of Hegel's self-consciousness. (Bloom's distinction concerning Dante, taken from John Freccero—who discusses Dante's relation to Virgil—is worthy of special attention, although it raises questions about the justification for Bloom's periodizations.) I will return to these matters in chapter 8.

The importance of chiasmus in de Man's accounts of literary history may be seen (among other places) in "Tropes (Rilke)," in *Allegories of Reading: Figural Language in Rousseau, Nietzsche, Rilke, and Proust* (New Haven: Yale University Press, 1979), pp. 20–56, and, in more practical fashion, in "Literary History and Literary Modernity," in *Blindness and Insight: Essays in the Rhetoric of Contemporary Criticism*, 2d ed. (London: Methuen, 1983), pp. 142–65, especially where de Man places "the steady fluctuation of an entity away from and toward its own mode of being" in his definition of literary history (pp. 163–65). Brook Thomas, *The New Historicism and Other Old-Fashioned Topics* (Princeton: Princeton University Press, 1991), pp. 183–97 (and throughout), has discussed Greenblatt's characteristic use of "that favorite new historicist figure—chiasmus."

7. Hegel, *Philosophy of Right*, section 220. In reproducing this passage I have followed Stanley Cavell's lead in eliding the words " . . . and this has its proper actuality in the court of law," after the word "scene," since they draw attention away from the scene itself, as if we are now viewing another scene (which we are not doing), and from the character of the language used to constitute the primary scene. See Cavell, *The Claim of Reason: Wittgenstein, Skepticism, Morality, and Tragedy* (New York: Oxford University Press, 1979), p. 475.

8. See Knox's note, pp. 310–11, clarifying that "itself" is "not the ego . . . but negativity," so that for Hegel the individual is "self-related negativity."

9. We should be clear that the scene of Hegel's oppositional "moment" signifies a mechanical or spatial picture, not a passage of time. For this purpose we can retrieve here part of J. R. Morell's comment, cited by J. Sibree, on Hegel's use of the term *moment:* "This term was borrowed from mechanics by Hegel (see his 'Wissenschaft der Logik,' Vol. 3, P. 104, Ed. 1841). He employs it to denote the contending forces which are mutually dependent, and whose contradiction forms an equation." See Hegel's *The Philosophy of History*, p. iv. Hegel, in fact, describes in detail the back-and-forth vectors of the smaller "moments" which make up the larger "moment [of] the concrete concept of freedom" that we see in the scene of revenge. Here is the passage at greater length: "Indeterminacy is . . . only a negation in contrast with the determinate, with finitude; the ego is this solitude and absolute negation. The indeterminate will is to this extent just as one sided as the will rooted in sheer determinacy.

"What is properly called the will includes in itself both the preceding moments. The ego as such is in the first place pure activity, the universal which is by itself. But this universal determines itself and to that extent is no longer by itself but *posits itself as an other* and ceases to be the universal. Now the third moment is that, *in its restriction, in this other,* the will is by itself; in determining itself it still remains by itself and does not cease to keep hold of the universal. . . . In this determinacy a man should not feel himself determined; on the contrary, since *he treats the other as other,* it is there that he first arrives at the feeling of his own self-hood. Thus freedom lies neither in indeterminacy nor in determinacy; it is *both of these at once*" (*PR*, sections 6, 7, additions; emphases added). Hegel's model may leave us wondering about the exclusiveness of this freedom, if self-consciousness, as the universal, can "in its restriction" posit "itself as other." Within his oppositional model of universal self-consciousness we may well feel, that is, that Hegel does not offer a persuasive meaning for the moment in which, he claims, his properly self-conscious man "treats the other as other." He provides no obvious specification of such treatment, at least not of treatment that expresses something about the other. Thus here too for Hegel thought expresses itself as the Force of subsuming the other, or the place for the other, within the self. What Hegel calls "both of these at once" seems to disappear according to plan into "Force proper." We remain within the scene of universal punishment, which is a process of mirroring or "speculation" constitutive of thought itself. At best, thought is understood here as a redefined scene of universal revenge. In this oppositional model, punishment is inflicted in the instantaneous attainment to self-consciousness.

10. Some readers seem to have had no misgivings about the "death" and "violence"— as Hegel names them in the Introduction to the *Phenomenology*—that take place in his scene of thought (section 80). Heidegger, for example, speaks of the death and violence as if they were experienced solely by the self that is in the process of achieving self-consciousness. Meditating upon the general locus of this scene in the *Phenomenology*, he seems to see no hidden moral costs when he declares it to be "the characteristic moment of the historical process in which the history of the formation of consciousness comes to pass." See Heidegger, *Hegel's Concept of Experience*, p. 76. (Heidegger earlier makes clear that the formation of consciousness he is discussing is Hegel's characteristic arrival in "the land of self-consciousness" [p. 28].) It is true that Heidegger is directly commenting only on Hegel's remarks on "death" and "violence" in the Introduction to the *Phenomenology*, though it seems impossible to suppose that Heidegger can have forgotten the scene of punishment which (among other things) Hegel's remarks anticipate. Heidegger writes, "The uprooting is the death of natural consciousness. In this constant dying consciousness sacrifices itself, so that it may by the sacrifice gain its resurrection into its own nature. . . . The violence is the prevalence of the restless tension within consciousness itself. . . ."

"[This] presentation of phenomenal knowledge is skepticism in its consummation. In accomplishing itself it works itself out in detail. The presentation produces itself as such, instead of merely entering on the scene" (pp. 80, 84). He paraphrases Hegel's chiasmus as the "mutual distinction between natural and real knowledge" within consciousness itself: the "restless tension that pits [A] the natural against [B] the real and [B] the real against [A] the natural" (p. 77).

11. Cavell, *The Claim of Reason*, pp. 475–76.

12. Ibid., p. 476.

13. Hegel gives us cause for wondering, indeed, what the special function, or even special right, of the philosopher may be in establishing the Idea. In Gans's addition to this paragraph from Hegel's lectures, Hegel drives home the right of "heroic coercion" with all the force of his Idealism of punishment or Force, which for him simultaneously constitutes the founding of the state and the birth of universal self-consciousness. The passage may seem to offer safeguards against claims for special rights of coercion by modern heroes, but the safeguards are perhaps less clear than may at first appear: "Once the state has been founded, there can no longer be any heroes. They come on the scene only in uncivilized conditions. . . . The heroes who founded states . . . did not do this as their recognized right, and their conduct still has the appearance of being their particular will. But as the higher right of the Idea against nature, this heroic coercion is a rightful coercion." Does Hegel, even with his straight lines of history, imagine that the state is everywhere founded once and for all, or does he assume that "uncivilized conditions" might (say, in periods of convulsion in German history—such as, on a small scale, Hegel experienced in his own lifetime) sometimes recur, so that "heroic coercion" can once again be "rightful coercion"? It would be reasonable to wonder whether the sentences reproduced by Gans are not particularly interesting because they reflect Hegel's conception of what his own enacting of universal self-consciousness may have to contribute as a privileged heroic repetition, unfolding, and actualization—in renewed uncivilized conditions—of the early heroic history of self-consciousness. Confirmation of Hegel's thinking about continued heroic activity of this kind seems to be present in

The Philosophy of History at moments when Hegel expands his definition of heroes to "thinking men." He speaks of those "great historical men"—who "may be called Heroes"—"whose own particular aims involve those large issues which are the will of the World-Spirit." See *The Philosophy of History*, trans. J. Sibree, pp. 30–32. The passage is arguably self-referential on a grand scale (including the famous banner, cited more fully below, "I have added—and Goethe repeated it ten years later . . . ").

14. *The Philosophy of History*, pp. 10–11.

15. See note 2.

16. Incidentally, the two sections immediately following Hegel's scene of punishment in the *Philosophy of Right* are clearly concerned with Roman civil law. On this concern in these two sections of the *Philosophy of Right*, see Shklar, *Freedom and Independence*, p. 205.

17. Readers of Erwin Panofsky will recognize my echoing of his statement about Virgil's first eclogue: "With only slight exaggeration one might say that he 'discovered' the evening." See *Meaning in the Visual Arts* (Garden City: Anchor Books, 1955), p. 300.

18. Shklar, *Freedom and Independence*, p. 88.

19. Those men "may be called Heroes," says Hegel, who were not only practical but "thinking men, who had an insight into the requirements of the time—*what was ripe for development*. This was the very Truth for their age, for their world; the species next in order, so to speak, and which was already formed in the womb of time" (*The Philosophy of History*, p. 30).

20. See Hegel's diary entries for 1 and 4 January in *Frühe Schriften I*, ed. Friedhelm Nicolin and Gisela Schüler (Hamburg: Felix Meiner, 1989), pp. 31–32. Yet Hegel's scattered comments on Virgil's merits as an epic poet, particularly by comparison with Homer's, are generally either lukewarm or inexplicably hostile. One comment is especially interesting for the form of hostility that it takes, namely, an irritation with the way in which Virgil's epic does not respect the separateness of Homer. This occurs in the early *Differenz des Fichte'schen und Schelling'schen Systems der Philosophie:* "wenn Virgil den Homer für eine solche Vorübung für sich und sein verfeinertes Zeitalter betrachtet hat, so ist sein Werk dafür eine Nachübung geblieben." (Quoted from the text in the *Jenaer Kritische Schriften*, ed. Hartmut Buchner and Otto Pöggeler [Hamburg: Felix Meiner, 1968], p. 12.) We might ask what the difference is between a Virgilian "Nachübung" and a Hegelian Phenomenology, especially once we have inventoried the latter's citations.

21. I cite the *Aeneid* from H. Rushton Fairclough's Loeb edition and translation (Cambridge: Harvard University Press, 1986).

22. See note 3.

23. In *Hegel* (Cambridge: Cambridge University Press, 1975), p. 155, Charles Taylor's formulation is that "death . . . invites the negation in thought which is the return to the universal."

24. This was published in Kojève's *Introduction à la Lecture de Hegel* (1939; 2d ed., Paris: Gallimard, 1947). I quote from the partial translation in Alexandre Kojève, *Introduction to the Reading of Hegel: Lectures on the Phenomenology of Spirit Assembled by Raymond Queneau*, ed. Allan Bloom, trans. James H. Nichols, Jr. (Ithaca: Cornell University Press, 1980), which, however, does not include Kojève's Appendix II, "The Idea of Death in the Philosophy of Hegel." In part, Kojève was able to achieve his new perspectives by attending to clarifications of Hegel's ideas available in his Jena manuscripts; in part, by following the reading of this topic in the *Phenomenology of Spirit* that he found in Heidegger's meditation on death in *Being and Time*. Yet Kojève's explication of Hegel's ideas on death in the *Phenomenology* are in no sense imposed from the outside. Kojève realized that in remarks such as the ones just cited Hegel declares his conviction that "death is . . . the genuine motor of the dialectical movement" that constitutes self-consciousness (*Introduction to the Reading of Hegel*, p. 253). Kojève reminded students

of Hegel that even before the *Phenomenology* Hegel had written of "the faculty of death" exercised by the "Subject." Wherever Hegel speaks of activities of the "negative-or-negating Absolute, pure freedom" (cited by Kojève, p. 247, from Hegel's essay on "Natural Right" [1802]), which he also calls the "doubling" effected by "negativity," he is speaking silently of "the faculty of death." I cite, for rereading as an account of the faculty of death, the following famous passage about negativity and doubling in Hegel's preface to the *Phenomenology* (section 18): "The living Substance is being which is in truth *Subject*, or, what is the same, is in truth actual only in so far as it is the movement of positing itself, or is the mediation of its self-othering with itself. This Substance is, as Subject, pure, *simple negativity*, and is for this very reason the bifurcation of the simple; it is the doubling which sets up opposition, and then again the negation of this indifferent diversity and of its antithesis [the immediate simplicity]. Only this self-*restoring* sameness, or this reflection in otherness within itself—not an *original* or *immediate* unity as such—is the True." We are thus reading about this faculty, and indeed about the drama of a certain experience of dying within life, in the present or "self-conscious Now," virtually everywhere within Hegel's thinking. If there is little or no pathos in Hegel's accounts of negativity or death that is because, as Kojève says, it has "nothing to do with an afterlife." On the contrary, Hegel believes that this experience of death can be reintegrated within the unity of self-consciousness. (See Kojève, pp. 246, 254.) In every experience of this kind of death within thought, self-consciousness "no less preserves itself." As Kojève was aware and as Gadamer has emphasized echoing Kojève, Hegel thus provides Heidegger with the understanding that "it is only death which can put the individual in authentic relationship with himself." This is Heidegger's concept of "Being towards Death" (Sein zum Tode). See H. G. Gadamer, *Hegel's Dialectic*, trans. P. Christopher Smith (New Haven: Yale University Press, 1976), p. 69n.

25. In Derrida's *Writing and Difference*, trans. Alan Bass (Chicago: University of Chicago Press, 1978), pp. 251–77.

26. Ibid., p. 258.

27. Ibid., p. 257.

28. Ibid., p. 276. He is referring specifically to "the figure of the slave," but as noted earlier the scene of the master and the slave is the consequence that Hegel follows out from the inequalities in the scene of Force and punishment.

29. Ibid., p. 262.

30. Cited in ibid., p. 263.

31. Ibid., p. 277.

32. Ibid., p. 258.

33. Bataille's notion of Hegel's use of "tradition" may only be the vulgar one that Marx already associates, reductively, with Hegel in the first two paragraphs of *The Eighteenth Brumaire of Louis Bonaparte*.

34. See Walter R. Johnson, *Darkness Visible: A Study of Vergil's "Aeneid"* (Berkeley: University of California Press, 1976), who affiliates himself with the main tenor of what he calls the "somewhat pessimistic Harvard school" of *Aeneid* criticism (p. 10), with Adam Parry's view in "The Two Voices of the *Aeneid*," *Arion* 2 (1963): 79–80, and with the interpretation of the poem's final episode provided by Hans R. Steiner, *Der Traum in der Aeneis*, Noctes Romanae 5 (Berlin and Stuttgart, 1952), pp. 72–75.

35. Following *Liddell and Scott's Greek-English Lexicon*, I have given "athroa pant' apotiseis" as "pay the penalty of all at once," whereas Lattimore translates "pay in a lump."

36. A verse-by-verse accounting of Virgil's thousands of echoes of Homer is available in Georg Nicholaus Knauer, *Die Aeneis und Homer: Studien zur poetischen Technik Vergils, mit Listen der Homerzitate in der Aeneis* [*Hypomnemata*, 7 (Göttingen: Vandenhoeck & Ruprecht, 1964)].

The correspondence between *Iliad* 22.270–72 (and 331–36) and *Aeneid* 12.947–49 is duly noted by Knauer. As C. J. Fordyce reminds us (ed., *Aeneid VII-VIII* [Oxford: Oxford University Press, 1977]), there is an obvious difference in metrical quantity, even in the nominative case, between the names of Pallas the young man and Pallas the goddess, yet it is difficult to avoid the sense, here, of a double evocation in Virgil's use of these names. Indeed, although they do not confront the poetic meaning of Virgil's citation of Homer's words in creating this intensely strange juncture, Roger Hornsby and William R. Nethercut have each noted evocations of this sort. (Hornsby, "The Armor of the Slain," *Philological Quarterly* 45 [1966]: 358–59 and *Patterns of Action in the Aeneid: An Interpretation of Virgil's Epic Similes* [Iowa City: University of Iowa Press, 1970], p. 87; Nethercut, "The Imagery of the *Aeneid*," *Classical Journal* 67 [1971]: 134–42.) Virgil's possible invocation of Pallas Athene at the end of the *Aeneid* has been extensively considered by Elisabeth Henry, *The Vigour of Prophecy: A Study of Virgil's Aeneid* (Carbondale: Southern Illinois University Press, 1989), pp. 90–107, who does not, however, see oppositions involved in Virgil's recalling the goddess who destroyed Hektor and to whom (as Henry points out) Virgil attributes the art of building the fatal Trojan horse (2.15). Henry argues that Virgil intends to realign the hostile goddess with the fortunes of the Trojans and Rome, although she acknowledges the paucity of evidence for a realignment of this kind.

37. Derrida, *Writing and Difference,*, pp. 276–77. Derrida makes an analogous point about hyperbolical doubt in "Cogito and the History of Madness," pp. 57–58.

38. *Theogony,* ll. 925–29. Hesiod seems to suggest (ll. 886–900) that the leaping forth takes even the mind of Zeus, the highest god, by surprise. (The names of Pallas Athene that Hesiod uses here are Tritogeneia and Atrytone.)

39. Cicero, *De Natura Deorum,* 3.59. See Karl Kerényi, *Athene: Virgin and Mother in Greek Religion,* trans. Murray Stein (Dallas: Spring, 1978), p. 63, and Walter Burkert, *Homo Necans: The Anthropology of Ancient Greek Sacrificial Ritual and Myth,* trans. Peter Bing (Berkeley: University of California Press, 1983), p. 67n, and more generally Burkert's discussion "The Sexualization of Ritual Killing: Maiden Sacrifice, Phallus Cult," pp. 58–72.

40. The *ballein,* to throw, of *hyperballein,* from which the word *hyperbole* is derived, may thus be part of a word game in the repetition of Pallas, *pallein,* to cast (lots).

41. Here are those lines:

> et laevo pressit pede talia fatus
> exanimem, rapiens immania pondera baltei
> impressumque nefas: una sub nocte iugali
> caesa manus iuvenum foede thalamique cruenti,
> quae Clonus Eurytides multo caelaverat auro.

[with his left foot he trod upon the dead, tearing away the belt's huge weight and the story of the crime thereon engraved—the youthful band foully slain on one nuptial night, and the chambers drenched with blood—which Clonus, son on Eurytus, had richly chased in gold.]

42. The possibility that Aeneas is responding to the scenes depicted on the baldric was pointed out by Kenneth Quinn, *Virgil's Aeneid: A Critical Description* (London: Routledge, 1968), p. 275.

43. The baldric picturing the forty-nine murderous Danaïdes doing their father's work becomes a sort of Gorgon badge of Pallas (Athene), though this badge is certainly not exclusively female in gender. Even to judge from Virgil's allusive division of the name Pallas between the male Pallas visible in the *Aeneid* and the female Pallas working in the *Iliad,* it seems likely that Virgil, following extensive mythological precedent (cf. Kerényi, *Athene: Virgin and Mother in Greek Religion,* esp. pp. 53–59), sees both the name and the badge as being each male

and female. Insofar as the Latin mythographers hoped to bring about a *translatio studii* of the Greek Palladium to Rome, Virgil's inscription of this deadly alienation within the image of the Palladium itself bespeaks a cultural commentary, on Greek as well as Roman civilization, of the most neutralizing kind.

CHAPTER 4. The Surrealism of "Respect" for Tradition

1. A modern example of the institutional claim for Virgil's paternalism and his monumentalizing of an achieved stasis in "the West" is Theodor Haecker, *Virgil, Father of the West,* trans. A. W. Wheen (London: Sheed & Ward, 1934), which Frank Kermode, *The Classic: Literary Images of Permanence and Change* (Cambridge: Harvard University Press, 1983), pp. 15–45, has shown exerted a limited but significant influence on T. S. Eliot.

2. Citations from Kant's "Analytic of the Sublime" in English are from *The Critique of Judgement,* trans. James Creed Meredith (Oxford: Clarendon, 1973); in German from *Kants Werke: Akademie-Textausgabe,* vol. 5 (Berlin: Walter de Gruyter, 1968).

3. What I am describing in Virgil's ways of constructing a continuous experience of time concurs with what Frank Kermode (in a Virgilian locution) terms *aevum*: that "variety of duration . . . in which things can be perpetual without being eternal": *The Sense of an Ending: Studies in the Theory of Fiction* (Oxford: Oxford University Press, 1967), p. 72. In fact, in the *Aeneid* the earlier revenge scene that I am about to discuss is specifically associated with a duration of *aevum*. This *aevum* seems to me inseparable from Virgil's imagining, and what may be called his continuous timing, of the final revenge scene.

4. Except for occasional choices of a more literal meaning, text and translations of the *Aeneid* are from the Loeb *Virgil,* trans. H. Rushton Fairclough, 2 vols. (London, 1960). Fairclough here has "unshaken" for "immobile," where I give "immovable."

5. Johnson, *Darkness Visible: A Study of Vergil's "Aeneid"* (Berkeley: University of California Press, 1976), p. 66.

6. From Homer's description of fleeing Hektor, in 22.199–201.

7. Johnson, *Darkness Visible,* pp. 98–99.

8. *Disappearance* is perhaps not the precisely right word here, but Virgil's striking shift from "saxum" to "lapis" may suggest an erosion or transformation in just such a direction.

9. Georg Nicholaus Knauer's generally exhaustive *Die Aeneis und Homer: Studien zur poetischen Technik Vergils, mit Listen der Homerzitate in der Aeneis* [*Hypomnemata,* 7 (Göttingen, 1964)] does not list this passage with its clearly related passages in Virgil and in Homer, though I cannot believe that the correspondences have previously gone unobserved.

10. Especially because of the chiastic structure of these lines (*sedem*:woodland thickets / forest:rock) I have assumed that the Tarpeian "sedem" primarily means "rock," secondarily "house." Fairclough gives "house."

11. Virgil describes Turnus as coming to this pass as inevitably and obliviously as when, "with mighty rush," a "rock from mountain-top rushes headlong, torn away by the blast" (12.684–89), thus already implying that not only Turnus's fate but also his identity is borne by the boundary stone that is to be torn *away* by the Fury.

12. Translations from Homer are from *The Iliad of Homer,* trans. Richmond Lattimore (Chicago: University of Chicago Press, 1961). I have used the name *Aineias* for Homer's character, *Aeneas* for Virgil's. To indicate at what general level of attention Virgil pored over this passage, it may be useful to recall one among many correspondences—or continuities— outside our immediate concern: Homer tells us that Aphrodite shields Aineias "with her

white [radiant] robe thrown in a fold in front" (l. 315). Virgil's Aeneas, on the way to the temple of Dido in book 1, encounters his mother disguised as a huntress, with "her flowing robes gathered in a knot" (l. 320). When, after the long interview, in which as usual she has failed to identify herself to her son, she turns to go, it is Aeneas's/Aineias's completely unspoken memory of "the white robe thrown in a fold in front" which helps give her away when the knot comes loose: "down to her feet fell her raiment. . . . He knew her as his mother . . . as she fled" (ll. 404–06). These corresponding verses are recorded in Knauer's lists. See also note 14 below.

13. A collateral subject of great interest here is Virgil's intricate play with Homer's intricate play with the mist, the temple, and the visual representation of Aineias, by means of which Aineias both exits and resumes history: see *Iliad* 5.445–52, 20.281–83, 325–41 together with *Aeneid*, 1.411–504.

14. See Søren Kierkegaard, *The Concept of Anxiety: A Simple Psychologically Orienting Deliberation on the Dogmatic Issue of Hereditary Sin*, ed. and trans. Reidar Thomte (Princeton: Princeton University Press, 1980), esp. p. 91. Kierkegaard asks us to abandon the notion that anxiety is about the past, even if that is its appearance. Anxiety is about the future, he insists, about what *will* happen to us, about the possible repetition in the future of what we may have once experienced or imagined, especially of the possibility that we will come to an end sooner rather than later and that we will then be swallowed by or become "Nothing." "The possible," he writes, "corresponds exactly to the future" that encompasses this Nothing. "For freedom," he says, "the possible is the future, and the future is for time the possible. To both of these corresponds anxiety in the individual life." In our experience of anxiety thus defined, we determine our orientation toward the future as well as the integrity and freedom of our consciousness and will. See also pp. 41–46, 81–90.

15. Even the gods recognize this unearthly, earthly sign: see, for example, 21.403–05. Another example of this divine acknowledgment of liminality is the gods' way of informing Priam that he can begin his mission for persuading Achilleus to return Hektor's body: Hermes the god of boundaries accosts Priam at a sacred boundary stone precisely at the boundary moment of day and night (cf. 24.349–52). See Walter Burkert's comment on this point in *Greek Religion*, trans. John Raffan (Cambridge: Harvard University Press, 1985), p. 157.

16. Derrida, *Of Grammatology*, trans. Gayatri Chakravorty Spivak (Baltimore: Johns Hopkins University Press), pp. 68–69.

17. See Adam Parry, "The Two Voices of the *Aeneid*," *Arion* 2 (1963): 79–80.

18. This is Aeneas's full formula: "Pallas te hoc volnere, Pallas / immolat et poenam scelerato ex sanguine sumit" (12.948–49): "'Tis Pallas, Pallas who with this stroke sacrifices thee, and takes atonement of thy guilty blood." On Virgil's two voices in other places, see Adam Parry in the essay noted above.

19. I especially have in mind here, as Virgil might have, Sophocles' recounting in *Oedipus at Colonus*, ll. 54–56, that in guaranteeing the foundation of Athens Oedipus disappears into the same rock "place" (khoros) from which chained Prometheus issued his prophecy for the continuity of Greek culture—and into which Prometheus and the chorus of *Prometheus Bound* vanish at the end of Aeschylus's tragedy.

20. A rich discussion of classical and Renaissance imitation is available in Thomas Greene, *The Light in Troy: Imitation and Discovery in Renaissance Poetry* (New Haven: Yale University Press, 1982). My divergences from Greene's views of how cultural transmission is achieved and experienced, for example, in Virgil's relation to Homer (p. 66), follow from my persuasion that sublime representation is a decisive factor in such transmission.

21. Erwin Panofsky, *Meaning in the Visual Arts* (Garden City, N.Y.: Doubleday, 1955), p. 300.

CHAPTER 5. Apostrophe in the Westering Sublime

1. Moshe Barasch, *The Language of Art: Studies in Interpretation* (New York: New York University Press, 1997), esp. pp. 10–24.

2. Where the experience of tradition is concerned, current erroneous assumptions about the workings of apostrophe are locatable in Jonathan Culler's influential essay "Apostrophe" (in *The Pursuit of Signs: Semiotics, Literature, Deconstruction* [London: Routledge, 1981]). In fact, Culler verges on an acknowledgment of the relation between the "sublime" "lineage" of apostrophe and the experience of tradition but then, following de Man, misses (or excludes) that experience or the experience of priority in any given culture. Culler consciously maintains an equivocal relation to what he calls the "poetic pretension" of the poet who uses apostrophe. This is the poet's pretension to being "the embodiment of poetic tradition." Describing this pretension, he notes, "Apostrophe is perhaps always an indirect invocation of the muse. Devoid of semantic reference, the *O* of apostrophe refers to other apostrophes and thus to the lineage and conventions of sublime poetry" (p. 143). But he expresses himself unequivocally about the experience, the "event" (p. 153) or "effect" (p. 154) that an apostrophe actually produces. He says that an apostrophe is "a temporality of writing . . . a special temporality which is the set of all moments at which writing can say 'now'" (p. 149). He is certain that experience of apostrophe's "*now* is not a moment in a temporal sequence" (p. 152) but "a fictive, discursive event" which is a "neutralization of time" in our "empirical lives" (pp. 153–54). His certainty on these points is accompanied by an equally certain, though unexplained, ethos. He says that apostrophe's "successes" in neutralizing time in this way "should be celebrated" (p. 154).

Even in the forms he has recorded them, Culler's certainties, which claim the notational purity of a mathematical "set," contradict the pretensions he describes in the poets who use apostrophe. The *O*'s of those poets' apostrophes, he recognizes, embody or refer to a "tradition" or a "lineage," terms which are meaningless without some concept of linearity or "temporal sequence." And his description of that pretension turns on a veiled equivocation, if not contradiction, in his use of the words *semantic* and *reference*. The "*O* of apostrophe" of these poets cannot be "devoid of semantic reference" if we can identify the fact that it "refers to other apostrophes" and to something that has been historically constituted and is known or experienced as "the lineage and conventions of sublime poetry." To imagine a historical content that dispenses with history is a form of mysticism or of archetypal myth, neither of which is consistent with Culler's convictions in his essay.

The difficulties generated by Culler's account of the experience of apostrophe as a "neutralization of time" can be overcome by supplementing it with an account of the larger experience of which the experience of uttering a single apostrophe, as he repeatedly notes, is only a part, at least in the apostrophes that draw his attention. Each such apostrophe is an experience or representation of partial withdrawal from experience or representation. The sublime is an experience or representation of an endless line, or lineage, of such partial withdrawals from experience or representation. It is not the experience of apostrophe itself, that is, but the experience of an endless line of apostrophes that achieves a special temporality. This is the temporality of a continuity of historical experience or tradition.

An ethos of historical experience or tradition may be that which Culler's apparently ethical celebration of the neutralization of time is meant to counter, though it may only be celebrating and enacting an act of repression. In his account of "post-enlightenment" apostrophe (p. 143) he claims that he experiences an ecstatic neutralization of the sequential and linear time of tradition. We would do well, however, to recall here the self-doubt raised by

Harold Bloom about the ecstatic "Counter-Sublime" of post-Enlightenment poetry: "Is all the *ekstasis*, the final step beyond, of Romantic vision only an intensity of repression previously unmatched in the history of the imagination? Is Romanticism after all only the waning of the Enlightenment?" (*The Anxiety of Influence* [New York: Oxford University Press, 1975], pp. 111–12). (I will return to these questions at the beginning of chapter 8.) And what do we say, in addition, if, or rather when, the picture of repression to which we have reduced or repressed the Enlightenment, or rather classical and neoclassical—and biblical—tradition turns out to be a freedom of historical experience par excellence? This is a freedom, and an *ekstasis*, that is achieved in repetitions of partial withdrawal of representation all along the classical and biblical lines of representation. In fact, romanticism itself mirrors and continues these lines of representation, despite its claims to having abandoned them. I will turn to this scene of countersublimes in the next chapter.

    3. At the close of the twentieth century it is perhaps impossible to speak of listening to the calling of language without seeming to refer to Heidegger. The account of such listening that I am offering here is not Heideggerian because what concerns me is the experience of the philological and historical line of language. This experience—which I view as the experience of tradition—has little or no meaning for Heidegger. (This may be seen in Heidegger's "The Anaximander Fragment," in *Early Greek Thinking*, trans. David Farrell Krell and Frank A. Capuzzi [New York: Harper & Row, 1984], pp. 13–58. With regard to the Anaximander text as well as other pre-Socratic texts and many of the later poetic texts to which Heidegger responds, including the Trakl poem mentioned below, Gerald R. Bruns comments on "the inaccessibility" of "reconstruction" of this kind, for Heidegger, in *Heidegger's Estrangements: Language, Truth, and Poetry in the Later Writings* [New Haven: Yale University Press, 1989], pp. 68–73. It is worth adding that Heidegger fails to consider a reconstruction of lineage even between Anaximander's scene of punishment and Hegel's, though Heidegger takes the time to criticize Hegel for his inattentiveness to "the Preplatonic and Presocratic philosophers" [pp. 15–16].) An experience of this kind may even be opposed to what Heidegger considers to be the "independent" status of "experience" and "self-consciousness." (See my first note in chapter 3.) Yet Heidegger's sensitivity to the possibility of such listening to language's speaking, which I am describing in historical terms, is relevant here. Culler reasons that we should not be embarrassed by the notion that "any versifier who wrote '*O* table'" might in fact approach "the condition of sublime poet" if the "brazenness" of his utterance were only sufficient to produce "the uncalculable force of an event" (p. 152). But the apostrophes that have the effect that interests Culler, and us, have far more than brazen force. These are the apostrophes of poets who both experience and represent, and celebrate, the continuity of apostrophe, therefore of historical experience, in their *O*'s of apostrophe, their embodiments of tradition. Within this line, apostrophe is an experience not only of voicing, but of listening as well. Heidegger in fact drives home the difference between the trivial case of the versifier who merely says, however brazenly, "*O* table" and an invocation of a table that begins to approach the condition of the sublime. Heidegger presents such a sublime case in his response to Georg Trakl's lyric "A Winter Evening." Among Trakl's verses are these three about a table:

    The table is for many laid.
    . . . .
    There lie, in limpid brightness shown,
    Upon the table bread and wine.

    Heidegger hears that the first of these verses, even its "emphatic 'is,'" "speaks in the mode of calling." He says that it brings "the ready table into that presence that is turned toward something absent." (However we invoke that "something absent" it must presumably have something to do with the "calling" of a sacrament, or parousia, of absence called into presence suggested by the "bread and wine" of the table or "altar" [Heidegger's word].) In the last two verses Heidegger hears that to which he responds in lyric verses addressed to an "us":

Man speaks only as he responds to language.
Language speaks.
Its speaking speaks for us in what has been spoken.

(See Martin Heidegger, *Poetry, Language, Thought,* trans. Albert Hofstadter [New York: Harper & Row, 1975], pp. 196, 199, 210.)

This sounds like a mysterious personification or theologizing of language. In the line of apostrophes that I will now trace, the invocation of the everyday calling of language—to listening to what it says even as one speaks it—is not mysterious but is no less demanding. In this line of apostrophes or callings it is possible, and even necessary, to reconstruct its lineage, and therefore a supposition of historical experience of that lineage, quite concretely. This lineage of listening and speaking is the Muse of apostrophe. Building upon Barbara Johnson's hypothesis, I will propose that the identity of the Muse of apostrophe is substantively maternal, that is (in my view), even in the classical and neoclassical line of apostrophe that was mostly voiced by male poets.

4. Geoffrey Tillotson, "Pope's 'Epistle to Harley': An Introduction and Analysis," in *Pope and His Contemporaries: Essays Presented to George Sherburn,* ed. James L. Clifford and Louis A. Landa (Oxford: Clarendon, 1949), p. 68. A full account of this echoing would have to pay close attention to apostrophes of Catullus, which are alluded to not only by Dryden's elegy but by passages in the *Aeneid* that Dryden here imitates. With regard to the anecdote, mentioned by Tillotson, that it was Swift who suggested to Pope the use of Dryden's Oldham materials, notice should also be taken of Swift's own extraordinary version of Virgil's apostrophe to Nisus and Euryalus in the closing moment of "The Battle of the Books."

5. For a survey of these and other apostrophes, see Elizabeth Block, "The Narrator Speaks: Apostrophe in Homer and Virgil," *Transactions of the American Philological Association* 112 (1982): 7–22.

6. The text of the *Iliad* is cited from the Loeb Classical Library edition, ed. A. T. Murray (Cambridge: Harvard University Press, 1988). Except for a few instances, indicated in the notes, all translations of Homer are from *The Iliad of Homer,* trans. Richmond Lattimore (Chicago: University of Chicago Press, 1961). Except in citing Pope's verse, I have normalized the names of Achilleus and Patroklos according to Lattimore's spellings.

7. Cited by Culler, "Apostrophe," p. 153. De Man's remarks appear in his discussion of Wordsworth's *Essay upon Epitaphs.* In the next chapter I will comment at some length on Wordsworth's essay and, to a lesser extent, on de Man's interpretation of it.

8. *The Iliad of Homer,* trans. Alexander Pope, ed. Maynard Mack et al. (London and New Haven: Methuen and Yale University Press, 1967). This is quite possibly the moment that Pope echoes at the end of his Epistle when his Muse, also acting with real courage, does not "fear to tell" of "one truly great" (ll. 39–40). (Tillotson, "Pope's 'Epistle to Harley,'" p. 75, cites Grattan's remark that writing the poem "required courage.") Interestingly, Kalchas's speaking at this juncture is the passage in the *Iliad* that Heidegger identifies as a lingering "within the expanse of unconcealment," a moving "away," he calls it, "from the sheer oppression of what lies before us, which is only present, away to what is absent." See Martin Heidegger, *Early Greek Thinking,* trans. David Farrell Krell and Frank A. Capuzzi (New York: Harper & Row, 1984), pp. 34–35.

9. See "Tradition in the Space of Negativity," in *Languages of the Unsayable: The Play of Negativity in Literature and Literary Theory*, ed. Sanford Budick and Wolfgang Iser (New York: Columbia University Press, 1989), pp. 311–14. I still believe that these contexts are highly significant for Homer's representation of apostrophe, but my understanding of the sublime lineage of apostrophe has substantially altered my view of how Homer's apostrophes function.

10. Barbara Johnson, "Apostrophe, Animation, and Abortion," in *Contemporary Literary Criticism: Literary and Cultural Studies*, ed. Robert Con Davis and Ronald Schleifer (Longman: New York, 1994), pp. 226–27; first published in *Diacritics* 16 (1986).

11. In this case I cite A. T. Murray's translation, which is closer to the literal than Lattimore's.

12. We find similar phenomena in Virgil's art of dense interconnection and what might be called intercorrection. In the instance of the apostrophe to Nisus and Euryalus the art of the *Aeneid* is shown by evenhandedly pairing this "Fortunati ambo" (fortunate pair) with pairs among Aeneas's provisional enemies, especially that of the poem's greatest runner, Camilla, and her "sister" Acca. In the moment of Camilla's fall upon the slippery place, she hands on to Turnus through Acca (11.823–27). In the pathos of Camilla's words to Acca there are evocations of other pairings: of Dido turning to her sister Anna; and of Aeneas inspired by the image of dead Marcellus, around whom, too, all has grown dim and dark ("nox atra caput tristi circumvolat umbra" / "black night hovers about his head with its mournful shade": 6.866). The most notable other pairing, however, is the one that Camilla calls for in her moment of handing on her mandamus ("mandata") or giving of the hand. Virgil pairs her with Turnus not only in their common fate as Italian heroes who fall, but in their sharing of the *Aeneid*'s concluding moment of apostrophe. The verse describing Turnus's death "moan" (12.952) repeats word for word the moan already described in Camilla in book 11, verse 831. As noted above, the same moment of crying out and turning away also joins Turnus and Camilla, with great exactitude, to Hektor's last breath in the *Iliad*: "His soul fleeting from his limbs was gone to Hades, bewailing her fate" (22.363; Murray's translation), and also to the exact same Homeric verse rendering the last breath of Patroklos (16.856).

13. John Dryden, *Of Dramatic Poesy and Other Critical Essays*, ed. George Watson (London: Dent, 1962), 2:199, 206. Dryden is citing the formula "manum de tabula . . . tollere" from Rapin's *Réflexions* (1671), XVI, where it is attributed to Apelles (though actually from Pliny).

14. See, for example, Watson's comment in *Of Dramatic Poesy and Other Critical Essays*, 1:xiv.

15. It is relevant here that the neoclassical historicism of Shakespeare's *Antony and Cleopatra*—a play brilliantly read by Dryden in his *All for Love; Or, The World Well Lost*—is also manifested in a projection of pagan and Christian counterworlds. See Frank Kermode's comments on Shakespeare's images of this kind in *The Riverside Shakespeare*, ed. G. Blakemore Evans et al. (Boston: Houghton Mifflin, 1974), p. 1344.

16. Tillotson's references to T. S. Eliot elsewhere in his essay may suggest that he thought of Eliot's doctrine of the impersonality of the poet—like perhaps Eliot's idea that the European tradition is a "mind" into which the depersonalized poet is absorbed—as being in no need or as insusceptible of further explanation. Eliot sets out and links both ideas in the first section of "Tradition and the Individual Talent."

17. Tillotson indeed attempts to qualify Eliot's edict banishing the poet from his poem by showing the importance of what he calls "occasion" or "place" in Pope's poetry (pp. 58–60). Tillotson could assume that the Eliot of *Four Quartets* (1943), with his departures into a more personal highlighting of occasion and place ("So, while the light fails / On a winter's afternoon, in a secluded chapel / History is now and England": "Little Gidding," ll. 235–37), would be especially sympathetic. Near the climax of Tillotson's essay, in any case, the

reference to Eliot in this vein delicately reminds the poet of his own response to England's emergency: "If Pope's poem is an occasional one, and one with an occasion of this status— a rough parallel in our own time would be to suppose that Mr. Eliot [i.e., the greatest English poet of his time] were presenting the poems of Sidney Keyes [died in the war, age twenty-one, in the same year that Eliot published *Four Quartets*] to Mr. Churchill [i.e., the hero of that emergency, now fallen from power]—it follows that we cannot forget the man, Pope" (p. 75).

18. Brower's remarks occur in his introduction to *The Iliad of Homer Translated by Alexander Pope*, ed. Reuben A. Brower and W. H. Bond (New York: Macmillan, 1965), pp. 19–20.

19. Pope places the verse from Horace's odes (IV.viii.28) as the epigraph to the volume of Parnell's poems and therefore, as well, to the epistle to Oxford which serves as the dedication of that volume. Pope, whose poetry everywhere shows an intense intimacy with Horace's poems, undoubtedly was aware that this particular verse and its expression of an apparent poetic commonplace was a turning point in Horace's poetic career. Horace had never before allowed himself to make this claim for his lyric poetry, a claim which until then was in Latin lyric even antithetical, as Eduard Fraenkel has said, to "the Roman conception of genuine *gloria*" (*Horace* [Oxford: Clarendon, 1966], p. 423). After making this claim Horace concludes his highly apostrophic ode with a series of examples of the Muses' power of conferring immortality. The ending of Pope's epistle mirrors this exercising of the power of "the Muse" (ll. 28ff.). Yet for Pope the justification and meaning of this claim, even after Horace has made it, are not at all self-evident; neither are the identity of the Muse and its way of actually creating a continuity of experience. In his epistle to Oxford Pope struggles to take part in and to clarify this identity and this continuity of experience.

20. Achilleus quoting Thetis: "leípsein pháos helíoio" (18.11), "should leave the light of the sun" (Murray); Thetis, with a different phrasing of the predicate: 18.61.

Dryden, *To the Memory of Mr. Oldham*

Farewel, too little and too lately known,
Whom I began to think and call my own;
For sure our Souls were near ally'd; and thine
Cast in the same Poetick mould with mine.
One common Note on either Lyre did strike,   5
And Knaves and Fools we both abhorr'd alike:
To the same Goal did both our Studies drive,
The last set out the soonest did arrive.
Thus *Nisus* fell upon the slippery place,
While his young Friend perform'd and won the Race.   10
O early ripe! to thy abundant store
What could advancing Age have added more?
It might (what Nature never gives the young)
Have taught the numbers of thy native Tongue.
But Satyr needs not those, and Wit will shine   15
Through the harsh cadence of a rugged line.
A noble Error, and but seldom made,
When Poets are by too much force betray'd.
Thy generous fruits, though gather'd ere their prime
Still shew'd a quickness; and maturing time   20
But mellows what we write to the dull sweets of Rime.
Once more, hail and farewel; farewel thou young,

But ah too short, *Marcellus* of our Tongue;
Thy Brows with Ivy, and with Laurels bound;
But Fate and gloomy Night encompass thee around.   25

Pope, *Epistle to Robert Earl of Oxford, and Earl Mortimer*

Such were the Notes, thy once-lov'd Poet sung,
'Till Death untimely stop'd his tuneful Tongue.
    Oh just beheld, and lost! admir'd, and mourn'd!
With softest Manners, gentlest Arts, adorn'd!
Blest in each Science, blest in ev'ry Strain!   5
Dear to the Muse, to HARLEY dear—in vain!
    For him, thou oft hast bid the World attend,
Fond to forget the Statesman in the Friend;
For *Swift* and him, despis'd the Farce of State,
The sober Follies of the Wise and Great;   10
Dextrous, the craving, fawning Crowd to quit,
And pleas'd to 'scape from Flattery to Wit.
    Absent or dead, still let a Friend be dear,
(A Sigh the Absent claims, the Dead a Tear)
Recall those Nights that clos'd thy toilsom Days,   15
Still hear thy *Parnell* in his living Lays:
Who careless, now, of Int'rest, Fame, or Fate,
Perhaps forgets that OXFORD e'er was Great;
Or deeming meanest what we greatest call,
Beholds thee glorious only in thy Fall.   20
    And sure if ought below the Seats Divine
Can touch Immortals, 'tis a Soul like thine:
A Soul supreme, in each hard Instance try'd,
Above all Pain, all Passion, and all Pride,
The Rage of Pow'r, the Blast of publick Breath,   25
The Lust of Lucre, and the Dread of Death.
    In vain to Desarts thy Retreat is made;
The Muse attends thee to the silent Shade:
'Tis hers, the brave Man's latest Steps to trace,
Re-judge his Acts, and dignify Disgrace.   30
When Int'rest calls off all her sneaking Train,
And all th' Oblig'd desert, and all the Vain;
She waits, or to the Scaffold, or the Cell,
When the last ling'ring Friend has bid farewel.
Ev'n now she shades thy Evening Walk with Bays,   35
(No Hireling she, no Prostitute to Praise)
Ev'n now, observant of the parting Ray,
Eyes the calm Sun-set of thy Various Day,
Thro' Fortune's Cloud One truly Great can see,
Nor fears to tell, that MORTIMER is He.   40

The text of Dryden's poem is cited from *The Poems and Fables of John Dryden*, ed. James Kinsley (London: Oxford University Press, 1962); of Pope's, from *The Poems of Alexander Pope*, ed. John Butt (New Haven: Yale University Press, 1963).

CHAPTER 6. Counterperiodization and the Colloquial

Epigraph: See nn. 16 and 17 below. I first published the materials of this chapter in "Chiasmus and the Making of Literary Tradition: The Case of Wordsworth and 'the days of Dryden and Pope,'" *ELH* 60 (1993): 961–87.

1. *Essays upon Epitaphs*, in the second volume of *The Prose Works of William Wordsworth*, ed. W. J. B. Owen and Jane Worthington Smyser, 3 vols. (Oxford: Clarendon, 1974), p. 79. Page numbers of further citations from this volume are indicated in parentheses within my text.

2. Henri Suhamy has recently emphasized this feature of shifting signs within the structure and movements of any chiasmus. He notes that in its mirror arrangement the binary terms, passing from one syntactic element to the next, as much *reflect* as oppose each other: *Les figures de style* (Paris: PUF, 1981), p. 78. Suhamy's observation is cited by Thomas Mermall, "The Chiasmus: Unamuno's Master Trope," *PMLA* 105 (1990): 252.

3. Mermall's essay, cited above, makes this claim not only on behalf of Unamuno but for the "modernist sensibility" in general. Octavio Paz is for Mermall another exemplar of the chiastic "spirit of modernity" (247).

4. Other recent discussions (not mentioned by Mermall) of chiasmus, besides de Man's (see n. 11), are those of Jerome Christensen, *Coleridge's Blessed Machine of Language* (Ithaca: Cornell University Press, 1981), pp. 26–27, 260–67, Stanley Corngold, "Metaphor and Chiasmus in Kafka," *Newsletter of the Kafka Society of America* 5 (1981): 23–31, Joshua Scodel, "The Affirmation of Paradox: A Reading of Montaigne's 'De la Phisionomie' (III:12)," *Yale French Studies* 64 (1983): 209–37, Jean Starobinski, "Sur l'emploi du chiasme dans 'Le Neveu de Rameau'," *Revue de Metaphysique et de Morale* 89 (1984): 182–96, and Andrzej Warminski, "Missed Crossing: Wordsworth's Apocalypses," *Modern Language Notes* 99 (1984): 983–1006. Except for de Man's essay, I have not related to these interesting commentaries on this occasion.

5. De Man, "Autobiography as De-Facement," in *The Rhetoric of Romanticism* (New York: Columbia University Press, 1984), pp. 67–81. Page numbers are given in parentheses within my text.

6. De Man, *Rhetoric of Romanticism*, pp. 80, 75.

7. Ibid., p. 70.

8. This middle chiasmus depends upon the fluidity of variables that is the condition of all three chiasmata in the lines of Dryden discussed below. These cases highlight the fact that in the ratios of chiasmus reciprocity actually includes the possibilities of both mutual correspondence and multiplicative inversion (i.e., AA = BB and AB = BA), so that the effect of chiasmus is a blending movement of opposition and reinforcement.

9. Wordsworth's poetry is cited from *The Poetical Works of Wordsworth*, ed. Thomas Hutchinson and Ernest de Selincourt (London: Oxford University Press, 1961). Hutchinson and de Selincourt print the epigraph in italics. Among other debts, it is clear that Milton's sonnets on his blindness have their place in Wordsworth's lines.

10. De Man, *Rhetoric of Romanticism*, p. 78.

11. I cite Dryden's poetry from *The Poems and Fables of John Dryden*, ed. James Kinsley (London: Oxford University Press, 1962). A whole book might be written about these eleven verses. Indeed, thirty years ago (almost in another life) I wrote such a book, although this is only half the book I would write now. In studying the aspects of negative theology which bear on the poem, I did not then take in the enabling force of negativity that makes these verses classic for English classicism. And I did not have more than the faintest glimpse of their vital correspondence with romanticism. (This was my Yale dissertation [1966] on *Reli-*

gio Laici, published as part of *Dryden and the Abyss of Light: A Study of Religio Laici and The Hind and the Panther* [New Haven: Yale University Press, 1970]).

12. In "Tropes (Rilke)," *Allegories of Reading: Figural Language in Rousseau, Nietzsche, Rilke, and Proust* (New Haven: Yale University Press, 1979), we find the following apparently substantive allegations: "The most classical of metaphors" is "conceived as a transfer from an inside to an outside space (or vice versa) by means of an analogical representation. This transfer then reveals a totalizing oneness that was originally hidden but which is fully revealed as soon as it is named and maintained in the figural language" (p. 35). "The classical schema [is] of a subject/object dialectic" (p. 38). "The traditional priority . . . located the depth of meaning in a referent conceived as an object or a consciousness of which the language is a more or less faithful reflection" (p. 45). De Man's claims for the modernity of Rilke's later use of chiasmus seem to contradict de Man's own skepticism concerning the claims of a modernity in "Literary History and Literary Modernity," in *Blindness and Insight: Essays in the Rhetoric of Contemporary Criticism,* 2d ed. (London: Methuen, 1983), pp. 142–65. In addition, in his comments on chiasmus in "Tropes (Rilke)" there seems to be a contradiction between de Man's pictures of (1) the figural elements of the chiasmus as "the poles around which the rotation of the chiasma takes place" (p. 40) and (2) the "void" or "lack that allows for the rotating motion of the polarities" (p. 49).

13. The details of such a close reading of this kind are my main concern in *Dryden and the Abyss of Light.* See, for example, the section on "Light and the Ground of Reason," pp. 97–103, and Appendix C.

14. *Rhetoric* 3.11.2–4.

15. For our inquiry into Dryden's thinking of absences and negative knowledge, it is of more than esoteric interest that, in addition to the inspiration of Boehme's *Ungrund,* Dryden was recollecting here a contemporary anticipation of a Kantian paradox at the end of the "Transcendental Analytic." In Kant the paradox is formulated as follows: "What our understanding acquires through this concept of a noumenon, is a negative extension; that is to say, understanding is not limited through sensibility; on the contrary, it itself limits sensibility by applying the term noumena to things in themselves (things not regarded as appearances). But in so doing it at the same time sets limits to itself, recognizing that it cannot know these noumena through any of the categories, and that it must therefore think them only under the title of an unknown something. . . . The problematic thought which leaves open a place for them [the noumena] serves only, *like an empty space,* for the limitation of empirical principles, without itself containing or revealing any other object of knowledge beyond the sphere of those principles" (*Critique of Pure Reason,* trans. Norman Kemp Smith [London: Macmillan, 1970], B 312–15; my emphasis). There are innumerable ways of formulating the Kantianism of the romantic period, but this surely is one of them. What interests me here is something I noted in *Dryden and the Abyss of Light* but had quite forgotten until I began to ponder Wordsworth's forgettings in the *Essays upon Epitaphs:* namely, that in the exordium of *Religio Laici* Dryden was already recollecting Richard Burthogge's startling anticipation of this particular Kantian paradox. I noted the detailed similarity between Dryden's exordium and a specific passage in Burthogge's *Causa Dei, Or An Apology For God* (1675) in *Dissertation Abstracts* 27:4216A. My discussion of Dryden's debt to Burthogge then appeared in *Dryden and the Abyss of Light* (1970). On Burthogge's anticipation of Kant, see Ernst Cassirer, *Das Erkenntnisproblem in der Philosophie und Wissenschaft der neueren Zeit* (Berlin: B. Cassirer, 1906), 1:464–73, Margaret W. Landes's introduction to her edition of *The Philosophical Writings of Richard Burthogge* (Chicago: University of Chicago Press, 1921), and George Boas, *Dominant Themes of Modern Philosophy* (New York: Ronald, 1957), pp. 253–59.

16. Landor is here referring to the lines of praise for Dryden's skeptical mind that he in-

cluded in his verse letter "To Wordsworth," published in *The Athenaeum* in February 1834, where he calls Dryden "the Bacon of the rhyming crew."

17. The letter to Robinson is now in the MSS collection of Dr. Williams's Library, London. Judging by internal references, the letter was probably written in 1836. The third sentence quoted in my text was excerpted and misquoted by Thomas Sadler, ed., *Diary, Reminiscences, and Correspondence of Henry Crabb Robinson* (Boston, 1870), 2:292 (and, from Sadler's misquotation, many times thereafter), who substituted the word *hymn* for *rhyme*. (He also reversed "eleven" and "first.") I am indebted to Colin Clarke of Dr. Williams's Library for having faith in my hunch that the MS containing Landor's full statement to Robinson was, indeed, somewhere in the library's MSS collection, for his personal labors in photographing the MS, and for being the first to realize that Sadler had misread Landor's word "rhyme" as "hymn." Landor's description of Dryden as the "Bacon of the rhyming crew" (see previous note) in the verses "To Wordsworth" (i.e., the "praise" to which Landor's letter to Robinson refers) confirms Clarke's spontaneous reading of the word "rhyme."

18. Dryden, lines 295–304 and 445–50.

19. For a different, highly interesting account of Wordsworth's relation to Pope, see Robert J. Griffin, "Wordsworth's Pope: The Language of His Former Heart," *ELH* 54 (1987): 695–715.

20. Wordsworth reminds us of Dr. Johnson's judgment that this is Pope's "most valuable" epitaph (p. 76), so that part of Wordsworth's aim is also to overturn the canons of that neoclassical judgment. See Samuel Johnson, *Lives of the English Poets* (London: Oxford University Press, 1964), 2:337. Here Pope's poetry is cited from *The Twickenham Edition of the Poems of Alexander Pope*, ed. John Butt et al., 11 vols. (London: Methuen: 1938–68).

21. *A Map of Misreading* (New York: Oxford University Press, 1975), p. 49.

22. On Bloom's material debt to Eliot, see Steven Gould Axelrod, "Harold Bloom's Enterprise," *Modern Philology* 81 (1984): 290–97. Bloom is drawn, indeed, to Emerson's idea of a "falling forward." This might have led Bloom toward a cosubjective dimension of literary relation. But Bloom chooses to contain Emerson's figure within what Bloom calls an intrapsychical "trick," lest (we may conjecture) it lead him back to Eliot's idea of benign influence. See *Agon* (New York: Oxford University Press, 1982), pp. 172–75. I mention here, again, the late moment in *The Anxiety of Influence* (New York: Oxford University Press, 1975) when Bloom asks the following crucial question, which, however, he fails to acknowledge is only half the question: "What of Blake's Counter-Sublime, and Wordsworth's? Is all the *ekstasis*, the final step beyond, of Romantic vision only an intensity of repression previously unmatched in the history of the imagination? Is Romanticism after all only the waning of the Enlightenment?" (pp. 111–12). (I will return to these questions once more in chapter 8.) If Wordsworth's relationship to the Enlightenment is itself not antithetical but chiastic, then the question which sets us on our quest must be countersolar as well as solar—a waxing and waning, and then a waning and waxing. These countermovements and interdependecies of chiasmus provide another reason for reexamining Bloom's assertion that "every post-enlightenment master moves, not towards a sharing-with-others . . . but towards a being-with-oneself" (p. 123). Like Wordsworth and de Man, Bloom forgets the poetry of neoclassicism as well as the chiasmus in which the days of romanticism and neoclassicism are written together.

23. On the "negative way" of Wordsworth's major verse, see Geoffrey H. Hartman, *Wordsworth's Poetry 1787–1814* (New Haven: Yale University Press, 1964), pp. 33–69.

24. Wordsworth may have had some sense that he was excluding evidence of Pope's poetic awareness of the cancer which killed Elizabeth Corbet, but he seems to have written it off as indirection of expression and avoidance of suffering: "The Epitaph now before us

owes what exemption it may have from these defects in its general plan to the excruciating disease of which the Lady died; but it too is liable to the same censure; and is, like the rest, further objectionable in this: namely, that the thoughts have their nature changed and moulded by the vicious expression in which they are entangled, to an excess rendering them wholly unfit for the place which they occupy" (p. 77). It is difficult to decide how much Wordsworth was forgetting at this particular moment, but it was likely a good deal.

25. "Tropes (Rilke)," in *Allegories of Reading*, p. 49. De Man continues, "Experiences, like . . . figural objects, must contain a void or a lack if they are to be converted into figures. . . . Hence the prevalence of a thematics of negative experiences in Rilke's poetry. . . . the totalization of subjective experience must lead to a positive assertion that only chiasmus can reveal. The reversal of a negativity into a promise, the ambivalent thematic strategy of the *Duino Elegies*, allows for a linguistic play that is analogous to that in the most discreet of the *New Poems*" (p. 50). De Man specifies a "mutual reflexive substitution" between the "two subjects" which are mirror halves of the same subject and which thus "constitutes the subject" (*Rhetoric of Romanticism*, p. 70).

26. De Man, *Rhetoric of Romanticism*, pp. 76–77. Frances Ferguson, *Wordsworth: Language as Counter-Spirit* (New Haven: Yale University Press, 1977), p. 166, similarly speaks of "Wordsworth's rejection of [Popeian] antithesis and his adoption of a complex series of reciprocal relationships." In her discussion of Wordsworth's idea of the counterspirit Ferguson describes a "doubling of consciousness" within "an internal dialectic" (pp. xiv, xvii). In this sense, Ferguson's concern, like de Man's, is with what Bloom calls the "intra-psychical."

27. De Man, *Rhetoric of Romanticism*, pp. 75–76.

28. Pope later chose the word "reserve" for a closely parallel context, even joining it to a decorum of forgetting as well as to the image of refining gold and character. This appears in "Of the Characters of Women" in lines which he calls (in a footnote) "The Picture of an estimable Woman, with the best kind of contrarieties." Pope began writing these lines two years after the Corbet epitaph. We recall that in the *Essays upon Epitaphs* Wordsworth explicitly refers—at least twice (pp. 56 and 80)—to Pope's "Of the Characters of Women." Here are Pope's lines:

> Reserve with Frankness, Art with Truth ally'd
> Courage with Softness, Modesty with Pride. . . .
> This Phoebus promis'd (I forget the year)
> When those blue eyes first open'd on the sphere; . . .
> The gen'rous God, who Wit and Gold refines,
> And ripens Spirits as he ripens Mines,
> Kept Dross for Duchesses, the world shall know it,
> To you gave Sense, Good-humour, and a Poet.
> (ll. 277–92)

29. In the 1730 publication of the epitaph Pope's title was only "Epitaph on Mrs. Elizabeth Corbett"—where, as in the actual family name, there are two *t*'s and where there is no naming of the disease or its location. In 1735 he changed the title to "EPITAPH. *On Mrs.* CORBET, *Who dyed of a Cancer in her Breast.*"

30. The Twickenham editors mention a nineteenth-century conjecture (for which, as they point out, there is no hard evidence of any kind) that the Corbet epitaph may have originally been intended for Mrs. Cope, who also died of a cancer in her breast, close to the same time as Mrs. Corbet, and who was better known to Pope than Mrs. Corbet. If this guess did turn out to be correct, it would not necessarily put in doubt an interpretation of the epitaph that depends on the play with the name Corbet, unless, of course, it could somehow be

shown that the lines, exactly as we have them, were meant for someone else. If there had been an early affiliation of these lines with Mrs. Cope it would, on the contrary, raise fascinating questions about why Pope ultimately chose "Corbet" over "Cope," in particular about the range of possible framings of absence which Pope may have originally envisioned for these lines in *cope* (e.g., an ecclesiastical vestment, a vault, a coffin, L. *cophinus*) that he eventually set aside or deepened in choosing *corbet*.

CHAPTER 7. The Reinvention of Desire

1. Since I am proposing a certain fluidity of these terms within the Western tradition, it is worth recalling here that the most famous modern statement of their meanings, Freud's "Mourning and Melancholia," opens with a "warning" that the "definition" of melancholia "fluctuates even in descriptive psychiatry" (*The Standard Edition of the Complete Psychological Works of Sigmund Freud*, trans. James Strachey et al., 24 vols. [London: Hogarth Press and the Institute of Psycho-Analysis, 1953–74], 14:243). The same could be said of modern definitions and descriptions of mourning. Part of the work of this chapter is to describe the sublime variant of melancholia that is constituted in the sublime experience (such as Kant schematizes) of what Freud calls "repetition" and "working-through" (12:150–56). Sublime melancholia confronts pathologies of "acting out" (12:151) which are manifested, I try to show, in attempting to recuperate loss not only in melancholia but also in a good deal of what passes for therapeutic mourning. These attempted recuperations of loss are both aspects of what I will call a vulgar melancholia. Sublime melancholia, moreover, is worked through simultaneously in the cultural and the personal spheres. In chapter 10 I will turn to Freud's own representations of sublime melancholia.

2. Kant, "Analytic of the Sublime": "brooding melancholy" (p. 121), "schwermüthigen Nachdenken" (p. 117); "an interesting sadness . . . melancholy (but not dispirited sadness)" (p. 130), "eine interessante Traurigkeit . . . Betrübniss (nicht niedergeschlagene Traurigkeit)" (pp. 127–28); "*freedom from affection (apatheia, phlegma in significatu bono)* in a mind that strenuously follows its unswerving principles is sublime" (p. 124), "*Affectlosigkeit (Apatheia, Phlegma in significatu bono)* eines seinen unwandelbaren Grundsätzen nachdrücklich nachgehenden Gemüths ist" (pp. 121–22). Citations from "The Analytic of the Sublime" in English are from *The Critique of Judgement*, trans. James Creed Meredith (Oxford: Clarendon, 1973); in German, from *Kants Werke: Akademie-Textausgabe*, vol. 5 (Berlin: Walter de Gruyter, 1968).

3. *The Gendering of Melancholia: Feminism, Psychoanalysis, and the Symbolics of Loss in Renaissance Literature* (Ithaca: Cornell University Press, 1992), p. 232.

4. Ibid., p. 19.

5. I cite Milton's poetry from *John Milton: Complete Shorter Poems*, ed. John Carey (London: Longman, 1971), and *John Milton: Paradise Lost*, ed. Alastair Fowler (London: Longman, 1971). Other places in "Il Penseroso" where Tasso's *Gerusalemme liberata* is alluded to are verses 88–96 and 151–54. For details, see *A Variorum Commentary on the Poems of John Milton*, vol. 2, part 1, ed. A. S. P. Woodhouse and Douglas Bush (London: Routledge, 1972).

6. This is one of my subjects in chapter 10.

7. Schiesari, *The Gendering of Melancholy*, pp. 228–29.

8. Cited by John McCole, *Walter Benjamin and the Antinomies of Tradition* (Ithaca: Cornell University Press, 1993), pp. 295, 298. Many of Benjamin's reflections on melancholy in *The Origin of German Tragic Drama*, trans. John Osborne (London: New Left Books, 1977), and in "Left Wing Melancholy," *Screen* 15 (1974): 28–32, could also be invoked in this context.

9. See "Comus," ll. 547–66 and "The Passion," stanza 6, as well as *Paradise Lost,* 4.598–604, 6.750ff., 7.197–217.

10. Edward Greenstein first made me aware of the varieties of muteness in Ezekiel.

11. *Paradise Lost,* 4.598–604, 7.197–217. The phrase "mute silence," which Milton had earlier used in "In Quintum Novembris" (l. 149: "per muta silentia"), is from Ovid, *Metamorphoses* 7.184.

12. Hegel, *The Phenomenology of Spirit,* trans. A. V. Miller (Oxford: Clarendon, 1977), section 163.

13. See Moshe Greenberg, "On Ezekiel's Dumbness," *Journal of Biblical Literature* 77 (1958): 101–05.

14. See Greenberg's itemization of such sources, *The Anchor Bible, Ezekiel, 1–20* (New York: Doubleday, 1983), pp. 55–58.

15. The word *hashmal* in this verse, also in 1:4 and 8:2 (there in the feminine form *hashmalah*), is unique to Ezekiel in the Bible. Of unknown etymology or meaning, it is translated "elektron" in the Septuagint, "electrum" in the Vulgate, hence "amber" in English.

16. This is Greenberg's translation in *Anchor Bible, Ezekiel, 1–20.*

17. On the history of the metamorphosis of the wheels of the chariot into a class of angels, see Greenberg, *Anchor Bible, Ezekiel, 1–20,* pp. 205–06.

18. As it happens we have suggestive evidence of Milton's realization that his representation must repeat Ezekiel's way of leaving the destruction largely unrepresented. Some months before composing "Il Penseroso" Milton had said it all in a "pensive" poem, "The Passion," which he left (as the endnote said) "unfinished":

> See, see the chariot, and those rushing wheels,
> That whirled the prophet up at Chebar flood,
> My spirit some transporting cherub feels,
> To bear me where the towers of Salem stood,
> Once glorious towers, now sunk in guiltless blood:
> There doth my soul in holy vision sit
> In pensive trance, and anguish, and ecstatic fit. (stanza VI)

Paradoxically, this image of Ezekiel's chariot of destruction is unfinished—misses the mark of ecstatic pensiveness—because it embodies no principle of *manum de tabula,* or representational deficit. In "Il Penseroso" Milton has achieved the sublime power of the unfinished or partially withdrawn, or undrawn, representation. Indeed, remarkably enough, in *Paradise Lost,* 6.751, Milton puns precisely to this effect, speaking of Ezekiel's "Wheel within Wheel undrawn."

19. Greenberg, *Anchor Bible, Ezekiel, 1–20,* p. 172.

20. Ibid., pp. 297–99.

21. Descartes, *Philosophical Essays,* trans. Laurence J. Lafleur (New York: Bobbs-Merrill, 1964), p. 110. See my comment on this point in chapter 1, p. 5–6 and n. 8.

22. Considering the biblical aspects of Kant's picture of sublime experience, it is not surprising that in the course of explaining the indispensability of self-deprivation for sublime experience and of mentioning the special efficacy of representations that show their own inadequacy as representation he says that the Decalogue commandment against graven images is in itself the most sublime passage in the Hebrew Bible. Kant specifies that this commandment entails a "removal" or deprivation of all initially imagined representation, in this sense a "negative presentation" (he cites, "Thou shalt not make unto thee any graven image, or any likeness of any thing that is in heaven or on earth, or under the earth"). Kant makes clear that this removal is totally different from a topos of mere inexpressibility. Yet Kant shows no interest in the fact that this same commandment is the recorded beginning of the

line for the husband-wife topos of faithfulness to this line of language. (See *The Critique of Judgement*, trans. Meredith, p. 127.) Sometimes, incidentally, these commandments are numbered as two different commandments, but they are one commandment in Luther's Bible, as they are also in the Vulgate.

23. Moshe Idel has pointed out to me that in kabbalistic writings the gendering of the *hashmal* and *hashmalah* is unmistakable, as in the *Zohar Chadash*, chapter Yitro.

24. The translation of these verses is again Greenberg's, except that I have now changed "fire surrounding it" to the more literal "fire surrounding her." Greenberg, of course, notes the feminine pronoun in his commentary.

25. The intervening matter here is "Like the appearance of the bow that is in a cloud on a rainy day such was the appearance of the surrounding radiance." It is possible to see a masculine figuration in the bow, as has been proposed by Howard Eilberg-Schwartz, *God's Phallus and Other Problems for Men and Monotheism* (Boston: Beacon, 1994), pp. 179–82, but (quite aside from the fact that this phallic symbol, if it is that, is semicircular and therefore strongly suggestive of a vaginal symbol—or of the covenant of peace between God and humankind, husband and wife) one should also then note the feminine image of the "cloud on a rainy day" in which the bow is couched. After the chiastic cross-gendering in the previous verse and considering the commonplace associations of God's presence with the image of the cloud (cf. Ez. 10:3), there is no obvious reason to give the element of the bow more importance than the cloud in characterizing the divine nature.

26. That this gender distribution is not accidental is shown by the fact that in verse 1.4 fire is also given as both feminine and masculine. In Ezekiel's inaugural vision there is arguably a substantial cross-gendering of "ruach," or spirit itself, as has recently been surveyed by Helen Shlüngel-Straumann, "Ruach und Gender-Frage am Beispiel der Visionen beim Propheten Ezechiel," in *On Reading Prophetic Texts: Gender-Specific and Related Studies,* ed. Bob Becking and Meinder Dijkstra (Leiden: Brill, 1996), pp. 201–15.

27. *Phenomenology of Spirit*, section 508.

28. Hegel, *Philosophy of Right,* trans. T. M. Knox (London: Oxford University Press, 1967). Knox and the German text that he translates (*Grundlinien der Philosophie des Rechts,* ed. Georg Lasson [Leipzig: Meiner, 1921]) do not reproduce the phrase "I will repay," although Hegel's comment on this verse is specifically on the word "repay" (in which Hegel italicizes the element of repetition). In fact, this error of omission—whether it is Hegel's oversight or that of his editors—defeats the meaning, and the explication of turning or chiastic form, of the passage. In chapter 3 I commented on the connection between chiasmus and revenge in Hegel's derivation of self-consciousness.

29. Here and in the next citation, from Deuteronomy, I have reproduced the emphatically chiastic arrangement of the Hebrew. Both the Vulgate and Luther preserve Ezekiel's chiastic arrangement in 25:14.

30. With regard to the divine track of this staking of one's life—or of divine revenge—it is difficult not to feel that the image and imitation of Christ's trial by death in the Passion is somewhere in the background of Hegel's thought.

31. *The Critique of Judgement,* trans. Meredith, p. 123.

32. T. S. Eliot's blindness to the sublimity of Milton's poetry is painfully obvious in the elaboration of his absurd (and cruel) remark that "Milton may be said never to have seen anything." In *Paradise Lost,* Eliot claims, "a dislocation takes place, through the hypertrophy of the auditory imagination at the expense of the visual and tactile" (*Milton: Two Studies* [London: Faber, 1968], pp. 11–18).

33. Elsewhere too Milton hears and represents Philomel's silence within song as a commonplace of her melancholy. See *Comus,* 545–66, and *Paradise Lost,* 4.600–04.

34. Robert Hertz, "The Pre-eminence of the Right Hand: A Study in Religious Polar-

ity," trans. Rodney Needham, in *Right and Left: Essays on Dual Symbolic Classification*, ed. Rodney Needham (Chicago: University of Chicago Press, 1973), pp. 3–31.

35. *The Works of Sir Thomas Browne*, ed. Geoffrey Keynes (London: Faber, 1928), 3:24, 21. (*Pseudodoxia Epidemica* or *Vulgar Errors*, book 4, chapter 5.)

36. Ezekiel represents his own vicitmized status as a forced *muteness* and forced lying on the *left* side. God says to him, "I shall make your tongue stick to your palate so that you will be dumb. . . . You, lie down on your left side and place the iniquity of the house of Israel on it" (3:26–4:4)—that is, before he can move toward rectification or redemption by lying on his right side, but Ezekiel apparently remains dumb, on his left (see 4:9). (The commonplace status of this straining against dextrality that Milton cites from Ezekiel is confirmed by the fact that at virtually the same moment that Milton composed "Il Penseroso" [1629–31] Rembrandt painted his iconography of melancholia, the so-called *Jeremiah* [actually, as we have seen, Ezekiel as well] *Lamenting the Destruction of Jerusalem* [1630], dumbstricken, lying on his left side. Rembrandt follows these verses of Ezekiel even more closely than Milton, showing the prophet beside the iron wall and as if beside his own picturing of the destruction of Jerusalem—just as God requires of him) (4:1–4).

37. It is difficult to imagine, then, that when Milton *moves off* the verse "The cherub Contemplation" to his next verse, "And the mute Silence hist along," he is not reinscribing (like a scribe) an element of this moment in Ezekiel. Both in Ezekiel and in Milton the destructiveness of a unilateral eroticism, especially of an erotic drive in representation, is a central topic. The idolatrous male abominations to which Ezekiel refers are specified a few verses earlier. They are fertility rites combined with sun worship: at the eastern "entrance to YHWH's temple . . . were about twenty-five men whose backs were to YHWH's temple and whose faces were turned east and they were prostrating themselves to the sun" and (obscenely) reaching "the vine branches to their noses" (8:16–17). In the verses in "L'Allegro" which are the phallicizing counterpart to the Ezekelian counterphallicizing verses of "Il Penseroso" Milton represents the phallic drive "right against the eastern gate, / Where the great sun begins his state, / Robed in flames and amber light" ("L'Allegro," ll. 59–61). To hear such complexities in Milton's language is not to reject the usual gloss on the eastern gate from Oberon's phrase describing the sunrise in *Midsummer Night's Dream*, 3.2.391, "the eastern gate, all fiery red." But Shakespeare's paganized, picturesque usage corresponds to only the apparently innocuous half of Milton's vision. That vision oscillates between "L'Allegro" and "Il Penseroso" and in fact already vibrates complexly in "L'Allegro." Ezekiel's vision of the pathology of language and its possible antidote, Milton suggests, is all along the "chiefest" placing of blame in these poems. This is to suppose that in "L'Allegro" Milton has opened the way for our memory of Ezekiel's (God's) excoriation of the abominations against the eastern gate, with their worship of what Milton calls the "amber" sun and the phallicism that would displace the worship of the God of a nonmaterial, *hashmal* (amber) light and of cross-gendered fiery loins. I am proposing the possibility that, with his own scribe's kit on his loins, Milton too moves off "the cherub" from his own immediately previous verse and that his succeeding couplet then makes a versifying X (suspending dextrality) in the chiasmus which inscribes this histing or sighing.

Without reference to Ezekiel, A. W. Verity long ago registered that Milton's verb "hist" is "probably an imperative . . . answering to *bring* in l. 51. It seems to mean 'bring the mute Silence with you'": *Milton's Ode on the Morning of Christ's Nativity, L'Allegro, and Lycidas* (Cambridge: Cambridge University Press, 1906). This understanding of "hist" fits neatly into Milton's citation of God's imperative of the "sigh" and its mark in Ezekiel. (In keeping with the effectively endless cultural line of Milton's referentiality, this is the place to wonder whether his verse "And the mute Silence hist along" might be related, directly or indirectly, to the gloss on Ezekiel's *hashmal* as *hash* and *mal*, meaning move along and murmur, in Talmud [Babylonian] *Hagiga*, 3ab.)

38. See G. A. Cooke, *A Critical and Exegetical Commentary on the Book of Ezekiel* (Edinburgh: Clark, 1960).

CHAPTER 8. Self-Endangerment and Obliviousness in "Personal Culture"

1. Hegel, *The Phenomenology of Spirit*, trans. A. V. Miller (Oxford: Clarendon, 1977), section 8; hereafter cited in text as *PS* and section number.

2. Harold Bloom, *The Anxiety of Influence: A Theory of Poetry* (New York: Oxford University Press, 1973), pp. 123, 67.

3. Ibid., pp. 111–12.

4. Cited by M. H. Abrams in *Natural Supernaturalism: Tradition and Revolution in Romantic Literature* (New York: Norton, 1971), p. 506n.

5. Nietzsche's sense of the "manifold," applied to Goethe, is very much in conflict with Kant's "unity of consciousness . . . in knowledge of the manifold" or a priori "synthesis of apprehension . . . to a transcendental unity" (*Critique of Pure Reason*, ed. Norman Kemp Smith [London: Macmillan, 1993], A107–08). For an exposition of Kant's concept of the manifold and of later concepts of the manifold (though not of Nietzsche's), see Michael Podro, *The Manifold in Perception: Theories of Art from Kant to Hildebrand* (Oxford: Clarendon, 1972).

6. Nietzsche, *Beyond Good and Evil: Prelude to a Philosophy of the Future*, trans. R. J. Hollingdale (London: Penguin, 1990), 244. Numbers refer to Nietzsche's section divisions.

7. For a glimpse of Schiller's philosophical interest in chiasmus as well as the possible reciprocal relation of this interest to Goethe's artistic practice, see Elizabeth M. Wilkinson's and L. A. Willoughby's introduction to their edition and translation of Schiller's *On the Aesthetic Education of Man: In a Series of Letters* (Oxford: Clarendon, 1982), esp. pp. lxviii–lxxii, xci–xcv, and cxcv–cxcvi.

8. In this instance I have offered my own literal translation, but the other translations from *Faust* included here are those of Philip Wayne (London: Penguin, 1979).

9. In *Faust* as a whole this "Geisterreich" reaches one kind of climax in the chiasmus of female and male, living and departed, sung by the Chorus Mysticus in the closing verses of the tragedy. I will briefly return to these lines later.

10. Unless otherwise noted translations of *Torquato Tasso* are from the version of Alan and Sandy Brownjohn (London: Angel Books, 1985). Goethe's plays are quoted from *Gedenkausgabe der Werke, Briefe und Gespräche*, ed. Ernst Beutler (Zurich: Artemis, 1962), vols. 5, 6.

11. The Italian text is that of *La Gerusalemme Liberata*, ed. Giovanni Getto (Brescia: La Scuola, 1967). I cite the literal prose translation of Ralph Nash, *Jerusalem Delivered* (Detroit: Wayne State University Press, 1987), though I arrange Nash's prose according to Tasso's lineation.

12. Praising the Princess and the Duke, she says, "Ein edler Mensch *zieht edle Menschen an* / Und weiss sie festzuhalten, wie ihr tut. / Um deinen Bruder und um dich verbinden / Gemüter sich, die euer würdig sind, / Und ihr seid eurer grossen Väter wert" (ll. 59–63; emphasis added).

13. Erich Auerbach, *Mimesis: The Representation of Reality in Western Literature*, trans. Willard Trask (1946; Princeton: Princeton University Press, 1971), pp. 444–45, 451.

14. Nash translates "gemiti" as "groans."

15. In chapter 7 of the *Vita Nuova*. I am indebted to Lawrence Besserman for showing me this parallel in Dante, especially since it raises Tasso's usage virtually to the level of a topos. In "A Note on the Sources of Chaucer's *Troilus* V, 540–613," *The Chaucer Review* 24 (1990): 306–07, Besserman has shown that in the "Proemio" to the *Filostrato* Boccaccio explicitly invokes the opening lament of Lamentations to bemoan the loss of his beloved: "O

how solitary abideth the city that before was full of people and a mistress among the nations!"

16. Auerbach, *Mimesis,* pp. 444, 452.

17. Ibid., pp. 447, 449–50.

18. Ibid., p. 452.

19. Johann Peter Eckermann, *Conversations with Goethe,* trans. Gisela C. O'Brien (New York: Ungar, 1964), p. 121; entry for July 15, 1827.

20. Nietzsche, *Beyond Good and Evil,* 251. From my own experience I flatter myself to think that this is a remark to which I, as a Jew, can happily take exception, but the form of Nietzsche's argument in the shadow of Goethe's picture of the manifold no doubt has real, general value which applies, in all directions, to the avoidances among cultures.

21. See chapter 1, note 22.

22. The fact that this passage comments on Hegel's scene of victimization was noted by Stanley Cavell, *The Claim of Reason: Wittgenstein, Skepticism, Morality, and Tragedy* (New York: Oxford University Press, 1979), pp. 475–76.

23. Hegel, *The Philosophy of History,* trans. J. Sibree (New York: Dover, 1956), p. 32.

24. See Nietzsche's invocation of *Faust,* ll. 1607–11, in section 13 of *The Birth of Tragedy.*

25. This version given by Brownjohn is not literal, yet it accurately captures, I believe, the complex countermovements within the couplet. The first-level meaning of these verses is—as Goethe surely intended—extraordinarily difficult to pin down.

26. Tasso, *Jerusalem Delivered,* trans. Ralph Nash, p. 474.

27. See Nietzsche, *The Birth of Tragedy,* section 4.

28. In fact, it is just here that Auerbach's bias toward "realism" comes in again in our story, this time in relation to his work as one of the foremost modern explicators of the workings of Christian typology. Auerbach insisted that Christian typological interpretation was totally different from and far superior to the "allegorical" interpretation of the Jews, precisely because of the "dramatic actuality" of the "fulfillment" created in Christian typology (*Scenes from the Drama of European Literature: Six Essays,* trans. Ralph Manheim [New York, 1959], pp. 51–55). I have elsewhere questioned whether the dimension of fulfillment in Christian typology is, in many highly significant cases, as closed or temporally located as Auerbach claims; and I have suggested some of the ways in which ancient Jewish texts very much already invent a typological-antitypological interpretation of the open kind employed in many Christian texts (see "Milton and the Scene of Interpretation: From Typology toward Midrash," in *Midrash and Literature,* ed. Geoffrey H. Hartman and Sanford Budick [New Haven: Yale University Press, 1986], pp. 195–212). In the present instance from Lamentations we witness an ancient Jewish form of typology which suggests, ironically enough, that in his own way Auerbach too was oblivious to the mind of the Jews that is part of the manifold of mind within the German and the European mind. (In a way that seems to me valuable, though somewhat neglectful of the achieved temporality of Christian typology, James J. Paxson, "A Theory of Biblical Typology in the Middle Ages," *Exemplaria* 3 [1991]: 379–83, has used de Man's perspectives on allegory and deconstruction to question Auerbach's account.)

CHAPTER 9. The Modernity of Learning

Epigraph: English versions of Baudelaire's criticism are from *Baudelaire: Selected Writings on Art and Artists,* trans. P. E. Charvet (Cambridge: Cambridge University Press, 1981), here from pp. 303 and 323, except that in the first excerpt I have given Baudelaire's "lieux communs" as "commonplaces" where Charvet has "commonplace things," and in the second excerpt I have given Baudelaire's "coupable" as "culpable" where Charvet has "sinful." Citations from Baudelaire's critical texts are from *Curiosités esthétiques: L'Art romantique, et autres Œuvres critiques,* ed. Henri Lemaitre (Paris: Garnier, 1962), in which the passages translated here appear on pp. 325–26 and 395.

1. De Man, *Blindness and Insight: Essays in the Rhetoric of Contemporary Criticism,* second edition (London: Methuen, 1983), pp. 142–65.

2. Ibid., pp. 148, 150.

3. Ibid., pp. 161–62.

4. In note 24 I comment on de Man's analysis of this term.

5. Baudelaire, *Curiosités esthétiques: L'Art romantique, et autres Œuvres critiques,* ed. Lemaitre, pp. 339, 325, 395; *Baudelaire: Selected Writings on Art and Artists,* trans. Charvet, pp. 312, 303, 323.

6. Kant, *The Critique of Judgement,* trans. James Creed Meredith (Oxford: Clarendon, 1973), p. 91.

7. The text of the poem and the translation (which I have modified) are taken from *Baudelaire,* ed. and trans. Francis Scarfe (London: Penguin, 1961), pp. 17–18.

8. Lee Johnson, *The Paintings of Eugène Delacroix: A Critical Catalogue* (Oxford: Clarendon, 1986), 3:89.

9. It is thus referred to repeatedly (especially by Tasso) in the text (act 2, scene iv), though Alfonso has sentenced Tasso to a self-supervised form of house arrest.

10. I quote from the second printing, 1827: Goethe, *Torquato Tasso,* anon. trans., in *Chefs-D'Oeuvre des Théâtres Étrangers* (Paris: Rapilly, 1827) 2:384 (opening of act 4, scene 1).

11. *Curiosités esthétiques: L'Art romantique, et autres Œuvres critiques,* ed. Lemaitre, pp. 326–27; *Baudelaire: Selected Writings on Art and Artists,* trans. Charvet, p. 304.

12. Goethe, *Torquato Tasso,* in *Chefs-D'Oeuvre des Théâtres Étrangers* 2:385.

13. Unless otherwise indicated, English translations of *Torquato Tasso* are from the version of Alan and Sandy Brownjohn (London: Angel Books, 1985). Goethe's German text is quoted from *Gedenkausgabe der Werke, Briefe und Gespräche,* ed. Ernst Beutler (Zurich: Artemis, 1962), vol. 5.

14. Within a discussion of the *roulant* it is appropriate to mention that Goethe's language extensively recirculates, from before Tasso's epic, the details of Virgil's representation of the Dira, or bird-demon, that flits and screams at doomed Turnus (*Aeneid* 12.843–68).

15. Goethe, *Torquato Tasso,* in *Chefs-D'Oeuvre des Théâtres Étrangers* 2:319 (act 1, scene 3).

16. *Jérusalem délivrée,* trans. le prince Lebrun (Paris, 1817).

17. The literal English version is from Tasso, *Jerusalem Delivered,* trans. Ralph Nash (Detroit: Wayne State University Press, 1987).

18. Tancred's "senses and countenance," Tasso tells us, are filled "with death": "The living man lies languishing like to the dead, in color, in silence, in attitude and in blood" (*G.L.,* 12:70). On Delacroix's coloration of Tasso, Delacroix's generally appreciative contemporary Eugène Bareste remarked—not understanding the provenience of the figure—"La couleur . . . est malheureusement terne et grise." In fact, from the same lack of awareness Bareste wrote of the deployment of Tasso's legs: "Nous regrettons que les jambes du Tasse soient attachées avec si peu de soin, et que le dessin soit si négligé." These comments are cited without protest by Johnson, ed., *The Paintings of Eugène Delacroix: A Critical Catalogue* 3:89.

19. *L'Oeuvre Complet de Eugène Delacroix: Peintures Dessins Gravures Lithographes Catalogué et Reproduit par Alfred Robaut,* commenté par Ernest Chesneau, ouvrage publié avec la collaboration de Fernand Calmettes (Paris: Charavay, 1885), p. 54. I have searched for the sketch in the Cabinet des Dessins of the Louvre, where the curator of the collection believes Robaut probably reproduced it, but the original sketch has apparently been lost.

20. For the leaning on the left hand as well as the urn in the iconography of melancholia, see, for example, Chaperon's, Feti's, and Castiglione's paintings of *Melancholy*, which are reproduced in Raymond Klibansky, Erwin Panofsky, and Fritz Saxl, *Saturn and Melancholy: Studies in the History of Natural Philosophy, Religion, and Art* (1964; Kraus Reprint: Nendeln / Leichtenstein, 1979), plates 134, 135, 136.

21. Goethe, *Torquato Tasso*, in *Chefs-D'Oeuvre des Théatres Étrangers* 2:305 (act 1, scene 1).

22. Karlheinz Stierle, *Ästhetische Rationalität: Kunstwerk und Werkbegriff* (Munich: Fink, 1996), p. 175, notes, in "Les Phares," a different instance of Baudelaire's wordplay with Delacroix's name: "Delacroix, lac de sang."

23. Erich Auerbach, "Philology and *Weltliteratur*," trans. Maire and Edward Said, *Centennial Review* 13 (1969): 15–16.

24. De Man makes a good deal of what he claims is an "incompatability" in Baudelaire's use of the word "représentation" in the following passage, of which de Man quotes the last sentence: "Le passé est intéressant non seulement par la beauté qu'ont su en extraire les artistes pour qui il était le présent, mais aussi comme passé, pour sa valeur historique. Il en est de même du présent. Le plaisir que nous retirons de la représentation du présent tient non seulement à la beauté dont il peut être revêtu, mais aussi à sa qualité essentielle de présent" (*Curiosités esthétiques: L'Art romantique, et autres Œuvres critiques*, ed. Lemaitre, p. 454). ["The past is interesting, not only because of the beauty that the artists for whom it was the present were able to extract from it, but also as past, for its historical value. The same applies to the present. The pleasure we derive from the representation of the present is due, not only to the beauty it can be clothed in, but also to its essential quality of being the present" (*Baudelaire: Selected Writings on Art and Artists*, trans. Charvet, p. 391). De Man alleges that Baudelaire does not see the following "paradox" or "incompatability": "The paradox of the problem is potentially contained in the formula 'représentation du présent,' which combines a repetitive with an instantaneous pattern without apparent awareness of the incompatability" (156). I suggest that the truly complex terms in Baudelaire's usages here are "extraire" (to extract) and "nous retirons" (we derive or extract). The incompatability that de Man sees in the formula "représentation du présent" is seen to be the focus of Baudelaire's own struggle once we understand "extraire" and "retirons" as operations in the past or present that are carried out in a succession of distinct moments, so that for Baudelaire the experience of the present of a sublime line of representation—the only kind that interests Baudelaire—is necessarily of what I have termed priority.

CHAPTER 10. Limping: Freud's Experience of Death

1. Citations from Freud's works are from *Sigmund Freud: Gesammelte Werke Chronologisch Geordnet*, 18 vols. (London: Imago, 1940–52), of which the page numbers are given within my text after the abbreviation *GW*, or, in English, from *The Standard Edition of the Complete Psychological Works of Sigmund Freud*, trans. James Strachey et al., 24 vols. (London: Hogarth Press and the Institute of Psycho-Analysis, 1953–74), of which the page numbers are given within my text after the abbreviation *SE*. In *Beyond the Pleasure Principle* Freud's uses of the word "Gedankengang" are to be found in *GW* 13:39, 60, 61, 64 and *SE* 18:37, 56 (twice), 59. At least the first of these is worth quoting here because it was written last and then placed first. This was done in 1925, five years after the original publication. Freud had now begun to *correct* his dualism (he was to make it even more correct later). His retrospective placement of the term "Gedankengang" in this key position, precisely when he had misgivings about the vulnerability he had incurred by following this line of thought, deserves special attention: "Man

möge nicht übersehen, dass das folgende die Entwicklung eines extremen Gedankenganges ist, der späterhin, wenn die Sexualtriebe in Betracht gezogen werden, Einschränkung und Berichtigung findet" (*GW* 13:39n.). "The reader should not overlook the fact that what follows is the development of an extreme line of thought. Later on, when account is taken of the sexual instincts, it will be found that the necessary limitations and corrections are applied to it" (*SE* 18:37n.). (Strachey regularly translates "Gedankengang" as "line of thought." He also uses this phrase on two occasions, pp. 58 and 60, when Freud's word is not "Gedankengang.") In *Beyond the Pleasure Principle* Freud uses the term *death instinct* (Todestrieb) most often in the plural but occasionally also in the singular (for example, twice on *SE* 18:54; *GW* 13:58).

2. Jean Laplanche, *Life and Death in Psychoanalysis,* trans. Jeffrey Mehlman (Baltimore: Johns Hopkins University Press, 1976), pp. 122–23. Two other distinguished interpreters of *Beyond the Pleasure Principle* who have found it impossible to credit Freud's "dualism" of life instincts and death instincts are Jacques Derrida, *The Post Card: From Socrates to Freud and Beyond,* trans. Alan Bass (Chicago: University of Chicago Press, 1987; French edition, 1980), pp. 259–409, esp. pp. 366–67, and Harold Bloom, "Freud's Concepts of Defense and the Poetic Will," in *The Literary Freud: Mechanisms of Defense and the Poetic Will,* ed. Joseph H. Smith (New Haven: Yale University Press, 1980), pp. 1–28.

3. Twenty-five years earlier he had quoted the verses in a letter to Wilhelm Fliess. See Sigmund Freud, *Briefe an Wilhelm Fliess 1887–1904,* ed. Jeffrey Moussaieff Masson (Frankfurt am Main: Fischer, 1986), p. 150; letter of 20 October 1895. In the letter Freud remembers "Sünde" as "Schande." The correction of the error in the citation that concludes *Beyond the Pleasure Principle* suggests that Freud had in the meanwhile gone back to Rückert's text.

4. I quote from the fourth edition of *Die Verwandlungen des Abu Seid von Serug oder die Makamen des Hariri,* trans. Friedrich Rückert (Stuttgart: Gottaschen, 1864).

5. See George J. Makari, "A History of Freud's First Concept of Transference," *International Review of Psycho-Analysis* 19 (1992): 415, who is citing a paper given by John Kerr at the History of Psychiatry Seminar of the Payne Whitney Clinic in 1990..

6. Laplanche, *Life and Death in Psychoanalysis,* trans. Mehlman, p. 122, in fact observes that Freud's "major piece of supporting evidence" for the death instinct and the repetition compulsion is "the psychoanalytic phenomenon par excellence: transference."

7. Tasso is quoted from *La Gerusalemme Liberata,* ed. Giovanni Getto (Brescia, 1967). In English I cite the literal prose translation of Ralph Nash, *Jerusalem Delivered* (Detroit: Wayne State University Press, 1987).

8. Jean Laplanche, *Life and Death in Psychoanalysis,* trans. Mehlman, p. 117. See below pp. 191–93 for remarks on the phrases of Freud that prompt Laplanche's question.

9. Hegel, *The Phenomenology of Spirit,* trans. A. V. Miller (Oxford: Clarendon, 1977); cited in text as *PS* and section number.

10. Michael S. Roth, *Psycho-Analysis as History: Negation and Freedom in Freud* (Ithaca: Cornell University Press, 1987), pp. 99–133. My quotations are from pp. 131–32. Roth's description of Hegel's dialectical reconciliation emphasizes "forgiveness" in the "redemption" that issues from "the struggle between two individuals." As I emphasized in chapter 3, this redemption in the "trial by death" of the individual is for Hegel also a matter of justified penal violence and ascendancy.

11. Hans Blumenberg, *The Legitimacy of the Modern Age,* trans. Robert M. Wallace (Cambridge: MIT Press, 1983), pp. 440, 441, 447, 451. In the present chapter it is worth noting Blumenberg's observation that "Torquato Tasso in his *Liberated Jerusalem* could view and evaluate the passage beyond the pillars of Hercules anew, in a clear allusion to the twenty-sixth canto of the *Inferno,* because in the meantime Columbus had reached and set foot upon the *nuova terra.* The self-confirmation of human curiosity has become the form of its legitima-

tion" (pp. 339–40). In tandem with our contemplation of the occasioning of Freud's freedom of curiosity, we need to note the sublime experience of a line of culture which Tasso's verse creates in order for him to gain access to curiosity. This Tassovian curiosity is perhaps less directly self-confirmed (and less dependent on Columbus's voyage) than Blumenberg suggests.

12. See, for example, *SE* 12:155; *GW* 10:135.

13. Laplanche, *Life and Death in Psychoanalysis,* trans. Mehlman, p. 117.

14. Ibid., pp. 114, 116, 109, 124.

15. Ibid., p. 124.

16. Arthur Schopenhauer, *The World as Will and Representation,* trans. E. F. J. Payne (New York: Dover, 1969), 2 vols., 1:378–86. In contemplating the differences between Schopenhauer's and his own conceptions of a death drive, and between Schopenhauer's aim in "conversion" (or "resignation") of the will and his own interest in the transference, Freud's identification of the scene in Tasso's *Gerusalemme liberata* as his exemplum of "behavior in the transference" (*SE* 18:22) may in part be a response to Schopenhauer's challenging way of instancing moments in Goethe's *Faust,* and then, secondarily, in Goethe's *Torquato Tasso* (1:396). "I know of no other description in poetry," says Schopenhauer, that "brings to us the essential point of that conversion so distinctly" (1:393).

17. Cited, to other ends, by Laplanche, *Life and Death in Psychoanalysis,* trans. Mehlman, p. 130. For a recent discussion of Freud's concept of ideogenic paralysis, see M. MacMillan, "Freud and Janet on Organic and Hysterical Paralysis: A Mystery Solved?" *International Review of Psycho-Analysis* 17 (1990): 189–203.

18. Laplanche, *Life and Death in Psychoanalysis,* trans. Mehlman, p. 110.

19. Ibid., p. 117.

20. See Paul de Man, *Allegories of Reading: Figural Language in Rousseau, Nietzsche, Rilke, and Proust* (New Haven: Yale University Press, 1979), pp. 44–46.

21. Without reference to Laplanche, Jean Starobinski's *"Acheronta Movebo,"* trans. Françoise Meltzer in *The Trial(s) of Psychoanalysis,* ed. Françoise Meltzer (Chicago: University of Chicago Press, 1988), pp. 273–86, has deepened our sense of Freud's Virgilian lineage.

22. For this sentence I have departed from the *SE* translation in order to reproduce Freud's juxtaposition of clauses.

23. *GW* 13:21; *SE* 18:22.

24. Tasso makes this dying-away thematically explicit when he says that Tancred is filled "with death" after killing Clorinda in their actual (first and only) duel: "He did not die outright" (12.68); but "When he sees the gentle soul is gone, he relaxes that strength he had summoned up; and . . . fills with death his senses and his countenance. The living man lies languishing like to the dead, in color, in silence, in attitude and in blood" (12.70).

25. *Minutes of the Vienna Psychoanalytic Society, 1910–1911,* ed. Herman Nunberg and Ernst Federn, trans. M. Nunberg (New York: International Universities Press, 1974), 3:331.

26. Sabina Spielrein, "Die Destruktion als Ursache des Werdens," *Jahrbuch für Psychoanalytische und Psychopathologische Forschungen* 4 (1912): 479.

27. There may well be deep ironies and ambivalences for Freud in his exemplification of the death instincts from a work named with the phrase *Gerusalemme liberata.* Already in Tasso there is a highlighting of the irony that the peace of Jerusalem "Liberata" is achieved only in "slaughter" and "rivers" of blood [20.143–44].) This deliverance is in direct analogy for Tasso with the fact that Tancred, a Christian Crusader, "liberates" Clorinda, a beautiful Ethiopian Moslem, by killing her. It is the perfect Hegelian tyranny over the other. For Freud there was a particular significance, or power of ambivalence or limping, attached to the phrase "Jerusalem delivered." In *Civilization and its Discontents* (1930) Freud instances "the cap-

ture of Jerusalem by the pious Crusaders" (i.e., the same "Crusaders' army" mentioned in our passage from *Beyond the Pleasure Principle*) as an example of "*Homo homini lupus*," in other words, as an example of man's natural (Hobbesian) state as a wolfish creature devouring its own kind. The piety of the Crusaders, he is saying, is only homicide. "Jerusalem" is only the worst of excuses for giving play to the most lethal of instincts (*SE* 21:111–12). Viewed within the context of Freud's writings on calamitous civilization and catastrophic sexuality, the signs of imperialism and sadism in Tasso's scene are undeniable. By announcing that Tancred is hostage to "a repetition of the same fatality" Freud highlights a "Jerusalem" which is both the victim of repeated destructions and a battle cry of death and destruction.

CHAPTER 11. The Real in the Commonplace

Epigraph: Nathalie Sarraute, *Portrait d'un inconnu*, pref. Jean-Paul Sartre (1948; 2d ed. Paris: Gallimard, 1956). Citations in English are from *Portrait of a Man Unknown*, pref. Jean-Paul Sartre, tran. Maria Jolas (London: Calder, 1959). In some instances I have chosen a more literal rendering than Jolas supplies. For those who may not be familiar with the novel, Sartre's summary is a useful entrée and will, I hope, make my discussion more intelligible: "The author has introduced a sort of impassioned amateur detective who becomes fascinated by a perfectly ordinary couple—an old father and a daughter who is no longer very young—spies on them, pursues them and occasionally sees through them, even at a distance, by virtue of a sort of thought transference, without ever knowing very well either what he is after or what they are. He doesn't find anything, or *hardly* anything, and he gives up his investigation as a result of a metamorphosis" (p. viii).

1. Some instances of male representations of these kinds that we have seen are Ezekiel's vision of the Lord's loins, Homer's Thetis, Virgil's Danaïdes, Milton's Philomel, Pope's and Wordsworth's Corbet, Goethe's "Ewig-Weibliche," and Freud's (and Tasso's) Clorinda.

2. Patrocinio Schweikart, "Reading Ourselves: Toward a Feminist Theory of Reading," in *Contemporary Literary Criticism: Literary and Cultural Studies*, ed. Robert Con Davis and Ronald Schleifer (New York: Longman, 1994), p. 209.

3. The banality of the commonplace is, of course, itself a commonplace, most obviously (in modern literature at least) in the French novel, perhaps most intensely in Gustave Flaubert, though in the French novel and elsewhere the uses of that commonplace vary greatly. For the nineteenth-century history of the banalism, see Anne Herschberg-Pierrot, *Le dictionnaire des idées reçues de Flaubert* (Lille: Presses Universitaires de Lille, 1988). Stirling Haig, *Flaubert and the Gift of Speech: Dialogue and Discourse in Four "Modern" Novels* (Cambridge: Cambridge University Press, 1986), p. 122, contrasts (somewhat inexactly, to my mind) Sarraute's and Flaubert's uses of the banalism.

4. See, for example, pp. 74, 99, 220.

5. F. H. Bradley, *The Principles of Logic*, 2d ed. (London: Oxford University Press, 1922), 1:85–87.

6. Freud, *The Standard Edition of the Complete Psychological Works of Sigmund Freud*, trans. James Strachey et al. (London: Hogarth Press and the Institute of Psycho-Analysis, 1955), 18:22; hereafter cited as *SE* in text.

7. In Neil Hertz's rich chapter "The Notion of Blockage in the Literature of the Sublime," in *The End of the Line: Essays on Psychoanalysis and the Sublime* (New York: Columbia University Press, 1985), pp. 40–60, "sublime blockage" (p. 54) is said to be an example or symptom of "end-of-the-line structures" (p. 222). My account of the cultural sublime draws

closest to Hertz's views when he speaks of a sublime experience that is "thorough-going self-loss—not the recuperable baffled self associated with scenarios of blockage, but a more radical flux and dispersion of the subject" (p. 58). His description, however, of end-of-the-line structures is fundamentally different from my tracing of sublime representations which include the "dispersion of the subject" and which are constitutively bound up with (at least in Western traditions) the continuity of cultural lines. Hertz leads us to understand that, following de Man, he would regard representations of cultural continuity as an illusion or at least as marked by "unreadability." Thus, even when at this penultimate moment of *The End of the Line* he comes to ask, "What comes *after* the end of the line?" (pp. 22–23) his answer (as I understand it) is a feminist theory that is very different from the feminine sublime of culture that I am explicating in Sarraute. He does not imagine the possibility of access, for women any more than for men, to an experience of the continuity of the line that they themselves help create and sustain. Similarly, although Hertz's linkage (built to some extent on the work of Thomas Weiskel: pp. 49–53) of the sublime with Freud is highly suggestive, in my view it misses the way Freud's representation of sublime experience is itself constituted by a line of cultural experience.

8. Jolas translates "un traité de psychiatrie" (p. 28) as "a psychiatric handbook" (p. 29).

9. Ruth Z. Temple, *Nathalie Sarraute* (New York: Columbia University Press, 1968), p. 20.

10. A suggestion of this kind has recently been made by Celia Britton, *The Nouveau Roman: Fiction, Theory and Politics* (New York: St. Martin's, 1992), pp. 32–33.

11. See esp. pp. 320–25 of *Being and Nothingness: A Phenomenological Essay on Ontology*, trans. Hazel E. Barnes (New York: Washington Square Press, 1966).

12. We should recall here not only the electrifying effect of Kojève's Hegel lectures on the Paris of the 1930s but the series of writings on Hegel by Bataille, reaching a temporary climax in 1943 in *L'expérience intérieure* (1943; Paris: Gallimard, 1954). Echoing Bataille's accusations against Hegel, Lacan's accusation, in 1949, that the scene of punishment in the *Phenomenology of Spirit* was a representation of "murder" [in "The Mirror Stage as Formative of the Function of the I as Revealed in Psychoanalytic Experience," in *Ecrits: A Selection*, trans. Alan Sheridan (New York: Norton, 1977), p. 6] both frames and focuses this French engagement with Hegel's duel scene at the time Sarraute wrote *Portrait d'un inconnu*.

13. Hegel, *The Phenomenology of Spirit*, trans. A. V. Miller (Oxford: Clarendon, 1977); hereafter cited in text as *PS* and section number.

14. For Sarraute the superimposition of the insectile onto the human no doubt also expresses the horrific banality of the commonplace when it is devoid of "La Désinvolture" or the "other view" or experience of the sublime.

15. On page 253, n. 2 I have pointed to significant differences in outlook between the *Phenomenology* and the *Philosophy of Right*.

16. Bradley, *The Principles of Logic*, 1:86.

17. Nathalie Sarraute and Marc Saporta, "Portrait d'une inconnue, conversation biographique," *L'Arc* 95 (1984): 17–18.

18. Valerie Minogue, *Nathalie Sarraute and the War of Words: A Study of Five Novels* (Edinburgh: Edinburgh University Press, 1981), p. 7. Closely related to Sarraute's reclamation of tradition is her difference from the other, mostly male, authors of the *nouveau roman*. Susan Suleiman catalogues the "canonical features" of the *nouveau roman* as "discontinuity, *rupture*, auto-representation, the absolute refusal to 'signify' anything other than the process of its own elaboration," thereby creating the illusion of a "self-engendered text." Suleiman argues that the male-authored novels represent "the ultimate masculine fantasy, . . . self-engenderment" and that this fantasy is often represented in "repeated violation of the maternal or-

gans" (see Suleiman, "Reading Robbe-Grillet: Sadism and Text in *Projet pour une révolution à New York*," *Romanic Review* 68 [1977]: 44–45, 62). Sarraute's *Portrait d'un inconnu* represents a female opposite of this fantasy by repeatedly representing the commonplaceness of male scenes of victimization and the fallaciousness of male claims (within those commonplace scenes) to self-endgendered recovery or sublimation.

CHAPTER 12. Of the Fragment

1. "Maharal" is the acronym of Rabbi Loew of Prague (1525–1609), a prolific Torah scholar and philosopher. Today the Maharal is popularly associated with the most famous of the legends that describe the making of a golem, although no documents earlier than the nineteenth century have so far been identified that mention the Maharal's name in connection with the making of a golem. According to the Prague legend, when the Jews of that city were in mortal danger Rabbi Loew spoke the sacred words necessary to create a golem, in this case a protecting and avenging creature whose outline Rabbi Loew drew in the wet clay.

2. This is my translation from the Hebrew text cited in *Epitaphs from the Ancient Jewish Cemetery of Prague*, ed. Otto Muneles (Jerusalem: Israel Academy of Sciences and Humanities, 1988), p. 273:

וירפאו את ההרוס:
ושבר על שבר יחדיו ידבקו
תאומים מלמטה:
ויהי בשלום סכו למעלה
תחת כנפי השכינה

Muneles gives the references to Psalms and Sanhedrin, and the first reference to Exodus, noted below. To my knowledge there is no extant comment on the epitaph. For helpful comments on historical aspects of the present chapter I am grateful to Jacob Elbaum, Ezra Fleisher, Moshe Idel, and Sid Z. Leiman.

3. Paul de Man comments on the status of the speaker of epitaphic language in "Autobiography as De-Facement," in *The Rhetoric of Romanticism* (New York: Columbia University Press, 1984), pp. 67–81. I have explained the grounds of my disagreement with many of de Man's views on this and related subjects in chapters 3 and 6.

4. In modern thought a meditation on the concept of the fragment is particularly associated with the emergence of romanticism. See, for example, Philippe Lacoue-Labarthe and Jean-Luc Nancy, *The Literary Absolute: The Theory of Literature in German Romanticisim*, trans. Philip Barnard and Cheryl Lester (Albany: State University of New York Press, 1988), pp. 39–58. As far as I can tell, this meditation is usually rooted in an article of faith, namely, that human beings are endowed with the equivalent of a divine capacity for creating wholes out of fragments. A latter-day instance of this aspect of romanticism is Harold Bloom's concept of *tessera* (fragment): "*Tessera* . . . is completion and antithesis. . . . A poet antithetically completes his percursor" (p. 14). The achieved endpoint for Bloom is always a scene of recuperation by the strong writer. This applies, in a related way, to Bloom's concept of "*Apophrades*, or the return of the dead," in which the strong poet determines how her or his poem is "now *held* open to the precursor": see *The Anxiety of Influence: A Theory of Poetry* (New York: Oxford University Press, 1975), pp. 14–16. By contrast, the concept of the fragment that I am tracing in the cultural sublime is one in which the condition of the fragment is sustained (not least in the experience of death), rather than being turned into a new wholeness.

5. This is the meaning of *vayirapooh* that the epitaph logically requires, especially be-

cause of the image (or counterimage) of the whole tabernacle two sentences later. Yet it is clear from the history of commentary on this word that it is fraught with ambiguity of reference, both of subject and object.

6. Verses 8:21–22 and 9:1 in the Authorized or King James Version.

7. I have translated the difficult Hebrew word *kadarti,* literally, "I am made black" as "I am made melancholy," following the comments of Amos Chacham on Job 5:11 in his edition of *Job* (Jerusalem: Mossad Harav Kook, 1981). Perhaps it is also worth speculating that there is an analogy here with the notion, in the old physiology, that one is made black by black bile, the humor of melancholy.

8. Authorized Version 41:17.

9. The Maharal could himself follow the former reading of this verse, as, for example, in *Sefer Netzach Yisrael* (Jerusalem: Honig, 1960), p. 190.

10. A particularly relevant reference of a virtually archetypical nature is Exodus 25:20–22: "And the cherubim shall stretch forth their *wings above* covering the mercy seat with their wings, and their faces each to his brother toward the mercy seat. . . . And there I will meet with you, and I will commune with you from *above* the mercy seat." (This verse refers to the wings of the cherubim above the mercy seat, above the ark of the covenant, in the tabernacle. The word used here for "covering" is *sochachim,* from the same root as the word *sukah* [tabernacle].) There is also Ruth 2:12: "The Lord recompense your work, and a full reward be given to you from the Lord God of Israel, since you have come to trust *under* his *wings.*" (Boaz is here speaking to Ruth. This verse was particularly memorable in the exegetical tradition because the "full reward" for trusting *under* God's *wings* was understood as the birth of the Messiah from the house of David, Ruth and Boaz's direct descendant.)

11. In one place the Maharal twice invokes the opening phrase of Jeremiah's verse—in the form "he repaired the fragment easily"—as part of his denial of the arguments of his famous opponent, Azariah de' Rossi. Having accused de' Rossi of rending divine truth to bits, the Maharal offers a counterclaim that must be of special interest with regard to the inscription on the Maharal's tomb. He argues that the Land of Israel, Jerusalem, and the Tabernacle are not of that order of things which are "of the edge, where absence bonds," where "life" borders on "sheol," death; i.e., this entity, as opposed to the welter of earthly objects, is not a "fragment" (Maharal, *Be'er Ha-Golah* [London: Honig, 1964], the sixth Be'er). These are striking similarities with the materials and thematics of the inscription lines. Thus, it is possible that the first two lines of the inscription on the Maharal's tomb cite this fragment or another such fragment of the Maharal's own speaking, a fragment, therefore, of the Maharal's mind or consciousness. Yet, for reasons that I will elaborate later, I regard this possibility (i.e., of any bonding of a moment of citation with another moment of citation) as only a potential meaning, never an actual or completed one. For comments (motivated by concerns different from mine) on some of the concepts that come into play in the Maharal's argument with de' Rossi, see two essays of Jacob Elbaum, (in English) "Rabbi Judah Loew of Prague and His Attitude to the Aggadah," *Scripta Hierosolymitana* 22 (1971): 42–45, and (in Hebrew) "Ha-Maharal Miprague Vetorato," in *Parshioth Iyunioth Betoldoth Yisrael,* ed. Jacob Elbaum and Joseph Dan (Jerusalem: Magnes, n.d.), 2:46–48. These latter pages include notes on the passage I have mentioned in the Maharal's response to de' Rossi.

12. The very last word of these lines is similarly double. *Ha'schechina,* "the spirit," is a closely related cognate of the word *mishkan,* "tabernacle. In this sense *schechina* denotes the spirit that indwells, in the near aspect of God's being. At the same time, however, the meaning of this largely postexilic word is itself a consequence of the destruction of the Temple at Jerusalem, where the spirit of God had a settled home, a *mishkan.* In this other sense it denotes the spirit that we try to bring into our transient midst, from its place made indeterminate by the destruction.

13. The problem of the date of the first writing of this inscription on the Maharal's tombstone is addressed below.

14. Current reference points for such theories are J. L. Austin, *How to Do Things with Words* (New York: Oxford University Press, 1962), and Jacques Derrida, "Signature Event Context," in *Margins of Philosophy*, trans. Alan Bass (Brighton: Harvester, 1982), pp. 307–30.

15. Derrida's remarks on *Frömmigheit* and *Zusage* appear in an essay-length footnote to *Of Spirit: Heidegger and the Question*, trans. Geoffrey Bennington and Rachel Bowlby (Chicago: University of Chicago Press, 1989), pp. 129–36.

16. Stanley Cavell, "The Uncanniness of the Ordinary," in *In Quest of the Ordinary: Lines of Skepticism and Romanticism* (Chicago: University of Chicago Press, 1988), pp. 176, 172.

17. In "Counter-Philosophy and the Pawn of Voice," in *A Pitch of Philosophy: Autobiographical Exercises* (Cambridge: Harvard University Press, 1994), p. 126. Here I gratefully acknowledge that on the final pages of *A Pitch of Philosophy* Cavell has written moving words of epitaph about our son Yochanan.

18. Hegel, *Phenomenology of Spirit*, trans. A. V. Miller (Oxford: Clarendon, 1977), section 508.

19. See pages 46–58.

20. I cite Hegel's phrase from *Phänomenologie des Geistes* (Stuttgart: Reclam, 1987), p. 71.

21. For example, *Phenomenology of Spirit*, trans. Miller, sections 18 and 593, of which the latter appears within Hegel's discussion of Culture.

22. A straightforward exposition of the Maharal's use of these terms is available, in Hebrew, in Avraham Kariv's introduction to *Selected Writings of the Maharal of Prague*, 2 vols. (Jerusalem: Mossad Harav Kook, 1960).

23. This is to say: toward any fragment that can be heard and addressed using our given line of language.

24. It is as difficult to generalize about medieval rabbinic thought as about any other vast body of learning, but the climactic verse of the reading from the prophets—Joel 2:27— chosen by the rabbis for the Sabbath of Return (Repentance), immediately before the Day of Atonement, may provide a classic instance of that thought with regard to chiasmus. Here the turn (AB) and return (BA) of the chiastic form enacts the reunion of Israel and God. Equally, the self-consciousness achieved in the double turn is both God's self-declaration in the world and the knowledge essential for Israel's being: "And you will know

[A]	[B]
in the midst of Israel	am I

X

[B]	[A]
I am Jehovah	*your* God."

The fact that there is a sharp opposition, or paradox, between a national God ("in the midst of Israel," "*your* God") and a God who is the only God of the entire cosmos is acknowledged by the words following the chiasmus, as if insisting on attention to the antithetical elements: "And there is none else and my people will never be ashamed."

25. Hegel, *Philosophy of Right*, trans. T. M. Knox (London: Oxford University Press, 1967). Lest the bracketed phrase cause confusion, I will mention again that Knox and the German text that he translates (*Grundlinien der Philosophie des Rechts*, ed. Georg Lasson [Leipzig: Meiner, 1921]) do not reproduce the phrase "I will repay," although Hegel's comment on this verse is specifically on the word "repay" (in which Hegel italicizes the element of repetition). I refer the reader to pages 130–34 above for comments on the connection between chiasmus and revenge in Hegel's derivation of self-consciousness.

26. This is my translation from the text in *Epitaphs from the Ancient Jewish Cemetery of*

Prague, ed. Muneles, p. 273. The phrase (from the account of the epitaph verses) that I have given in single quotation marks, 'the unique lettering style of this inscription,' is likely the immediate point of the Aramaic phrase quoted (slightly rearranged) from Daniel 5:8 and from Babylonian Talmud Sanhedrin 22a: "lo kahalin mikra k'tava." Jay Harris has pointed out to me that the citing of the phrase probably refers to the passage in Sanhedrin in which the debate is only about knowing the style of lettering and distinctly not about knowing the words used. In the case of the tombstone inscription, therefore, the implication is that what was lost irrecoverably was an encoding of signs in certain highlightings of letters in the verses of the epitaph. Such highlighting was not unusual in these texts and is even rendered on some of the letters on the reverse of the stone where our epitaph verses occur. (One other change from a literal transcription: I have supplied C.E. dates for the Hebrew ones.)

27. See Gershom G. Scholem, *On the Kabbalah and its Symbolism,* trans. Ralph Manheim (New York: Schocken, 1965), "The Idea of a Golem," pp. 158–204, and Moshe Idel, *Golem: Jewish Magical and Mystical Traditions on the Artificial Anthropoid* (Albany: State University of New York Press, 1990), for rich surveys of the texts of this tradition. (Scholem and Idel do not discuss the epitaph text on the Maharal's tombstone.)

28. In making the tabernacle Bezalel himself was supposed to have made use of the *Book of Creation, Sefer Yetsirah,* the ancient text which, among other things, is at the heart of virtually all the traditions of golem making. The earthly correspondences of the fragments mentioned in the *Sefer Yetsirah* are visualized in great detail. They include, for example, the kidneys, liver, and perhaps even the pancreas. See *Sefer Yetzirah: The Book of Creation,* ed. and trans. Aryeh Kaplan (York Beach, Maine: Weiser, 1990), p. 214.

29. For the Jeremiah story, see Scholem, *On the Kabbalah and its Symbolism,* pp. 178–81.

30. Scholem, *On the Kabbalah and its Symbolism,* p. 188, quotes the phrase from the anonymous Spanish author of "Questions of the Old Man," *She'eloth ha-Zaken,* no. 97, Oxford MS. Neubauer, No. 2396, Fol. 53a. Where Ralph Manheim has given "creation of thought," translating Scholem's translation, "gedankliche Schöpfung," for the Hebrew original, *yetsirah mahshavtith,* I have proposed "thought creation," which reproduces the Spanish author's use of the term for the nature of the objects created. The German edition of Scholem's book is *Zur Kabbala und ihrer Symbolik* (Zurich: Rhein-Verlag, 1960). The phrase in question appears . on p. 243.

31. Jeremiah's phrases are closely related to Isaiah 57, especially verses 18–21. In fact, Isaiah 57 extensively suggests the impossibility of a human repairing of fragmentation. I should mention here the Maharal's pervasive division of the cosmos into three worlds and his placement of "peace" not in the highest but in the middle world, in other words, below heavenly perfection: see, for example, his discussion in *Netivoth Olam* (London: Honig, 1960; new and corrected printing, 1974), 1:202; chap. 3 of "Nativ HaEmeth." In the epitaph lines, similarly, three levels of the cosmos and the same placement of "peace" are indicated by "below" and by the "peace" "above" which is itself "under" the "wings of the spirit." As Kariv, *Selected Writings of the Maharal of Prague,* p. 21, emphasizes, for the Maharal the typical direction of miraculous contact between these worlds is from below to above, that is, initiated by human beings. In addition it should be noted that in the ancient *Book of Creation* these three direction words figure in the creation of the three-dimensionality of spiritual being. (On verse 1:13 of the *Book of Creation,* see *Sefer Yetzirah,* ed. Kaplan, pp. 80–87.) According to one of the best-known versions of the Prague legend, the Maharal is alleged to have used the *Book of Creation* in making the golem—quite conventionally, of course, for golem making: see the *Niflaoth Maharal* of Y. L. Rosenberg in *The Golem of Prague and Other Tales of Wonder* (Hebrew), ed. Eli Yassif (Jerusalem: Mossad Bialik, 1991), p. 76.

32. Some months after Yochanan died, my wife and I received a videotape of an inter-

view conducted at school a few weeks before his death. The interviewer asked Yochanan what he would do if, immediately after an attack by Arab terrorists—in which an Israeli soldier was wounded or killed—a pregnant Arab woman were to come aboard a public bus in which he was seated and in which all the other seats were taken. Would he offer her his seat? Thoughtfully, even with pain, Yochanan affirms that he certainly would give her his seat. "So what?!" he asks and exclaims. "How do I know that she's tied to that? Isn't she a human being?!"

Index